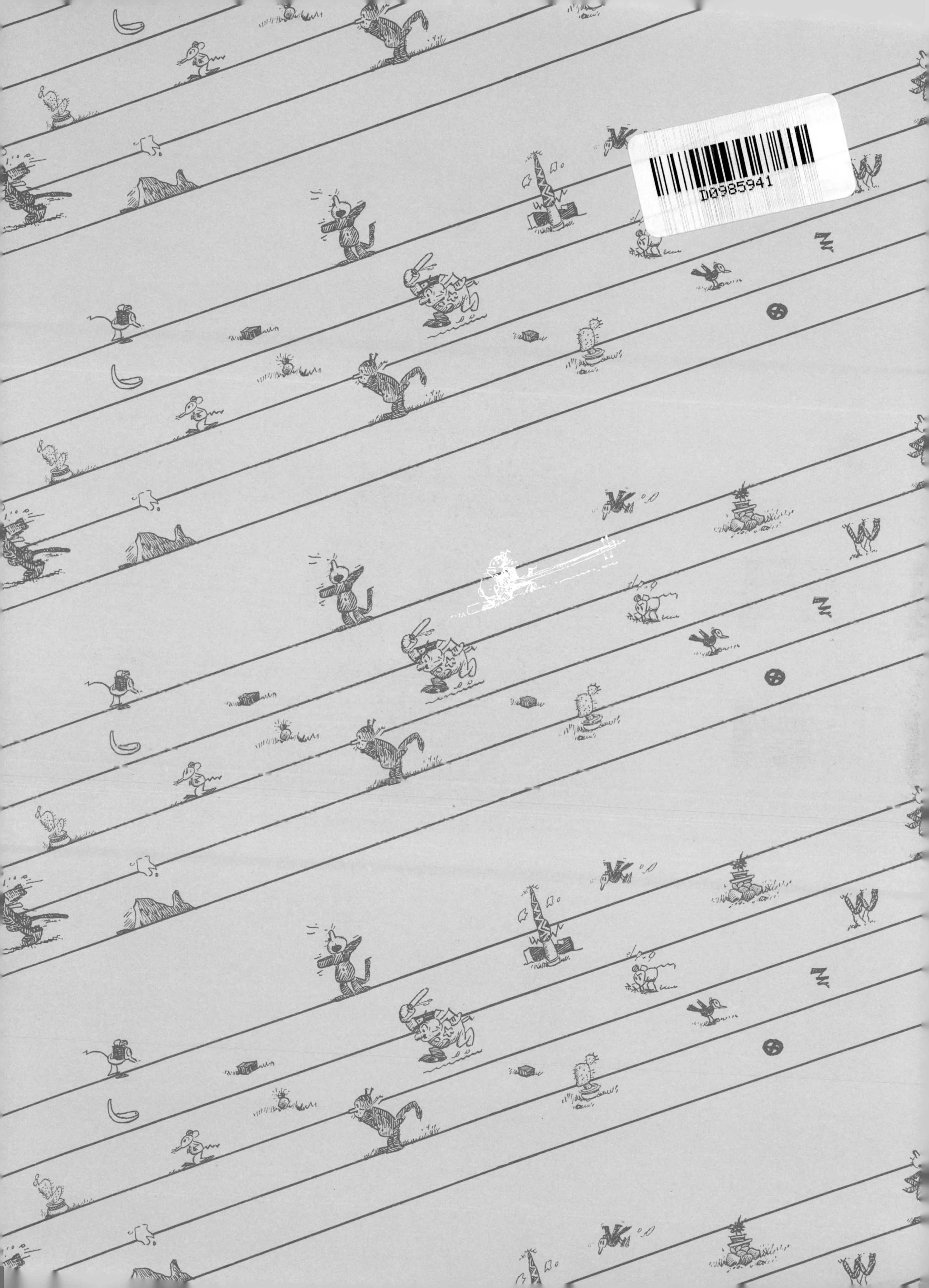

George Herriman, from the October/November 1902 issue of *Bookman* magazine.
The picture is autographed "Truly Yours Geo. Herriman '02" and accompanies
an article surveying the cartoonists of the day; Herriman is cited as promising, and
the essay includes a lengthy quotation from him about cartoonists sporting
non-poetic souls (cited on pages 36-37 of *The Comic Art of George Herriman*
by O'Connell, McDonnell and De Havenon; Abrams, 1986.)
Courtesy of and thanks to Robert L. Beerbohm.

KRAZY & IGNATZ.

by George Herriman.

"A Kat a'Lilt with Song."

Convening the Complete Full-Page Comic Strips,
with some extra Dailies.

1931-32.

Edited by Bill Blackbeard and Derya Ataker.

Fantagraphics Books, SEATTLE.

KRAZY KAT by He

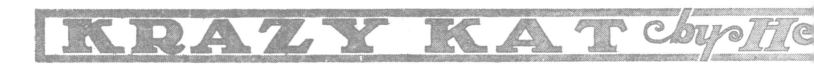

Published by Fantagraphics Books.
7563 Lake City Way North East,
Seattle, Washington, 98115, United States of America.

Edited and annotated by Bill Blackbeard and Derya Ataker.
Except where noted, all research materials appear courtesy of the San Francisco Academy of Cartoon Art.
Designed and Decorated by Chris Ware.
Production assistance and scanning by Paul Baresh.
Promoted by Eric Reynolds.
Published by Gary Groth and Kim Thompson.

For a free full-color catalogue of comics and cartooning, including many classic American newspaper strips, please telephone 1-800-657-1100. Our books may be viewed – and purchased – by consulting www.fantagraphics.com on your home terminal.

First Fantagraphics Books edition: April 2004.

ISBN 1-56097-594-6.

Printed in Canada by WestCan Printing Group, Winnipeg, Manitoba.

Special thanks to Robert L. Beerbohm
for his generous help in assembling this volume.

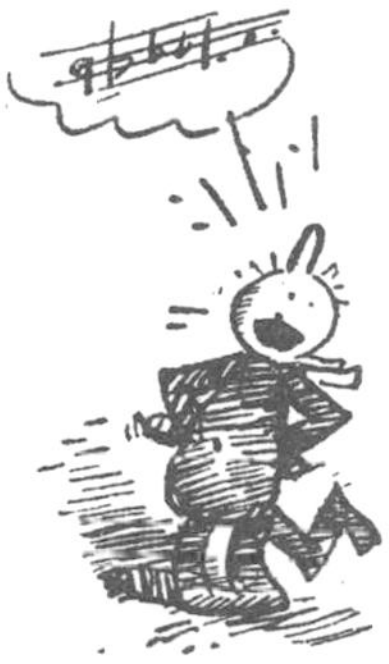

iman **KRAZY & IGNATZ.**

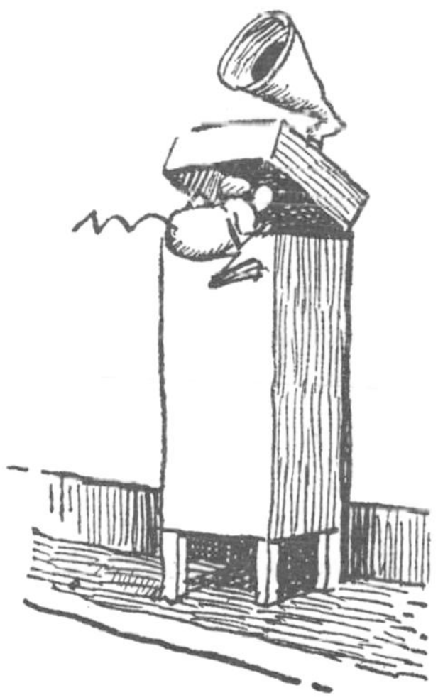

THE BARON AND THE DUKE.

Other Great Stuff Before the Bricks Zipped.

Introduction by Bill Blackbeard.

George Herriman was a Los Angeles boy almost from the start. Of the brief stint he and his parents spent in his birthplace, New Orleans, he remembered next to nothing, having been whisked across the continent as soon as his Greek immigrant father realized that the dark southern European hue of his family's skin identified them as blacks in the hyper-racist eyes of the Louisiana white elite — the very people he wanted as customers in the bakery he planned to open in the new country. Hearing from other Greeks that southern racism was then almost non-existent in black-free California, he packed up the roots he wanted to put down and followed the locomotive smoke to the sun and santanas of southern California, finding just the site he wanted for his bakery, where even the pinkest-hued citizens accepted him and his wife as Europeans. Here the budding boy cartoonist named George enjoyed growing up in the halcyon fresh air and sunshine of a big 1880s hamlet named Los Angeles, decades away from the smog and sprawl of the mega city to come.

For a kid who had early on discovered the delights of drawing funny pitchers that gained the frequent plaudits of other kids — and, wonderfully, adults — L.A. was a wonder town of constantly shifting urban panoramas made up of the new houses and downtown buildings that seemed to spring up overnight, so that no vista was quite the same

LOS ANGELES EXAMINER
BASEBALL AND
Terrible! Baron Mooch Labo
Y'SCORN MEH, HAY? VERY WELL TAWM McCAREY - REE-EE-MEM-BAH, HE WHO LAUGHS LAST - IRRITATES = VENGEANCE !!
GET OUT YOU FAT PEST
T. McCAREY
McCAREY'S PAVILION.
BOILER FACTORY
IRON WORKS
FINE. REPUTATION I'D HAVE, IF I COULDN'T GET THE BEST OF A 'RUBE WOT LETS HIMSELF GET TOUCHED FOR HIS SUNDAY SHINER -
ON - ON - I OUGHT TO BE UNDER THE PAVILION BEFORE THE SECOND PRELIM.
AH - TIS THE SOUND OF BATTLE, I MUST BE RIGHT UNDER THE RING -
BANG BANG BANGITY BONG BOW

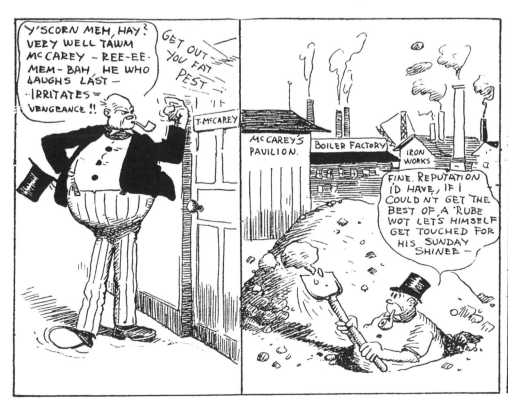

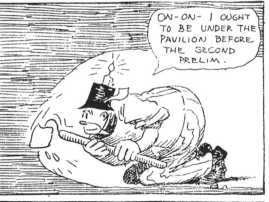

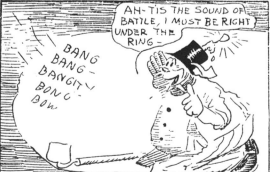

from one day to the next — why, it could almost change behind a kid's back during a game of aggies-out or hide-and-seek behind the coach houses. But the real magic for the sketchpad kid were the myriad comic drawings he soon discovered in the weekly cartoon magazines of the era — *Puck, Life, Judge, Punch*, among an array of others — where exquisitely funny artists filled the glossy pages with galleries of small gag drawings carrying a punch line or two, amid full-page sketches — often in full color! — that just made a cartooning kid's creative mouth water. These magazines, which could be looked at in barbershops or the city library (where they could be pursued far into the past through shelves of bound back issues), filled young George's gleefully intoxicated imagination with wondrous revelations of applicable drawing techniques that soon gave a unique and comically effective zest to his own cartoons. Loaded up with coverless back issues purchased in grubby, dusty, wholly delicious second-hand magazine shops for a penny each, paid for with earnings from delivering hot baked rolls and bread from the family bakery, George spent gas-lit evenings studying the treasured art that he knew was going to shape the rest of his life and take him into the elite ranks of the published cartoonists just as soon as the right editor —

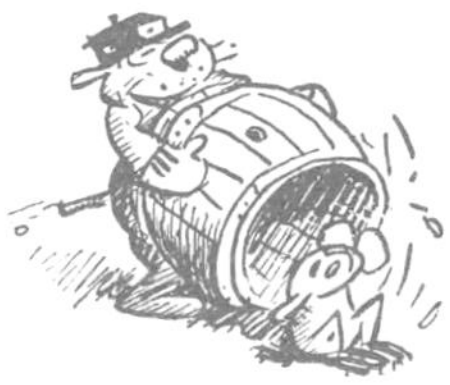

But as all young cartoonists learn at the outsets of their burgeoning careers, right editors are not commonly come by. Certainly when the young George followed the hallowed scent of newsprint to the racket and roar of the editorial offices of the *Los Angeles Herald* in 1895, he encountered only wrong editors, who hired the eager kid (cheap talent, of course) just to draw routine sketches of the recently deceased, newly opened store fronts, and similar grindingly dull work, while refusing to pay the least attention to the boy's comic pen apart from a guffaw, followed by a shake of the grizzled head, and "Not for this paper, kid; we don't print funny stuff." (Actually, the *Herald* was printing a couple of pages of cartoons in its Sunday edition while George labored at his battered desk, which constituted the sole furnishing of the paper's art department, which in turn consisted of George and a companionable cat. These color Sunday cartoons, however, were purchased from the McClure Syndicate, whose august rep assured the editors they were getting genuinely funny stuff for their money. The curly-headed staff artist, not yet eighteen, was a suffering, anguished, ignored Rodney Dangerfield, laboring over a painfully realistic drawing of an ice wagon horse whose cobblestone-caught hoof held up traffic for a rainy hour in a grubby subdivision called Hollywood.)

It was for the birds — the razzoos, in fact. And George walked in due time. The kid felt his days were better spent at the tilted board, fitting nibs and bringing increasingly skilled comicalities to ink-limned life, even if it meant lean pockets for the time being. (After all, starvation was no threat for a kid whose folks ran a first-rate bakery.) Then, toward the close of the century, those elusive, uninterested magazine editors at last became right editors, and a few checks began to nuzzle into George's family mailbox between the returned packets of art. Herriman cartoons, drawn in a freewheeling, eye-catching, and wholly individual style, began to turn up in the humor magazines, as well as in the gag cartoon pages of the Hearst Sunday paper chain. And George tried his luck with newspapers again in the early 1900s — first with the Hearst *New York American* for a year or so in a trial trip to the Apple, then back home with the *L.A. Times* for a few months, finally signing on at the Hearst *Los Angeles Examiner*, even as he had begun to introduce color

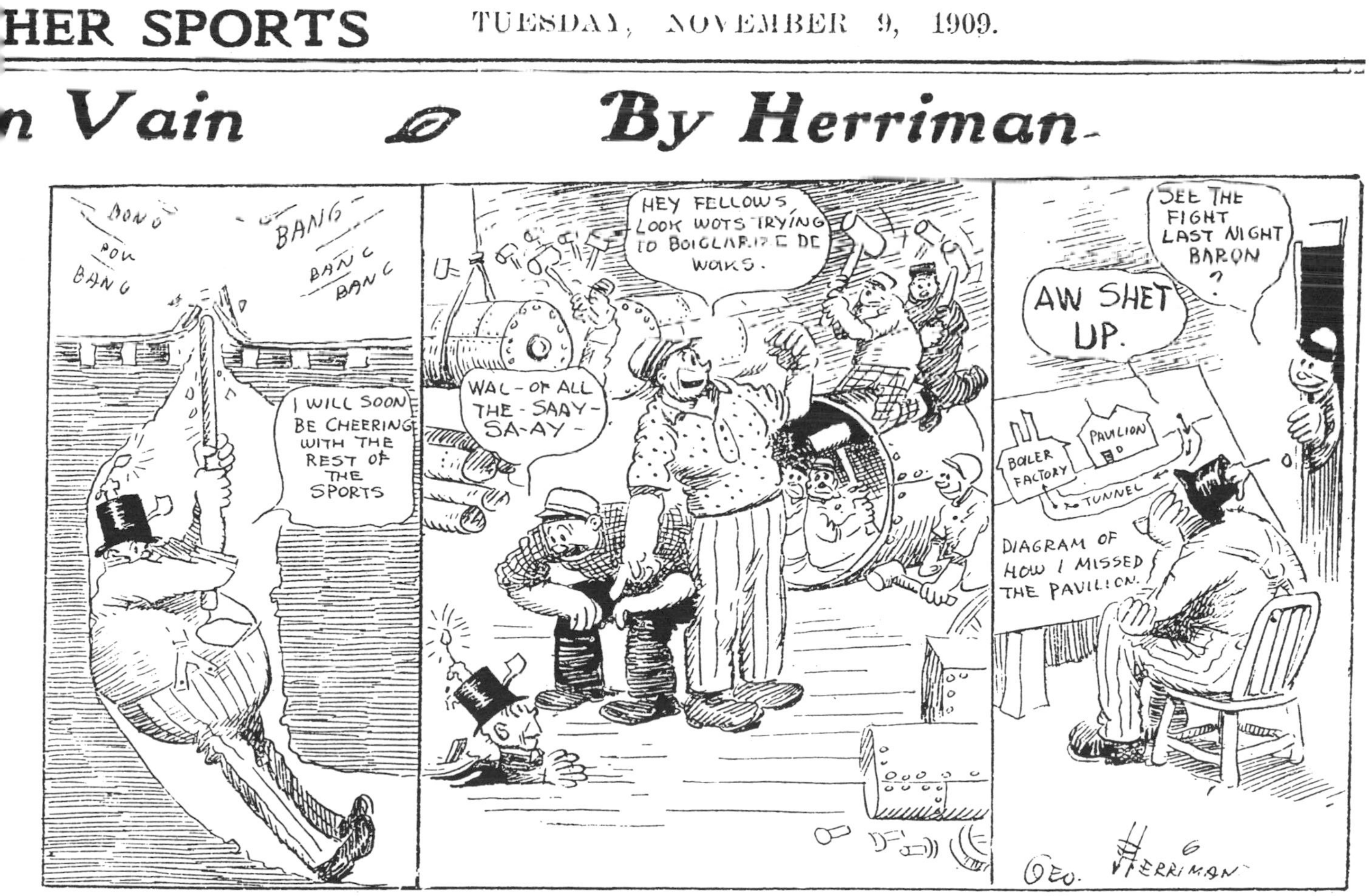
HER SPORTS
TUESDAY, NOVEMBER 9, 1909.
n Vain
By Herriman
DONG
POW
BANG
BANG
BANG BANG
I WILL SOON BE CHEERING WITH THE REST OF THE SPORTS
HEY FELLOWS LOOK WOTS TRYING TO BOIGLARIZE DE WAKS.
WAL - OF ALL THE - SAAY - SA-AY -
SEE THE FIGHT LAST NIGHT BARON ?
AW SHET UP.
BOILER FACTORY
PAVILION
TUNNEL
DIAGRAM OF HOW I MISSED THE PAVILION.
GEO. HERRIMAN

Herriman's engagingly krowded kanvas for this 1909 episode of *Baron Mooch* delighted the readers of Hearst's *Los Angeles Examiner*, who'd seen only much smaller panels in daily newspaper comics before.

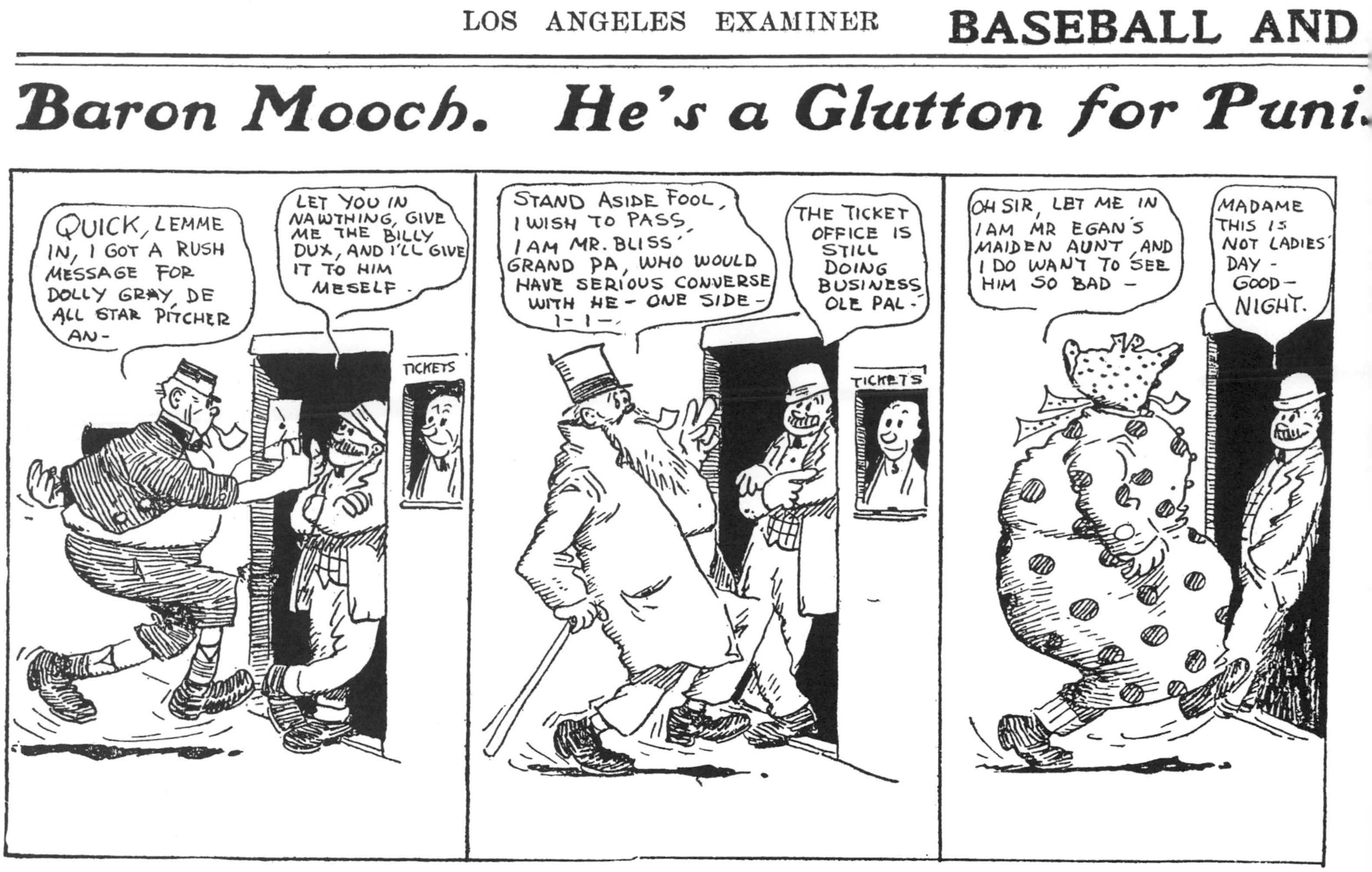
LOS ANGELES EXAMINER BASEBALL AND
Baron Mooch. He's a Glutton for Puni
QUICK, LEMME IN, I GOT A RUSH MESSAGE FOR DOLLY GRAY, DE ALL STAR PITCHER AN-
LET YOU IN NAWTHING, GIVE ME THE BILLY DUX, AND I'LL GIVE IT TO HIM MESELF.
TICKETS
STAND ASIDE FOOL, I WISH TO PASS, I AM MR. BLISS' GRAND PA, WHO WOULD HAVE SERIOUS CONVERSE WITH HE - ONE SIDE - 1-1-.
THE TICKET OFFICE IS STILL DOING BUSINESS OLE PAL.
TICKETS
OH SIR, LET ME IN I AM MR EGAN'S MAIDEN AUNT, AND I DO WANT TO SEE HIM SO BAD -
MADAME THIS IS NOT LADIES' DAY - GOOD - NIGHT.

Sunday comic strips into such national markets as the *New York World* and the World Color Printing Co. But he remained no comic strip hero in his own hometown; the *Times* wanted him only as a political cartoonist, with his graphics dictated by the paper's editors, while the brand new *Examiner,* the latest title in the Hearst chain, wanted him to do sport page cartoons and comic treatments of goings-on about town. But no comic strips, thanks.

By 1907, George's stunning cartoons had made the *Examiner* the most attractive newspaper in town. Often given a half page or more to fill in exquisite comic detail, the young artist followed his graphic fancy around town, from the diamond to the turf, having a grand old freewheeling good time. Life had never been better. George had discovered Dickens and Lewis Carroll and Thackeray, superb story-tellers whose tales were often co-created with the most gifted comic artists of their time. Dickens would toil over the drawing board with cartoon illustrators like Cruikshank and Browne (Phiz) to get the graphic portrayal of a character like Sairey Gamp or Mr Pecksniff exactly right, considering his novel illustrations an integral part of his books. (In our desolate time, publishers have no knowledge of this and routinely reprint Dickens sans the crucial cartoon art.) George reveled over these novel combinations of art and text and longed to tell stories involving his own comic characters developed in depth over time, just as the best Hearst Sunday newspaper cartoonists had been doing since the start of the new century. His spot gag Sunday page work for the *World* Sunday paper and the World syndicate conformed to the simplistic kiddie jokes those outlets wanted but failed to provide the space over time he knew he needed.

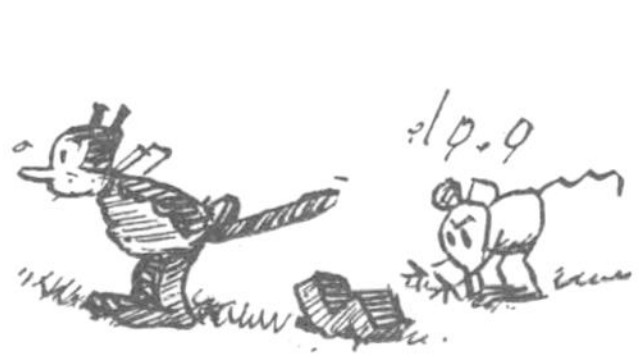

The problem was that George wanted to develop comic characters in anecdote-linked narratives published every day — in a daily comic strip, in short — and such a thing was simply not to be found in the newspapers of 1907. Most editors thought that comic strips were for kids on Sunday, while they were editing daily papers for adults. Moses Koenigsberg, Hearst's feature editor on the *Chicago American*, however, thought a strip narrative aimed at the readership of the daily sports page — making fun of the anguish many horse players went through every day at the tracks when their sure-thing steeds turned into last-place nags, if focused on one desperate loser day by day — might kindle popular interest in the readers of an evening sex-murder-and-sports-finals gazette like the *American*.

A young cartoonist named Clare Briggs, later to be famed for his Mr. and Mrs. Sunday page, was given the job of developing such a strip in 1903, which he called A. Piker Clerk after his crazed bachelor horseplayer. With the added notion of having Clerk's pick for the net day's races be an actual horse, the strip was initially a reader hit, but stumbled in the stretch when it was crowded out of many of the *American*'s ten daily editions because of incoming news, the paper's editors considering their reporters' hot scoops of greater worth than a sports page "filler." Thus many readers who wanted to learn how Clerk did with his latest picks and what ponies he had picked for the next day, were unable to find out. A daily strip that couldn't be read every day by everybody was a born loser, and Clerk galloped into quick oblivion.

But other editorial eyes had been opened in San Francisco by the Clerk innovation, and when a just-hired young comic artist named Bud

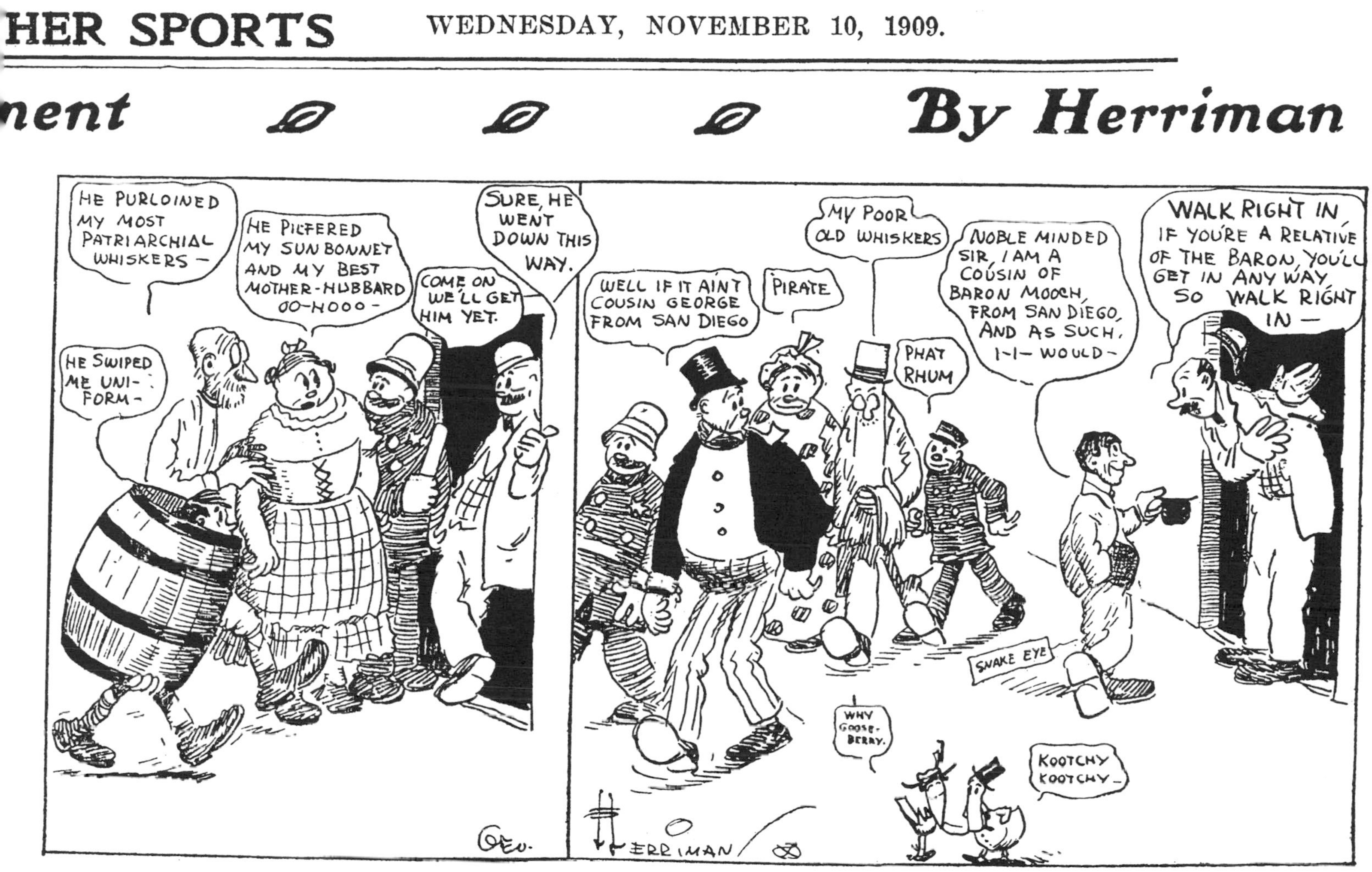
HER SPORTS
WEDNESDAY, NOVEMBER 10, 1909.
nent
By Herriman
HE PURLOINED MY MOST PATRIARCHIAL WHISKERS -
HE PILFERED MY SUN BONNET AND MY BEST MOTHER-HUBBARD OO-HOOO -
SURE, HE WENT DOWN THIS WAY.
COME ON WE'LL GET HIM YET.
HE SWIPED ME UNI-FORM -
GEO.
MY POOR OLD WHISKERS
WELL IF IT AINT COUSIN GEORGE FROM SAN DIEGO
PIRATE
NOBLE MINDED SIR, I AM A COUSIN OF BARON MOOCH, FROM SAN DIEGO, AND AS SUCH, I-I- WOULD -
PHAT RHUM
WALK RIGHT IN, IF YOU'RE A RELATIVE OF THE BARON, YOU'LL GET IN ANY WAY, SO WALK RIGHT IN -
SNAKE EYE
WHY GOOSE-BERRY.
KOOTCHY KOOTCHY
HERRIMAN

Fisher suggested to the sports editor of *San Francisco Chronicle* in 1907 that the Clerk strip might stand a retread job if it had an assured daily sinecure in the *Chron*'s sports section, he was taken up on the offer and Fisher's A. Mutt (a married Clerk) pursued his daily desperation on the racing results and schedules page — to almost immediate acclaim after Fisher's initial few picks turned out (incredibly) to be winners.

Needless to say, George spotted the *Chronicle*'s innovation, read about the paper's quick boast of an actual rise in circulation in A. Mutt's first week, and made the obvious proposal to his editors. And lo, it came to pass that on December 10, 1907, less than a month after the inauguration of A. Mutt, a yet-to-be-named cartoon horse-player in resplendent garb amazed readers of the *L.A. Examiner* by doing funny and desperate things through five successive panel spots framed in the paper's sports pages, all very amusingly limned by boy George. Like Mutt, the quickly named Mr. Proones (star of *Mr. Proones the Plunger*) was wed, but seemed a good deal better off: Proones believed in putting on flash among his raffish fellow bettors. Unlike Mutt, however, Proones was not functionally linked to picking winners every day — George had been given a looser rein on his pioneering weekday strip and quickly pursued his own broadly thematic but sharply differentiated daily gags, some getting Proones as far from the actual track locale as George could swing it. But those delicious daily gags came to an abrupt halt a bare two weeks after their inception and now no one knows why — probably an editor with the Last Word on such things simply felt the experimental strip had failed to properly mimic the successful *A. Mutt* formula and had certainly not goosed the paper's circulation in the same way. So it was back to random single panel sports and news art for George for a while. Nevertheless, the young cartoonist had made a bit of comic strip history in two ways — one, by drawing the second of the first two acknowledged daily newspaper strips to run more than a week, and two, by creating the image of Little Jeff in his short, bristly moustached Proones: an image to be adopted (certainly with a now unrecorded bow to George) by Fisher a few months later in *A. Mutt* (as a madhouse denizen, no less), and to be developed as the small member of the lifetime buddyship of Mutt and Jeff.

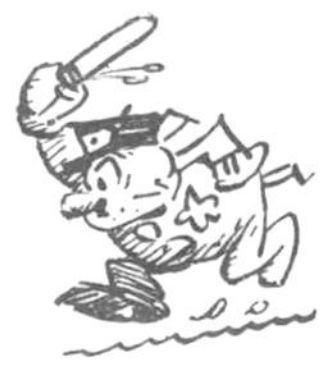

We can only guess what got George's next comic strip (the long-lived and widely popular *Baron Mooch*) into the *Examiner* in 1909 after a two-year stint of artistry-as-usual, but it's intriguing to speculate. We know that Hearst had been publishing small-panel comic strips by a number of artists on the editorial pages of his morning papers since the early 1900s, most notably Gus Mager's *Monks*, but these were not prominently placed and never appeared more than three days a week apiece when they ran — and often one or another title might not appear for weeks. These strip vignettes, together with Fisher's *A. Mutt* (by now *Mutt and Jeff*), had effectively shaken the general newspaper taboo on daily comic strips, while Hearst was about to shatter it completely with a full page of large-paneled strips in his *New York Evening Journal* in 1912. There was an editorial awareness in the *L.A. Examiner* that the times were certainly a-changin', and it is likely serious attention was paid to some sample Mooch episodes backed up with a strong pitch by George — "Look, it's a class act, chief — Mooch is a steal from Wilkins Micawber in Dickens' *David Copperfield*, fer gosh sakes. A great comic bum — the greatest. It'll be lowbrow enough for the sports readers, but there'll be some cute highbrow stuff, too. A funny duck quoting Shakespeare, like that. Those strips the boss is running are getting a real public these days, and hell, *Mutt and Jeff* is really big — " (Of course you and I, good reader, know that Herriman was above such slangy *Front Page*-style gab, but in the newspapers of the time, you didn't let the rest of the crew know it. Fun enough to speculate, though, and in fact the confab may well have gone very much like this.)

Whatever happened, the first spectacularly placed large-panel *Baron Mooch* episode (it ran completely across the top of a sports page) socked the readers on Monday, September 27, 1909, and — possibly amazingly to some — the next episode turned up the next day, then another on Wednesday, and so right through the week, to come back the next Monday for a repeat performance. This was terrific. Great comedy, a great character (who even announced, "They say I look like Wilkins Micawber" in one early episode), and highly detailed comic art, was a sensation in L.A., and caught the highly amused eye of William Randolph in his flagship office at the New York American. The boss was in the habit of going through every edition of all of his papers every day, and *Baron Mooch* hit him front and center. He was not long in mulling over plans for this superb comic strip talent, what with his developing plans about the upcoming daily comic strip page — the first in the country! — that would grace all of his afternoon dailies early in the next decade.

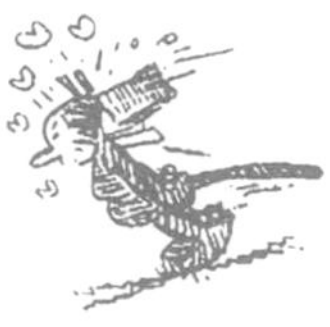

George, of course, was in creative bliss with the new strip. His inherent fancy for the comic grotesque and bizarre was running at full throttle in Mooch. Ideas piled up in his head, more than he could use for months to come. Inspiration was not only easy, it ran rampant, just as it did in the novels of his mentor in matters fictional, Dickens. The new comic strip form was made to order for such an unfettered talent, and George was its avatar. *Mooch* was a work for any age, a classic work that was to be a mere prelude for the greater work to come. But even in the relatively few months George had to work on *Mooch* he managed to conceive of a further step into high comedy — a world of avian characters centered on the enlarged activities of Gooseberry Sprigg, the Duck duke, whom he had kept on the sidelines in *Mooch* as a casual (and marvelously funny) kibitzer on the disastrous antics of the strip's voracious hero. In short, inspired by the *Examiner*'s need to editorially glorify and promote one of the nation's first aviation shows, which was to unlimber pilots and creaky aircraft in L.A. for a good two weeks, George created Coconino County, the future realm of Krazy Kat, as a background for Sprigg and his tangle-winged cohorts to participate in their version of the air show. The brilliantly comic Sprigg strip did it for Hearst. Even though it would be a year or more before his daily comic page would be ready to go, he damnall wanted this fantastic comic genius in New York to develop a strip for national Hearst paper distribution.

Below: the world's first look at Coconino County's krazy kountenance occurred in Herriman's *Gooseberry Sprigg*, sampled here from a 1909 *L. A. Examiner* Sports page.

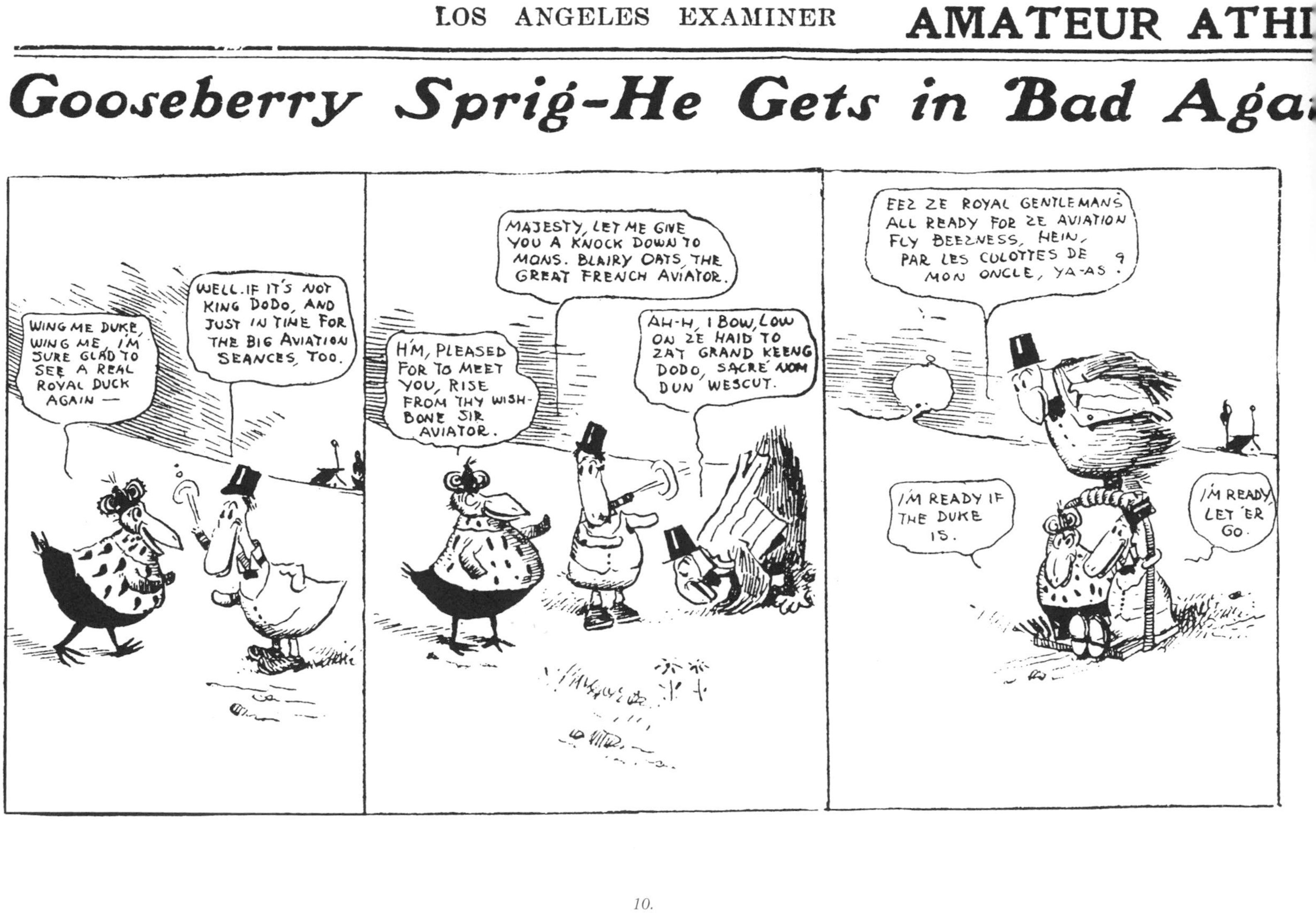
LOS ANGELES EXAMINER
AMATEUR ATHI
Gooseberry Sprig-He Gets in Bad Aga
WING ME DUKE, WING ME, I'M SURE GLAD TO SEE A REAL ROYAL DUCK AGAIN —
WELL. IF IT'S NOT KING DODO, AND JUST IN TIME FOR THE BIG AVIATION SEANCES, TOO.
MAJESTY, LET ME GIVE YOU A KNOCK DOWN TO MONS. BLAIRY OATS, THE GREAT FRENCH AVIATOR.
H'M, PLEASED FOR TO MEET YOU, RISE FROM THY WISH-BONE SIR AVIATOR.
AH-H, I BOW, LOW ON ZE HAID TO ZAT GRAND KEENG DODO, SACRÉ NOM DUN WESCUT.
EEZ ZE ROYAL GENTLEMANS ALL READY FOR ZE AVIATION FLY BEEZNESS, HEIN, PAR LES CULOTTES DE MON ONCLE, YA-AS?
I'M READY IF THE DUKE IS.
I'M READY, LET 'ER GO.

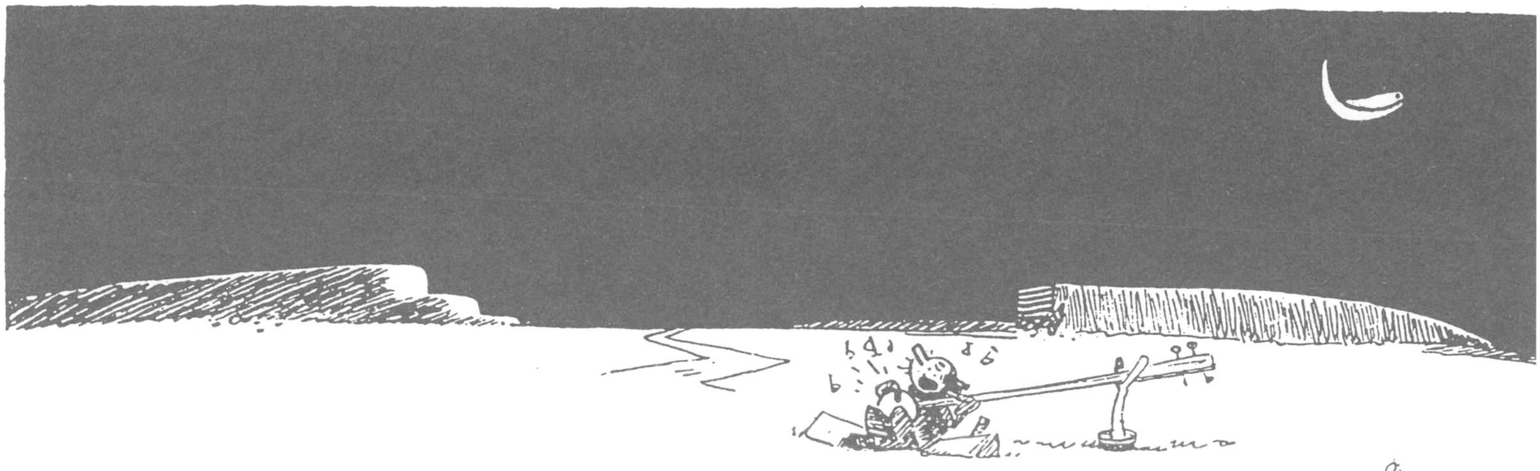

At Hearst's urgent beck, George left L.A. to develop the boss's idea for a first-rate family gag strip, the Dingbat Family epic that quickly became the masterful fantasy called *The Family Upstairs* — a unique comic strip that was at once two strips, in which the forlorn Krazy Kat character (first introduced briefly in *Mooch* in a meeting with Sprigg) would develop in great comic company with a sadistic mouse, a protective and kat-enamored kop, and an occasional look-in by the ineffable Sprigg — all of which will be discussed in the next volume of *Krazy and Ignatz*, with nifty specimens of the great strips involved, and a little more about the one-of-a-kind comic strip talent that wrought drawing board wonder of a kind never seen before.

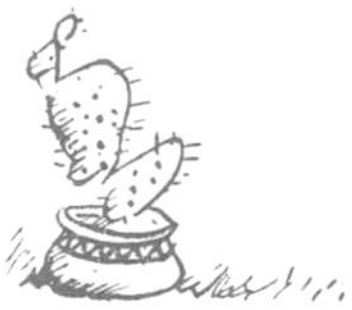

Drums and cymbals and katkalls! The komplete runs of Baron Mooch and Gooseberry Sprigg, full size as published in 1909 and 1910, can be found reprinted in the first volume of ***By George! The Komplete Daily Komik Strips of George Herriman,*** *edited by Bill Black-beard, available from specproductions@msn.com. Ask for Andy Feigery, publisher.*

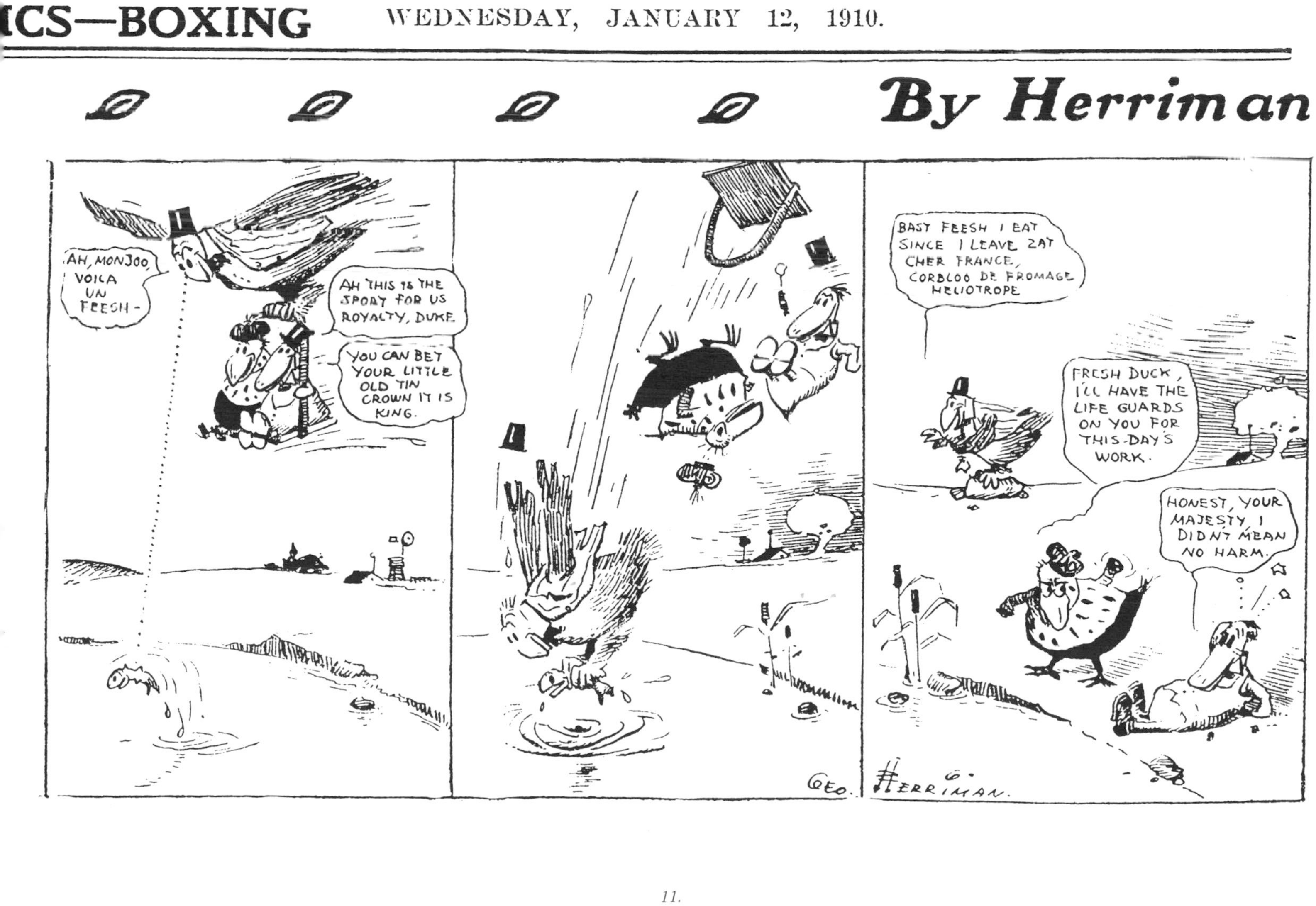
ICS—BOXING
WEDNESDAY, JANUARY 12, 1910.
By Herriman
AH, MONJOO, VOILA UN FEESH -
AH THIS IS THE SPORT FOR US ROYALTY, DUKE
YOU CAN BET YOUR LITTLE OLD TIN CROWN IT IS KING.
BAST FEESH I EAT SINCE I LEAVE ZAT CHER FRANCE, CORBLOO DE FROMAGE HELIOTROPE
FRESH DUCK, I'LL HAVE THE LIFE GUARDS ON YOU FOR THIS-DAY'S WORK.
HONEST, YOUR MAJESTY, I DIDN'T MEAN NO HARM.
GEO. HERRIMAN.

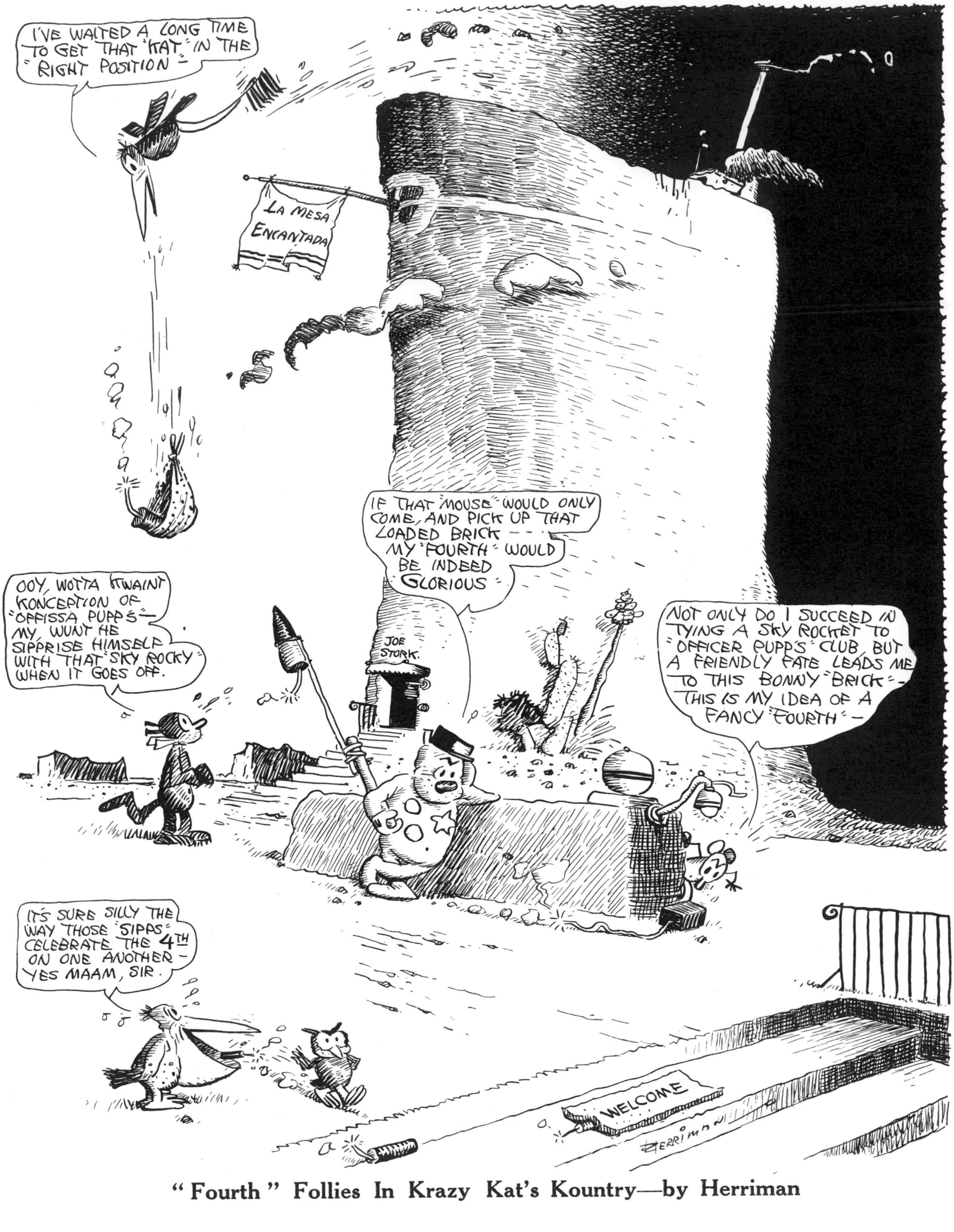
I'VE WAITED A LONG TIME TO GET THAT KAT IN THE RIGHT POSITION -
LA MESA ENCANTADA
IF THAT MOUSE WOULD ONLY COME, AND PICK UP THAT LOADED BRICK --- MY FOURTH WOULD BE INDEED GLORIOUS
OOY, WOTTA KWAINT KONCEPTION OF OFFISSA PUPP'S — MY, WUNT HE SIPPRISE HIMSELF WITH THAT SKY ROCKY WHEN IT GOES OFF.
JOE STORK.
NOT ONLY DO I SUCCEED IN TYING A SKY ROCKET TO OFFICER PUPP'S CLUB, BUT A FRIENDLY FATE LEADS ME TO THIS BONNY BRICK - THIS IS MY IDEA OF A FANCY FOURTH -
IT'S SURE SILLY THE WAY THOSE SIPPS CELEBRATE THE 4TH ON ONE ANOTHER - YES MAAM, SIR.
WELCOME
HERRIMAN

"Fourth" Follies In Krazy Kat's Kountry—by Herriman

A drawing done especially for the July 1923 issue of *Circulation* magazine, a monthly King Features publication sent out to newspaper editors advertising its columnists and syndicated features — most particularly its cartoonists. Courtesy of and thanks to Robert L. Beerbohm.

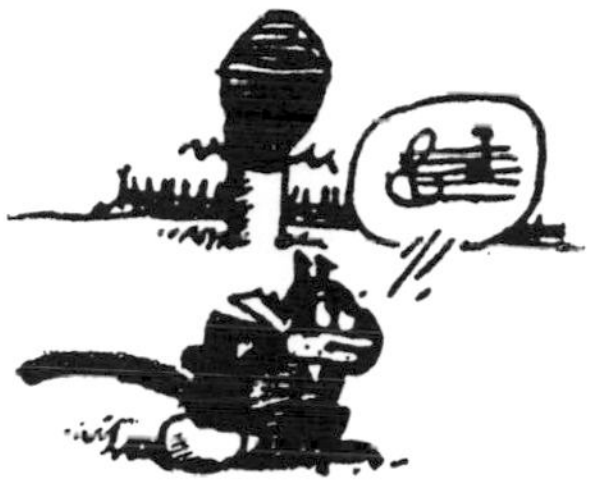

1931.

Readers, please note: an Ignatz "dingbat" placed below a strip indicates a relevant or related footnote at the volume's end for that particular selection, all to be found in the "Ignatz Debaffler" section.

KRAZY KAT *By Herriman.*

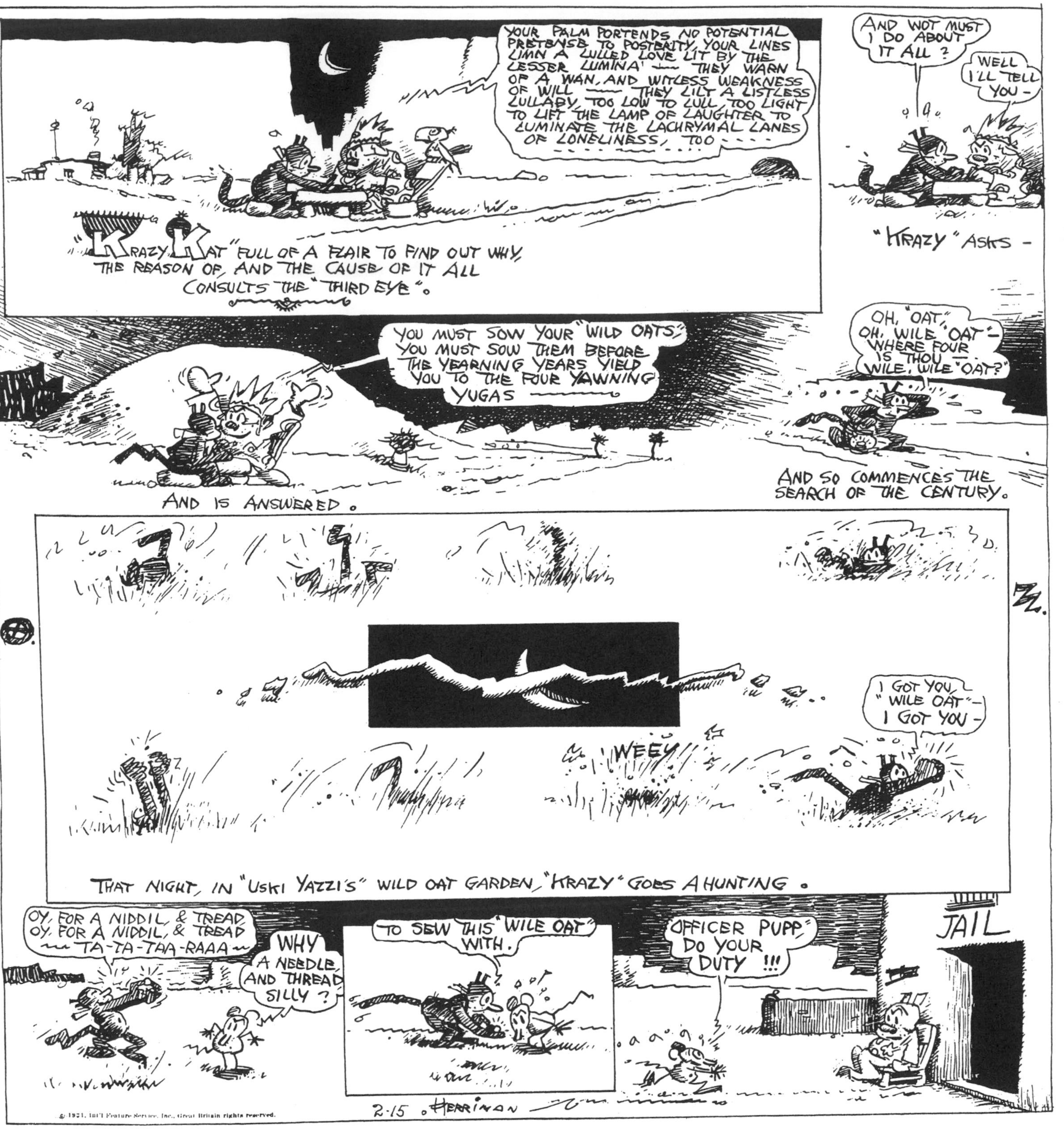

YOUR PALM PORTENDS NO POTENTIAL PRETENSE TO POSTERITY, YOUR LINES LIMN A LULLED LOVE LIT BY THE LESSER LUMINA' — THEY WARN OF A WAN, AND WITLESS WEAKNESS OF WILL — THEY LILT A LISTLESS LULLABY, TOO LOW TO LULL, TOO LIGHT TO LIFT THE LAMP OF LAUGHTER TO LUMINATE THE LACHRYMAL LANES OF LONELINESS, TOO - - - -
"KRAZY KAT" FULL OF A FLAIR TO FIND OUT WHY, THE REASON OF, AND THE CAUSE OF IT ALL CONSULTS THE "THIRD EYE".
AND WOT MUST I DO ABOUT IT ALL ?
WELL I'LL TELL YOU -
"KRAZY" ASKS -
YOU MUST SOW YOUR "WILD OATS", YOU MUST SOW THEM BEFORE THE YEARNING YEARS YIELD YOU TO THE FOUR YAWNING YUGAS
AND IS ANSWERED.
OH, "OAT," OH, WILE "OAT" — WHERE FOUR IS THOU — WILE, WILE "OAT?"
AND SO COMMENCES THE SEARCH OF THE CENTURY.
I GOT YOU, "WILE OAT" — I GOT YOU -
WEEY
THAT NIGHT, IN "USKI YAZZI'S" WILD OAT GARDEN, "KRAZY" GOES A HUNTING.
OY, FOR A NIDDIL, & TREAD OY, FOR A NIDDIL, & TREAD — TA-TA-TAA-RAAA
WHY A NEEDLE AND THREAD SILLY ?
TO SEW THIS "WILE OAT" WITH.
OFFICER PUPP, DO YOUR DUTY !!!
JAIL
© 1931, Int'l Feature Service, Inc., Great Britain rights reserved.
2-15 HERRIMAN

February 15th, 1931.

KRAZY KAT *By Herriman*

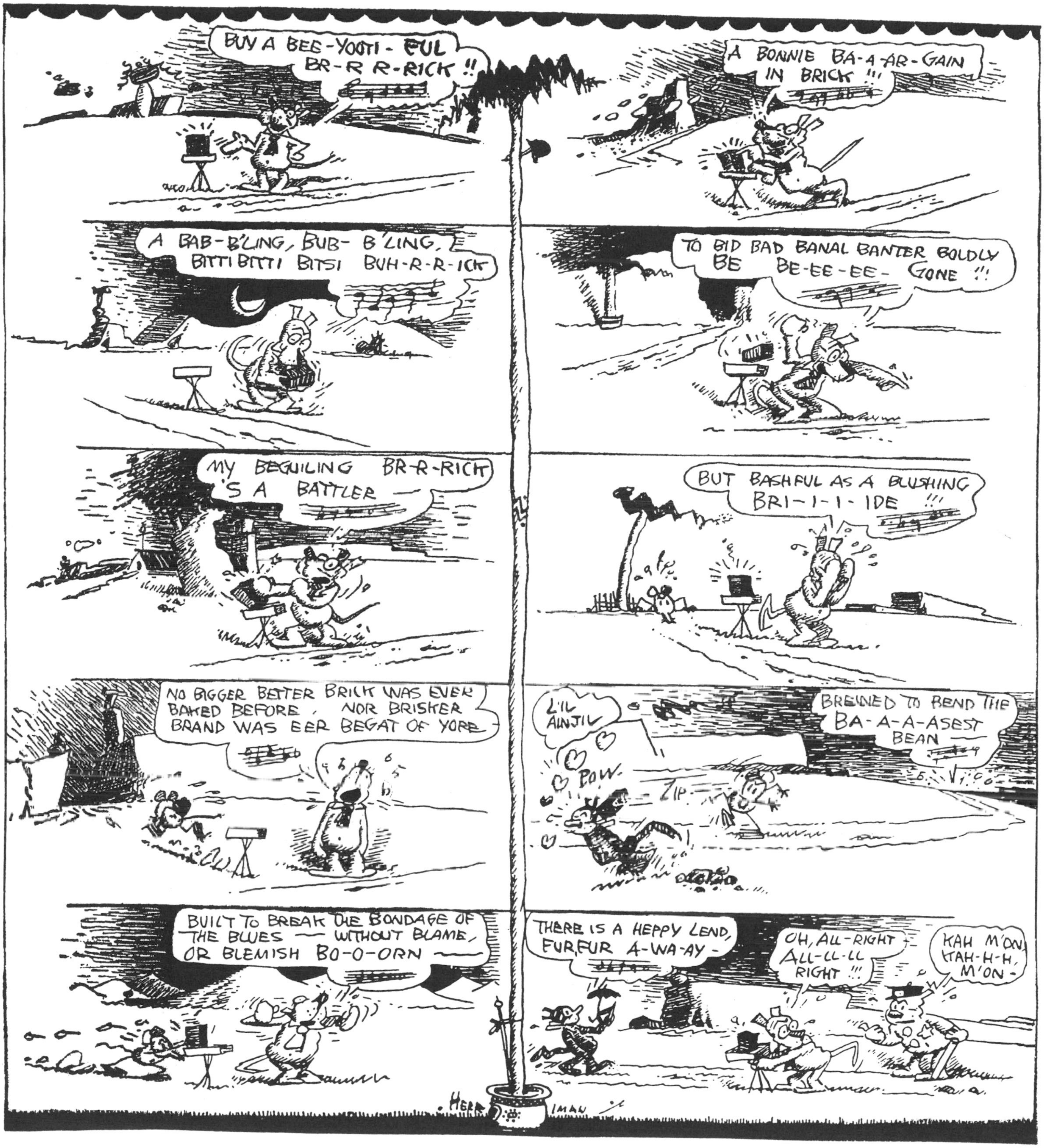
BUY A BEE-YOOTI-FUL BR-R R-RICK !!
A BONNIE BA-A-AR-GAIN IN BRICK !!!
A BAB-B'LING, BUB-B'LING, BITTI BITTI BITSI BUH-R-R-ICK
TO BID BAD BANAL BANTER BOLDLY BE BE-EE-EE- GONE !!!
MY BEGUILING BR-R-RICK 'S A BATTLER
BUT BASHFUL AS A BLUSHING BRI-I-I-IDE !!!
NO BIGGER BETTER BRICK WAS EVER BAKED BEFORE, NOR BRISKER BRAND WAS E'ER BEGAT OF YORE
L'IL AINJIL
POW
ZIP
BREWED TO BEND THE BA-A-A-ASEST BEAN
BUILT TO BREAK THE BONDAGE OF THE BLUES — WITHOUT BLAME, OR BLEMISH BO-O-ORN
THERE IS A HEPPY LEND, FUR, FUR A-WA-AY -
OH, ALL-RIGHT ALL-LL-LL RIGHT !!!
KAH M'ON, KAH-H-H, M'ON -
HERRIMAN

February 22nd, 1931.

KRAZY KAT *By Herriman*

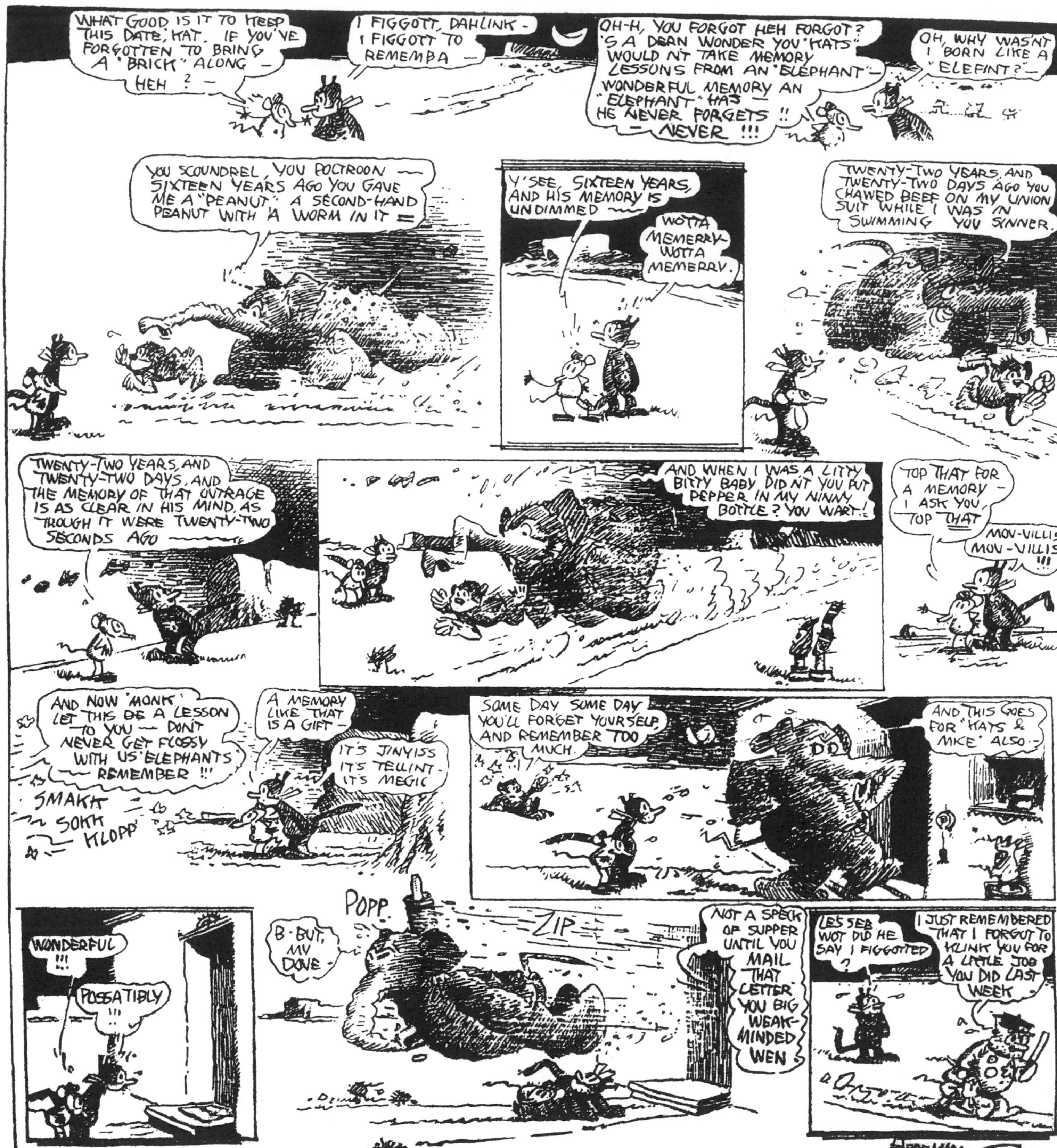

WHAT GOOD IS IT TO KEEP THIS DATE, KAT. IF YOU'VE FORGOTTEN TO BRING A "BRICK" ALONG — HEH ? —
I FIGGOTT, DAHLINK — I FIGGOTT TO REMEMBA —
OH-H, YOU FORGOT HEH FORGOT? 'S A DERN WONDER YOU "KATS" WOULD N'T TAKE MEMORY LESSONS FROM AN "ELEPHANT" — WONDERFUL MEMORY AN "ELEPHANT" HAS — HE NEVER FORGETS !! — NEVER !!!
OH, WHY WASN'T I BORN LIKE A "ELEFINT?" —
YOU SCOUNDREL, YOU POLTROON — SIXTEEN YEARS AGO YOU GAVE ME A "PEANUT" A SECOND-HAND PEANUT WITH A WORM IN IT =
Y'SEE, SIXTEEN YEARS, AND HIS MEMORY IS UNDIMMED —
WOTTA MEMERRY — WOTTA MEMERRY.
TWENTY-TWO YEARS, AND TWENTY-TWO DAYS AGO YOU CHAWED BEEF ON MY UNION SUIT WHILE I WAS IN SWIMMING YOU SINNER.
TWENTY-TWO YEARS, AND TWENTY-TWO DAYS, AND THE MEMORY OF THAT OUTRAGE IS AS CLEAR IN HIS MIND, AS THOUGH IT WERE TWENTY-TWO SECONDS AGO —
AND WHEN I WAS A LITTY BITTY BABY DID N'T YOU PUT PEPPER IN MY NINNY BOTTLE? YOU WART!
TOP THAT FOR A MEMORY — I ASK YOU, TOP THAT
MOV-VILLIS MOV-VILLIS !!!
AND NOW "MONK" LET THIS BE A LESSON TO YOU — DON'T NEVER GET FLOSSY WITH US "ELEPHANTS" — REMEMBER !!"
SMAKK
SOKK
KLOPP
A MEMORY LIKE THAT IS A GIFT —
IT'S JINYISS IT'S TELLINT — IT'S MEGIC
SOME DAY SOME DAY YOU'LL FORGET YOURSELF, AND REMEMBER TOO MUCH.
AND THIS GOES FOR "KATS & MIKE" ALSO —
WONDERFUL !!!
POSSATIBLY !!!
POPP.
B-BUT, MY DOVE —
ZIP
NOT A SPECK OF SUPPER UNTIL YOU MAIL THAT LETTER YOU BIG WEAK-MINDED WEN
LES SEE WOT DID HE SAY I FIGGOTTED ?
I JUST REMEMBERED THAT I FORGOT TO KLINK YOU FOR A LITTLE JOB YOU DID LAST WEEK
HERRIMAN

March 1st, 1931.

KRAZY KAT By Herriman

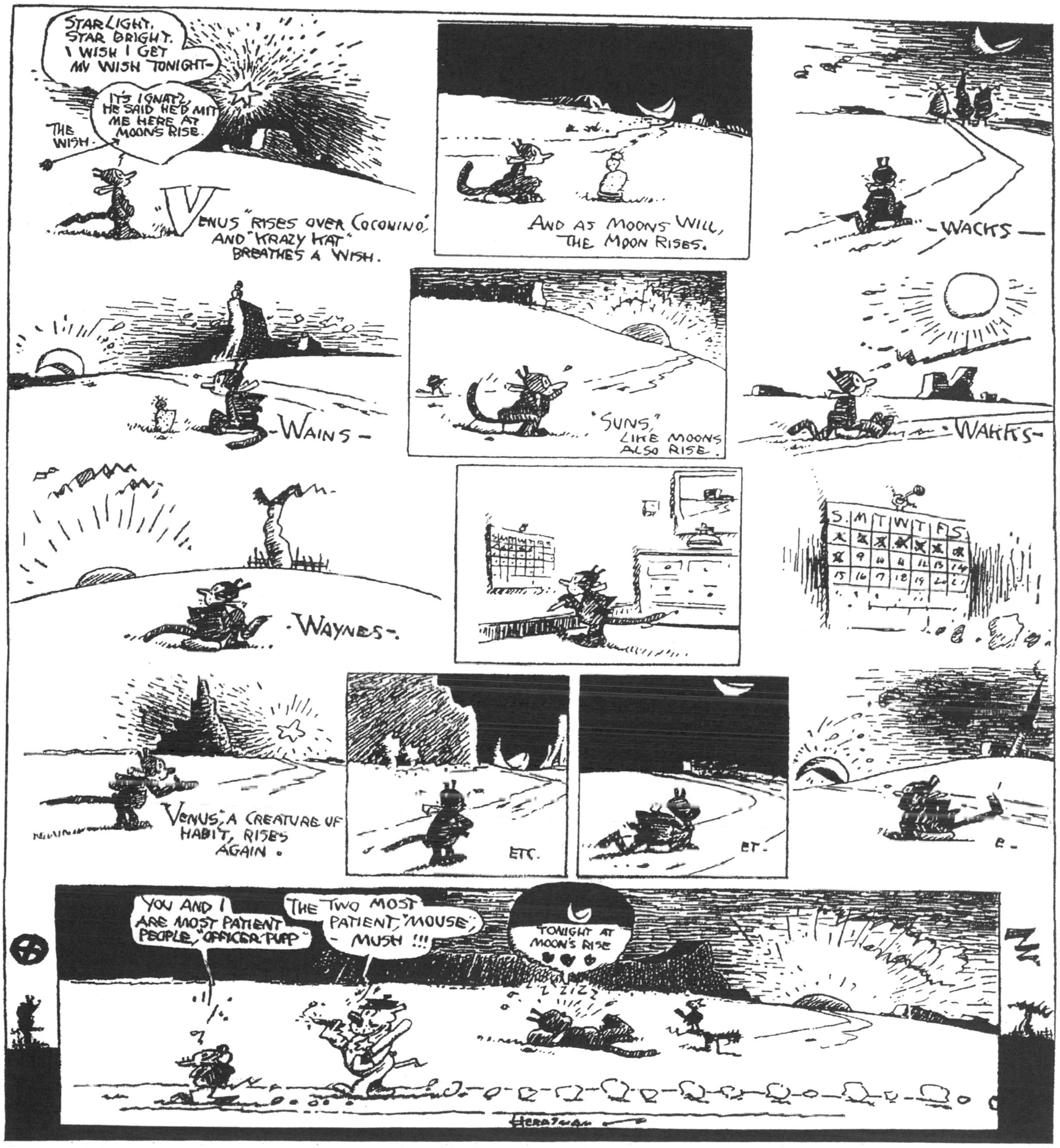

STAR LIGHT, STAR BRIGHT. I WISH I GET MY WISH TONIGHT—
IT'S IGNATZ, HE SAID HE'D MIT ME HERE AT MOON'S RISE.
THE WISH.
"VENUS" RISES OVER COCONINO, AND "KRAZY KAT" BREATHES A WISH.
AND AS MOONS WILL, THE MOON RISES.
-WACKS-
-WAINS-
"SUNS," LIKE MOONS ALSO RISE.
-WAKKS-
-WAYNES-.
S M T W T F S
VENUS, A CREATURE OF HABIT, RISES AGAIN.
ETC.
ET-
E-
YOU AND I ARE MOST PATIENT PEOPLE, "OFFICER PUPP"
THE TWO MOST PATIENT, "MOUSE", - MUSH !!!
TONIGHT AT MOON'S RISE
Z Z Z I Z Z
HERRIMAN

March 8th, 1931.

KRAZY KAT By Herriman

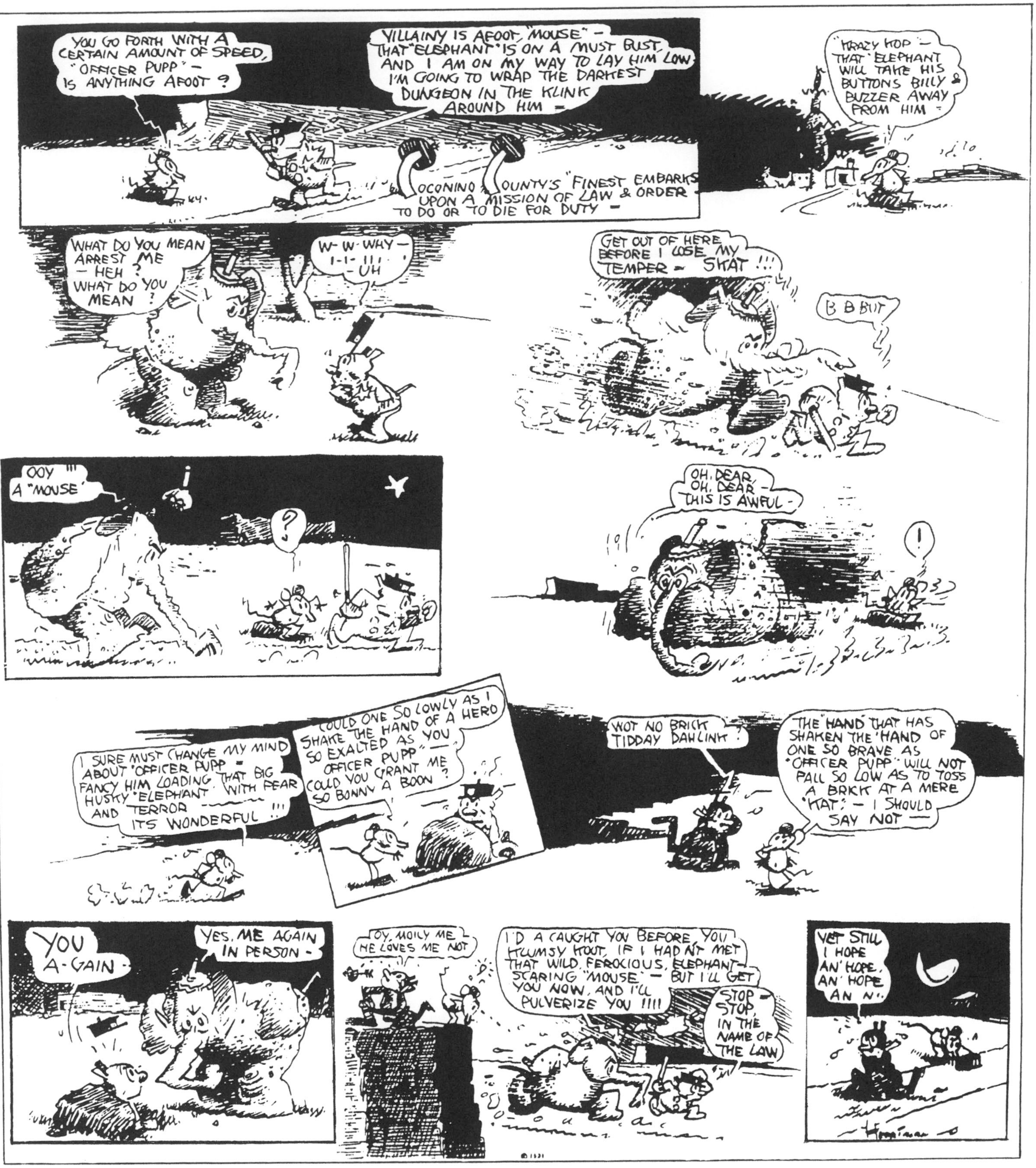

YOU GO FORTH WITH A CERTAIN AMOUNT OF SPEED, "OFFICER PUPP" — IS ANYTHING AFOOT ?
VILLAINY IS AFOOT, "MOUSE" — THAT "ELEPHANT" IS ON A MUST BUST, AND I AM ON MY WAY TO LAY HIM LOW. I'M GOING TO WRAP THE DARKEST DUNGEON IN THE KLINK AROUND HIM —
OCONINO COUNTY'S "FINEST" EMBARKS UPON A MISSION OF LAW & ORDER — TO DO OR TO DIE FOR DUTY —
"KRAZY KOP" — THAT "ELEPHANT" WILL TAKE HIS BUTTONS BILLY & BUZZER AWAY FROM HIM —
WHAT DO YOU MEAN ARREST ME — HEH ? WHAT DO YOU MEAN ?
W-W-WHY — I-I-III — UH
GET OUT OF HERE BEFORE I LOSE MY TEMPER — SKAT !!!
B B BUT
OOY !!! A "MOUSE"
?
OH, DEAR, OH, DEAR — THIS IS AWFUL —
!
I SURE MUST CHANGE MY MIND ABOUT "OFFICER PUPP" — FANCY HIM LOADING THAT BIG HUSKY "ELEPHANT" WITH FEAR AND TERROR — ITS WONDERFUL !!!
COULD ONE SO LOWLY AS I SHAKE THE HAND OF A HERO SO EXALTED AS YOU "OFFICER PUPP" — COULD YOU GRANT ME SO BONNY A BOON ?
WOT NO BRICK TIDDAY DAHLINK ?
THE "HAND" THAT HAS SHAKEN THE "HAND" OF ONE SO BRAVE AS "OFFICER PUPP" WILL NOT FALL SO LOW AS TO TOSS A BRICK AT A MERE "KAT" — I SHOULD SAY NOT —
YOU A-GAIN
YES, ME AGAIN IN PERSON —
OY, MOILY ME — HE LOVES ME NOT
I'D A CAUGHT YOU BEFORE, YOU KLUMSY KOUT, IF I HAD'NT MET THAT WILD, FEROCIOUS, ELEPHANT-SCARING "MOUSE" — BUT I'LL GET YOU NOW, AND I'LL PULVERIZE YOU !!!!
STOP — STOP, IN THE NAME OF THE LAW
YET STILL I HOPE AN' HOPE, AN' HOPE AN' —
Herriman
© 1931

March 15th, 1931.

KRAZY KAT *By Herriman*

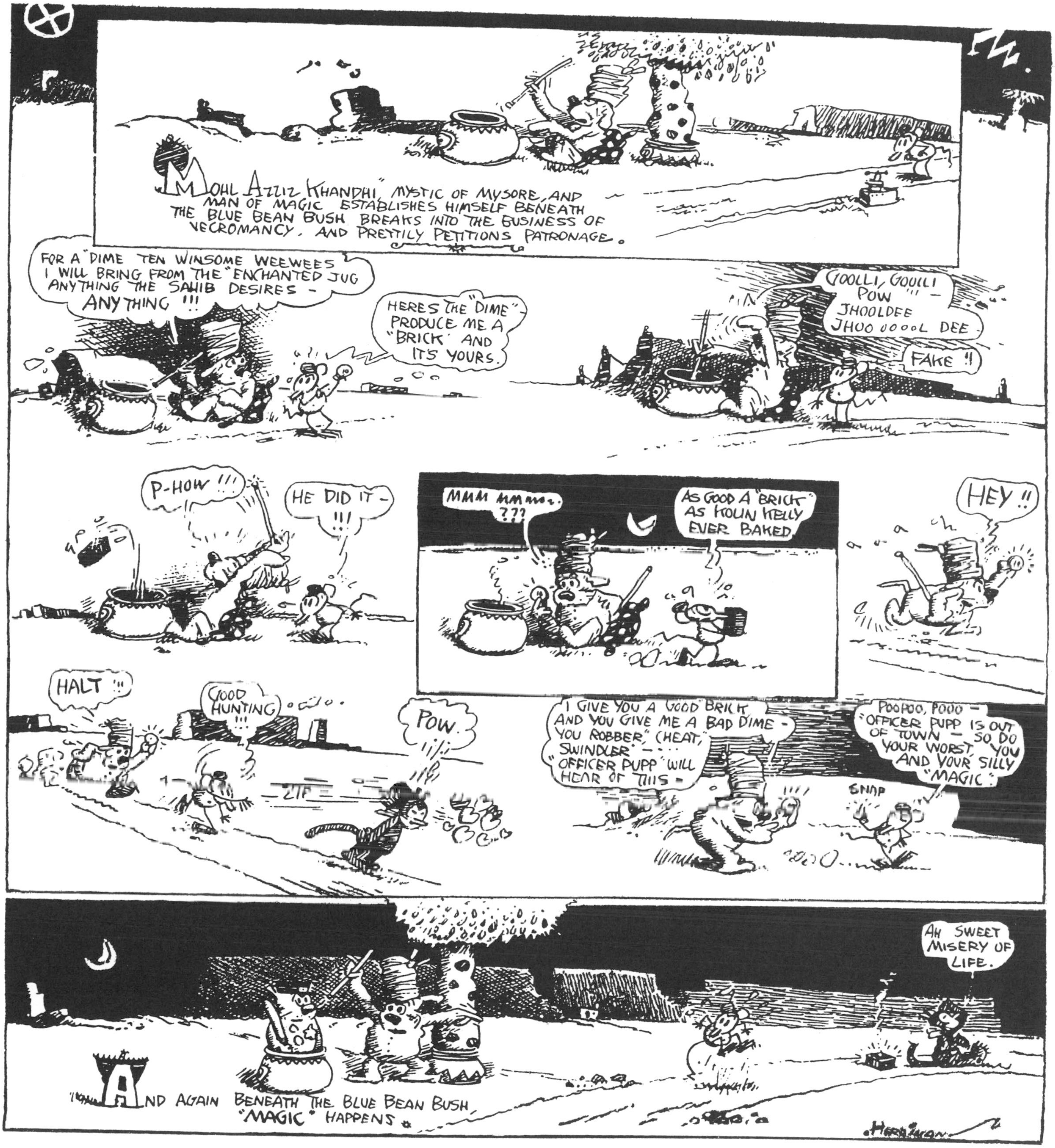

MOHL AZZIZ KHANDHI, MYSTIC OF MYSORE, AND MAN OF MAGIC ESTABLISHES HIMSELF BENEATH THE BLUE BEAN BUSH BREAKS INTO THE BUSINESS OF NECROMANCY, AND PRETTILY PETITIONS PATRONAGE.
FOR A "DIME" TEN WINSOME WEEWEES I WILL BRING FROM THE "ENCHANTED JUG" ANYTHING THE SAHIB DESIRES - ANYTHING !!!
HERES THE "DIME" PRODUCE ME A "BRICK" AND ITS YOURS.
GOOLLI, GOULLI POW !!! - JHOOLDEE JHOO OOOOL DEE.
FAKE !!
P-HOW !!!
HE DID IT - !!!
MMM MMMMM ???
AS GOOD A "BRICK" AS KOLIN KELLY EVER BAKED
HEY !!
HALT !!!
GOOD HUNTING !!!
ZIP
POW.
I GIVE YOU A GOOD BRICK AND YOU GIVE ME A BAD DIME - YOU ROBBER, CHEAT, SWINDLER - - "OFFICER PUPP" WILL HEAR OF THIS -
POOPOO, POOO - "OFFICER PUPP" IS OUT OF TOWN - SO DO YOUR WORST, YOU AND YOUR SILLY "MAGIC".
SNAP
AH SWEET MISERY OF LIFE.
AND AGAIN BENEATH THE BLUE BEAN BUSH "MAGIC" HAPPENS.
Herriman

March 22nd, 1931.

KRAZY KAT By Herriman

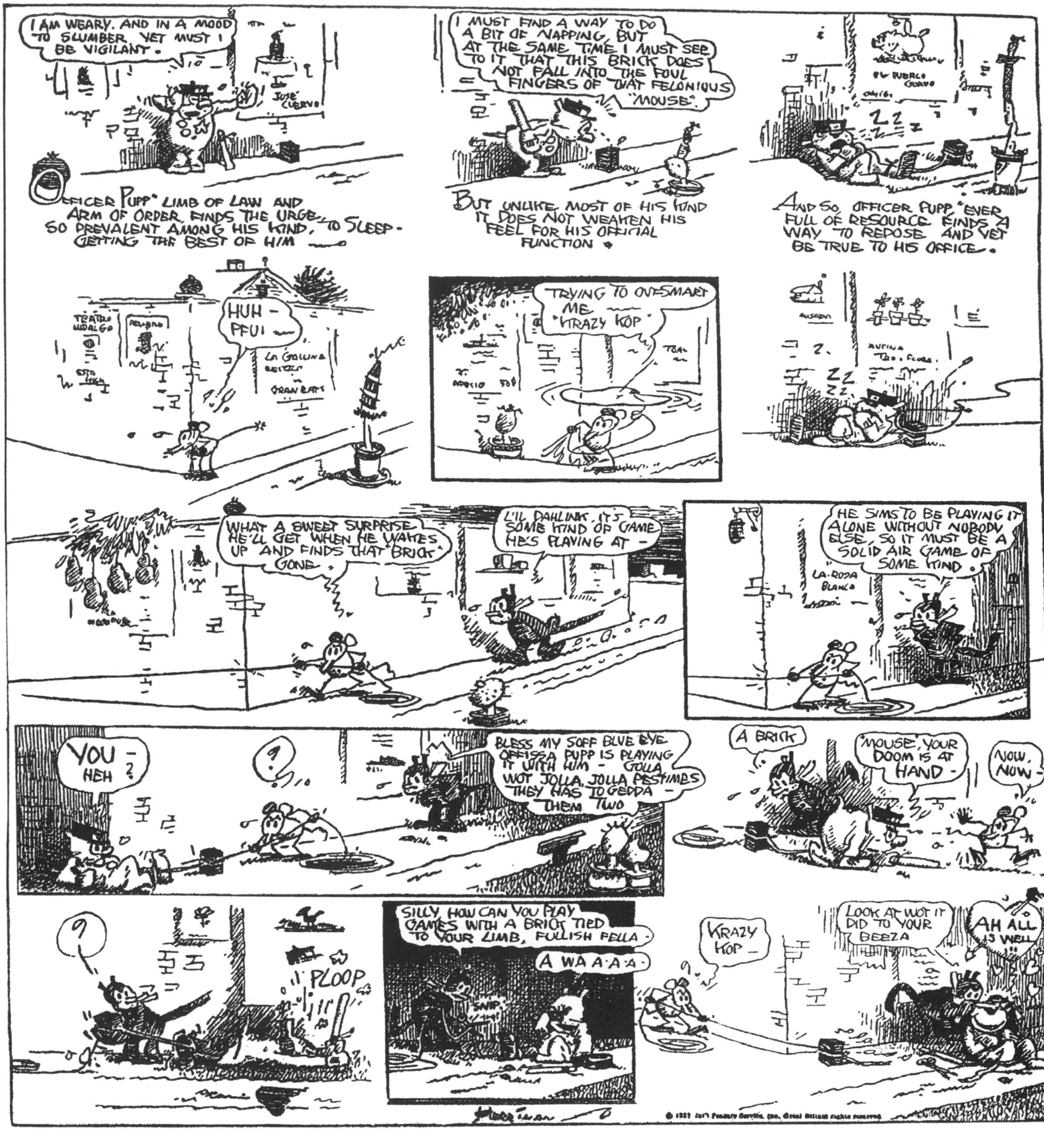

I AM WEARY, AND IN A MOOD TO SLUMBER, YET MUST I BE VIGILANT.
OFFICER "PUPP" LIMB OF LAW AND ARM OF ORDER, FINDS THE URGE, SO PREVALENT AMONG HIS KIND, TO SLEEP - GETTING THE BEST OF HIM
I MUST FIND A WAY TO DO A BIT OF NAPPING, BUT AT THE SAME TIME I MUST SEE TO IT THAT THIS BRICK DOES NOT FALL INTO THE FOUL FINGERS OF THAT FELONIOUS "MOUSE".
BUT UNLIKE MOST OF HIS KIND IT DOES NOT WEAKEN HIS FEEL FOR HIS OFFICIAL FUNCTION
AND SO, OFFICER PUPP, "EVER FULL OF RESOURCE" FINDS A WAY TO REPOSE AND YET BE TRUE TO HIS OFFICE.
HUH - PFUI -
TRYING TO OUTSMART ME - "KRAZY KOP"
WHAT A SWEET SURPRISE HE'LL GET WHEN HE WAKES UP AND FINDS THAT BRICK GONE.
L'IL DAHLINK, IT'S SOME KIND OF GAME HE'S PLAYING AT -
HE SIMS TO BE PLAYING IT ALONE WITHOUT NOBODY ELSE, SO IT MUST BE A SOLID AIR GAME OF SOME KIND.
YOU - HEH ?
?
BLESS MY SOFF BLUE EYE OFFISSA PUPP IS PLAYING IT WITH HIM - GOLLA WOT JOLLA, JOLLA PESTIMES THEY HAS TO GEDDA - THEM TWO
A BRICK
"MOUSE", YOUR DOOM IS AT HAND -
NOW, NOW -
?
PLOOP
SILLY, HOW CAN YOU PLAY GAMES WITH A BRICK TIED TO YOUR LIMB, FULLISH FELLA -
A WA A-A-A
SNIP
KRAZY KOP -
LOOK AT WOT IT DID TO YOUR BEEZA
AH ALL IS WELL

March 29th, 1931.

KRAZY KAT *By Herriman*

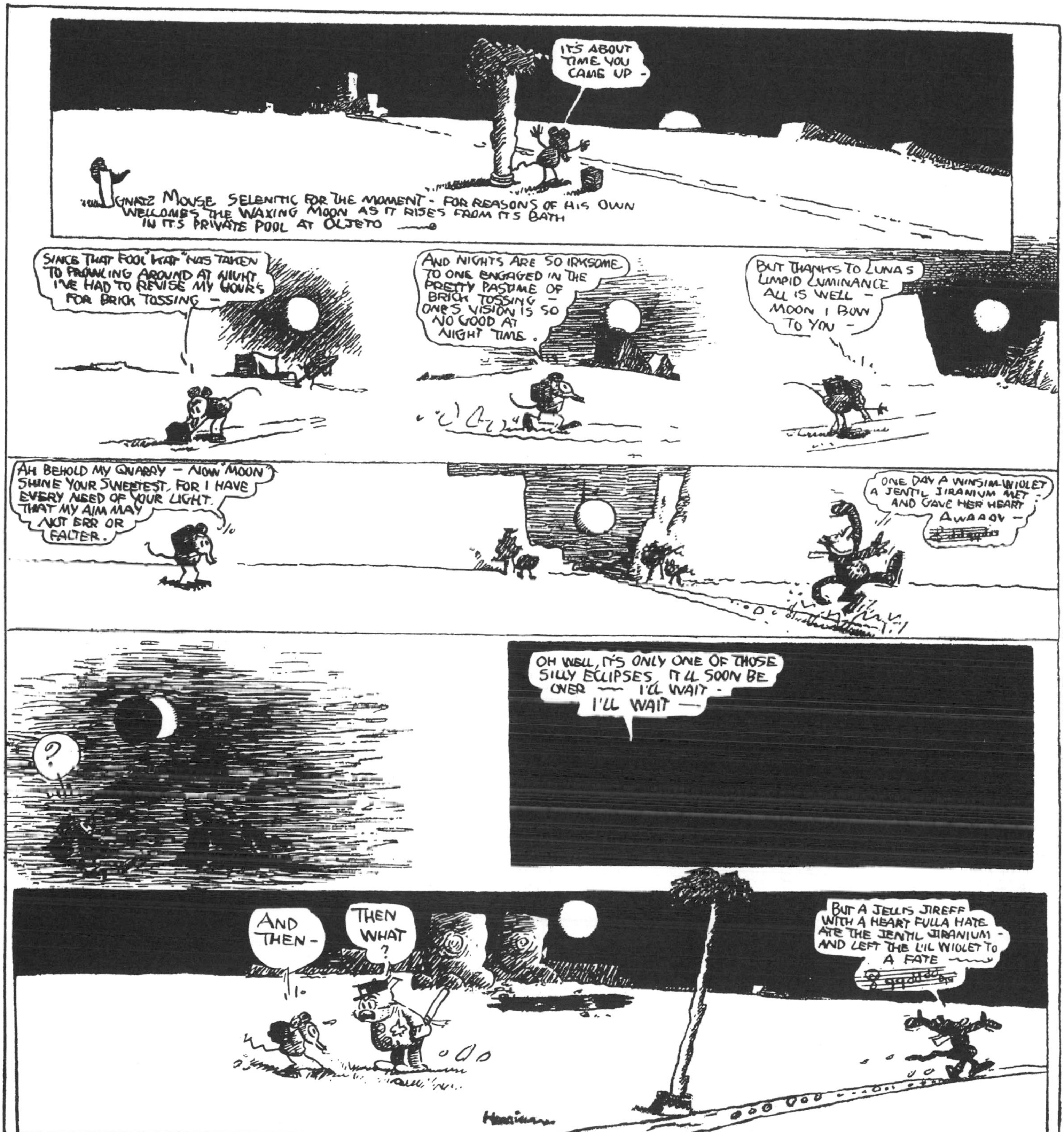

IT'S ABOUT TIME YOU CAME UP -
IGNATZ MOUSE SELENITIC FOR THE MOMENT - FOR REASONS OF HIS OWN WELCOMES THE WAXING MOON AS IT RISES FROM ITS BATH IN ITS PRIVATE POOL AT OLJETO
SINCE THAT FOOL "KAT" HAS TAKEN TO PROWLING AROUND AT NIGHT I'VE HAD TO REVISE MY HOURS FOR BRICK TOSSING -
AND NIGHTS ARE SO IRKSOME TO ONE ENGAGED IN THE PRETTY PASTIME OF BRICK TOSSING - ONE'S VISION IS SO NO GOOD AT NIGHT TIME.
BUT THANKS TO LUNA'S LIMPID LUMINANCE ALL IS WELL - MOON I BOW TO YOU -
AH BEHOLD MY QUARRY - NOW "MOON" SHINE YOUR SWEETEST, FOR I HAVE EVERY NEED OF YOUR LIGHT. THAT MY AIM MAY NOT ERR OR FALTER.
ONE DAY A WINSIM WIOLET A JENTIL JIRANIUM MET - AND GAVE HER HEART AWAAAY -
?
OH WELL, IT'S ONLY ONE OF THOSE SILLY ECLIPSES IT'LL SOON BE OVER — I'LL WAIT - I'LL WAIT —
AND THEN -
THEN WHAT ?
BUT A JELLIS JIREFF WITH A HEART FULLA HATE ATE THE JENTIL JIRANIUM - AND LEFT THE LIL WIOLET TO A FATE
Herriman

April 19th, 1931.

KRAZY KAT *By Herriman*

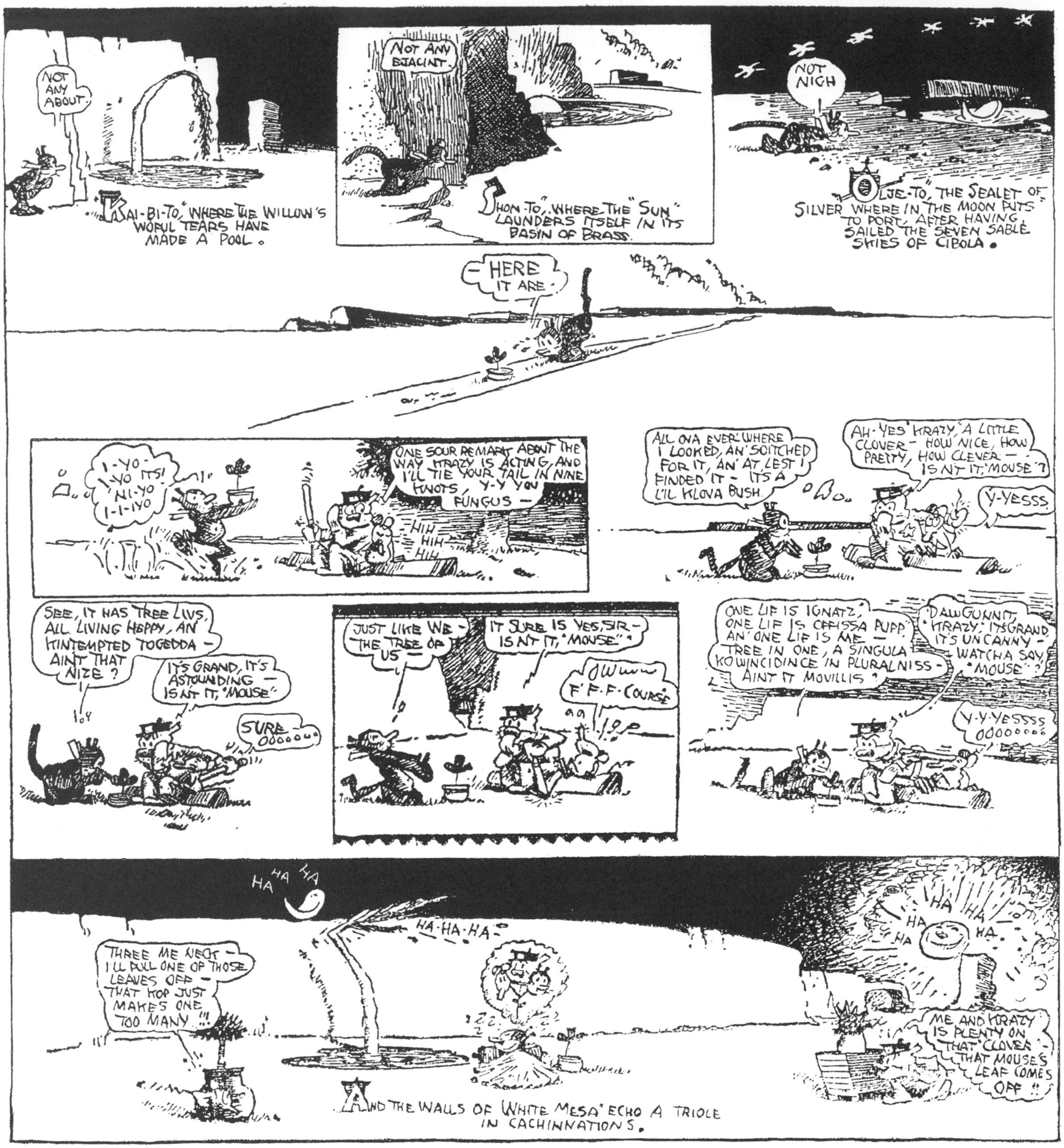
NOT ANY ABOUT.
KAI-BI-TO," WHERE THE WILLOW'S WOFUL TEARS HAVE MADE A POOL.
NOT ANY BJACINT.
SHON-TO," WHERE THE "SUN" LAUNDERS ITSELF IN ITS BASIN OF BRASS.
NOT NIGH
OLJE-TO," THE SEALET OF SILVER WHERE IN THE MOON PUTS TO PORT, AFTER HAVING SAILED THE SEVEN SABLE SKIES OF CIBOLA.
HERE IT ARE.
I-YO-I-YO ITS! NI-YO I-I-IYO
ONE SOUR REMARK ABOUT THE WAY KRAZY IS ACTING, AND I'LL TIE YOUR TAIL IN NINE KNOTS, Y-Y YOU FUNGUS—
HIH HIH HIH
ALL OVA EVER WHERE I LOOKED, AN' SCITCHED FOR IT, AN' AT LEST I FINDED IT — ITS A L'IL KLOVA BUSH.
AH-YES KRAZY, A LITTLE CLOVER — HOW NICE, HOW PRETTY, HOW CLEVER — IS N'T IT, "MOUSE"?
Y-YESSS
SEE, IT HAS TREE LIVS, ALL LIVING HEPPY, AN KINTEMPTED TOGEDDA — AIN'T THAT NIZE?
IT'S GRAND, IT'S ASTOUNDING — IS N'T IT, "MOUSE"
SURE — OOOOOOO
JUST LIKE WE THE TREE OF US —
IT SURE IS YES, SIR — IS N'T IT, "MOUSE"?
OWWW F'F-F-COURSE
ONE LIF IS IGNATZ, ONE LIF IS OFFISSA PUPP, AN' ONE LIF IS ME — TREE IN ONE, A SINGULA KOWINCIDINCE IN PLURALNISS — AIN'T IT MOVILLIS?
DAW GUNNIT, KRAZY, IT'S GRAND, IT'S UNCANNY — WATCHA SAY, "MOUSE"?
Y-Y-YESSSS OOOOOOO
HA HA HA
HA-HA-HA
THREE ME NECK — I'LL PULL ONE OF THOSE LEAVES OFF — THAT KOP JUST MAKES ONE TOO MANY!!
ZZZ
HA HA HA HA HA
ME AND KRAZY IS PLENTY ON THAT CLOVER — THAT MOUSE'S LEAF COMES OFF!!
AND THE WALLS OF WHITE MESA ECHO A TRIOLE IN CACHINNATIONS.

April 26th, 1931.

KRAZY KAT By Herriman.

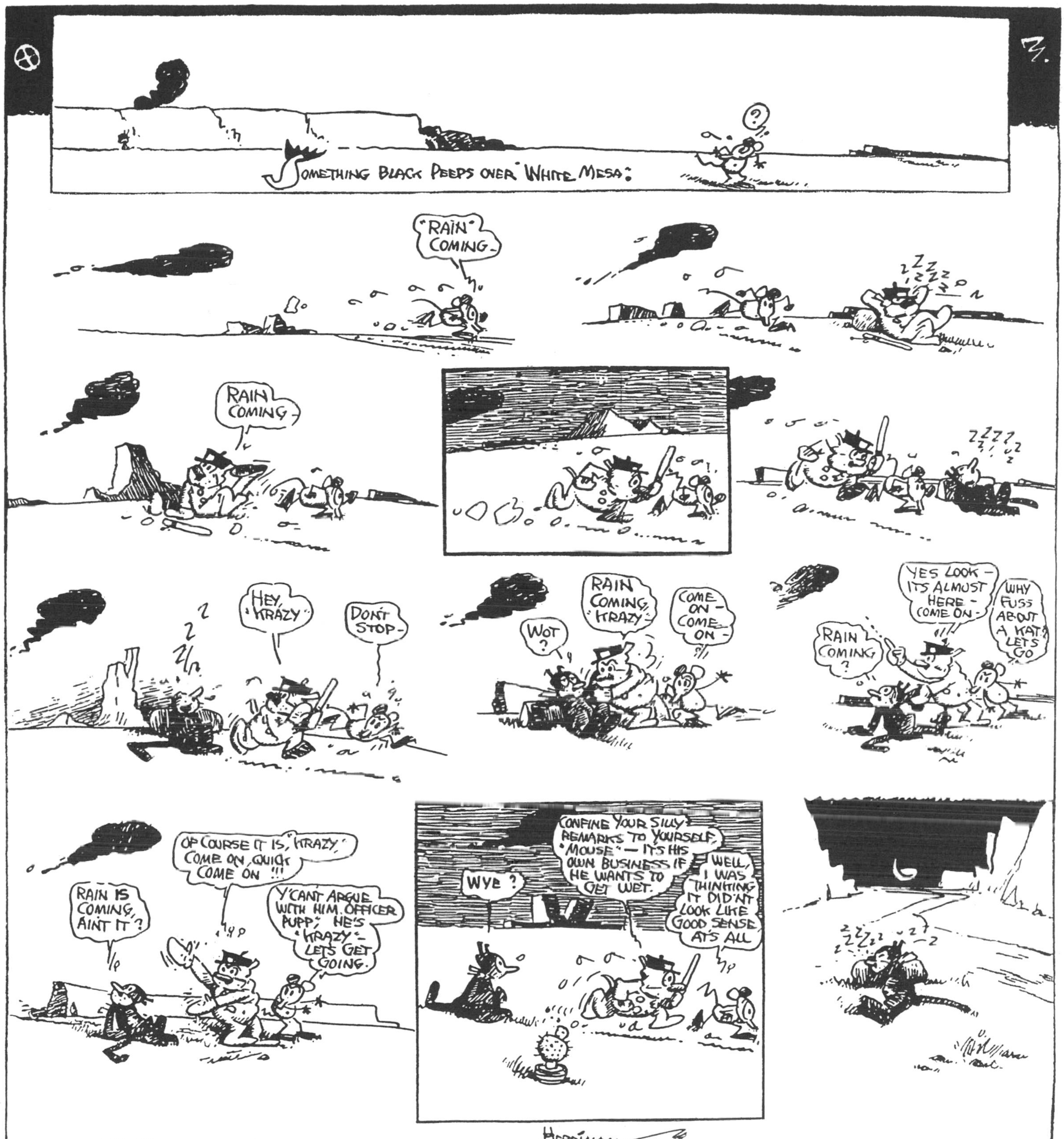

Something Black Peeps over White Mesa:
?
"RAIN" COMING -
RAIN COMING -
HEY, "KRAZY"
DON'T STOP -
WOT ?
RAIN COMING, "KRAZY"
COME ON - COME ON -
RAIN COMING ?
YES LOOK - ITS ALMOST HERE - COME ON -
WHY FUSS ABOUT A KAT? LETS GO
RAIN IS COMING, AINT IT ?
OF COURSE IT IS, "KRAZY" COME ON, QUICK COME ON !!!
Y'CANT ARGUE WITH HIM, OFFICER PUPP, HE'S "KRAZY" - LETS GET GOING.
WYE ?
CONFINE YOUR SILLY REMARKS TO YOURSELF "MOUSE" - ITS HIS OWN BUSINESS IF HE WANTS TO GET WET.
WELL, I WAS THINKING IT DIDN'T LOOK LIKE GOOD SENSE AT'S ALL
HERRIMAN

May 3rd, 1931.

KRAZY KAT *By Herriman.*

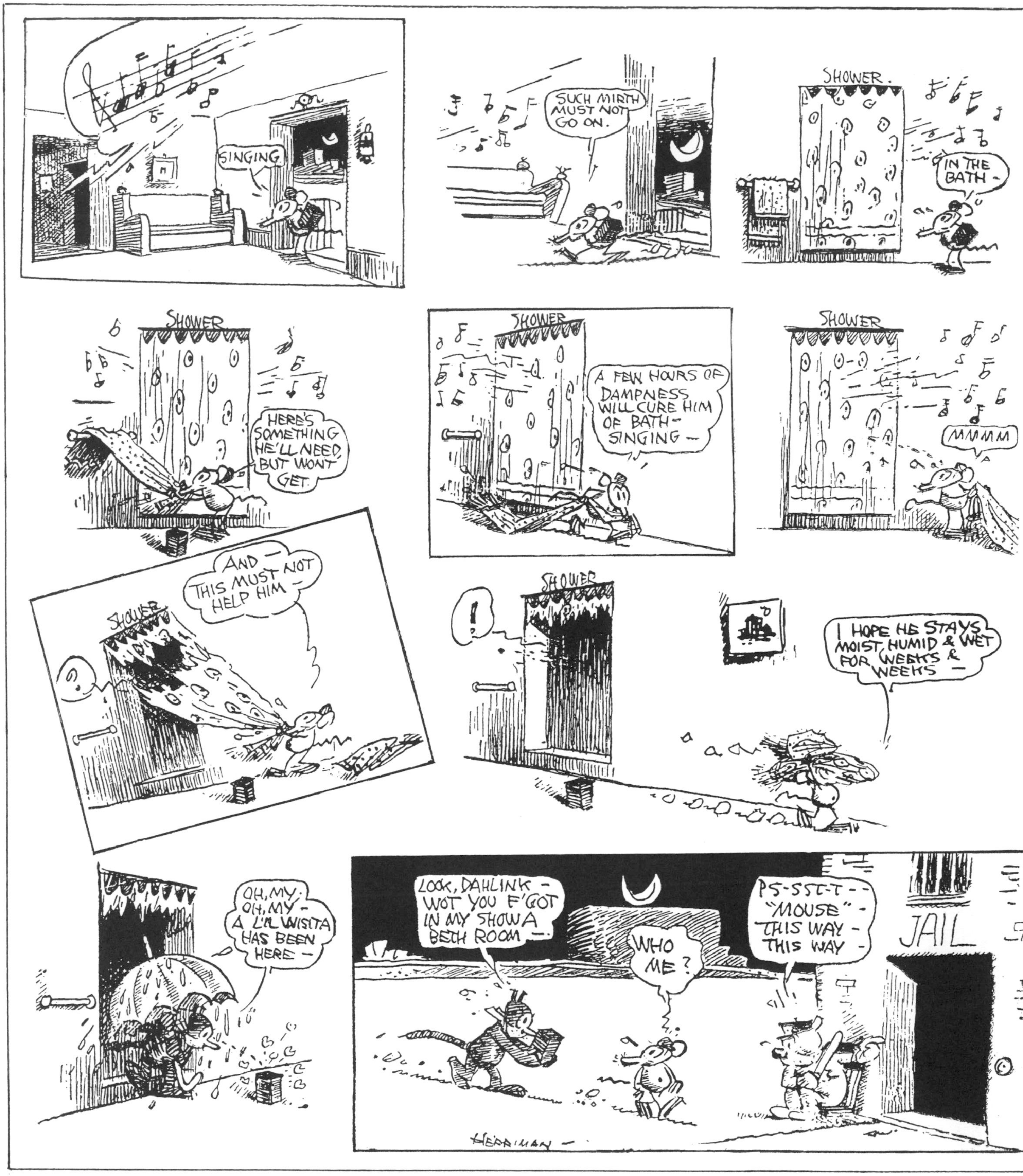
SINGING
SUCH MIRTH MUST NOT GO ON.
SHOWER.
IN THE BATH -
SHOWER
HERE'S SOMETHING HE'LL NEED, BUT WON'T GET.
SHOWER
A FEW HOURS OF DAMPNESS WILL CURE HIM OF BATH-SINGING -
SHOWER
MMMM
AND - THIS MUST NOT HELP HIM -
SHOWER
SHOWER
I HOPE HE STAYS MOIST, HUMID & WET FOR WEEKS & WEEKS -
OH, MY. OH, MY - A L'IL WISITA HAS BEEN HERE -
LOOK, DAHLINK - WOT YOU F'GOT IN MY SHOWA BETH ROOM -
WHO ME?
PS-SST-T - "MOUSE" - THIS WAY - THIS WAY -
JAIL
HERRIMAN -

May 10th, 1931.

KRAZY KAT By Herriman

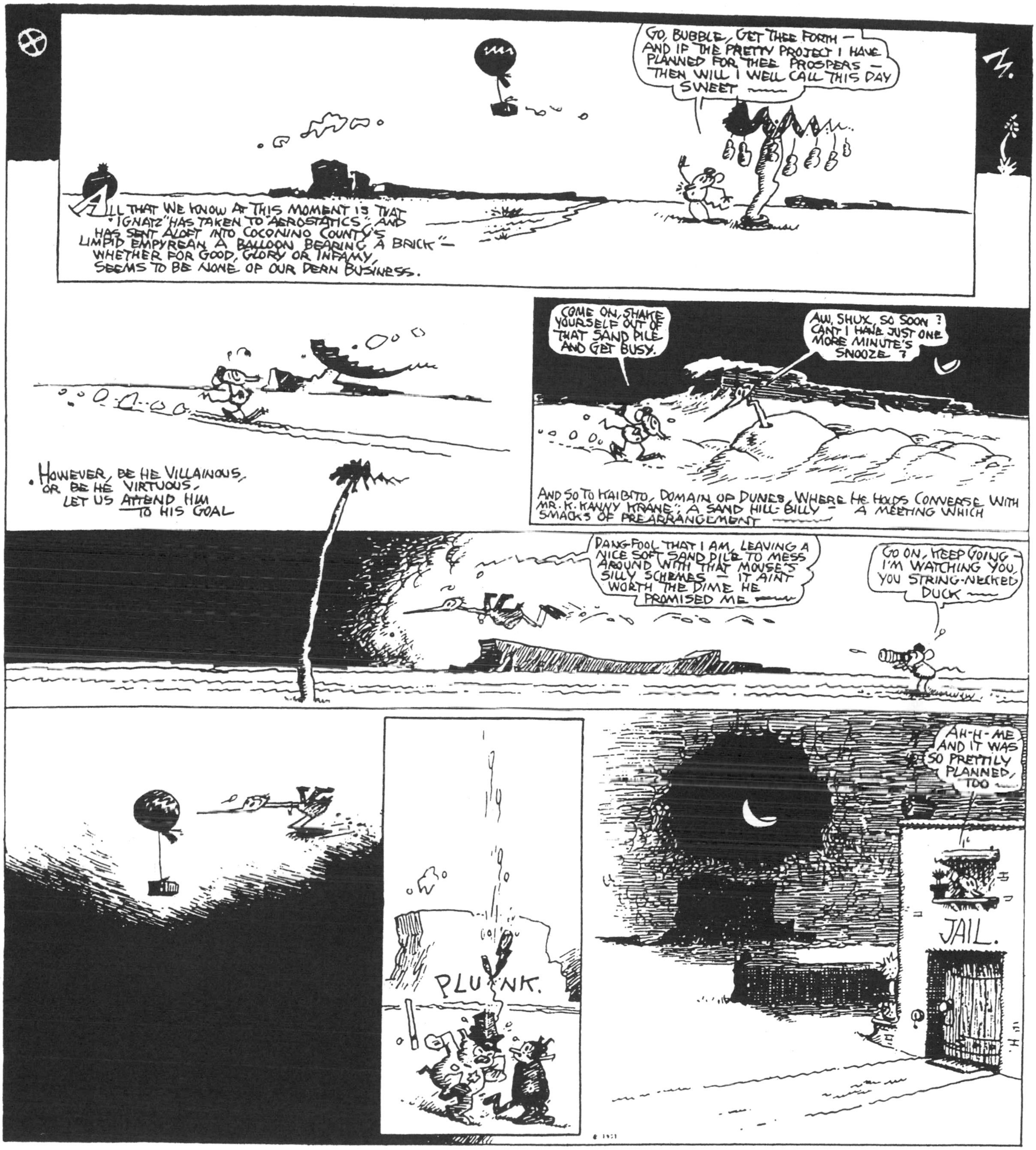

GO, BUBBLE, GET THEE FORTH — AND IF THE PRETTY PROJECT I HAVE PLANNED FOR THEE PROSPERS — THEN WILL I WELL CALL THIS DAY SWEET ——
ALL THAT WE KNOW AT THIS MOMENT IS THAT "IGNATZ" HAS TAKEN TO "AEROSTATICS", AND HAS SENT ALOFT INTO COCONINO COUNTY'S LIMPID EMPYREAN A BALLOON BEARING A BRICK — WHETHER FOR GOOD, GLORY OR INFAMY, SEEMS TO BE NONE OF OUR DERN BUSINESS.
HOWEVER, BE HE VILLAINOUS, OR BE HE VIRTUOUS, LET US ATTEND HIM TO HIS GOAL
COME ON, SHAKE YOURSELF OUT OF THAT SAND PILE AND GET BUSY.
AW, SHUX, SO SOON? CAN'T I HAVE JUST ONE MORE MINUTE'S SNOOZE?
AND SO TO KAIBITO, DOMAIN OF DUNES, WHERE HE HOLDS CONVERSE WITH MR. K. KANNY KRANE, A SAND HILL BILLY — A MEETING WHICH SMACKS OF PREARRANGEMENT
DANG-FOOL THAT I AM, LEAVING A NICE SOFT SAND PILE TO MESS AROUND WITH THAT MOUSE'S SILLY SCHEMES — IT AINT WORTH THE DIME HE PROMISED ME ——
GO ON, KEEP GOING — I'M WATCHING YOU, YOU STRING-NECKED DUCK ——
PLUNK.
AH-H-ME AND IT WAS SO PRETTILY PLANNED, TOO ——
JAIL.

May 17th, 1931.

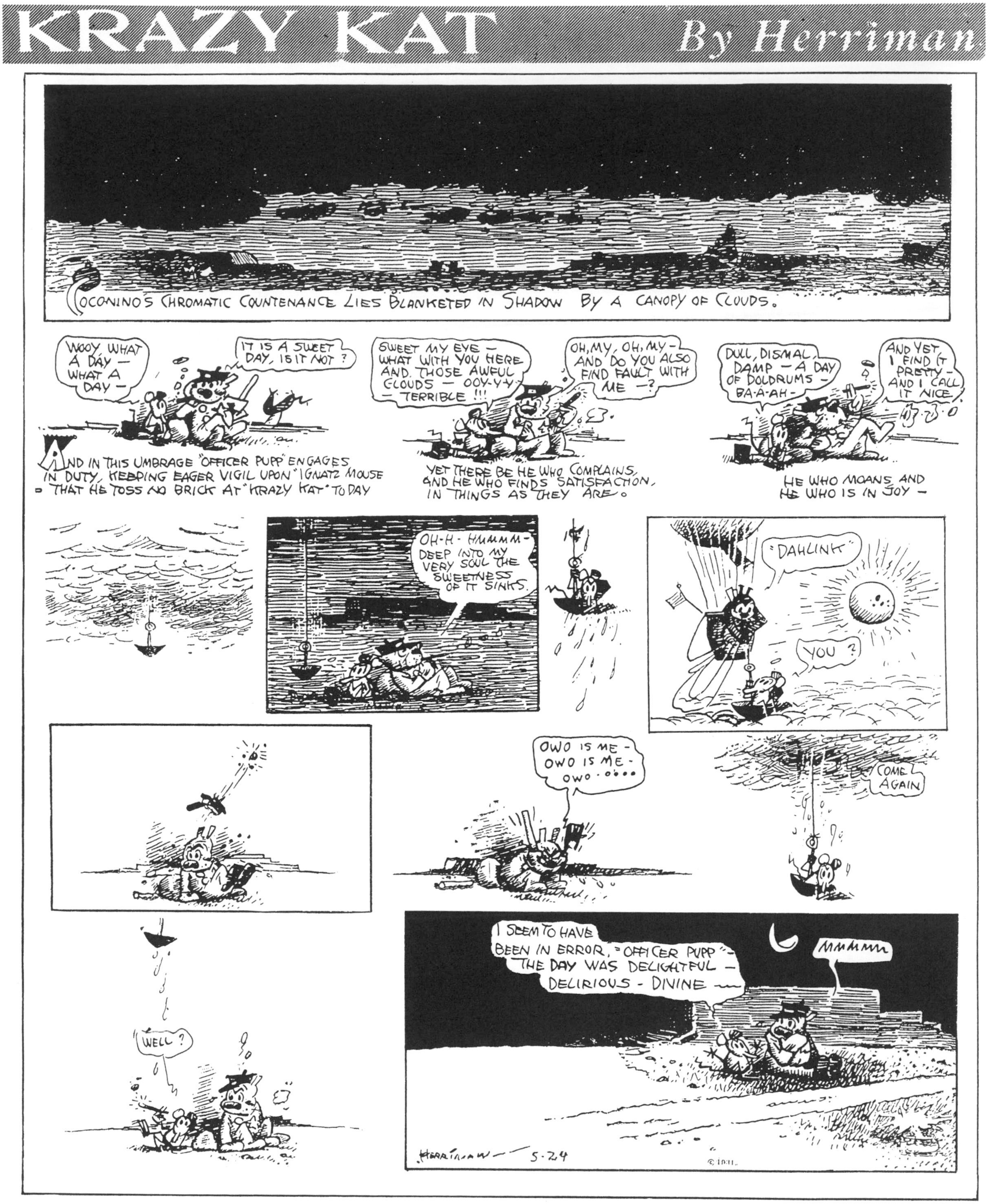
KRAZY KAT By Herriman
COCONINO'S CHROMATIC COUNTENANCE LIES BLANKETED IN SHADOW BY A CANOPY OF CLOUDS.
WOOY, WHAT A DAY — WHAT A DAY —
IT IS A SWEET DAY, IS IT NOT?
AND IN THIS UMBRAGE "OFFICER PUPP" ENGAGES IN DUTY, KEEPING EAGER VIGIL UPON "IGNATZ MOUSE" - THAT HE TOSS NO BRICK AT "KRAZY KAT" TO DAY
SWEET MY EYE — WHAT WITH YOU HERE AND THOSE AWFUL CLOUDS — OOY-Y-Y — TERRIBLE !!!
OH, MY, OH, MY — AND DO YOU ALSO FIND FAULT WITH ME —?
YET THERE BE HE WHO COMPLAINS, AND HE WHO FINDS SATISFACTION, IN THINGS AS THEY ARE.
DULL, DISMAL, DAMP — A DAY OF DOLDRUMS — BA-A-AH —
AND YET I FIND IT PRETTY — AND I CALL IT NICE.
HE WHO MOANS, AND HE WHO IS IN JOY —
OH-H- HMMMM — DEEP INTO MY VERY SOUL THE SWEETNESS OF IT SINKS.
"DAHLINK"
YOU?
OWO IS ME — OWO IS ME — OWO....
COME AGAIN
WELL?
I SEEM TO HAVE BEEN IN ERROR, "OFFICER PUPP" — THE DAY WAS DELIGHTFUL — DELIRIOUS — DIVINE —
MMMMM
HERRIMAN — 5-24

May 24th, 1931.

KRAZY KAT By Herriman

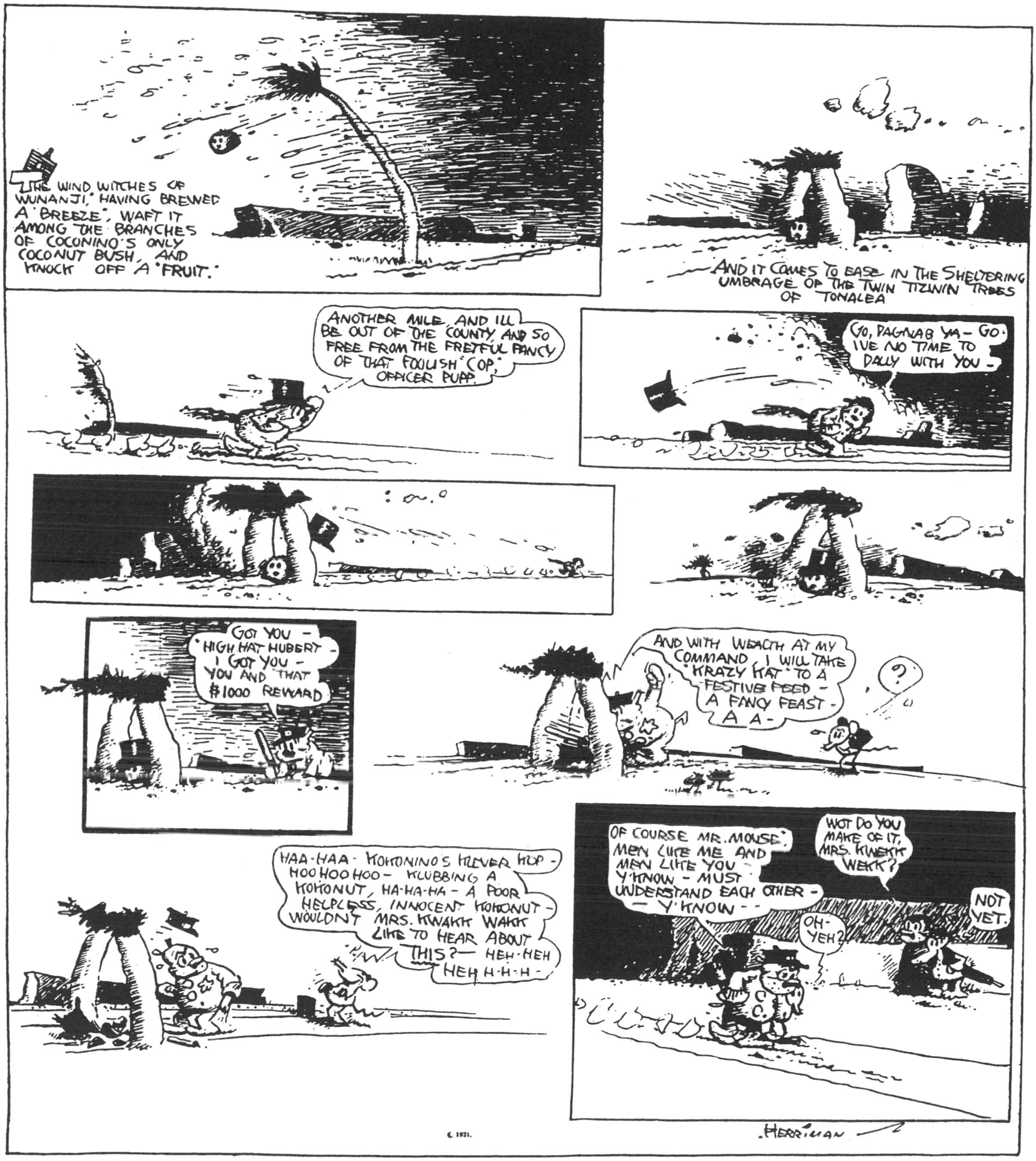

THE WIND WITCHES OF WUNANJI, HAVING BREWED A "BREEZE", WAFT IT AMONG THE BRANCHES OF COCONINO'S ONLY COCONUT BUSH, AND KNOCK OFF A "FRUIT."
AND IT COMES TO EASE IN THE SHELTERING UMBRAGE OF THE TWIN TIZWIN TREES OF TONALEA
ANOTHER MILE, AND I'LL BE OUT OF THE COUNTY, AND SO FREE FROM THE FRETFUL FANCY OF THAT FOOLISH "COP," OFFICER PUPP.
GO, PAGNAB YA - GO - I'VE NO TIME TO DALLY WITH YOU -
GOT YOU - "HIGH HAT HUBERT" - I GOT YOU - YOU AND THAT $1000 REWARD
AND WITH WEALTH AT MY COMMAND, I WILL TAKE "KRAZY KAT" TO A FESTIVE FEED - A FANCY FEAST - A A -
?
HAA-HAA - KOKONINO'S KLEVER KOP - HOO HOO HOO - KLUBBING A KOKONUT, HA-HA-HA - A POOR HELPLESS, INNOCENT KOKONUT - WOULDN'T MRS. KWAKK WAKK LIKE TO HEAR ABOUT THIS? — HEH-HEH HEH H-H-H -
OF COURSE MR. MOUSE, MEN LIKE ME AND MEN LIKE YOU - Y'KNOW - MUST UNDERSTAND EACH OTHER - — Y'KNOW - -
OH-YEH?
WOT DO YOU MAKE OF IT, MRS. KWAKK WAKK?
NOT YET.
© 1931.
HERRIMAN

May 31st, 1931.

KRAZY KAT *By Herriman*

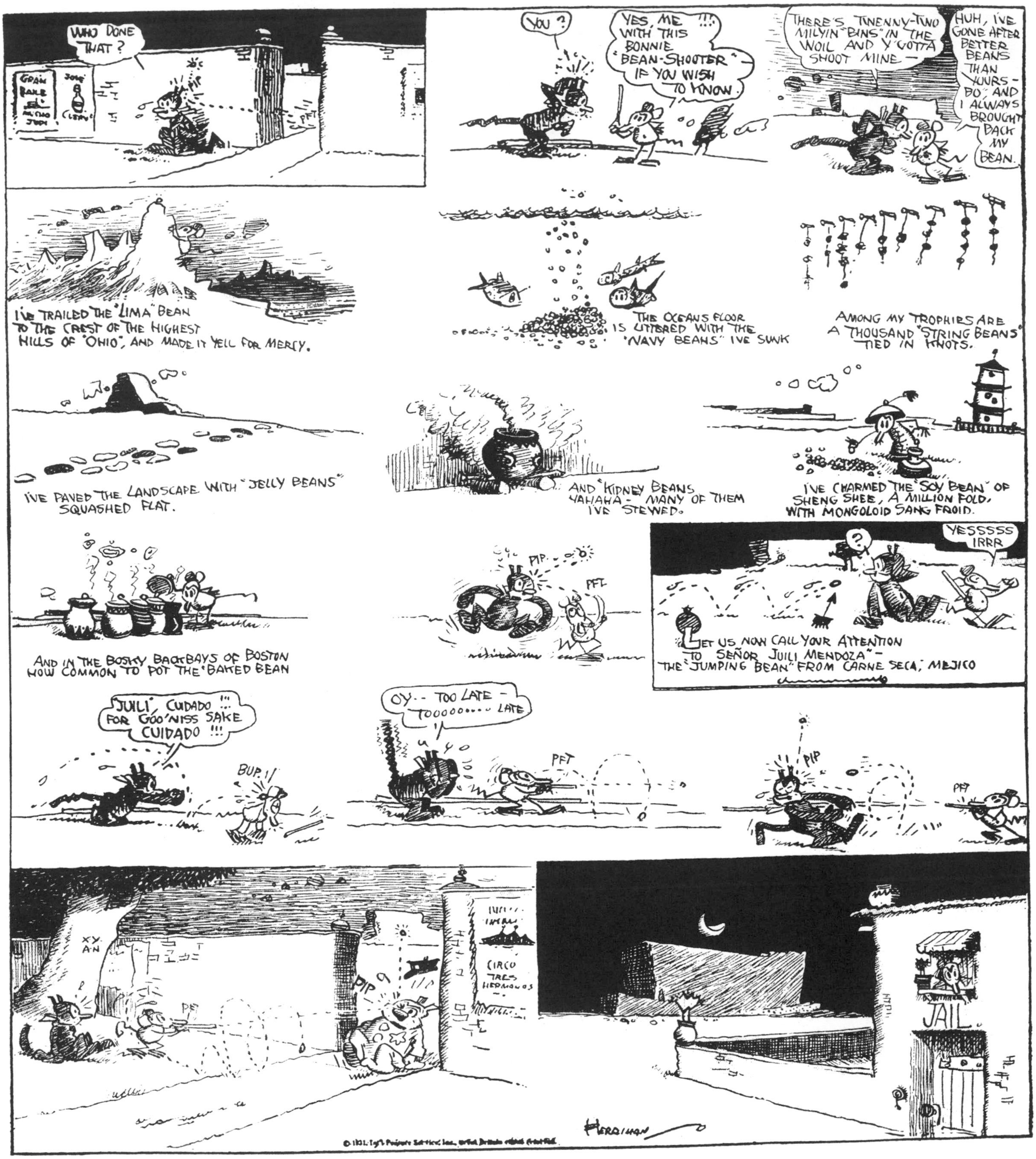
WHO DONE THAT ?
PIP
PFT
YOU ?
YES, ME !!! WITH THIS BONNIE "BEAN-SHOOTER" — IF YOU WISH TO KNOW.
THERE'S TWENNY-TWO MILYIN "BINS" IN THE WOIL AND Y'GOTTA SHOOT MINE —
HUH, I'VE GONE AFTER BETTER BEANS THAN YOURS "BO", AND I ALWAYS BROUGHT BACK MY BEAN.
I'VE TRAILED THE "LIMA" BEAN TO THE CREST OF THE HIGHEST HILLS OF "OHIO", AND MADE IT YELL FOR MERCY.
THE OCEANS FLOOR IS LITTERED WITH THE "NAVY BEANS" I'VE SUNK
AMONG MY TROPHIES ARE A THOUSAND "STRING BEANS" TIED IN KNOTS.
I'VE PAVED THE LANDSCAPE WITH "JELLY BEANS" SQUASHED FLAT.
AND "KIDNEY BEANS" HAHAHA — MANY OF THEM I'VE STEWED.
I'VE CHARMED THE "SOY BEAN" OF SHENG SHEE, A MILLION FOLD, WITH MONGOLOID SANG FROID.
AND IN THE BOSKY BACKBAYS OF BOSTON HOW COMMON TO POT THE "BAKED BEAN"
PIP
PFT
YESSSSS IRRR
LET US NOW CALL YOUR ATTENTION TO SEÑOR JUILI MENDOZA" — THE "JUMPING BEAN" FROM CARNE SECA, MEJICO
"JUILI", CUIDADO !!! FOR GOO'NISS SAKE CUIDADO !!!
BUP !!
OY.. TOO LATE — TOOOOOOO.... LATE
PFT
PIP
PFT
PIP
PFT
CIRCO TRES HERMANOS
JAIL
HERRIMAN

June 7th, 1931.

KRAZY KAT *By Herriman*

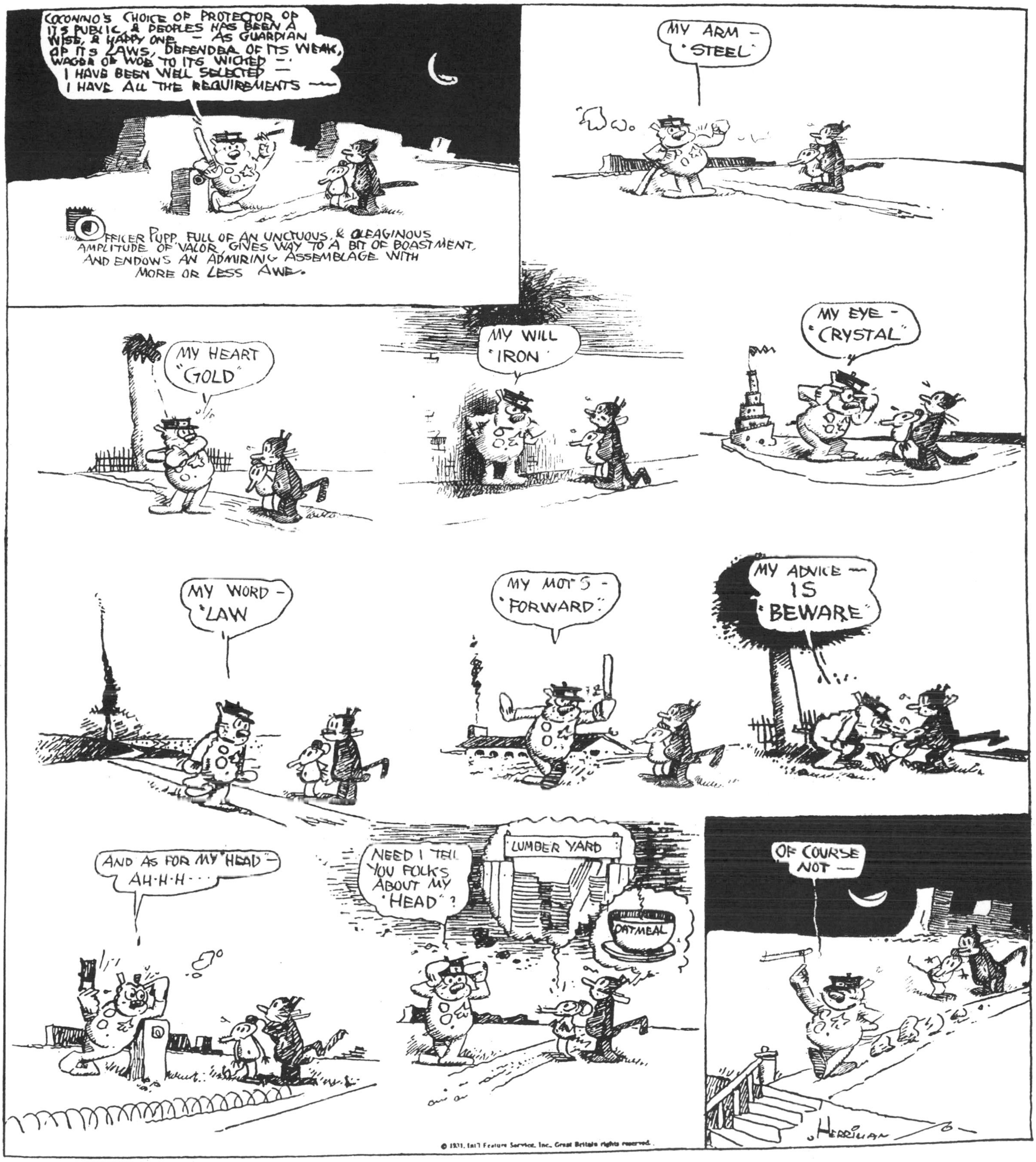

COCONINO'S CHOICE OF PROTECTOR OF ITS PUBLIC, & PEOPLES HAS BEEN A WISE, & HAPPY ONE — AS GUARDIAN OF ITS LAWS, DEFENDER OF ITS WEAK, WAGER OF WOE TO ITS WICKED — I HAVE BEEN WELL SELECTED — I HAVE ALL THE REQUIREMENTS —
OFFICER PUPP, FULL OF AN UNCTUOUS, & OLEAGINOUS AMPLITUDE OF VALOR, GIVES WAY TO A BIT OF BOASTMENT, AND ENDOWS AN ADMIRING ASSEMBLAGE WITH MORE OR LESS AWE.
MY ARM — "STEEL"
MY HEART "GOLD"
MY WILL "IRON"
MY EYE — "CRYSTAL"
MY WORD — "LAW"
MY MOTTO — "FORWARD"
MY ADVICE — IS "BEWARE"
AND AS FOR MY "HEAD" — AH-H-H . . .
NEED I TELL YOU FOLKS ABOUT MY "HEAD"?
LUMBER YARD
OATMEAL
OF COURSE NOT —
HERRIMAN
© 1931, Int'l Feature Service, Inc., Great Britain rights reserved.

June 14th, 1931.

KRAZY KAT *By Herriman*

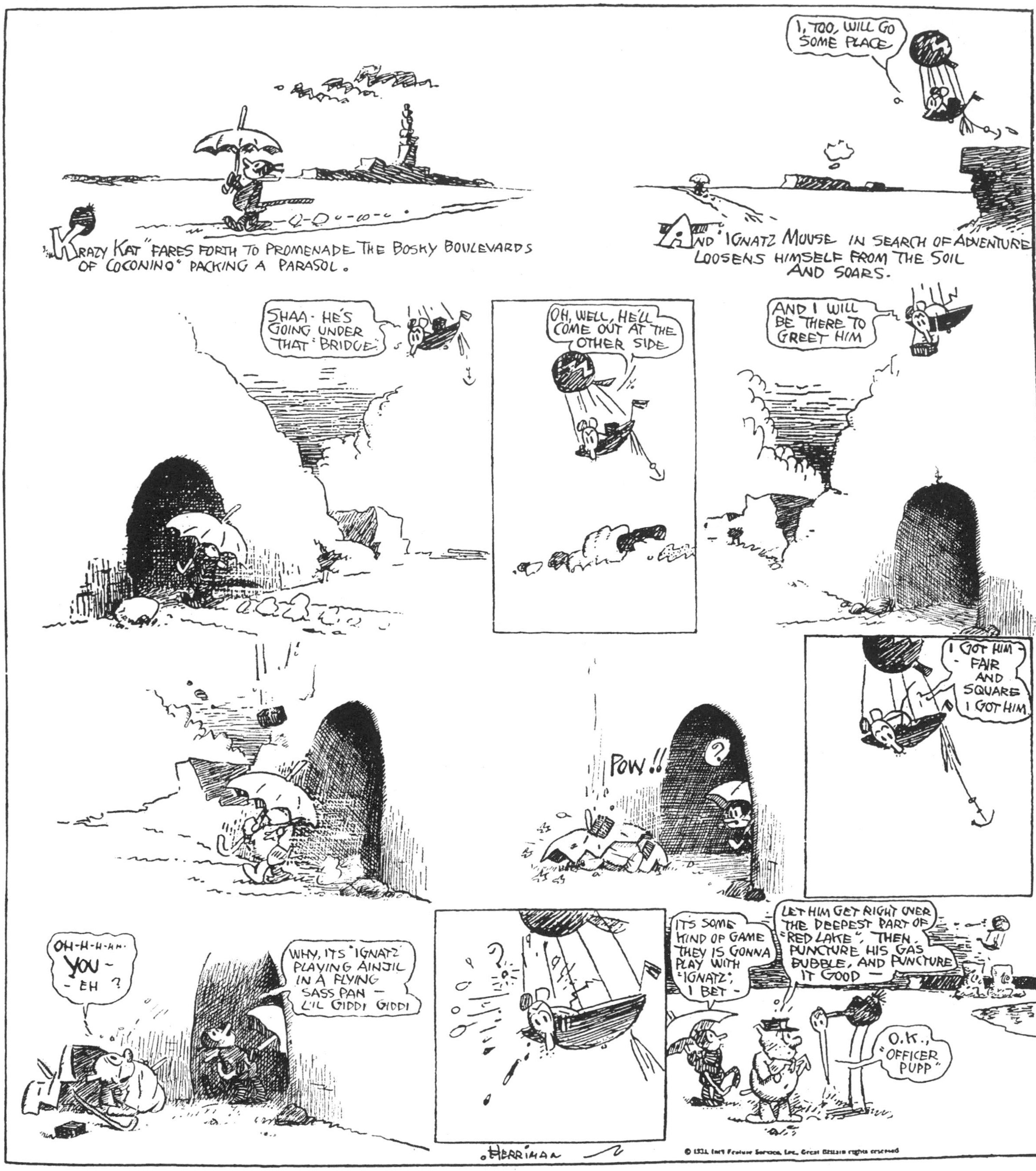

"KRAZY KAT" FARES FORTH TO PROMENADE THE BOSKY BOULEVARDS OF COCONINO" PACKING A PARASOL.
I, TOO, WILL GO SOME PLACE
AND "IGNATZ MOUSE IN SEARCH OF ADVENTURE LOOSENS HIMSELF FROM THE SOIL AND SOARS.
SHAA- HE'S GOING UNDER THAT "BRIDGE"
OH, WELL, HE'LL COME OUT AT THE OTHER SIDE
AND I WILL BE THERE TO GREET HIM
I GOT HIM - FAIR AND SQUARE I GOT HIM.
POW!!
?
OH-H-H-HH. YOU - EH ?
WHY, ITS "IGNATZ" PLAYING AINJIL IN A FLYING SASS PAN - L'IL GIDDI GIDDI
?
ITS SOME KIND OF GAME THEY IS GONNA PLAY WITH "IGNATZ", I BET -
LET HIM GET RIGHT OVER THE DEEPEST PART OF "RED LAKE", THEN, PUNCTURE HIS GAS BUBBLE, AND PUNCTURE IT GOOD -
O.K., "OFFICER PUPP"
HERRIMAN

June 21st, 1931.

KRAZY KAT *By Herriman*

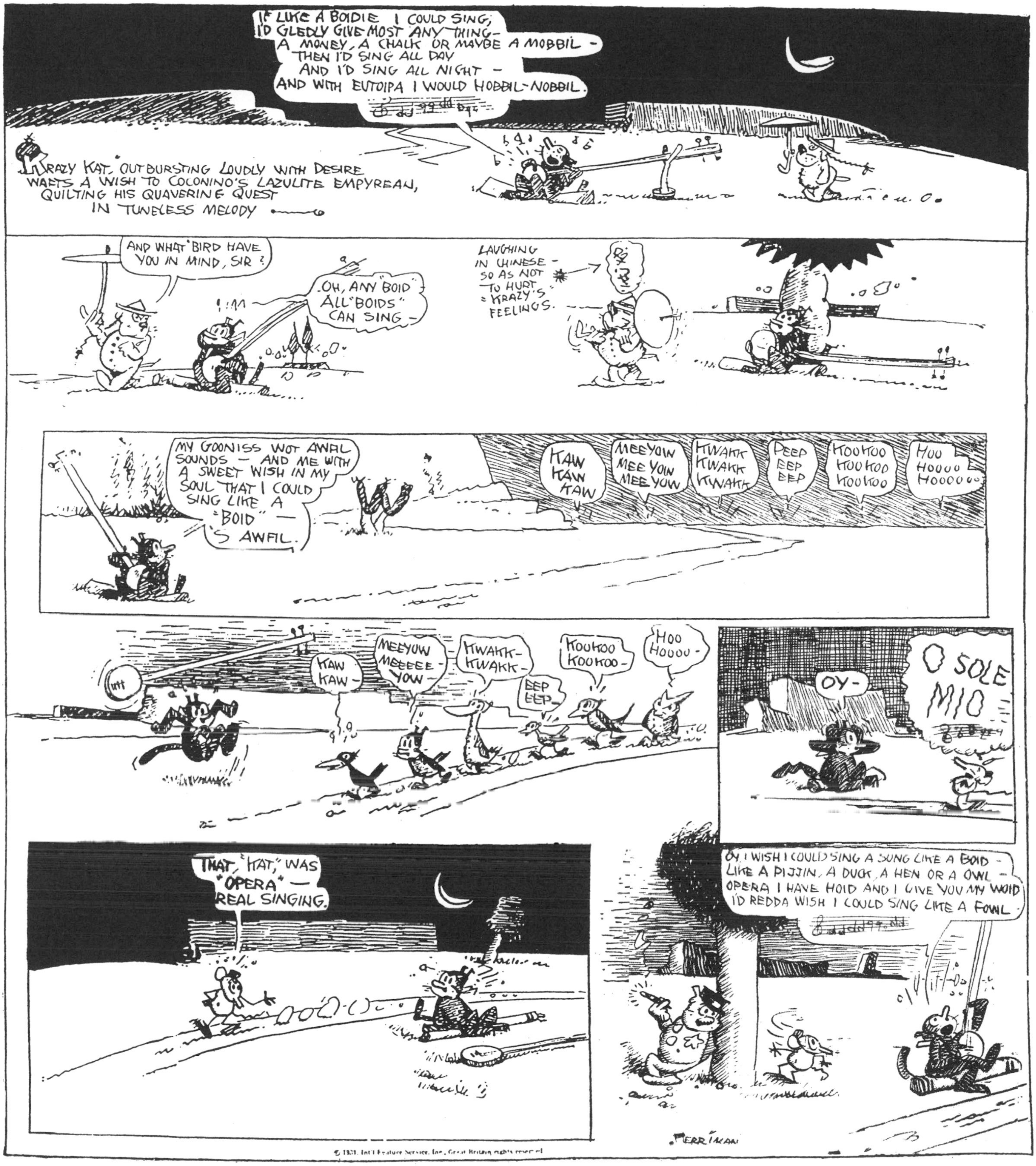

IF LIKE A BOIDIE I COULD SING, I'D GLEDLY GIVE MOST ANY THING – A MONEY, A CHALK OR MAYBE A MOBBIL – THEN I'D SING ALL DAY AND I'D SING ALL NIGHT – AND WITH EUTOIPA I WOULD HOBBIL-NOBBIL.
KRAZY KAT, OUTBURSTING LOUDLY WITH DESIRE WAFTS A WISH TO COCONINO'S LAZULITE EMPYREAN, QUILTING HIS QUAVERINE QUEST IN TUNELESS MELODY
AND WHAT "BIRD" HAVE YOU IN MIND, SIR?
OH, ANY "BOID" – ALL "BOIDS" CAN SING –
LAUGHING IN CHINESE – SO AS NOT TO HURT "KRAZY'S" FEELINGS.
MY GOONISS WOT AWFUL SOUNDS – AND ME WITH A SWEET WISH IN MY SOUL THAT I COULD SING LIKE A "BOID" – 'S AWFIL.
KAW KAW KAW
MEEYOW MEE YOW MEE YOW
KWAKK KWAKK KWAKK
PEEP EEP EEP
KOOKOO KOOKOO KOOKOO
HOO HOOOO HOOOOOO
KAW KAW –
MEEYOW MEEEEE – YOW
KWAKK – KWAKK –
EEP EEP –
KOOKOO KOOKOO –
HOO HOOOO –
OY –
O SOLE MIO
THAT "KAT," WAS "OPERA" – REAL SINGING.
OY, I WISH I COULD SING A SONG LIKE A BOID – LIKE A PIJJIN, A DUCK, A HEN OR A OWL – OPERA I HAVE HOID AND I GIVE YOU MY WOID I'D REDDA WISH I COULD SING LIKE A FOWL –
HERRIMAN

June 28th, 1931.

KRAZY KAT *By Herriman*

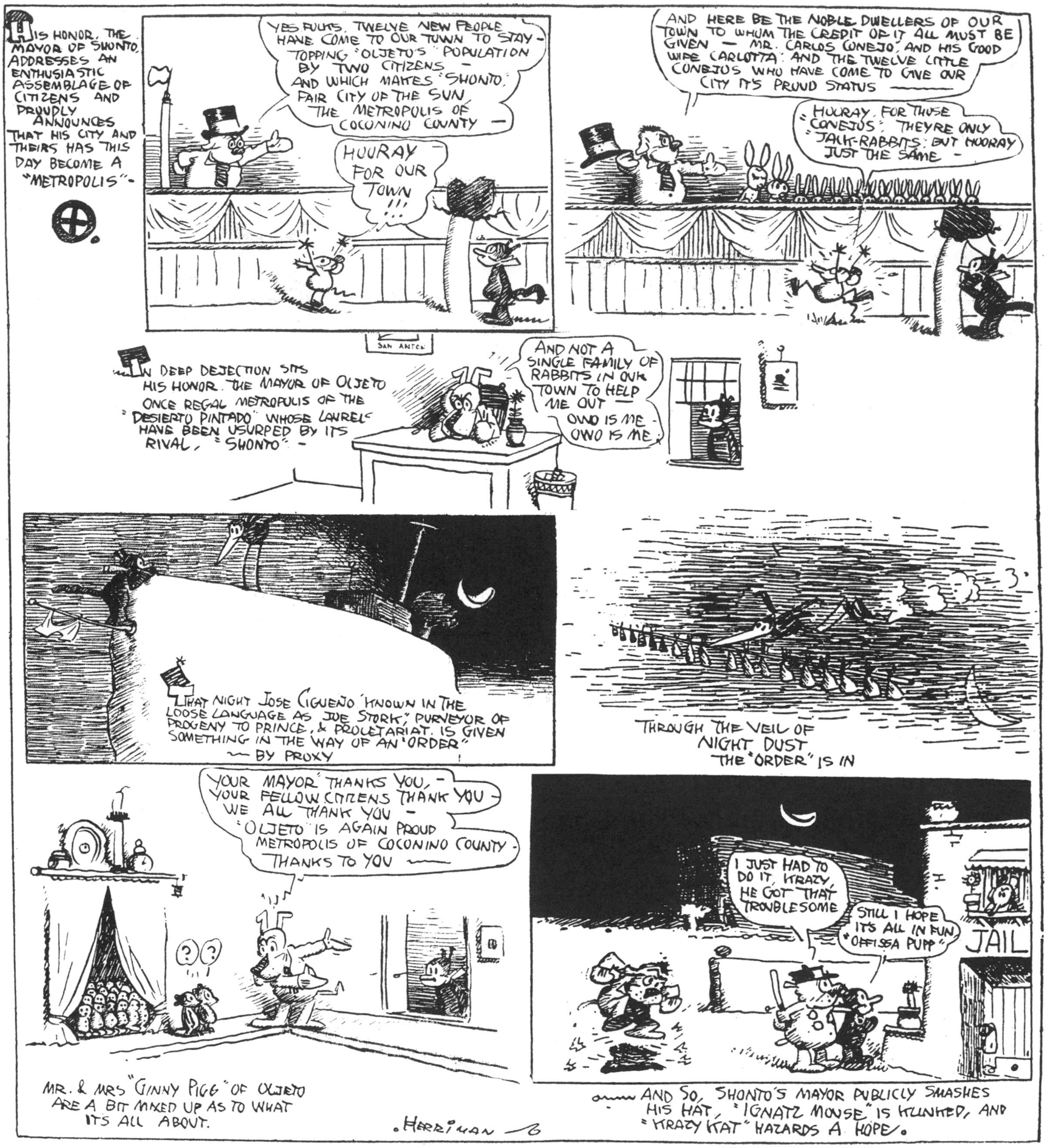

His honor, the mayor of Shonto, addresses an enthusiastic assemblage of citizens and proudly announces that his city and theirs has this day become a "metropolis" -
Yes folks, twelve new people have come to our town to stay - topping "Oljeto's" population by two citizens - and which makes "Shonto," fair city of the sun, the metropolis of Coconino County -
Hooray for our town !!!
And here be the noble dwellers of our town to whom the credit of it all must be given - Mr. Carlos Conejo, and his good wife Carlotta, and the twelve little conejos who have come to give our city it's proud status
Hooray for those "conejos," they're only "jack-rabbits," but hooray just the same -
In deep dejection sits his honor, the Mayor of Oljeto once regal metropolis of the "Desierto Pintado" whose laurels have been usurped by its rival, "Shonto" -
And not a single family of rabbits in our town to help me out - owo is me - owo is me
San Anton
That night Jose Cigueño (known in the loose language as "Joe Stork," purveyor of progeny to prince, & proletariat, is given something in the way of an "order" - by proxy
Through the veil of night, dust the "order" is in
Your mayor thanks you, - your fellow citizens thank you - we all thank you - "Oljeto" is again proud metropolis of Coconino County - thanks to you
Mr. & Mrs "Ginny Pigg" of Oljeto are a bit mixed up as to what it's all about.
I just had to do it, Krazy, he got that troublesome
Still I hope it's all in fun "Offissa Pupp"
JAIL
And so, Shonto's mayor publicly smashes his hat, "Ignatz Mouse" is klunked, and "Krazy Kat" hazards a hope.
Herriman

July 12th, 1931.

KRAZY KAT *By Herriman*

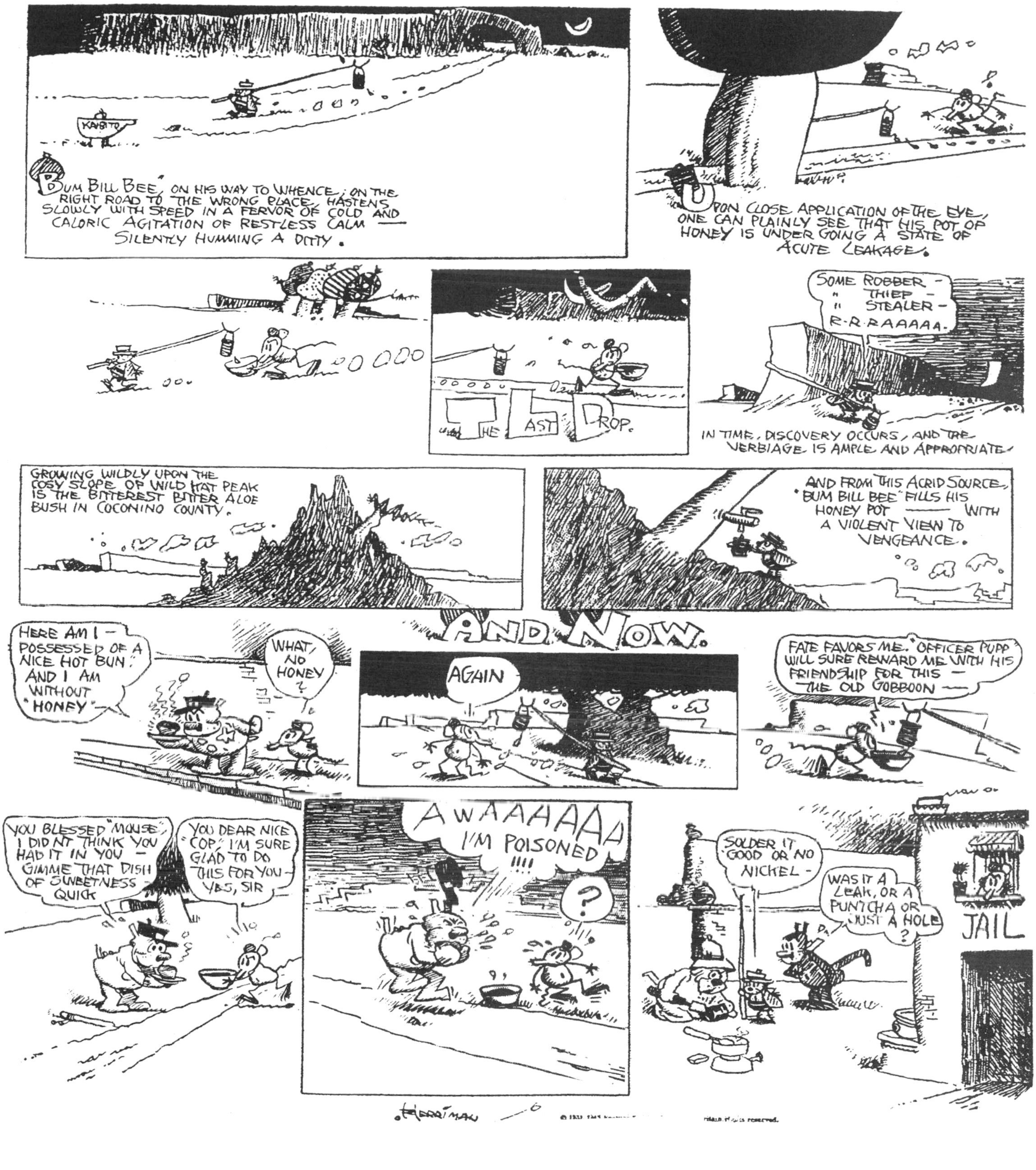

KABITO
"Bum Bill Bee," on his way to whence, on the right road to the wrong place, hastens slowly with speed in a fervor of cold and caloric agitation of restless calm — silently humming a ditty.
Upon close application of the eye, one can plainly see that his pot of honey is under going a state of acute leakage.
The Last Drop.
Some robber — " thief — " stealer — R-R-RAAAAAA.
In time, discovery occurs, and the verbiage is ample and appropriate.
Growing wildly upon the cosy slope of Wild Hat Peak is the bitterest bitter aloe bush in Coconino County.
And from this acrid source, Bum Bill Bee fills his honey pot —— with a violent view to vengeance.
And Now.
Here am I — possessed of a nice hot bun, and I am without "honey" —
What, no honey ?
Again
Fate favors me. "Officer Pupp" will sure reward me with his friendship for this — the old gobboon —
You blessed "mouse," I didn't think you had it in you — gimme that dish of sweetness — quick
You dear nice "cop," I'm sure glad to do this for you — yes, sir
AWAAAAAA I'm poisoned !!!!
?
Solder it good or no nickel —
Was it a leak, or a puncha or just a hole ?
JAIL
Herriman

August 16th, 1931.

KRAZY KAT *By Herriman*

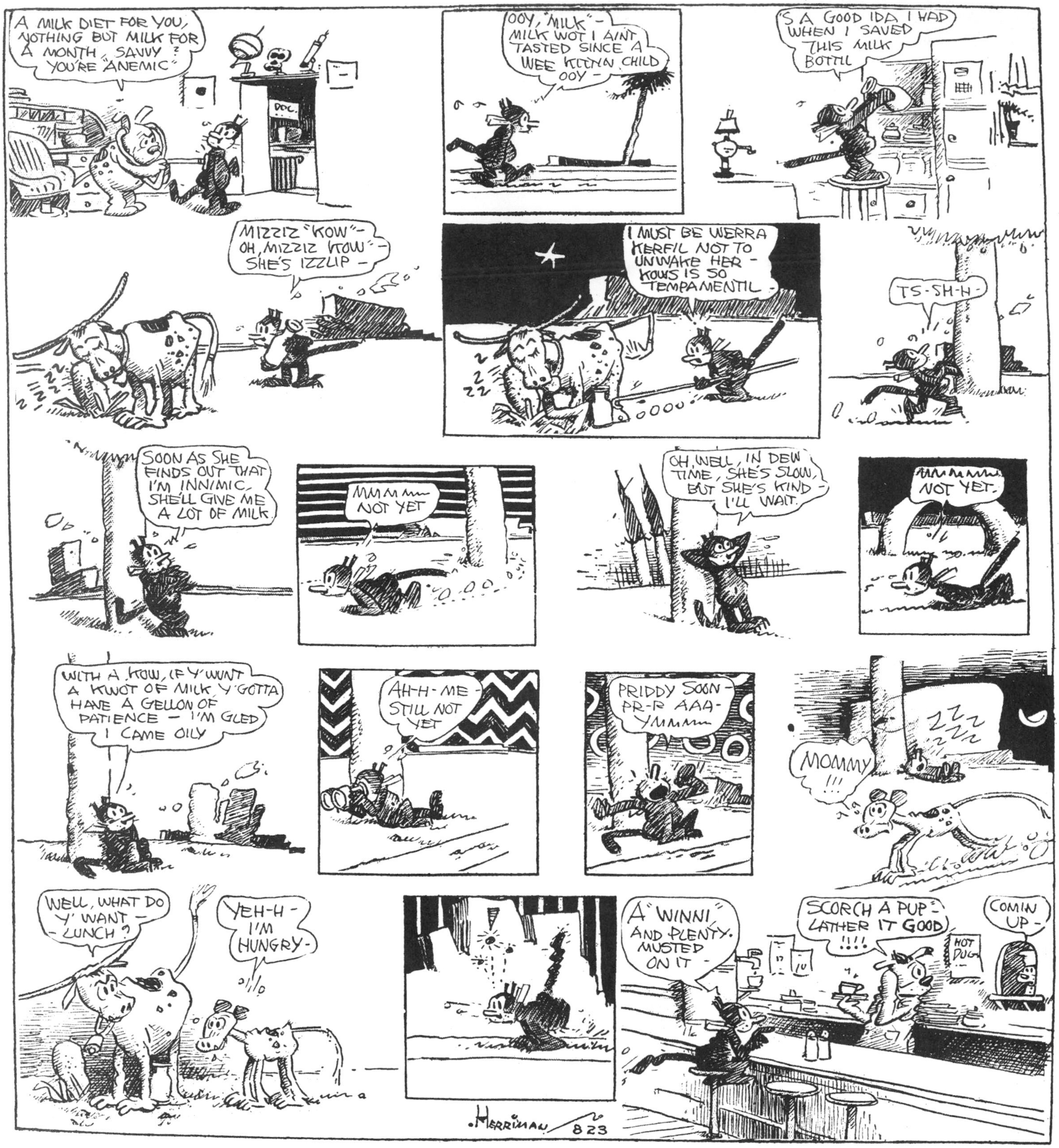

A MILK DIET FOR YOU, NOTHING BUT MILK FOR A MONTH, SAVVY? YOU'RE ANEMIC
DOC.
OOY, "MILK" - MILK WOT I AIN'T TASTED SINCE A WEE KITTIN CHILD OOY -
'S A GOOD IDA I HAD WHEN I SAVED THIS MILK BOTTIL
MIZZIZ "KOW" - OH, MIZZIZ KOW - SHE'S IZZLIP -
I MUST BE WERRA KERFIL NOT TO UNWAKE HER - KOWS IS SO TEMPAMENTIL
TS-SH-H
SOON AS SHE FINDS OUT THAT I'M INNIMIC, SHE'LL GIVE ME A LOT OF MILK
MMMM NOT YET
OH, WELL, IN DEW TIME, SHE'S SLOW, BUT SHE'S KIND I'LL WAIT.
MMMMM NOT YET.
WITH A KOW, IF Y' WUNT A KWOT OF MILK, Y' GOTTA HAVE A GELLON OF PATIENCE - I'M GLED I CAME OILY
AH-H- ME STILL NOT YET
PRIDDY SOON - PR-R AAA-YMMMM
MOMMY !!!
WELL, WHAT DO Y' WANT - LUNCH?
YEH-H - I'M HUNGRY -
A "WINNI" AND PLENTY MUSTED ON IT -
SCORCH A PUP - LATHER IT GOOD !!!!
COMIN UP -
HOT DUG
HERRIMAN 8 23

August 23rd, 1931.

KRAZY KAT *By Herriman*

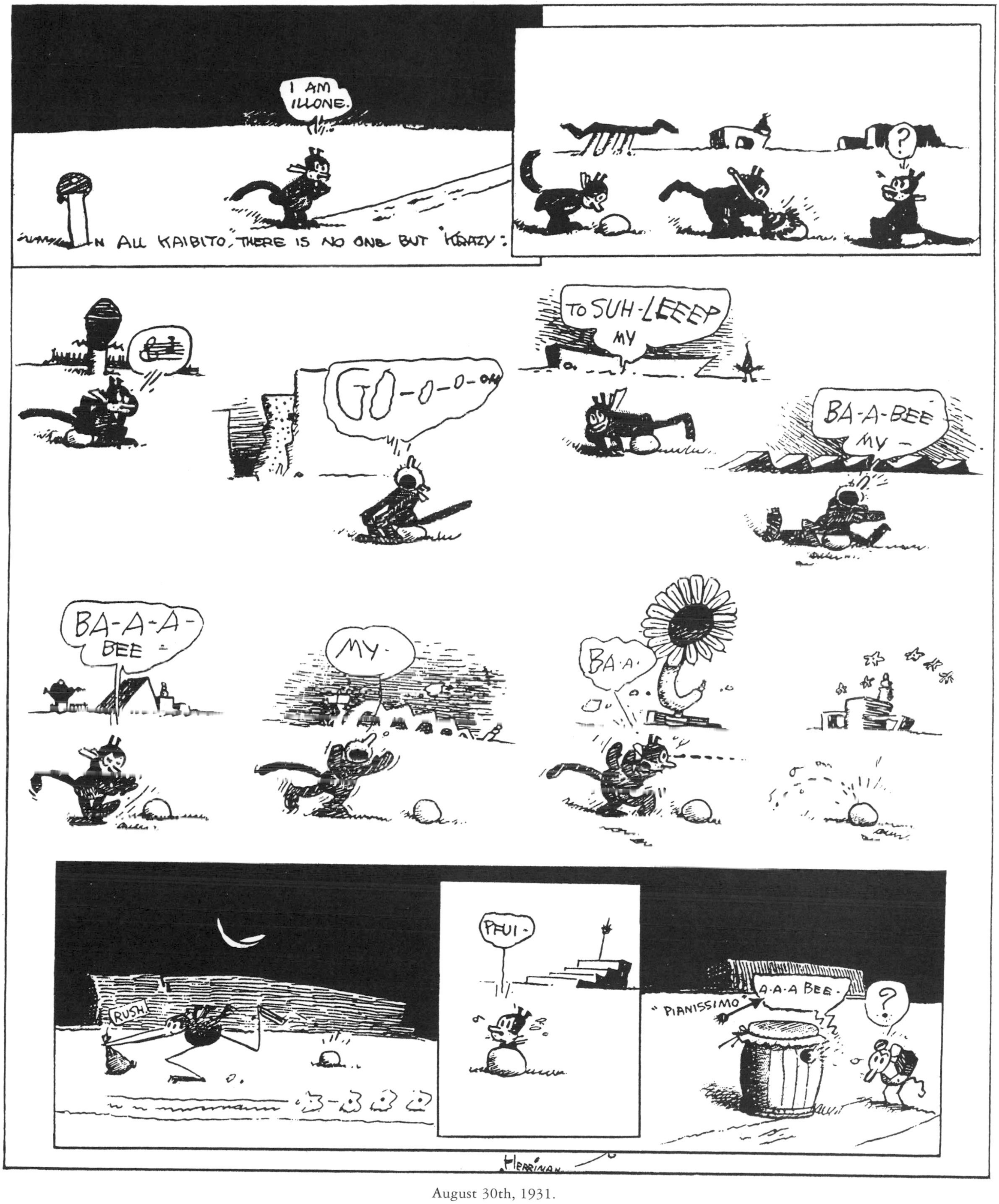
I AM ILLONE.
N ALL KAIBITO, THERE IS NO ONE BUT KRAZY:
?
GO-O-O-OH
TO SUH-LEEEP MY
BA-A-BEE MY -
BA-A-A- BEE
MY-
BA-A-
RUSH.
PFUI-
"PIANISSIMO"
A-A-A BEE-
?
HERRIMAN

August 30th, 1931.

KRAZY KAT By Herriman

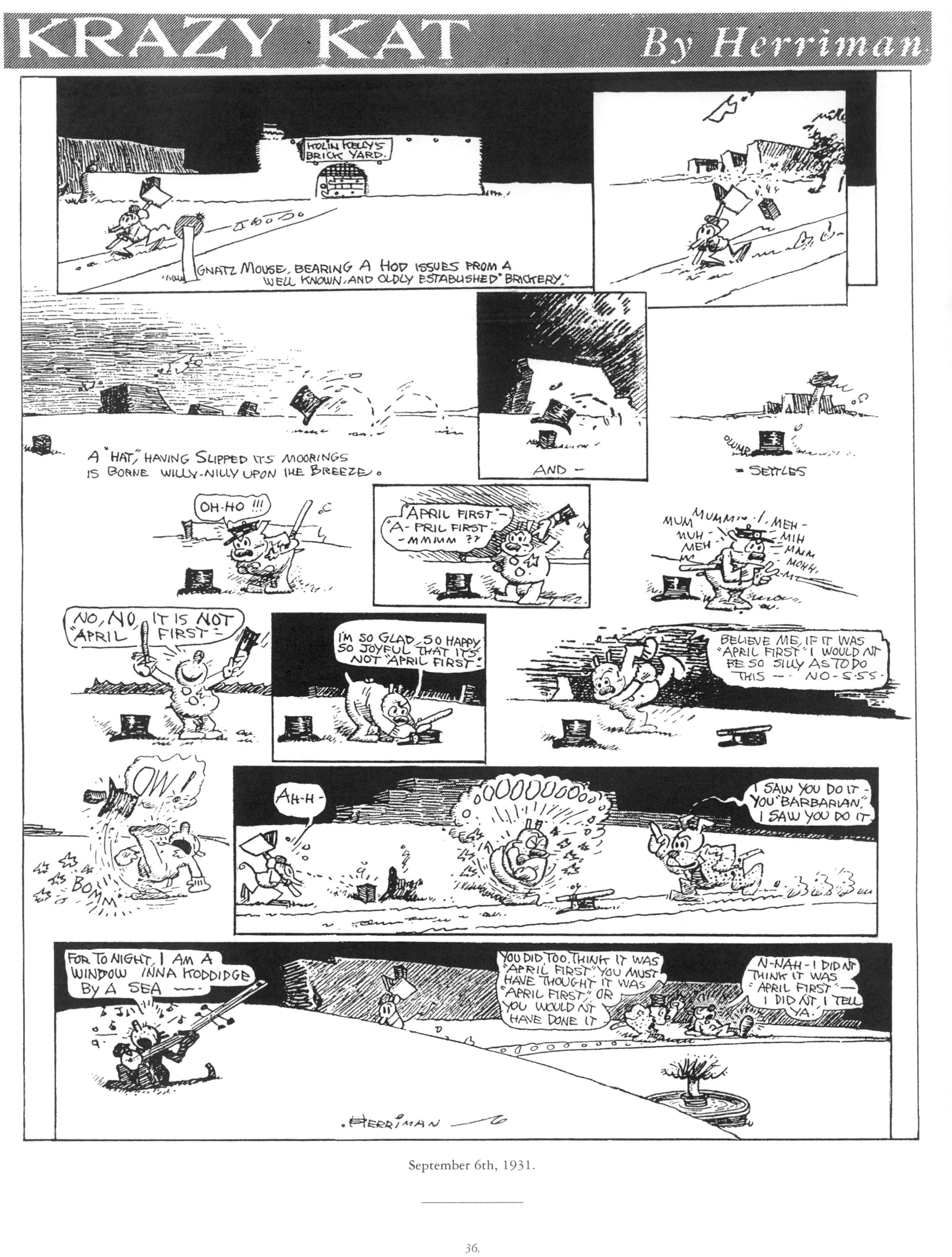

KOLIN KELLY'S BRICK YARD.
GNATZ MOUSE, BEARING A HOD ISSUES FROM A WELL KNOWN, AND OLDLY ESTABLISHED "BRICKERY."
A "HAT," HAVING SLIPPED ITS MOORINGS IS BORNE WILLY-NILLY UPON THE BREEZE.
AND -
- SETTLES
OH-HO !!!
"APRIL FIRST" - "A-PRIL FIRST" - MMMM ??
MUM MUMMM - / - MEH - MUH - MIH MEH - MMM MOHH - M -
NO, NO, IT IS NOT "APRIL FIRST" -
I'M SO GLAD, SO HAPPY SO JOYFUL THAT IT'S NOT "APRIL FIRST" -
BELIEVE ME, IF IT WAS "APRIL FIRST" I WOULD N'T BE SO SILLY AS TO DO THIS - - NO-S-SS
OW!
BOMM
AH-H -
OOOOOOOOOO
I SAW YOU DO IT - YOU "BARBARIAN," I SAW YOU DO IT
FOR TO NIGHT, I AM A WINDOW INNA KODDIDGE BY A SEA -
YOU DID TOO. THINK IT WAS "APRIL FIRST." YOU MUST HAVE THOUGHT IT WAS "APRIL FIRST," OR YOU WOULD N'T HAVE DONE IT
N-NAH - I DID N'T THINK IT WAS "APRIL FIRST" - I DID N'T, I TELL YA.
HERRIMAN

September 6th, 1931.

KRAZY KAT By Herriman

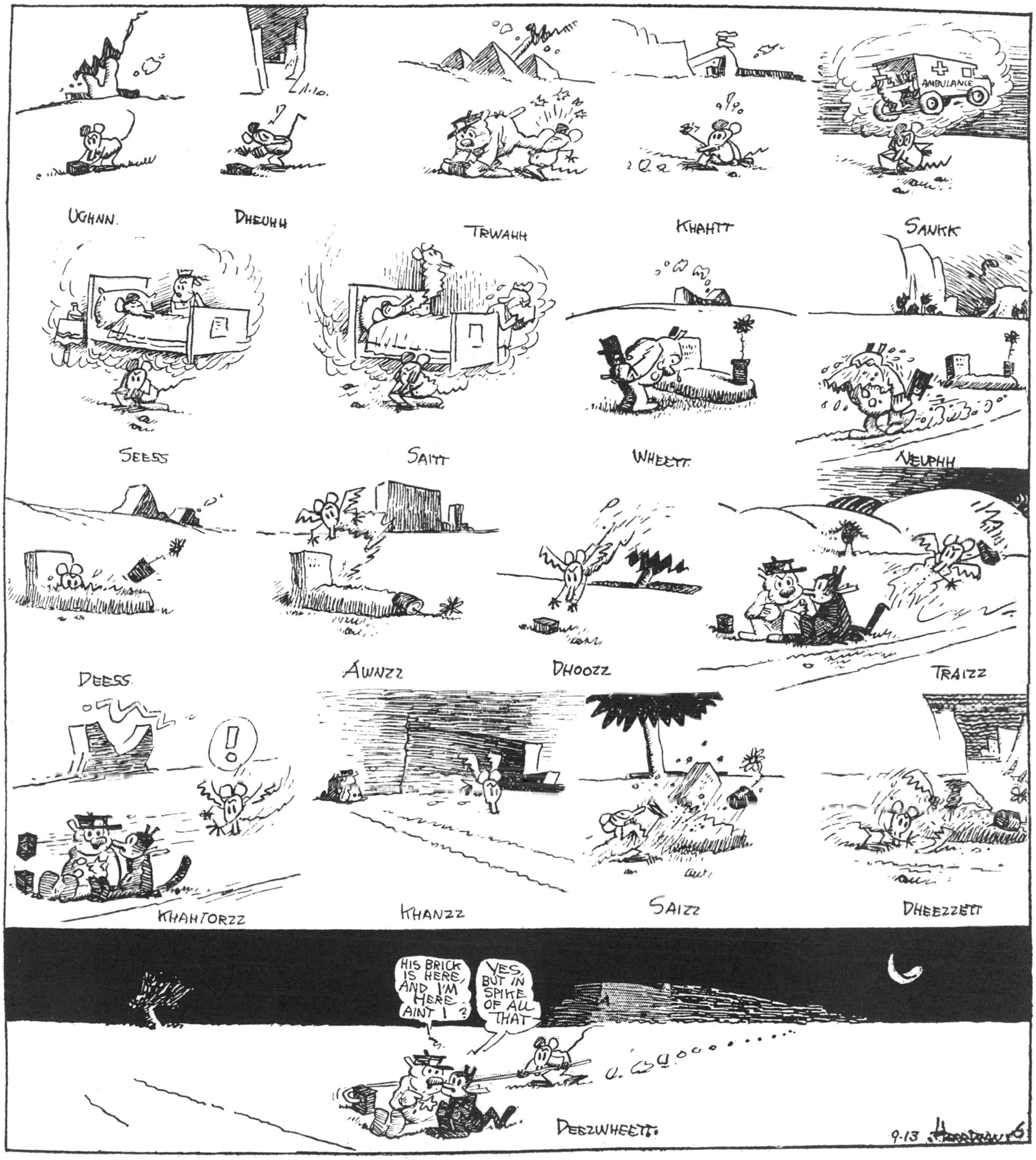

AMBULANCE
UGHNN.
DHEUHH
TRWAHH
KHAHTT
SANKK
SEESS
SAITT
WHEETT.
NEUPHH
DEESS.
AWNZZ
DHOOZZ
TRAIZZ
!
KHAHTORZZ
KHANZZ
SAIZZ
DHEEZZETT
HIS BRICK IS HERE, AND I'M HERE AINT I ?
YES, BUT IN SPIKE OF ALL THAT
DEEZWHEETT.
9-13 Herriman

September 13th, 1931.

KRAZY KAT *By Herriman*

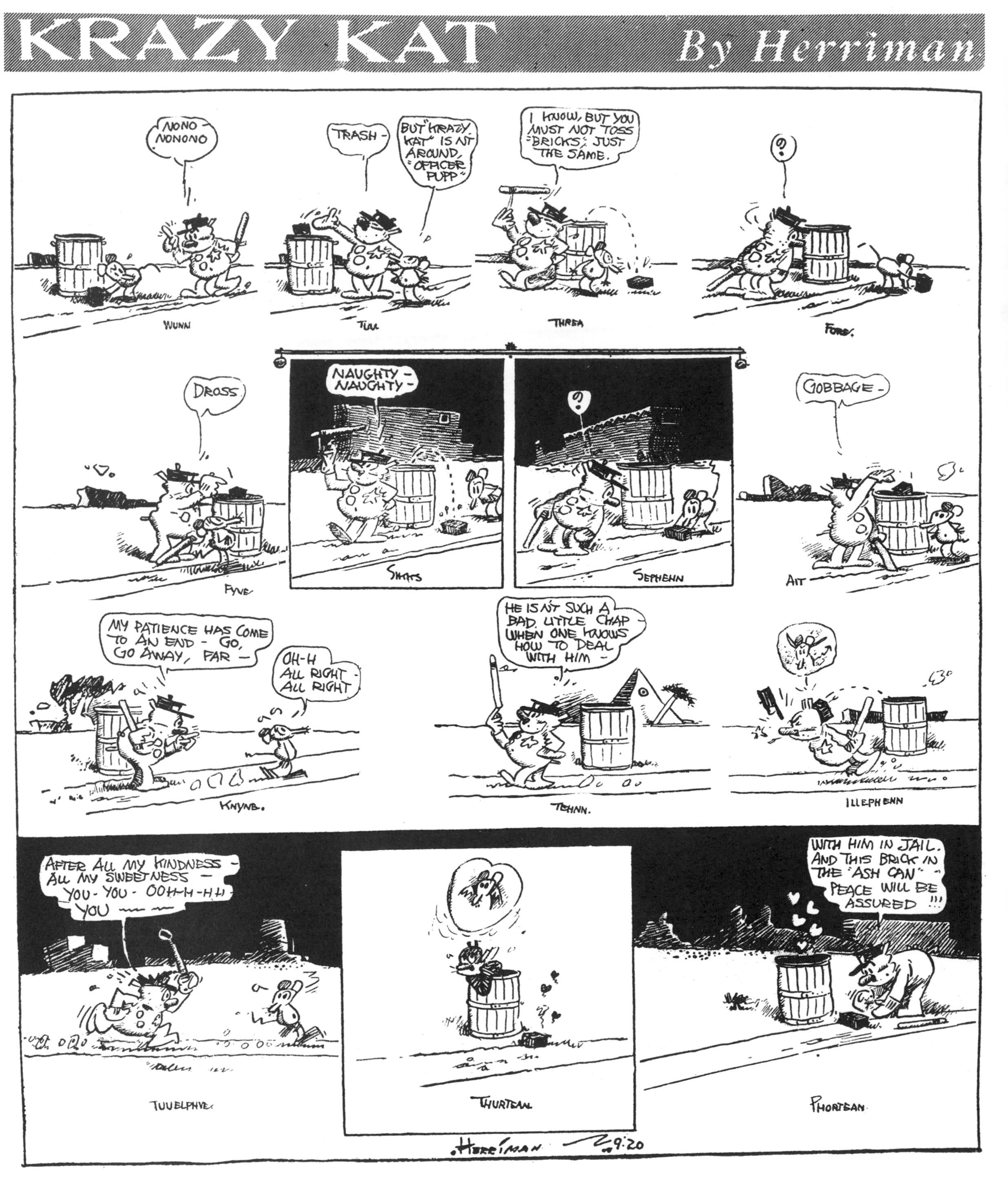
NONO - NONONO
WUNN
TRASH -
BUT "KRAZY KAT" IS N'T AROUND, "OFFICER PUPP"
I KNOW, BUT YOU MUST NOT TOSS "BRICKS," JUST THE SAME.
THREA
?
DROSS
FYVE
NAUGHTY - NAUGHTY -
?
SEPHENN
GOBBAGE -
AIT
MY PATIENCE HAS COME TO AN END - GO, GO AWAY, FAR -
OH-H ALL RIGHT - ALL RIGHT
HE IS N'T SUCH A BAD LITTLE CHAP - WHEN ONE KNOWS HOW TO DEAL WITH HIM -
TEHNN.
ILLEPHENN
AFTER ALL MY KINDNESS - ALL MY SWEETNESS - YOU - YOU - OOH-H-H-H YOU
WITH HIM IN JAIL, AND THIS BRICK IN THE "ASH CAN" - PEACE WILL BE ASSURED !!!
TUUELPHVE
THURTEAN
PHORTEAN
HERRIMAN 9.20

September 20th, 1931.

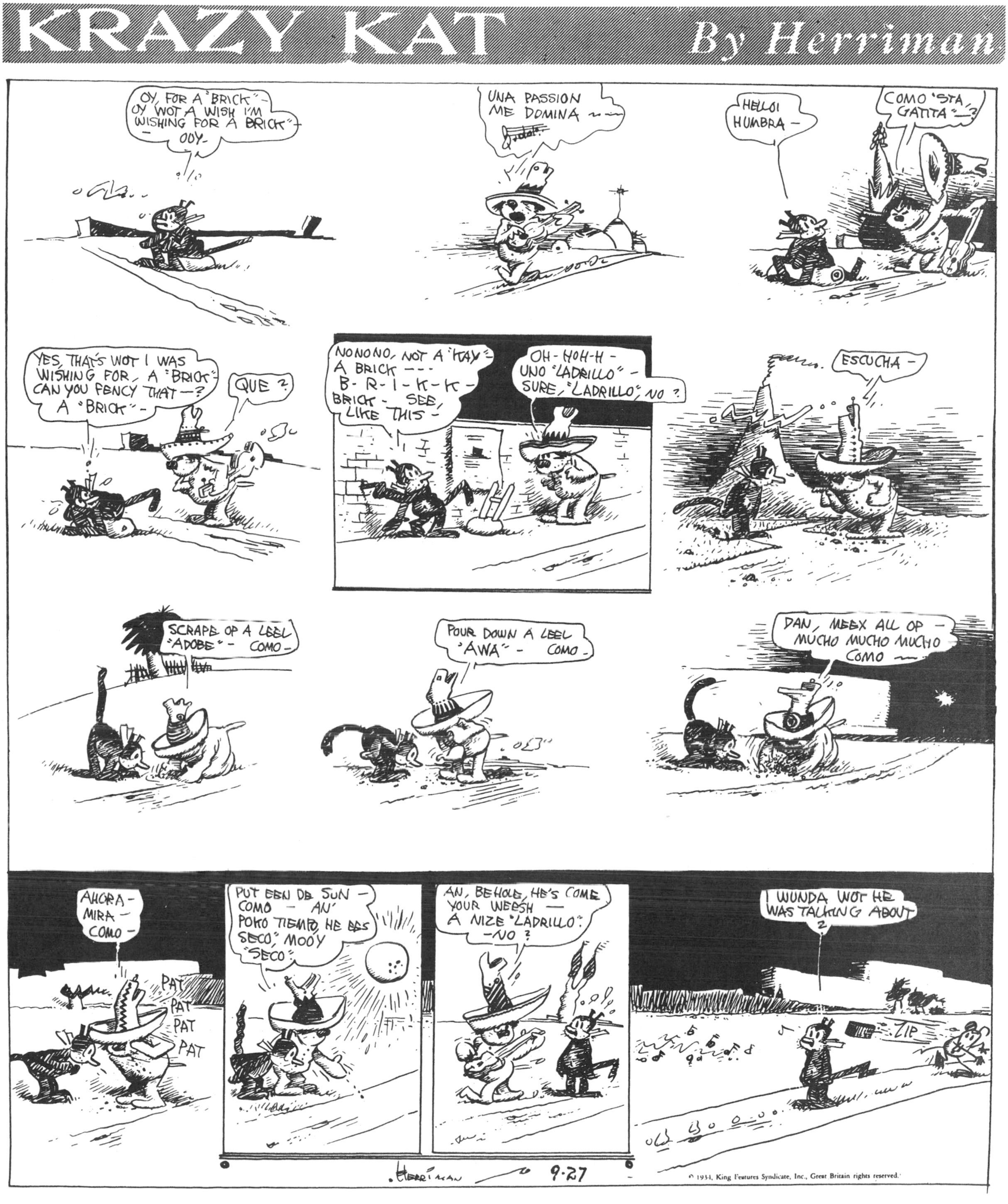
KRAZY KAT By Herriman
OY, FOR A "BRICK" – OY WOT A WISH I'M WISHING FOR A "BRICK" – OOY–
UNA PASSION ME DOMINA
HELLO! HUMBRA –
COMO 'STA GATITA –?
YES, THAT'S WOT I WAS WISHING FOR, A "BRICK" CAN YOU FENCY THAT –? A "BRICK" –
QUE ?
NONONO, NOT A "KAY" – A BRICK --- B-R-I-K-K – BRICK – SEE, LIKE THIS –
OH-HOH-H – UNO "LADRILLO" – SURE, "LADRILLO", NO ?
ESCUCHA –
SCRAPE OP A LEEL "ADOBE" – COMO –
POUR DOWN A LEEL "AWA" – COMO –
DAN, MEEX ALL OP – MUCHO MUCHO MUCHO COMO –
AHORA – MIRA – COMO –
PAT PAT PAT PAT
PUT EEN DE SUN – COMO – AN' POKO TIEMPO, HE EES SECO, MOOY "SECO"
AN, BEHOLE, HE'S COME YOUR WEESH – A NIZE "LADRILLO" –NO ?
I WUNDA WOT HE WAS TALKING ABOUT ?
ZIP
HERRIMAN 9-27
© 1931, King Features Syndicate, Inc., Great Britain rights reserved.

September 27th, 1931.

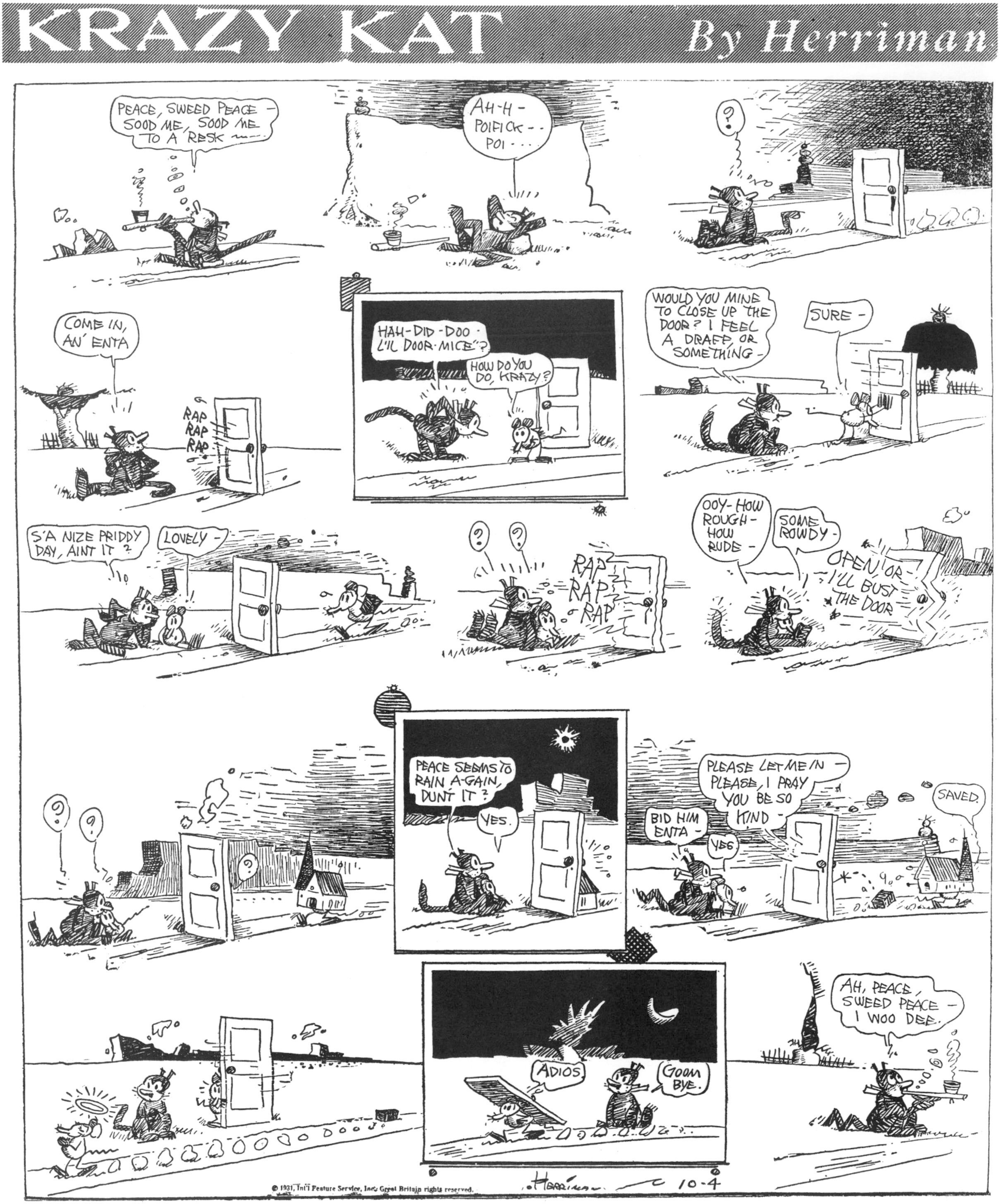
KRAZY KAT By Herriman
PEACE, SWEED PEACE – SOOD ME, SOOD ME TO A RESK –
AH-H – POIFICK – – POI – – –
?
COME IN, AN' ENTA
RAP RAP RAP
HAH-DID-DOO – L'IL DOOR-MICE"?
HOW DO YOU DO, KRAZY?
WOULD YOU MINE TO CLOSE UP THE DOOR? I FEEL A DRAFF, OR SOMETHING –
SURE –
S'A NIZE PRIDDY DAY, AINT IT ?
LOVELY –
? ?
RAP RAP RAP
OOY-HOW ROUGH-HOW RUDE –
SOME ROWDY –
OPEN, OR I'LL BUST THE DOOR
? ? ?
PEACE SEEMS TO RAIN A-GAIN, DUNT IT?
YES.
PLEASE LET ME IN – PLEASE, I PRAY YOU BE SO KIND –
BID HIM ENTA –
YES.
SAVED.
ADIOS
GOOM BYE.
AH, PEACE, SWEED PEACE – I WOO DEE.
© 1931, Int'l Feature Service, Inc. Great Britain rights reserved.
Herriman 10-4

October 4th, 1931.

KRAZY KAT By Herriman

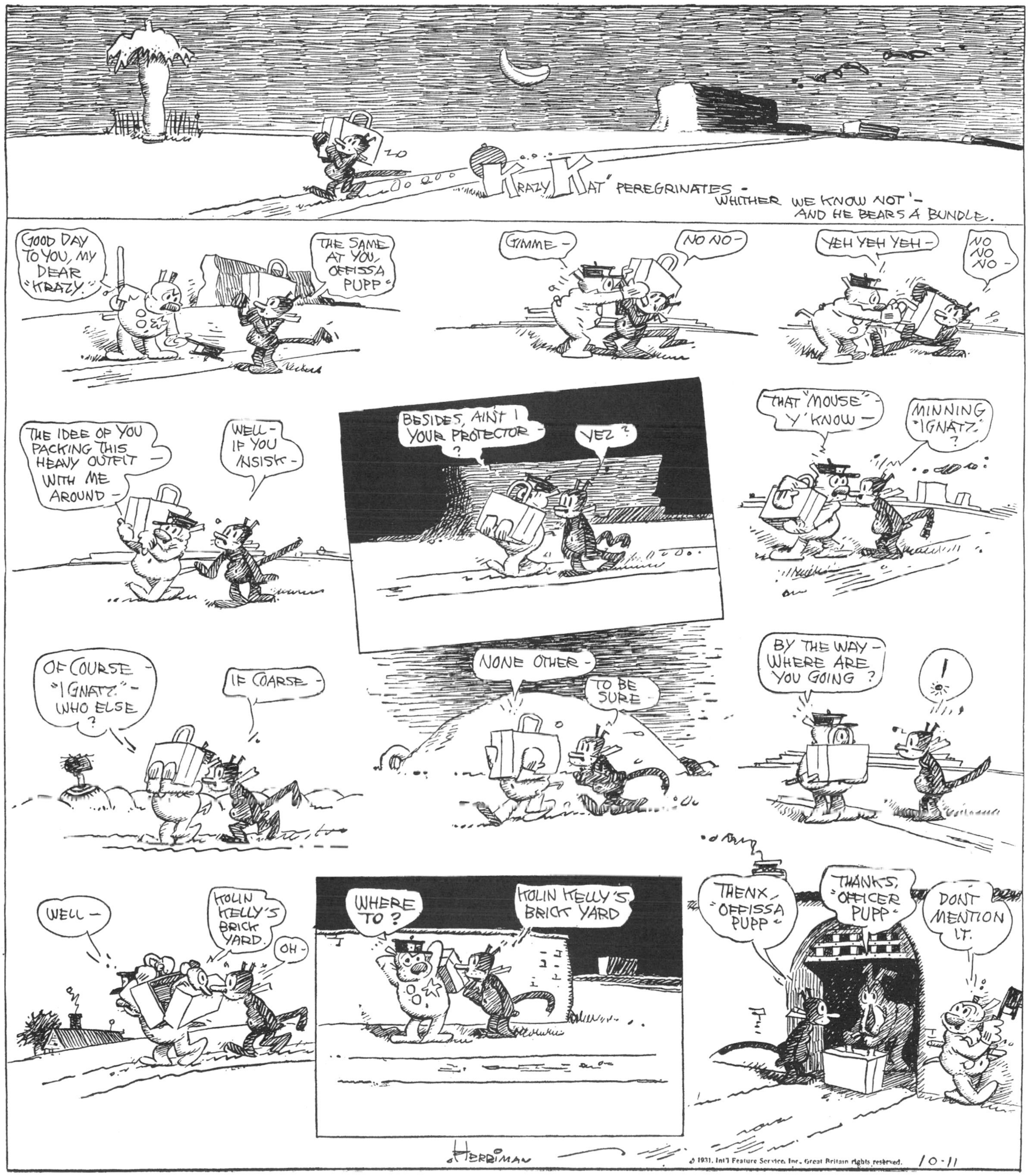
"KRAZY KAT" PEREGRINATES - WHITHER WE KNOW NOT - AND HE BEARS A BUNDLE.
GOOD DAY TO YOU, MY DEAR "KRAZY"
THE SAME AT YOU, OFFISSA PUPP
GIMME -
NO NO -
YEH YEH YEH -
NO NO NO -
THE IDEE OF YOU PACKING THIS HEAVY OUTFIT WITH ME AROUND -
WELL - IF YOU INSISK -
BESIDES, AIN'T I YOUR PROTECTOR ?
YEZ ?
THAT "MOUSE" Y'KNOW -
MINNING "IGNATZ" ?
OF COURSE "IGNATZ" - WHO ELSE ?
IF COARSE -
NONE OTHER -
TO BE SURE
BY THE WAY - WHERE ARE YOU GOING ?
!
WELL -
KOLIN KELLY'S BRICK YARD.
OH -
WHERE TO ?
KOLIN KELLY'S BRICK YARD
THENX, OFFISSA PUPP
THANKS, OFFICER PUPP
DONT MENTION IT.
HERRIMAN
© 1931, Int'l Feature Service, Inc., Great Britain rights reserved.
10-11

October 11th, 1931.

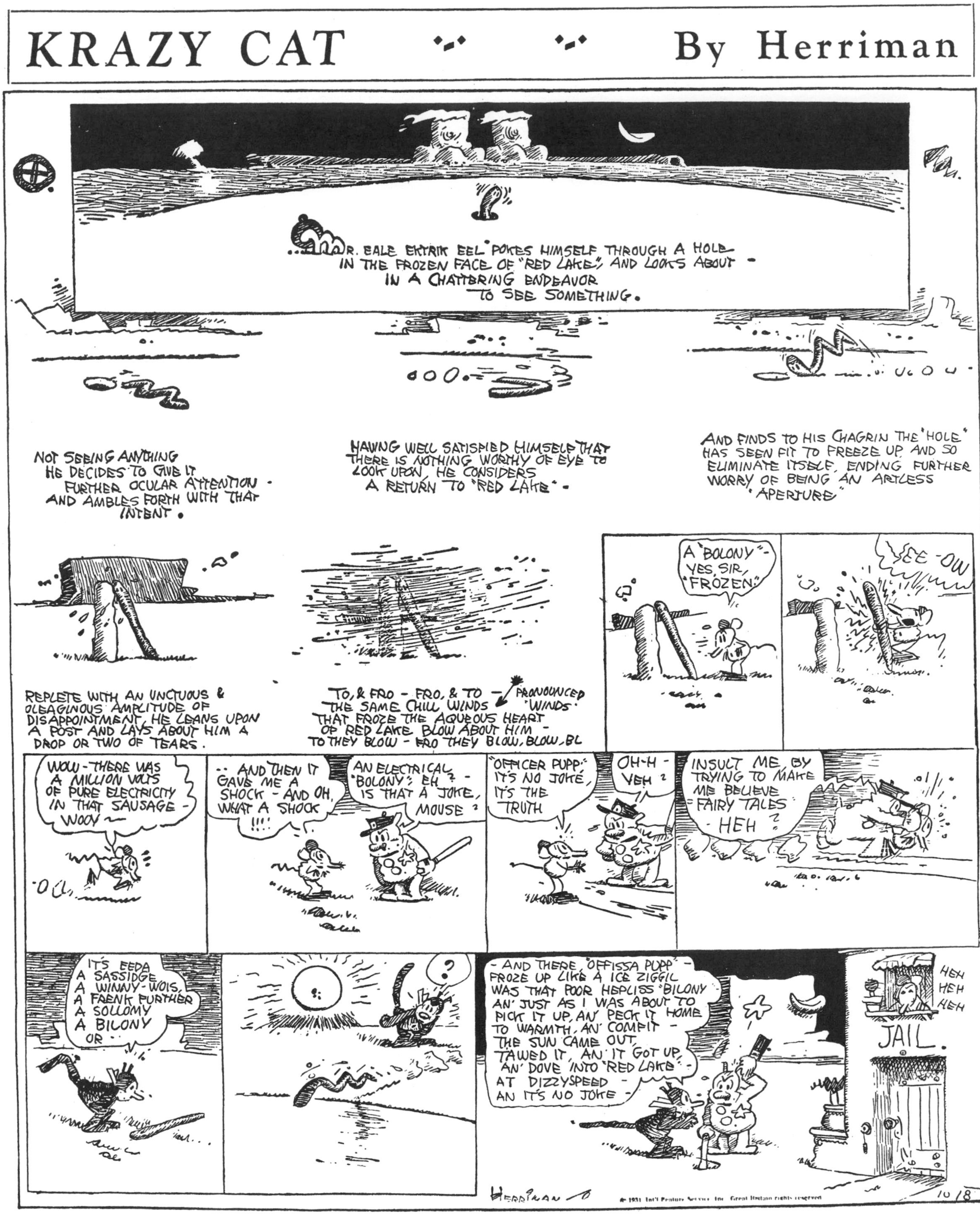
KRAZY CAT
By Herriman
MR. EALE EKTRIK EEL POKES HIMSELF THROUGH A HOLE IN THE FROZEN FACE OF "RED LAKE", AND LOOKS ABOUT - IN A CHATTERING ENDEAVOR TO SEE SOMETHING.
NOT SEEING ANYTHING HE DECIDES TO GIVE IT FURTHER OCULAR ATTENTION - AND AMBLES FORTH WITH THAT INTENT.
HAVING WELL SATISFIED HIMSELF THAT THERE IS NOTHING WORTHY OF EYE TO LOOK UPON, HE CONSIDERS A RETURN TO "RED LAKE" -
AND FINDS TO HIS CHAGRIN THE "HOLE" HAS SEEN FIT TO FREEZE UP, AND SO ELIMINATE ITSELF, ENDING FURTHER WORRY OF BEING AN ARTLESS "APERTURE"
REPLETE WITH AN UNCTUOUS & OLEAGINOUS AMPLITUDE OF DISAPPOINTMENT, HE LEANS UPON A POST AND LAYS ABOUT HIM A DROP OR TWO OF TEARS.
TO, & FRO - FRO, & TO - THE SAME CHILL WINDS THAT FROZE THE AQUEOUS HEART OF RED LAKE BLOW ABOUT HIM - TO THEY BLOW - FRO THEY BLOW, BLOW, BL
PRONOUNCED "WINDS"
A "BOLONY" - YES, SIR, "FROZEN"
SEE-OW
WOW - THERE WAS A MILLION VOLTS OF PURE ELECTRICITY IN THAT SAUSAGE - WOOY
- AND THEN IT GAVE ME A SHOCK - AND OH, WHAT A SHOCK !!!
AN ELECTRICAL "BOLONY", EH? IS THAT A JOKE, MOUSE?
"OFFICER PUPP" IT'S NO JOKE, IT'S THE TRUTH
OH-H YEH?
INSULT ME, BY TRYING TO MAKE ME BELIEVE FAIRY TALES - HEH?
IT'S EEDA A SASSIDGE, A WINNY-WOIS, A FRENK FURTHER A SOLLOMY A BILONY OR - -
?
- AND THERE, "OFFISSA PUPP" - FROZE UP LIKE A ICE ZIGGIL WAS THAT POOR HEPLISS "BILONY" AN' JUST AS I WAS ABOUT TO PICK IT UP, AN' PECK IT HOME TO WARMTH, AN' COMFIT - THE SUN CAME OUT, TAWED IT, AN' IT GOT UP, AN' DOVE INTO "RED LAKE" AT DIZZYSPEED - AN IT'S NO JOKE -
HEH HEH HEH
JAIL
HERRIMAN
© 1931 Int'l Feature Service, Inc. Great Britain rights reserved
10/18

October 18th, 1931.

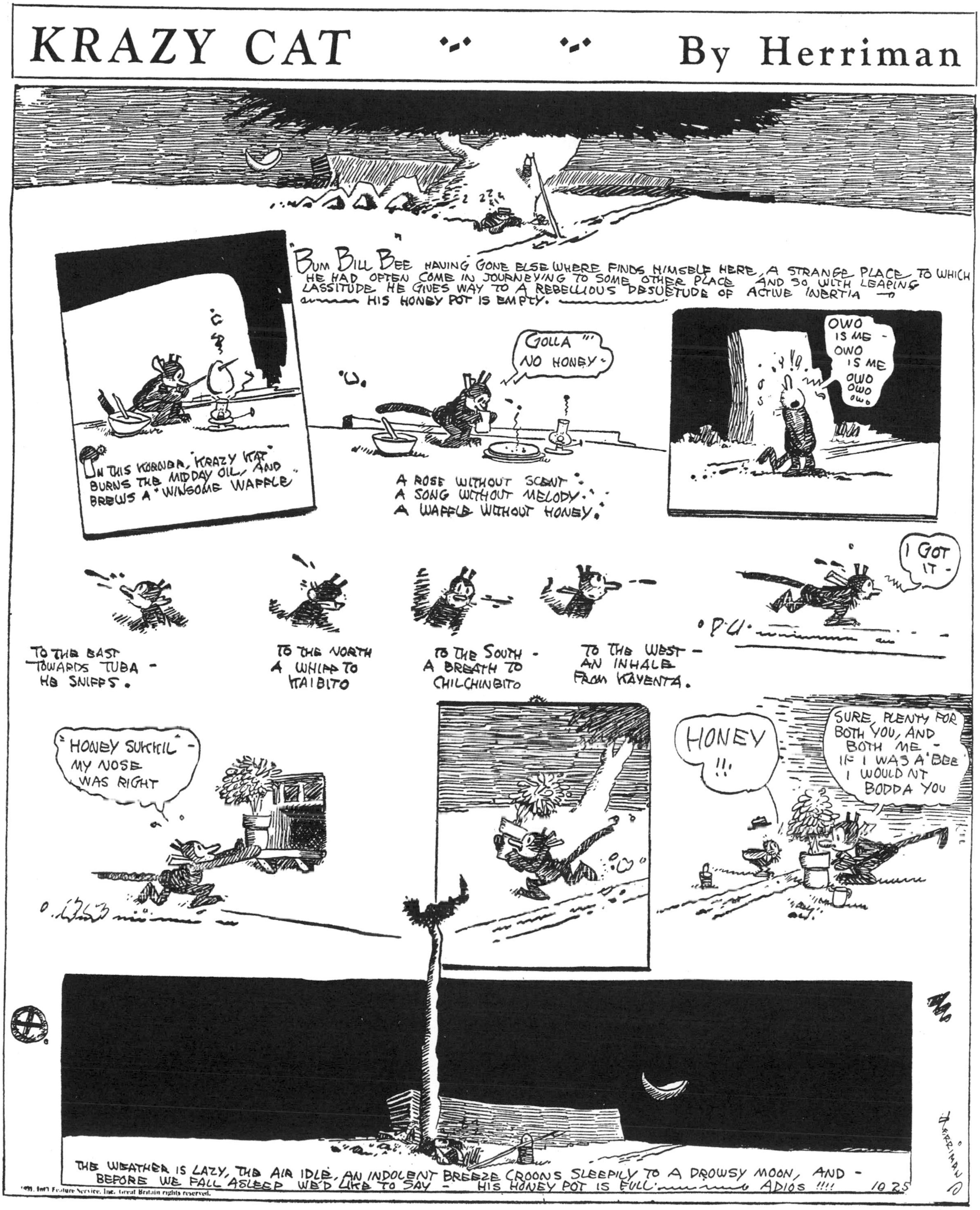
KRAZY CAT
By Herriman
"BUM BILL BEE" HAVING GONE ELSE WHERE FINDS HIMSELF HERE, A STRANGE PLACE TO WHICH HE HAD OFTEN COME IN JOURNEYING TO SOME OTHER PLACE AND SO WITH LEAPING LASSITUDE HE GIVES WAY TO A REBELLIOUS DESUETUDE OF ACTIVE INERTIA — HIS HONEY POT IS EMPTY.
IN THIS KORNER, "KRAZY KAT" BURNS THE MIDDAY OIL, AND BREWS A "WINSOME WAFFLE"
GOLLA NO HONEY
A ROSE WITHOUT SCENT
A SONG WITHOUT MELODY
A WAFFLE WITHOUT HONEY
OWO IS ME - OWO IS ME OWO OWO OWO
TO THE EAST TOWARDS TUBA - HE SNIFFS.
TO THE NORTH A WHIFF TO KAIBITO
TO THE SOUTH - A BREATH TO CHILCHINBITO
TO THE WEST - AN INHALE FROM KAYENTA.
I GOT IT -
HONEY SUKKIL - MY NOSE WAS RIGHT
HONEY !!!
SURE, PLENTY FOR BOTH YOU, AND BOTH ME - IF I WAS A 'BEE' I WOULD N'T BODDA YOU
THE WEATHER IS LAZY, THE AIR IDLE, AN INDOLENT BREEZE CROONS SLEEPILY TO A DROWSY MOON, AND - BEFORE WE FALL ASLEEP WE'D LIKE TO SAY - HIS HONEY POT IS FULL — ADIOS !!!!
10 25
HERRIMAN
Feature Service, Inc. Great Britain rights reserved.

October 25th, 1931.

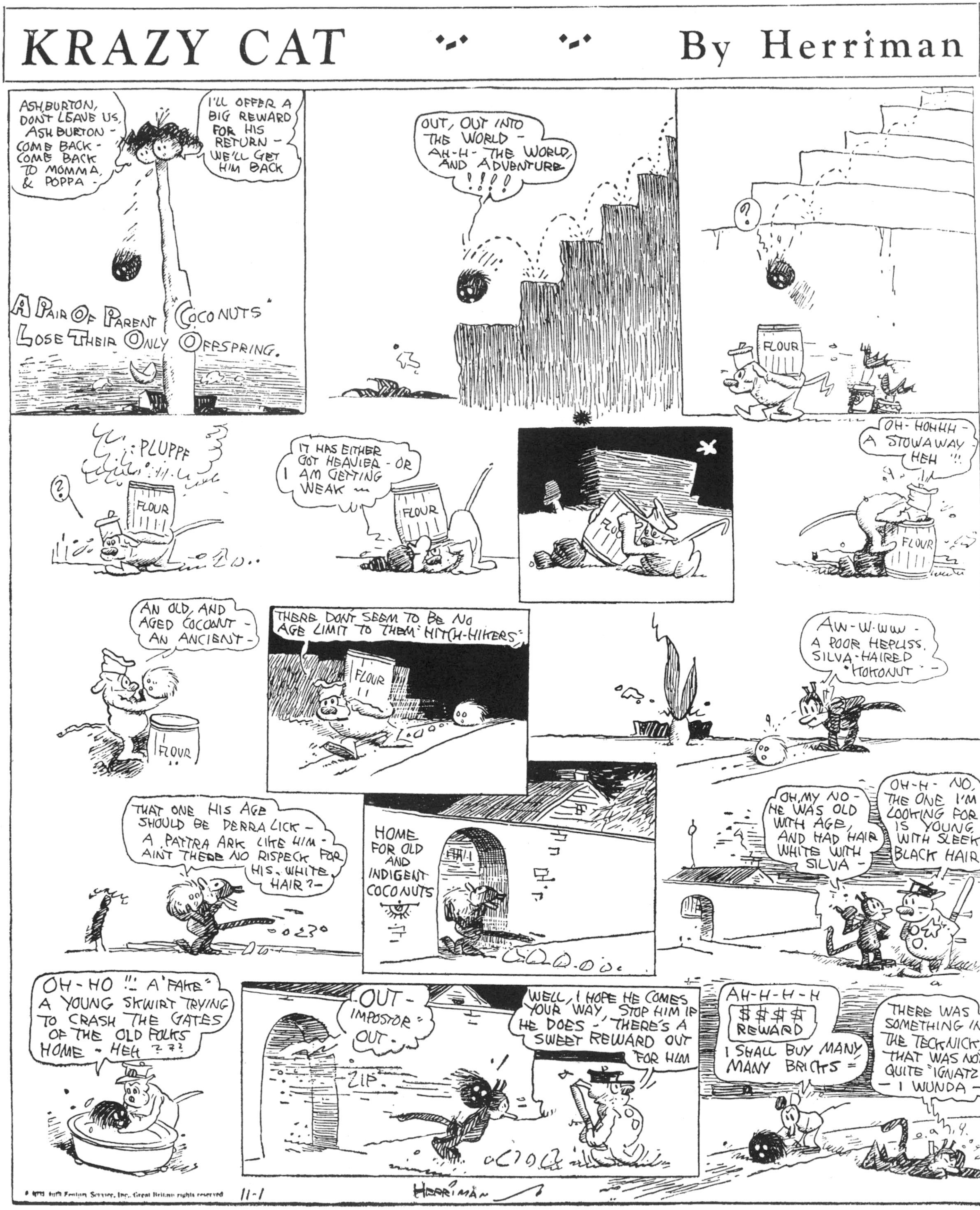
KRAZY CAT By Herriman
ASH BURTON, DON'T LEAVE US, ASH BURTON - COME BACK - COME BACK TO MOMMA, & POPPA -
I'LL OFFER A BIG REWARD FOR HIS RETURN - WE'LL GET HIM BACK
A PAIR OF PARENT "COCONUTS" LOSE THEIR ONLY OFFSPRING.
OUT, OUT INTO THE WORLD - AH-H - THE WORLD, AND ADVENTURE !!!!
?
FLOUR
PLUPPF
?
IT HAS EITHER GOT HEAVIER - OR I AM GETTING WEAK ---
OH - HOHHH - A STOWAWAY HEH !!!
AN OLD, AND AGED COCONUT - AN ANCIENT -
THERE DON'T SEEM TO BE NO AGE LIMIT TO THEM "HITCH-HIKERS"
AW-W-WW - A POOR HEPLISS, SILVA-HAIRED "KOKONUT" -
THAT ONE HIS AGE SHOULD BE DERRA LICK - A PATTRA ARK LIKE HIM - AINT THERE NO RISPECK FOR HIS, WHITE HAIR? -
HOME FOR OLD AND INDIGENT COCONUTS
OH, MY NO - HE WAS OLD WITH AGE, AND HAD HAIR WHITE WITH SILVA -
OH-H - NO, THE ONE I'M LOOKING FOR IS YOUNG, WITH SLEEK BLACK HAIR.
OH - HO !! A "FAKE" - A YOUNG SKWIRT TRYING TO CRASH THE GATES OF THE OLD FOLKS HOME - HEH ???
- OUT - IMPOSTOR - OUT -
ZIP
WELL, I HOPE HE COMES YOUR WAY, STOP HIM IF HE DOES - THERE'S A SWEET REWARD OUT FOR HIM
AH-H-H-H $$$$ REWARD I SHALL BUY MANY MANY BRICKS -
THERE WAS SOMETHING IN THE TECKNICK, THAT WAS NOT QUITE "IGNATZ" - I WUNDA -
11-1
HERRIMAN

November 1st, 1931.

KRAZY CAT ∴ By Herriman

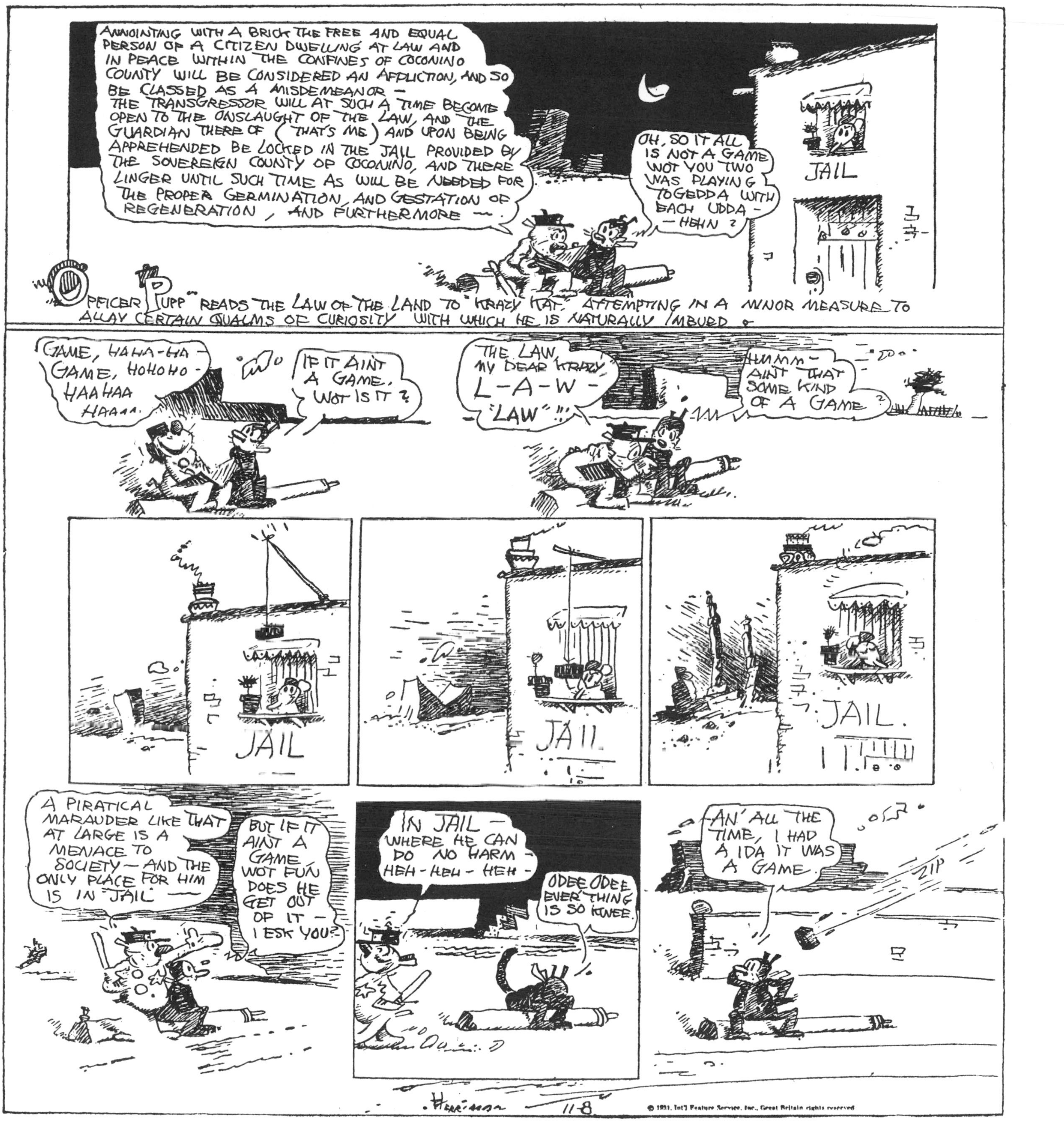
ANNOINTING WITH A BRICK THE FREE AND EQUAL PERSON OF A CITIZEN DWELLING AT LAW AND IN PEACE WITHIN THE CONFINES OF COCONINO COUNTY WILL BE CONSIDERED AN AFFLICTION, AND SO BE CLASSED AS A MISDEMEANOR — THE TRANSGRESSOR WILL AT SUCH A TIME BECOME OPEN TO THE ONSLAUGHT OF THE LAW, AND THE GUARDIAN THERE OF (THAT'S ME) AND UPON BEING APPREHENDED BE LOCKED IN THE JAIL PROVIDED BY THE SOVEREIGN COUNTY OF COCONINO, AND THERE LINGER UNTIL SUCH TIME AS WILL BE NEEDED FOR THE PROPER GERMINATION, AND GESTATION OF REGENERATION, AND FURTHERMORE —
OH, SO IT ALL IS NOT A GAME WOT YOU TWO WAS PLAYING TOGEDDA WITH EACH UDDA — HEHN?
JAIL
"OFFICER PUPP" READS THE LAW OF THE LAND TO "KRAZY KAT" ATTEMPTING IN A MINOR MEASURE TO ALLAY CERTAIN QUALMS OF CURIOSITY WITH WHICH HE IS NATURALLY IMBUED
GAME, HAHA-HA — GAME, HOHOHO — HAAHAA HAAAA.
IF IT AINT A GAME, WOT IS IT?
THE LAW, MY DEAR KRAZY L-A-W — "LAW"!!
HUMM — AINT THAT SOME KIND OF A GAME?
JAIL
JAIL
JAIL.
A PIRATICAL MARAUDER LIKE THAT AT LARGE IS A MENACE TO SOCIETY — AND THE ONLY PLACE FOR HIM IS IN "JAIL" —
BUT IF IT AINT A GAME WOT FUN DOES HE GET OUT OF IT — I ESK YOU?
IN JAIL — WHERE HE CAN DO NO HARM — HEH - HEH - HEH —
ODEE ODEE EVER'THING IS SO KWEE.
AN' ALL THE TIME, I HAD A IDA IT WAS A GAME.
ZIP
HERRIMAN 11-8
© 1931, Int'l Feature Service, Inc., Great Britain rights reserved

November 8th, 1931.

KRAZY CAT By Herriman

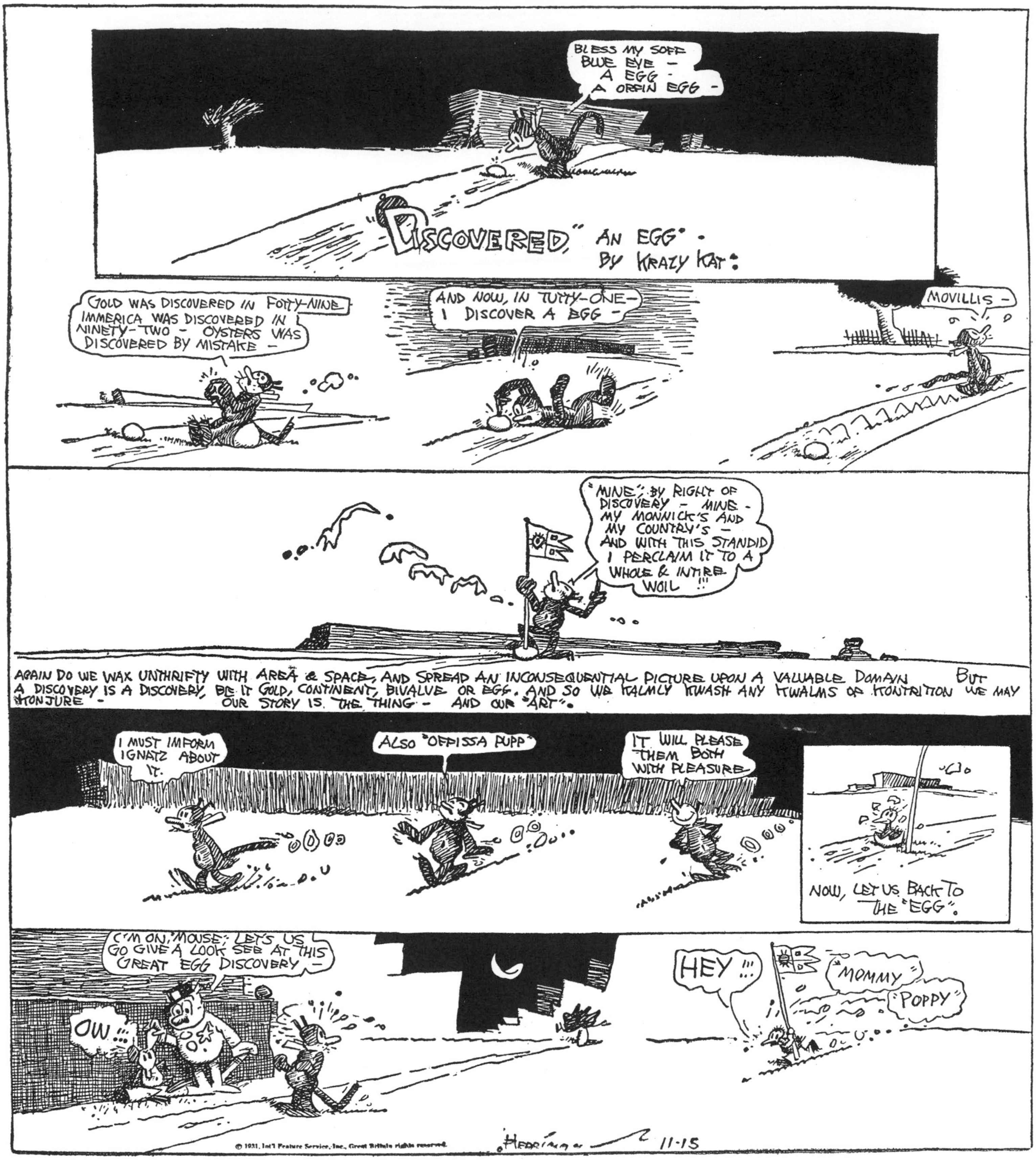

BLESS MY SOFF BLUE EYE — A EGG — A ORFIN EGG —
"DISCOVERED" AN EGG — BY KRAZY KAT:
GOLD WAS DISCOVERED IN FOTTY-NINE IMMERICA WAS DISCOVERED IN NINETY-TWO — OYSTERS WAS DISCOVERED BY MISTAKE —
AND NOW, IN TUTTY-ONE — I DISCOVER A EGG —
MOVILLIS —
"MINE", BY RIGHT OF DISCOVERY — MINE — MY MONNICK'S AND MY COUNTRY'S — AND WITH THIS STANDID I PERCLAIM IT TO A WHOLE & INTIRE WOIL !!!
AGAIN DO WE WAX UNTHRIFTY WITH AREA & SPACE, AND SPREAD AN INCONSEQUENTIAL PICTURE UPON A VALUABLE DOMAIN BUT A DISCOVERY IS A DISCOVERY, BE IT GOLD, CONTINENT, BIVALVE OR EGG. AND SO WE KALMLY KWASH ANY KWALMS OF KONTRITION WE MAY KONJURE — OUR STORY IS THE THING — AND OUR "ART".
I MUST IMFORM IGNATZ ABOUT IT.
ALSO "OFFISSA PUPP"
IT WILL PLEASE THEM BOTH WITH PLEASURE
NOW, LET US BACK TO THE "EGG".
C'M ON, MOUSE, LET'S US GO GIVE A LOOK SEE AT THIS GREAT EGG DISCOVERY —
OW !!!
HEY !!!
"MOMMY"
"POPPY"
© 1931, Int'l Feature Service, Inc., Great Britain rights reserved.
HERRIMAN 11-15

November 15th, 1931.

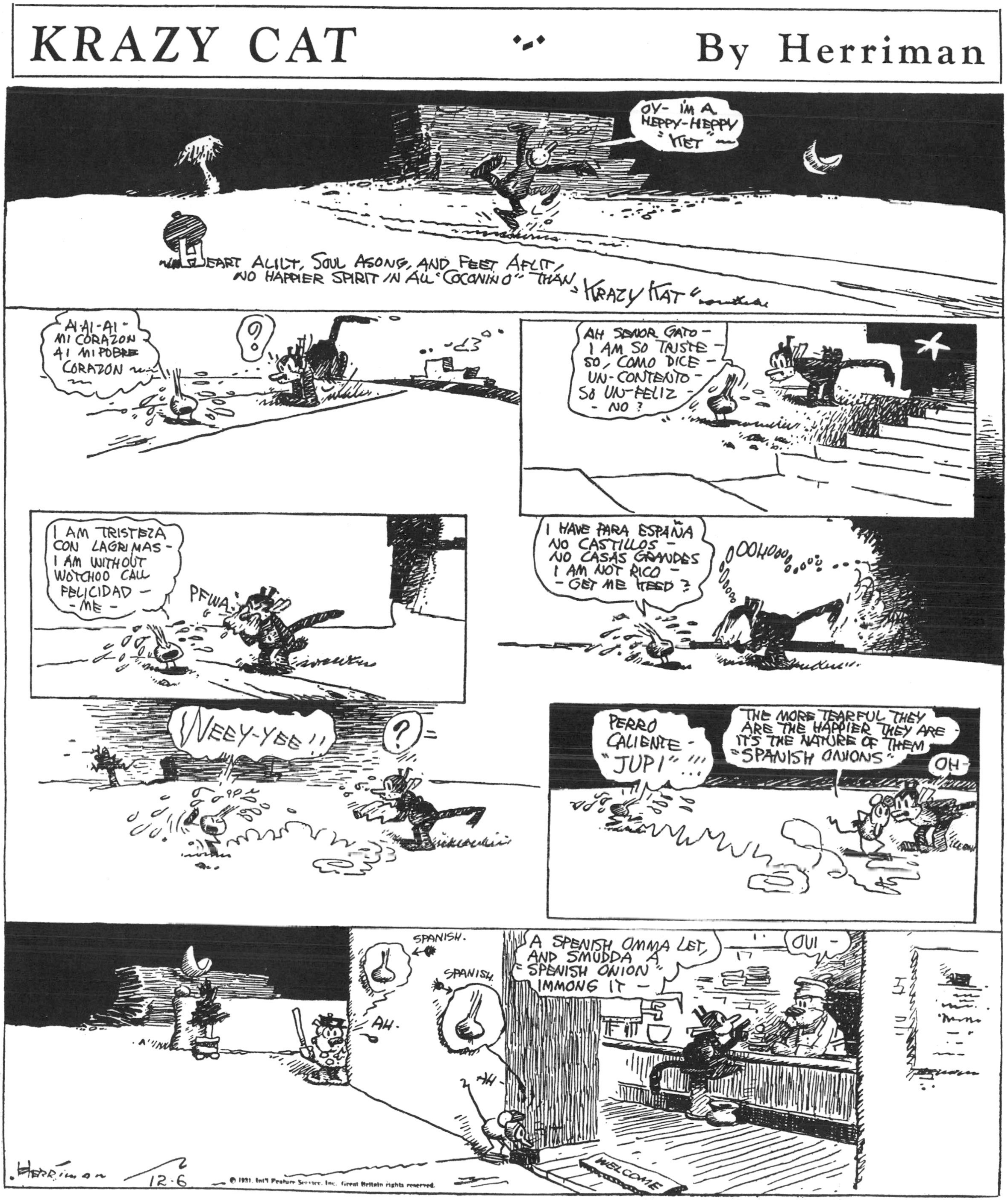

KRAZY CAT
By Herriman
OY- IM A HEPPY-HEPPY "KET"
HEART ALILT, SOUL ASONG, AND FEET AFLIT, NO HAPPIER SPIRIT IN ALL "COCONINO" THAN "KRAZY KAT"
AI-AI-AI MI CORAZON AI MI POBRE CORAZON
?
AH SENOR GATO - I AM SO TRISTE - SO, COMO DICE UN-CONTENTO - SO UN-FELIZ - NO?
I AM TRISTEZA CON LAGRIMAS - I AM WITHOUT WOTCHOO CALL FELICIDAD - ME -
PFWA
I HAVE PARA ESPAÑA NO CASTILLOS - NO CASAS GRANDES I AM NOT RICO - GET ME YEED?
OOHOOO
NEEY-YEE!!
?
PERRO CALIENTE - "JUPI"!!!
THE MORE TEARFUL THEY ARE THE HAPPIER THEY ARE IT'S THE NATURE OF THEM "SPANISH ONIONS"
OH -
SPANISH.
SPANISH.
AH-
A SPENISH OMMA LET, AND SMUDDA A SPENISH ONION IMMONG IT -
OUI -
WELCOME
HERRIMAN 12-6
© 1931, Int'l Feature Service, Inc. Great Britain rights reserved.

December 6th, 1931.

KRAZY CAT ❖ By Herriman

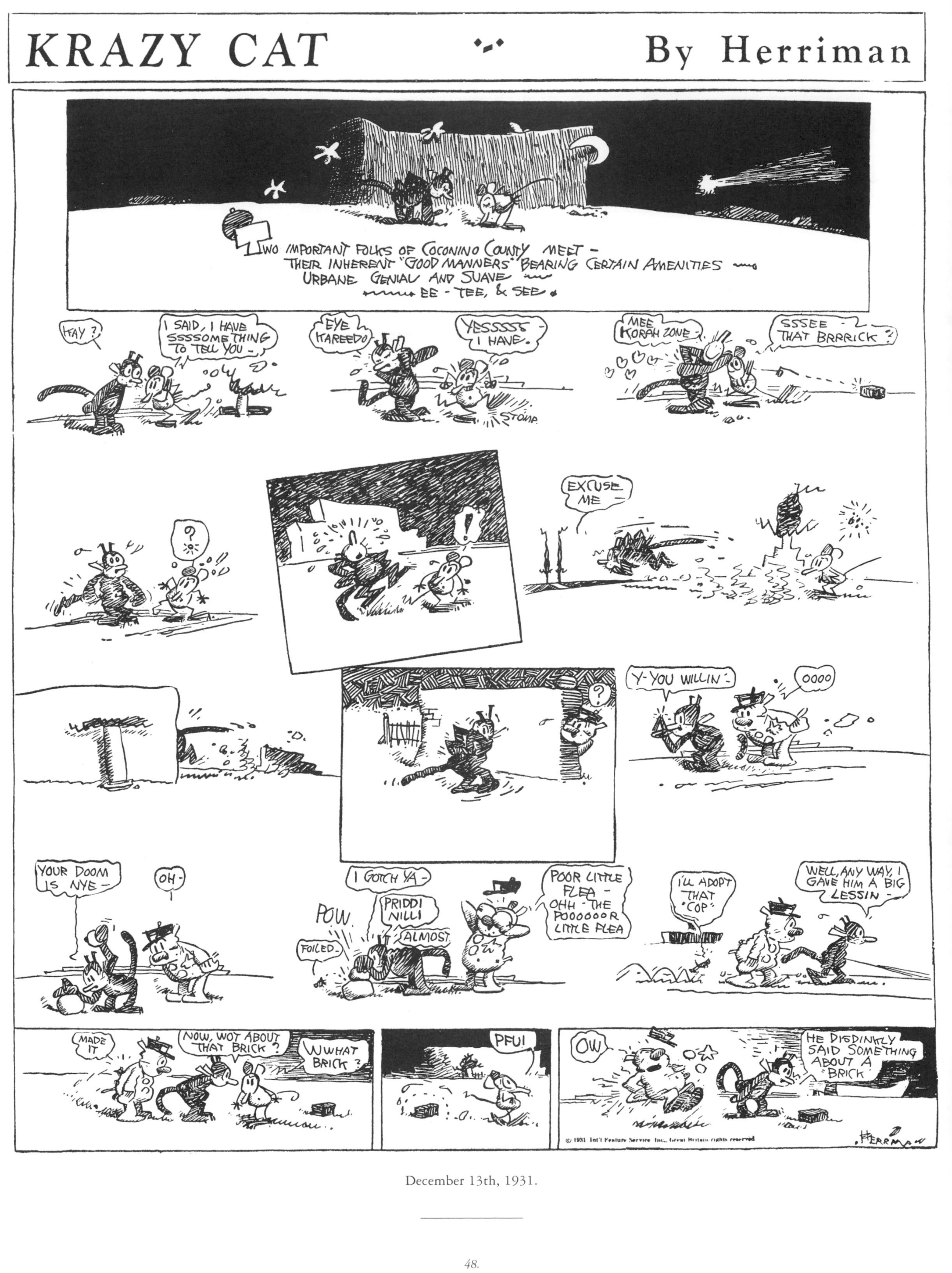

TWO IMPORTANT FOLKS OF COCONINO COUNTY MEET - THEIR INHERENT "GOOD MANNERS" BEARING CERTAIN AMENITIES — URBANE GENIAL AND SUAVE — — EE - TEE, & SEE
KAY ?
I SAID, I HAVE SSSSOMETHING TO TELL YOU -
EYE KAREEDO
YESSSSS I HAVE.
STOMP
MEE KORAH ZONE
SSSEE THAT BRRRICK ?
EXCUSE ME
Y-YOU WILLIN'-
OOOO
YOUR DOOM IS NYE -
OH -
I GOTCH YA -
POW
PRIDDI NILLI
ALMOST
FOILED
POOR LITTLE FLEA - OHH THE POOOOOOR LITTLE FLEA
I'LL ADOPT THAT 'COP'
WELL, ANY WAY, I GAVE HIM A BIG LESSIN -
MADE IT
NOW, WOT ABOUT THAT BRICK ?
WWHAT BRICK ?
PFUI
OW
HE DISDINKLY SAID SOMETHING ABOUT A BRICK
© 1931 Int'l Feature Service Inc., Great Britain rights reserved
HERRMAN

December 13th, 1931.

KRAZY CAT By Herriman

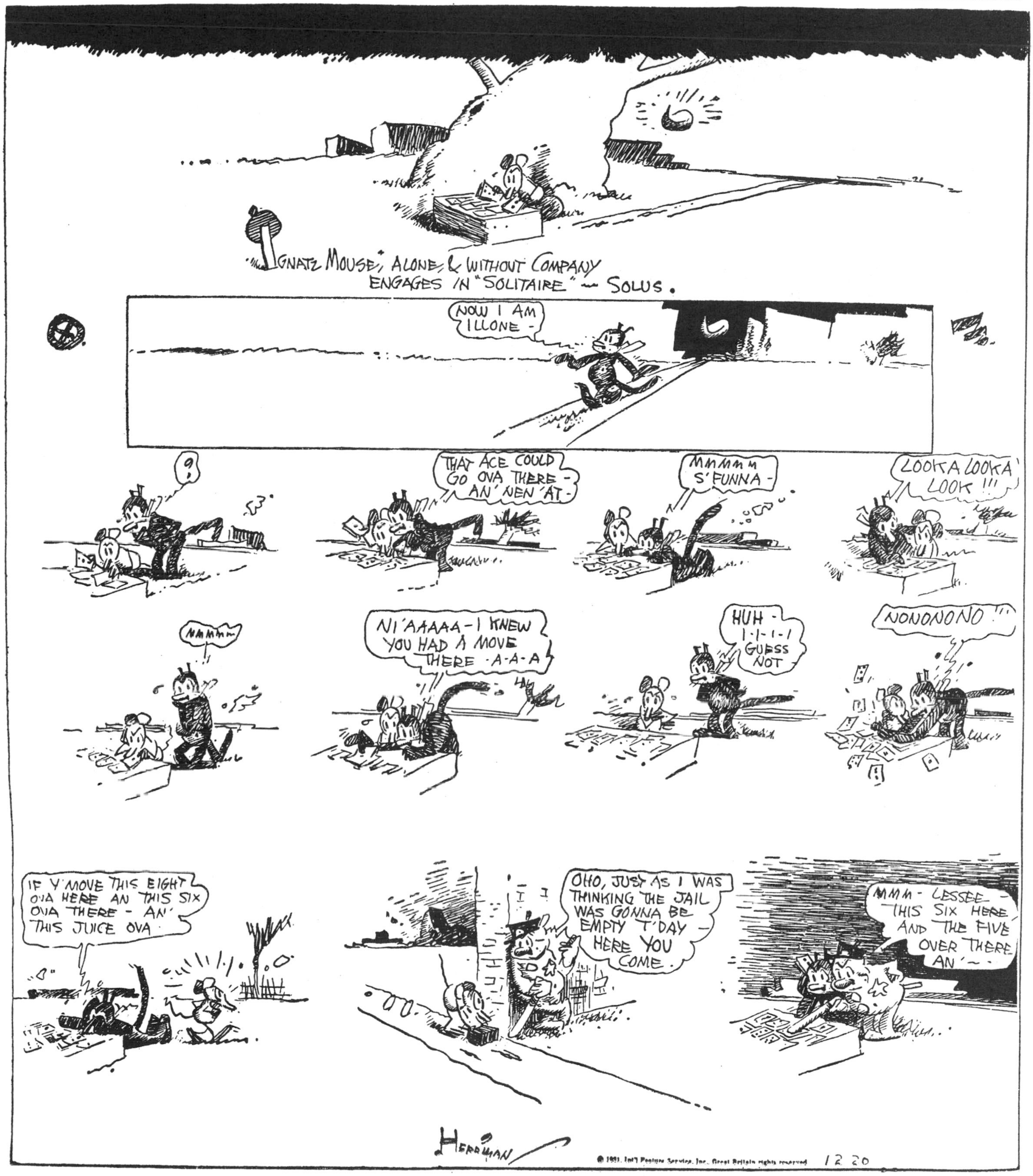

IGNATZ MOUSE, ALONE, & WITHOUT COMPANY ENGAGES IN "SOLITAIRE" ~ SOLUS.
NOW I AM ILLONE -
?
THAT ACE COULD GO OVA THERE - AN' NEN 'AT -
MMMMM S'FUNNA -
LOOKA LOOKA LOOK !!!
MMMMM
NI'AAAAA - I KNEW YOU HAD A MOVE THERE - A - A - A
HUH - I - I - I - I GUESS NOT
NONONONO !!!
IF Y' MOVE THIS EIGHT OVA HERE AN THIS SIX OVA THERE - AN' THIS JUICE OVA
OHO, JUST AS I WAS THINKING THE JAIL WAS GONNA BE EMPTY T'DAY - HERE YOU COME.
MMM - LESSEE - THIS SIX HERE AND THE FIVE OVER THERE AN' ~
HERRIMAN
12 20

December 20th, 1931.

KRAZY CAT — By Herriman

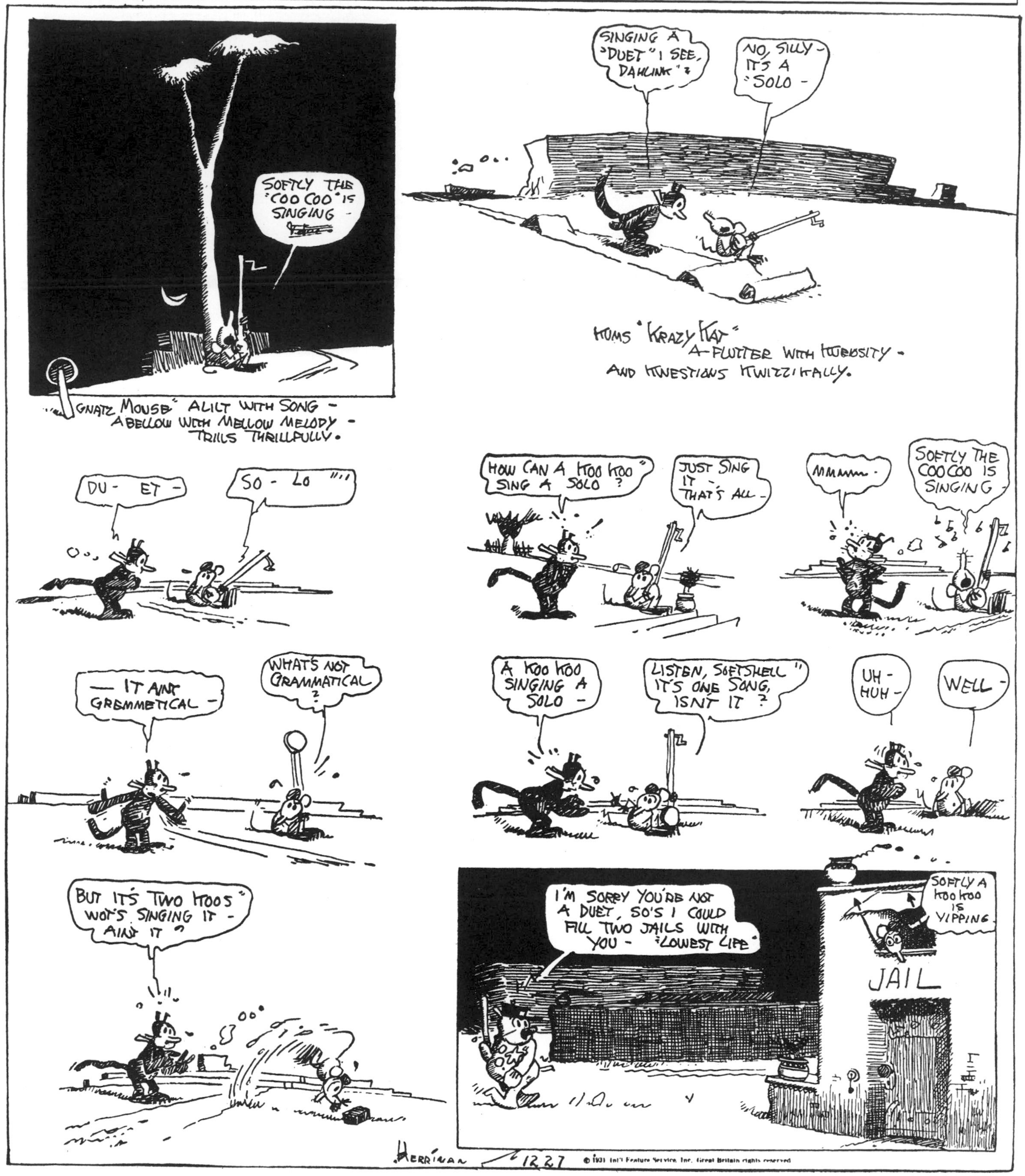

SOFTLY THE "COO COO" IS SINGING -
"IGNATZ MOUSE" ALILT WITH SONG - ABELLOW WITH MELLOW MELODY - TRILLS THRILLFULLY.
SINGING A "DUET" I SEE, DAHLINK"?
NO, SILLY - IT'S A "SOLO -
HUMS "KRAZY KAT" A-FLUTTER WITH KURIOSITY - AND KWESTIONS KWIZZIKALLY.
DU - ET -
SO - LO
HOW CAN A KOO KOO SING A SOLO ?
JUST SING IT - THAT'S ALL -
MMMMM -
SOFTLY THE COO COO IS SINGING -
— IT AINT GREMMETICAL -
WHAT'S NOT GRAMMATICAL ?
A KOO KOO SINGING A SOLO -
LISTEN, SOFTSHELL" IT'S ONE SONG, ISNT IT ?
UH - HUH -
WELL -
BUT IT'S TWO KOOS" WOT'S SINGING IT - AIN'T IT ?
I'M SORRY YOU'RE NOT A DUET, SO'S I COULD FILL TWO JAILS WITH YOU - "LOWEST LIFE"
SOFTLY A KOO KOO IS YIPPING
JAIL
HERRIMAN 12 27
© 1931 Int'l Feature Service, Inc. Great Britain rights reserved

December 27th, 1931.

1932.

KRAZY KAT By Herriman

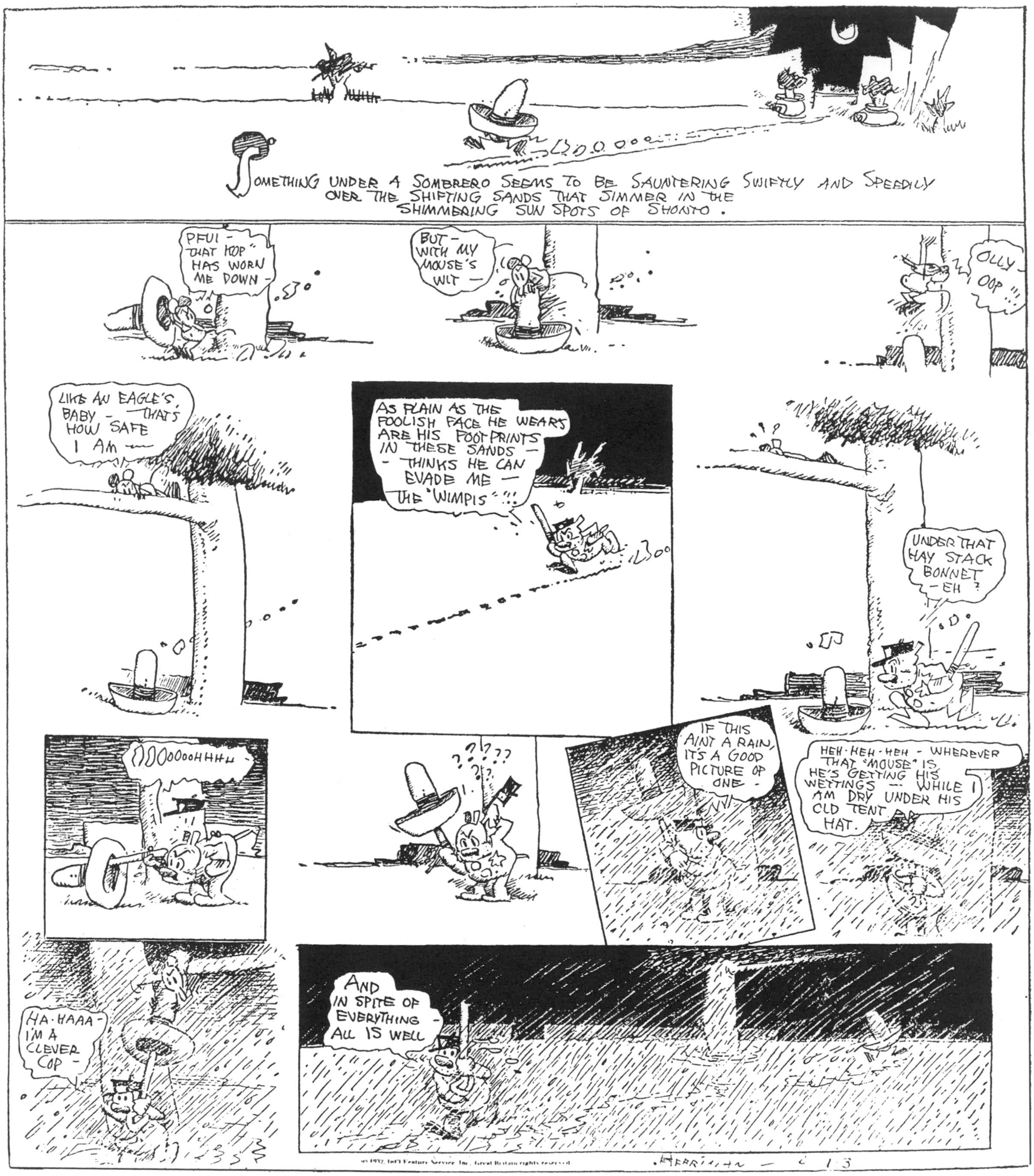

SOMETHING UNDER A SOMBRERO SEEMS TO BE SAUNTERING SWIFTLY AND SPEEDILY OVER THE SHIFTING SANDS THAT SIMMER IN THE SHIMMERING SUN SPOTS OF SHONTO.
PFUI - THAT "KOP" HAS WORN ME DOWN -
BUT - WITH MY MOUSE'S WIT -
OLLY OOP !!
LIKE AN EAGLE'S BABY - THAT'S HOW SAFE I AM -
AS PLAIN AS THE FOOLISH FACE HE WEARS ARE HIS FOOTPRINTS IN THESE SANDS - - THINKS HE CAN EVADE ME - THE "WIMPIS" !!
UNDER THAT HAY STACK BONNET - EH ?
OOOOOooHHHH
IF THIS AIN'T A RAIN, IT'S A GOOD PICTURE OF ONE -
HEH - HEH - HEH - WHEREVER THAT "MOUSE" IS, HE'S GETTING HIS WETTINGS - WHILE I AM DRY UNDER HIS OLD TENT HAT.
HA - HAAA - I'M A CLEVER COP -
AND IN SPITE OF EVERYTHING ALL IS WELL

January 3rd, 1932.

KRAZY KAT ⁘ ⁘ By Herriman

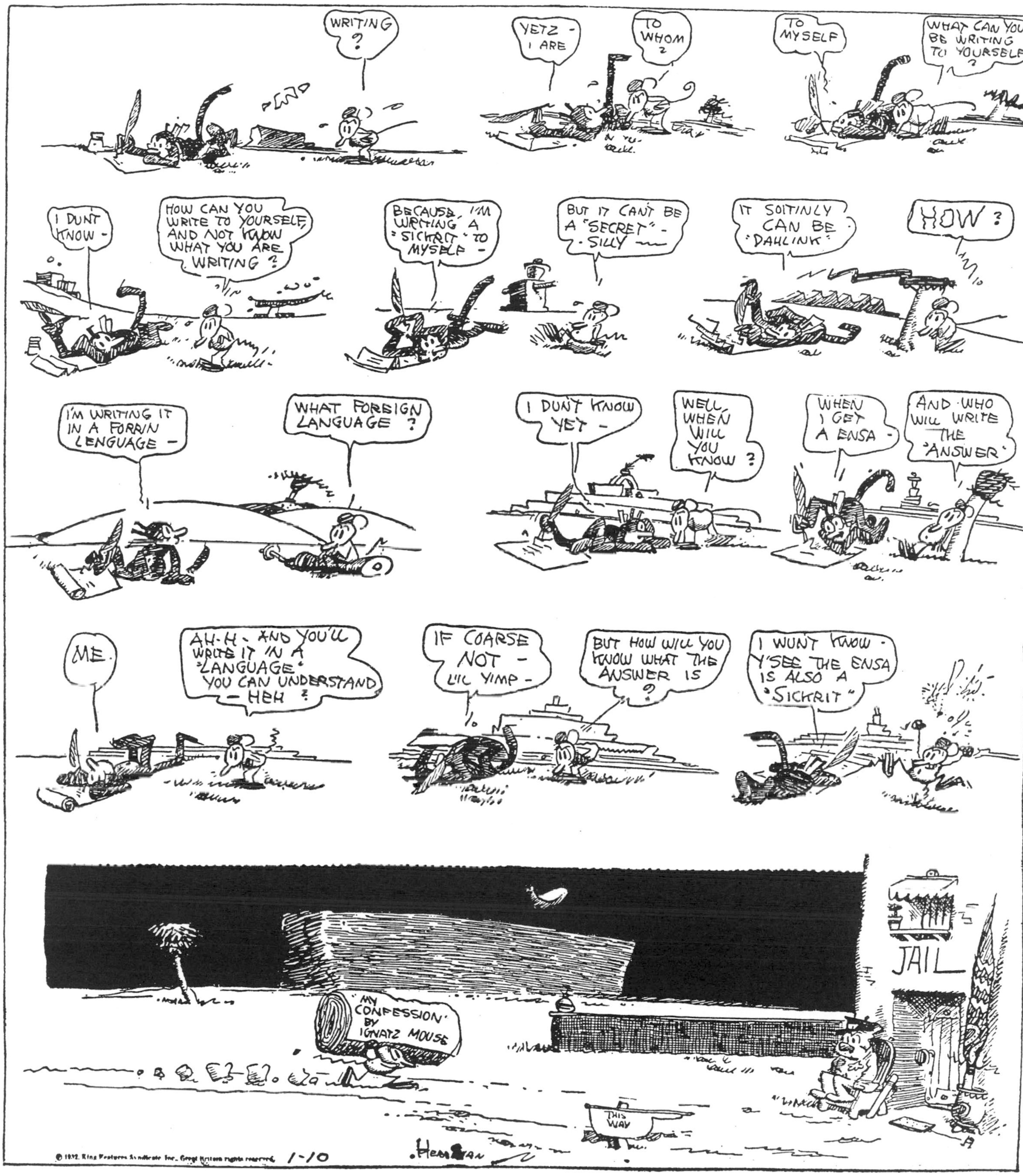
WRITING ?
YETZ - I ARE
TO WHOM ?
TO MYSELF
WHAT CAN YOU BE WRITING TO YOURSELF ?
I DUNT KNOW -
HOW CAN YOU WRITE TO YOURSELF, AND NOT KNOW WHAT YOU ARE WRITING ?
BECAUSE, I'M WRITING A "SICHRIT" TO MYSELF -
BUT IT CAN'T BE A "SECRET" - SILLY —
IT SOITINLY CAN BE "DAHLINK"
HOW ?
I'M WRITING IT IN A FORRIN LENGUAGE -
WHAT FOREIGN LANGUAGE ?
I DUN'T KNOW YET -
WELL, WHEN WILL YOU KNOW ?
WHEN I GET A ENSA -
AND WHO WILL WRITE THE "ANSWER"
ME.
AH-H - AND YOU'LL WRITE IT IN A "LANGUAGE" YOU CAN UNDERSTAND - HEH ?
IF COARSE NOT - LI'L YIMP -
BUT HOW WILL YOU KNOW WHAT THE ANSWER IS ?
I WUN'T KNOW - Y'SEE THE ENSA IS ALSO A "SICKRIT"
MY CONFESSION BY IGNATZ MOUSE
JAIL
THIS WAY
1-10

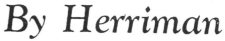

January 10th, 1932.

KRAZY KAT ⁘ ⁘ By Herriman

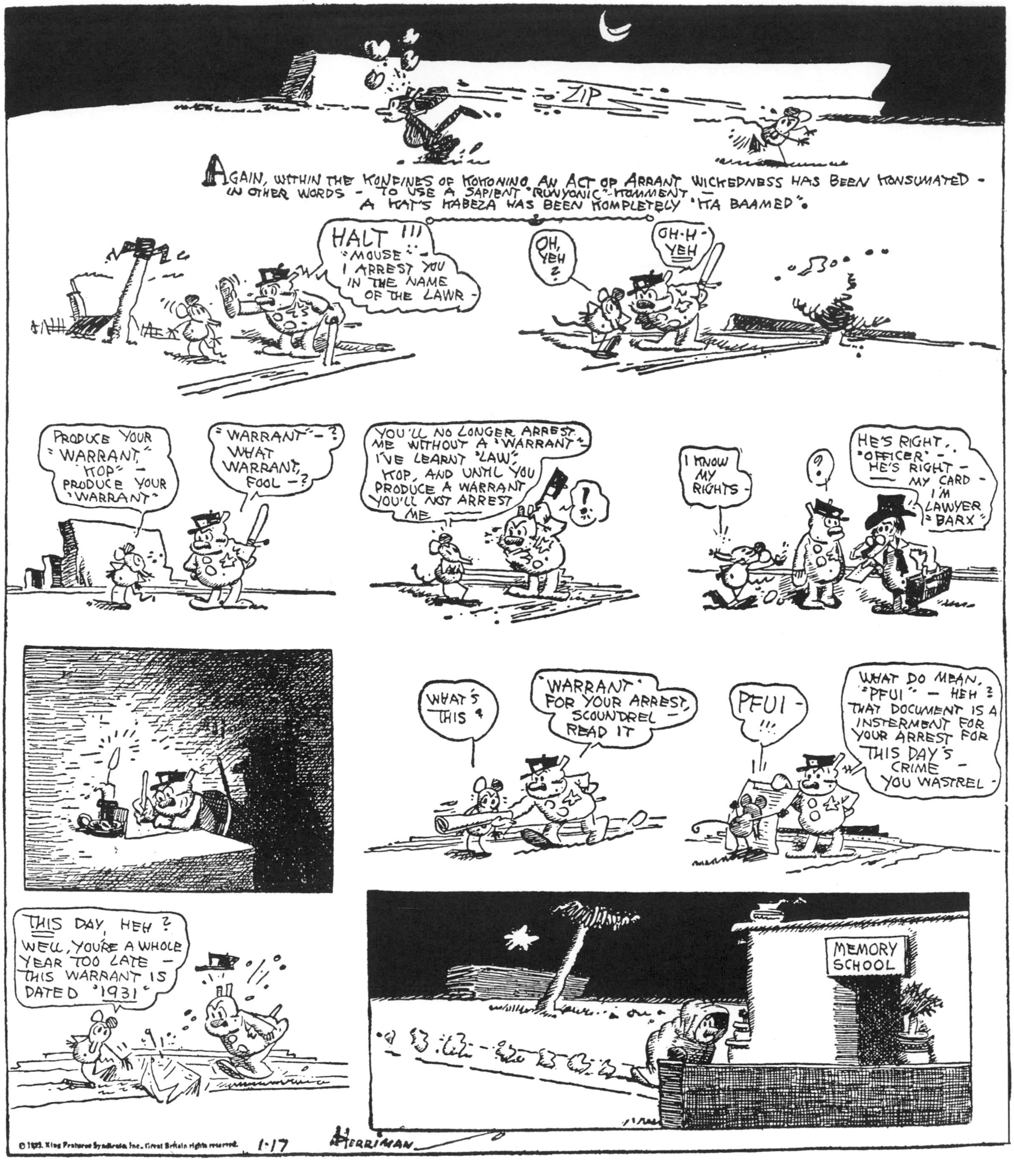

ZIP
AGAIN, WITHIN THE KONFINES OF KOKONINO AN ACT OP ARRANT WICKEDNESS HAS BEEN KONSUMATED - IN OTHER WORDS - TO USE A SAPIENT "RUNYONIC" KOMMENT - A KAT'S KABEZA HAS BEEN KOMPLETELY "KA BAAMED".
HALT !!! "MOUSE" - I ARREST YOU IN THE NAME OF THE LAWR -
OH, YEH ?
OH-H- YEH
PRODUCE YOUR "WARRANT," "KOP" - PRODUCE YOUR "WARRANT"
"WARRANT" - ? WHAT WARRANT, FOOL - ?
YOU'LL NO LONGER ARREST ME WITHOUT A "WARRANT" - I'VE LEARNT "LAW" KOP, AND UNTIL YOU PRODUCE A WARRANT YOU'LL NOT ARREST ME
!
I KNOW MY RIGHTS -
?
HE'S RIGHT, "OFFICER" - HE'S RIGHT - MY CARD - I'M LAWYER "BARX"
WHAT'S THIS ?
"WARRANT" FOR YOUR ARREST, SCOUNDREL - READ IT
PFUI - !!!
WHAT DO MEAN, "PFUI" - HEH ? THAT DOCUMENT IS A INSTERMENT FOR YOUR ARREST FOR THIS DAY'S CRIME - YOU WASTREL -
THIS DAY, HEH ? WELL, YOU'RE A WHOLE YEAR TOO LATE - THIS WARRANT IS DATED "1931"
MEMORY SCHOOL
1-17
HERRIMAN

January 17th, 1932.

KRAZY KAT ⁘ ⁘ By Herriman

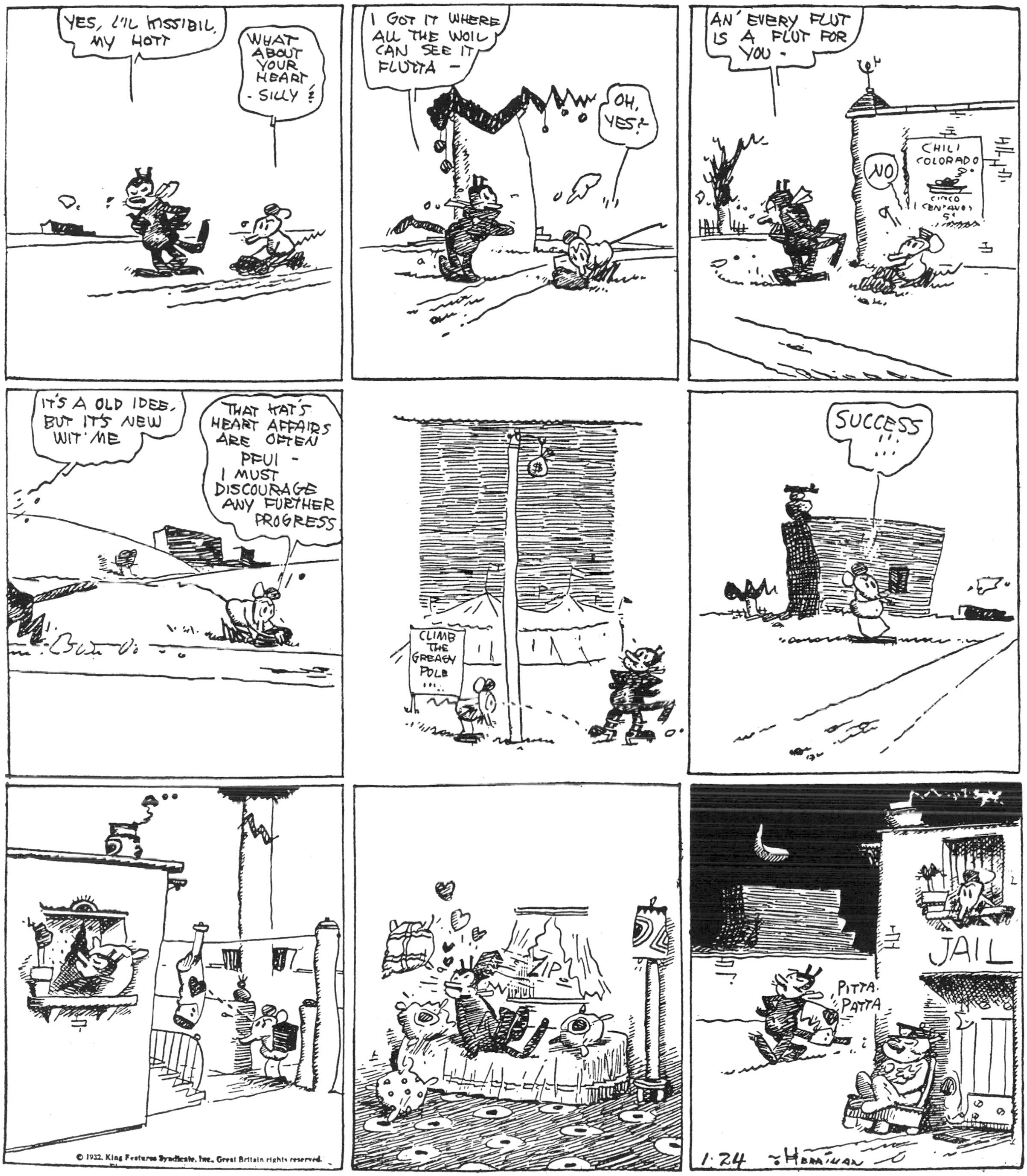

YES, L'IL KISSIBIL, MY HOTT
WHAT ABOUT YOUR HEART - SILLY ?
I GOT IT WHERE ALL THE WOIL CAN SEE IT FLUTTA —
OH, YES?
AN' EVERY FLUT IS A FLUT FOR YOU -
NO
CHILI COLORADO
CINCO CENTAVOS 5¢
IT'S A OLD IDEE, BUT IT'S NEW WIT' ME
THAT KAT'S HEART AFFAIRS ARE OFTEN PFUI - I MUST DISCOURAGE ANY FURTHER PROGRESS
CLIMB THE GREASY POLE ...
SUCCESS !!! ...
© 1932, King Features Syndicate, Inc., Great Britain rights reserved.
ZIP
JAIL
PITTA PATTA
1.24 HERRIMAN

January 24th, 1932.

KRAZY KAT ∴ ∴ By Herriman

OOY-YOOY- MY FAVARIT INSTERMINT OF MELLIDY A JUICE HOPP.
MARBLE KANYON
ZSLOOOO
THE HOMINY OF A AINJIL, SILLESS. CHILL MUSICALNISS -
BVEEEEMMM
ZUUUUMMM FUMMMM SWIMMMM
TZAAAAAA
?
GZONNNNZ YUMMM
OH.
STOP!
WOMM
YIMMMMMM
I SAID ---
S-S-STOP !!
HUMM
NOW, I'LL HAVE "PEACE" !!
FOR TOOOOOOO NIGHT --
I - YAMMA - WEE - HEE - DOH - ... EENNA - HOTTIDGE BY THE SEA
VLOOM
© 1932, King Features Syndicate, Inc., Great Britain rights reserved.
1-31
HERRIMAN

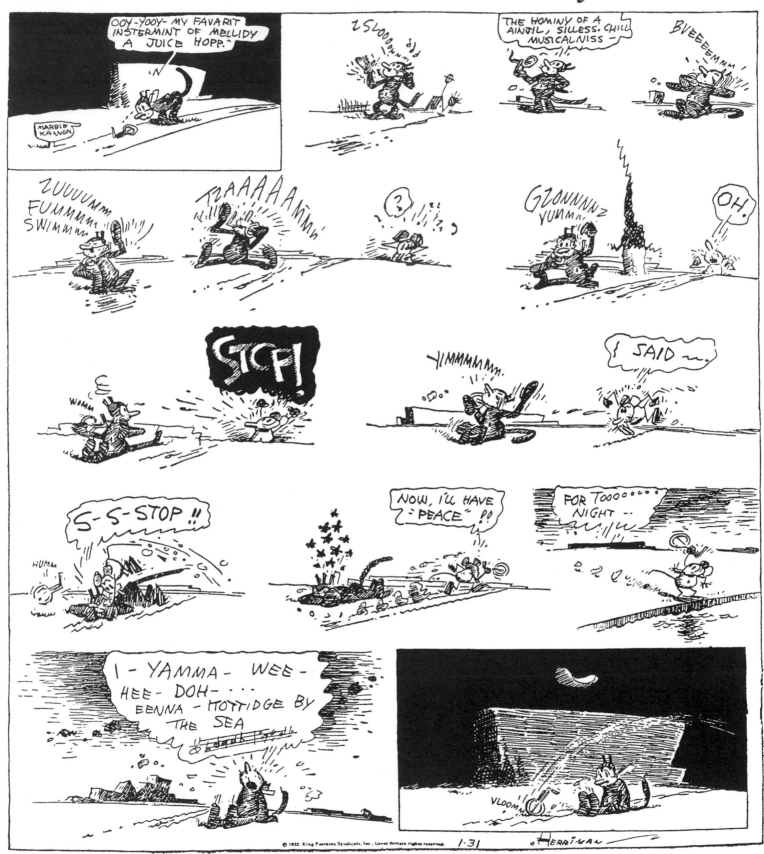

January 31st, 1932.

KRAZY KAT ⁘ ⁘ By Herriman

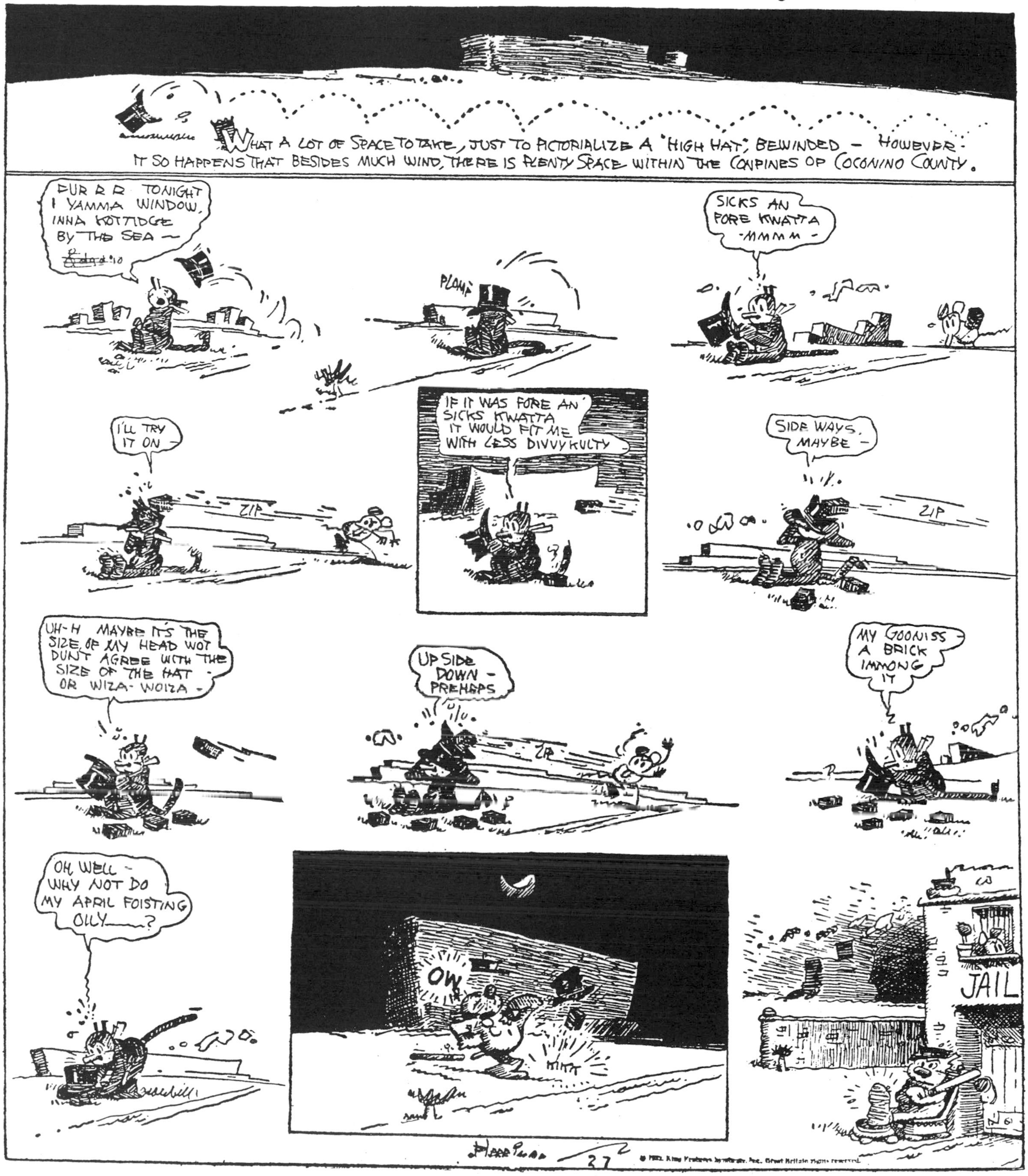

WHAT A LOT OF SPACE TO TAKE, JUST TO PICTORIALIZE A "HIGH HAT" BEWINDED – HOWEVER IT SO HAPPENS THAT BESIDES MUCH WIND, THERE IS PLENTY SPACE WITHIN THE CONFINES OF COCONINO COUNTY.
PUR R R TONIGHT I YAMMA WINDOW, INNA KOTTIDGE BY THE SEA –
PLOMP
SICKS AN FORE KWATTA – MMMM –
I'LL TRY IT ON –
ZIP
IF IT WAS FORE AN' SICKS KWATTA IT WOULD FIT ME WITH LESS DIVVYKULTY
SIDE WAYS, MAYBE –
ZIP
UH-H MAYBE IT'S THE SIZE OF MY HEAD WOT DUN'T AGREE WITH THE SIZE OF THE HAT – OR WIZA-WOIZA –
UP SIDE DOWN – PREHEPS
ZIP
MY GOONISS – A BRICK IMMONG IT
OH, WELL – WHY NOT DO MY APRIL FOISTING OILY——?
OW
JAIL
HERRIMAN 2-7

February 7th, 1932.

KRAZY KAT By Herriman

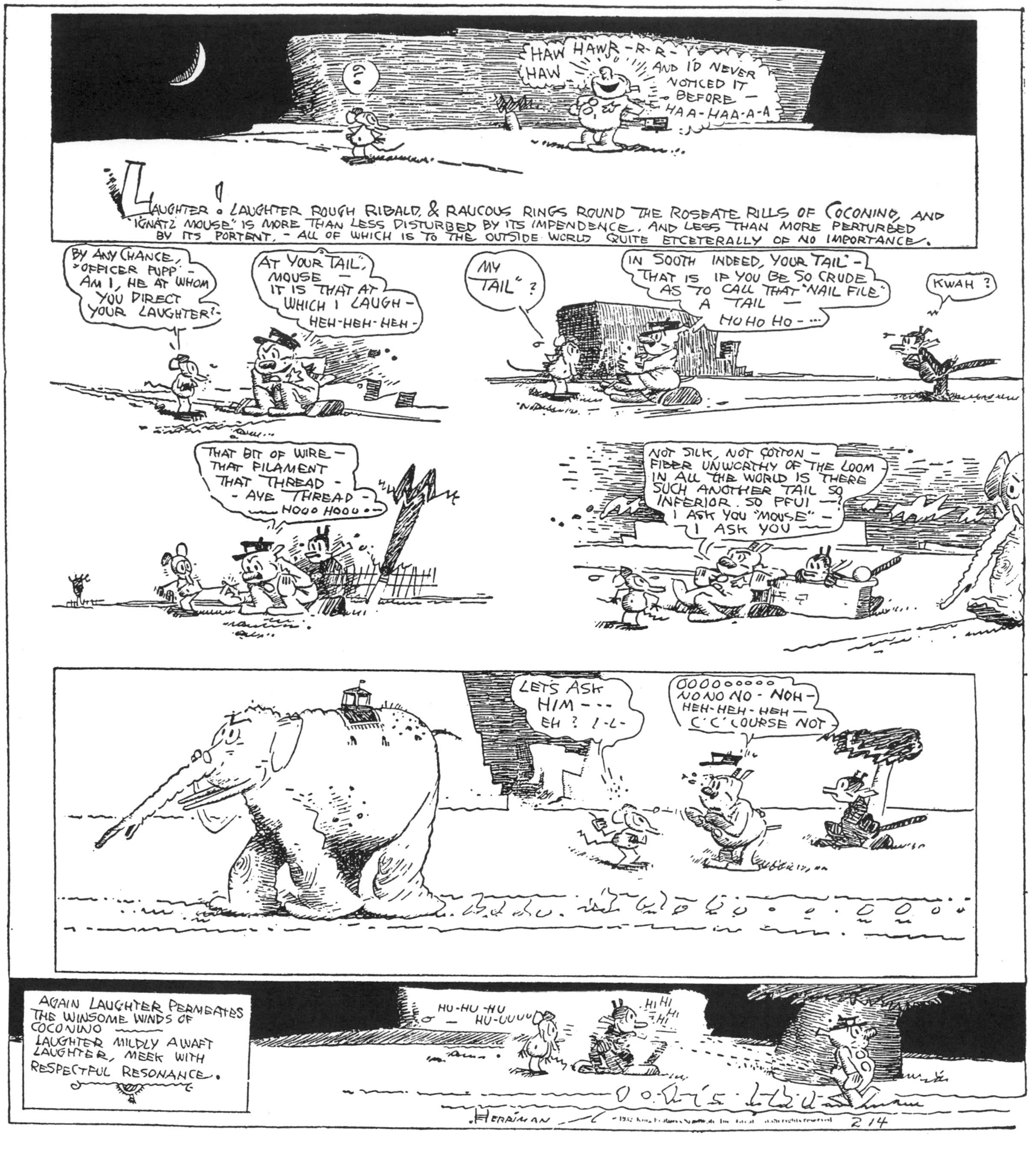
HAW HAWR-R-R-Y
HAW
AND I'D NEVER NOTICED IT BEFORE — HAA-HAA-A-A
?
LAUGHTER ! LAUGHTER ROUGH RIBALD, & RAUCOUS RINGS ROUND THE ROSEATE RILLS OF COCONINO, AND "IGNATZ MOUSE" IS MORE THAN LESS DISTURBED BY ITS IMPENDENCE, AND LESS THAN MORE PERTURBED BY ITS PORTENT, — ALL OF WHICH IS TO THE OUTSIDE WORLD QUITE ETCETERALLY OF NO IMPORTANCE.
BY ANY CHANCE, "OFFICER PUPP" AM I, HE AT WHOM YOU DIRECT YOUR LAUGHTER?
AT YOUR "TAIL", MOUSE — IT IS THAT AT WHICH I LAUGH — HEH-HEH-HEH —
MY "TAIL"?
IN SOOTH INDEED, YOUR "TAIL" — THAT IS IF YOU BE SO CRUDE AS TO CALL THAT "NAIL FILE" A TAIL — HO HO HO —
KWAH ?
THAT BIT OF WIRE — THAT FILAMENT THAT THREAD — AYE THREAD — HOOO HOOO —
NOT SILK, NOT COTTON — FIBER UNWORTHY OF THE LOOM — IN ALL THE WORLD IS THERE SUCH ANOTHER TAIL SO INFERIOR. SO PFUI —? I ASK YOU "MOUSE" — I ASK YOU
LET'S ASK HIM — — — EH ? I-L-
OOOOOOOOO NO NO NO - NOH - HEH-HEH-HEH — C'C'COURSE NOT
AGAIN LAUGHTER PERMEATES THE WINSOME WINDS OF COCONINO — LAUGHTER MILDLY AWAFT LAUGHTER, MEEK WITH RESPECTFUL RESONANCE.
HU-HU-HU — HU-UUUU
HI HI HI HI
HERRIMAN
2 14

February 14th, 1932.

KRAZY KAT ⁘ ⁘ By Herriman

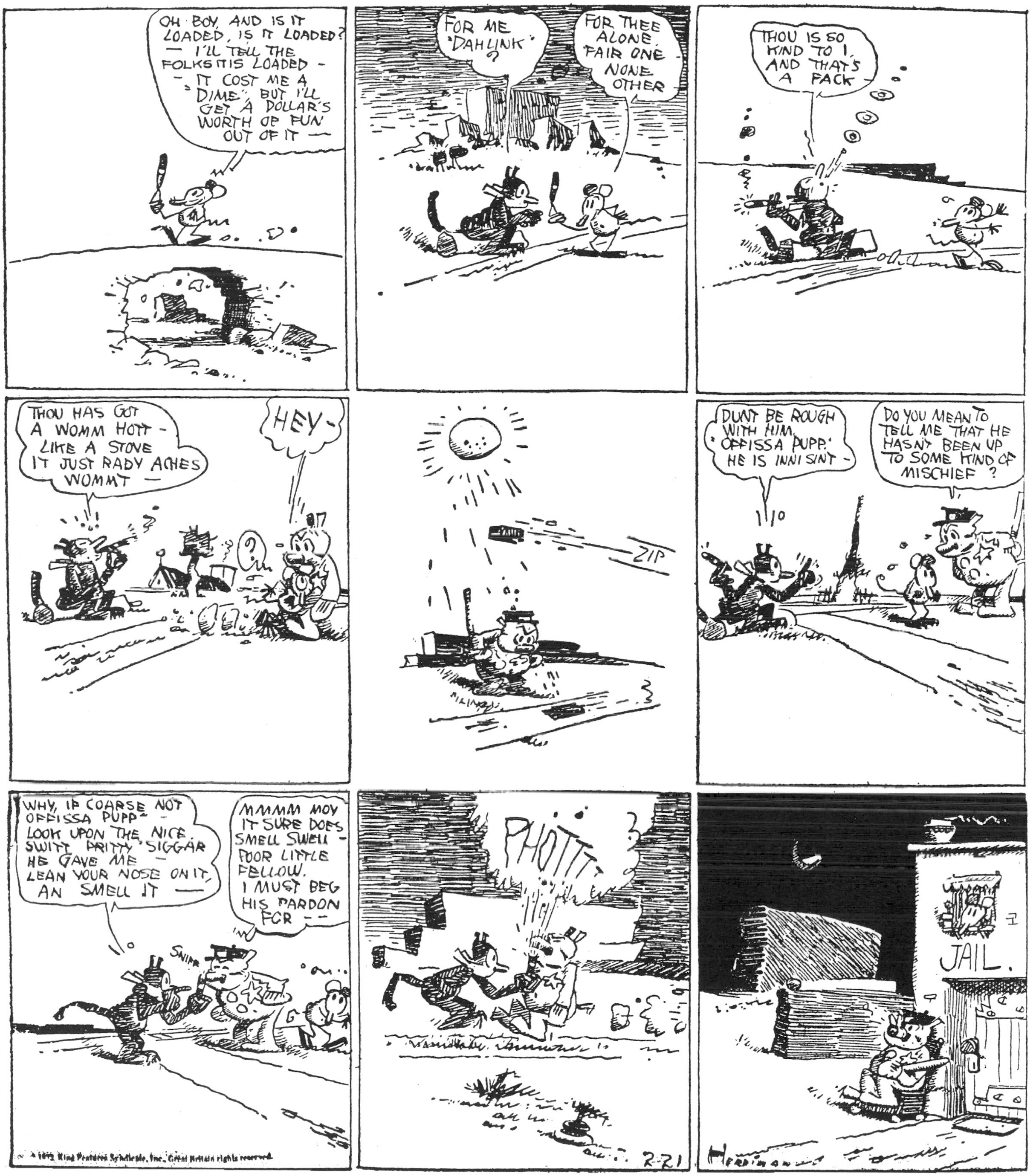

OH BOY, AND IS IT LOADED, IS IT LOADED? — I'LL TELL THE FOLKS IT IS LOADED — IT COST ME A DIME, BUT I'LL GET A DOLLAR'S WORTH OF FUN OUT OF IT —
FOR ME "DAHLINK"?
FOR THEE ALONE, FAIR ONE — NONE OTHER —
THOU IS SO KIND TO I, AND THAT'S A FACK —
THOU HAS GOT A WOMM HOTT — LIKE A STOVE — IT JUST RADY ACHES WOMMT —
HEY —
ZIP
DUNT BE ROUGH WITH HIM, OFFISSA PUPP. HE IS INNISINT —
DO YOU MEAN TO TELL ME THAT HE HASN'T BEEN UP TO SOME KIND OF MISCHIEF?
WHY, IF COARSE NOT OFFISSA PUPP — LOOK UPON THE NICE, SWITT, PRITTY SIGGAR HE GAVE ME — LEAN YOUR NOSE ON IT, AN SMELL IT —
SNIFF
MMMMM MOY IT SURE DOES SMELL SWELL — POOR LITTLE FELLOW. I MUST BEG HIS PARDON FOR — —
PHOTT
JAIL.
2-21
HERRIMAN

February 21st, 1932.

KRAZY KAT ⁘ ⁘ By Herriman

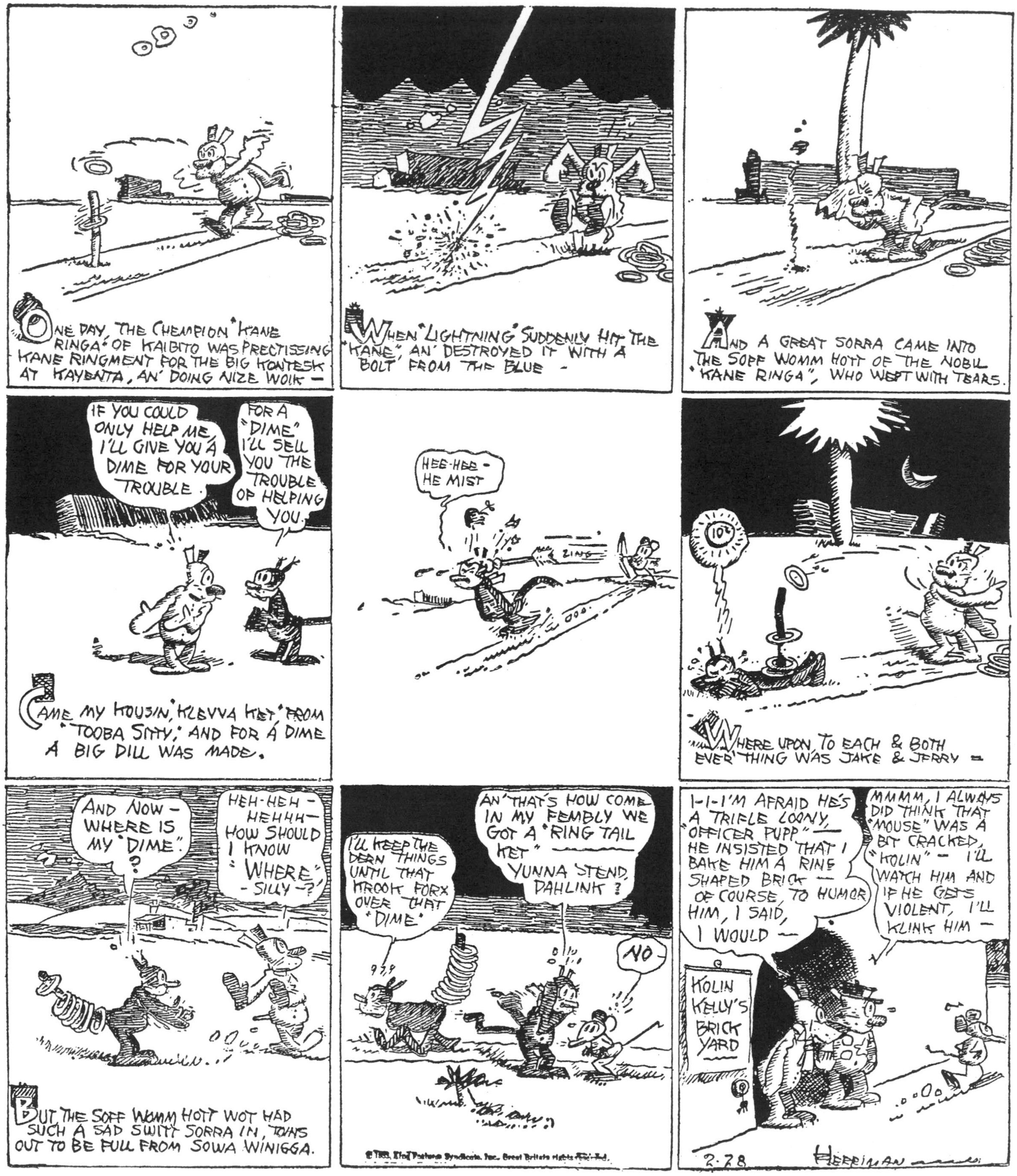

ONE DAY, THE CHEMPION "KANE RINGA" OF KAIBITO WAS PRECTISSING KANE RINGMENT FOR THE BIG KONTESK AT KAYENTA, AN' DOING NIZE WOIK –
WHEN "LIGHTNING" SUDDENLY HIT THE "KANE", AN' DESTROYED IT WITH A BOLT FROM THE BLUE –
AND A GREAT SORRA CAME INTO THE SOFF WOMM HOTT OF THE NOBIL "KANE RINGA", WHO WEPT WITH TEARS.
IF YOU COULD ONLY HELP ME, I'LL GIVE YOU A DIME FOR YOUR TROUBLE.
FOR A "DIME" I'LL SELL YOU THE TROUBLE OF HELPING YOU.
CAME MY KOUSIN, "KLEVVA KET," FROM "TOOBA SITTY," AND FOR A DIME A BIG DILL WAS MADE.
HEE-HEE – HE MIST
ZING
10¢
WHERE UPON, TO EACH & BOTH EVER' THING WAS JAKE & JERRY –
AND NOW – WHERE IS MY "DIME". ?
HEH-HEH – HEHHH – HOW SHOULD I KNOW "WHERE" – SILLY –?
BUT THE SOFF WOMM HOTT WOT HAD SUCH A SAD SWITT SORRA IN, TOINS OUT TO BE FULL FROM SOWA WINIGGA.
I'LL KEEP THE DERN THINGS UNTIL THAT KROOK FORKS OVER THAT "DIME"
AN' THAT'S HOW COME IN MY FEMBLY WE GOT A "RING TAIL KET" – YUNNA STEND, DAHLINK ?
NO –
I-I-I'M AFRAID HE'S A TRIFLE LOONY, "OFFICER PUPP" – HE INSISTED THAT I BAKE HIM A RING SHAPED BRICK – OF COURSE, TO HUMOR HIM, I SAID, I WOULD –
MMMM, I ALWAYS DID THINK THAT "MOUSE" WAS A BIT CRACKED, "KOLIN" – I'LL WATCH HIM AND IF HE GETS VIOLENT, I'LL KLINK HIM –
KOLIN KELLY'S BRICK YARD
2-28
HERRIMAN

February 28th, 1932.

KRAZY KAT ⁘ ⁘ By Herriman

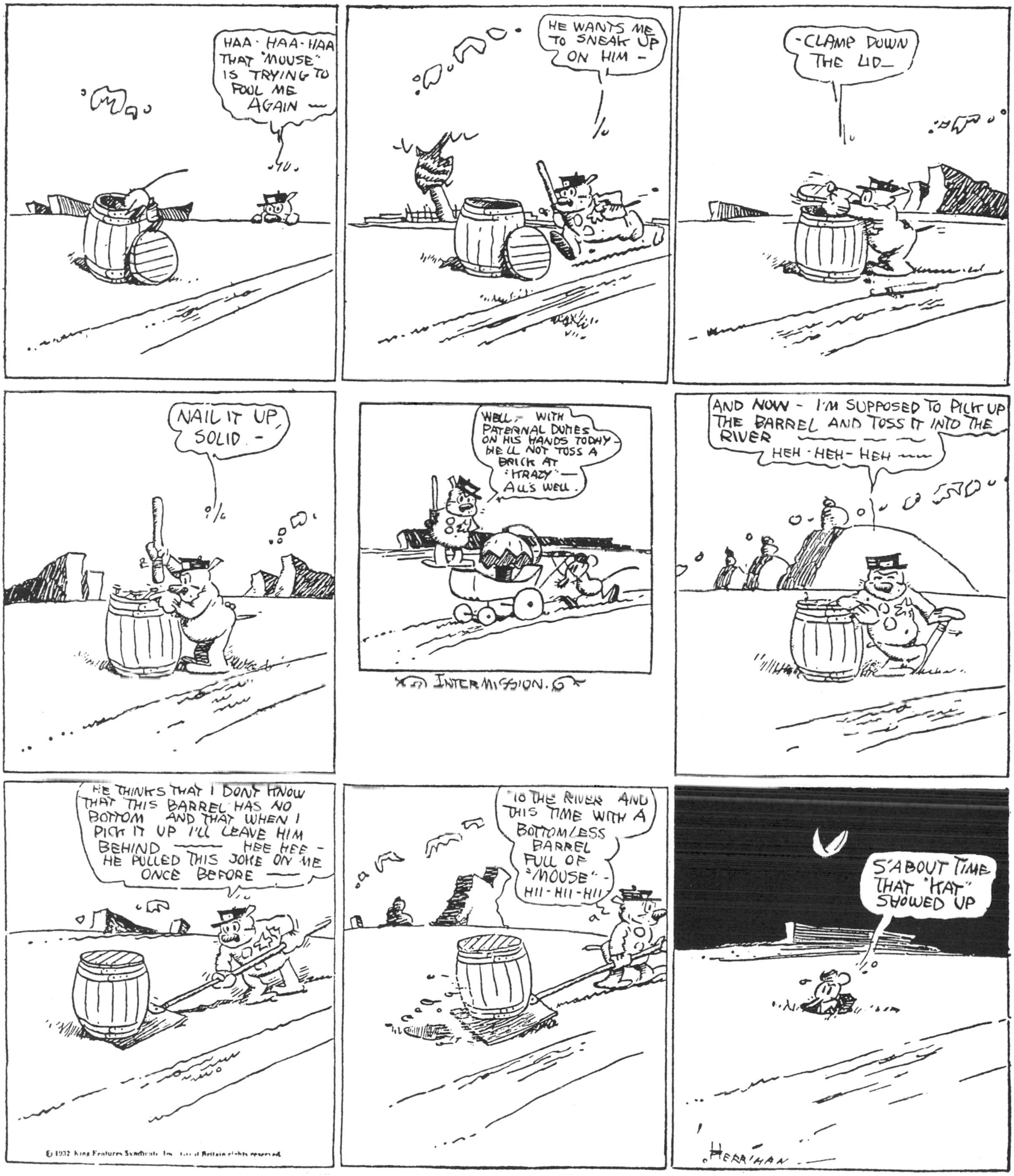
HAA-HAA-HAA THAT "MOUSE" IS TRYING TO FOOL ME AGAIN —
HE WANTS ME TO SNEAK UP ON HIM —
-CLAMP DOWN THE LID—
NAIL IT UP SOLID —
WELL,- WITH PATERNAL DUTIES ON HIS HANDS TODAY - HE'LL NOT TOSS A BRICK AT "KRAZY" — ALL'S WELL.
INTERMISSION.
AND NOW - I'M SUPPOSED TO PICK UP THE BARREL AND TOSS IT INTO THE RIVER — HEH-HEH-HEH —
HE THINKS THAT I DON'T KNOW THAT THIS BARREL HAS NO BOTTOM AND THAT WHEN I PICK IT UP I'LL LEAVE HIM BEHIND — HEE HEE - HE PULLED THIS JOKE ON ME ONCE BEFORE —
TO THE RIVER AND THIS TIME WITH A BOTTOMLESS BARREL FULL OF "MOUSE" - HII-HII-HII
S'ABOUT TIME THAT "KAT" SHOWED UP
HERRIMAN

March 6th, 1932.

KRAZY KAT ⁘ ⁘ By Herriman

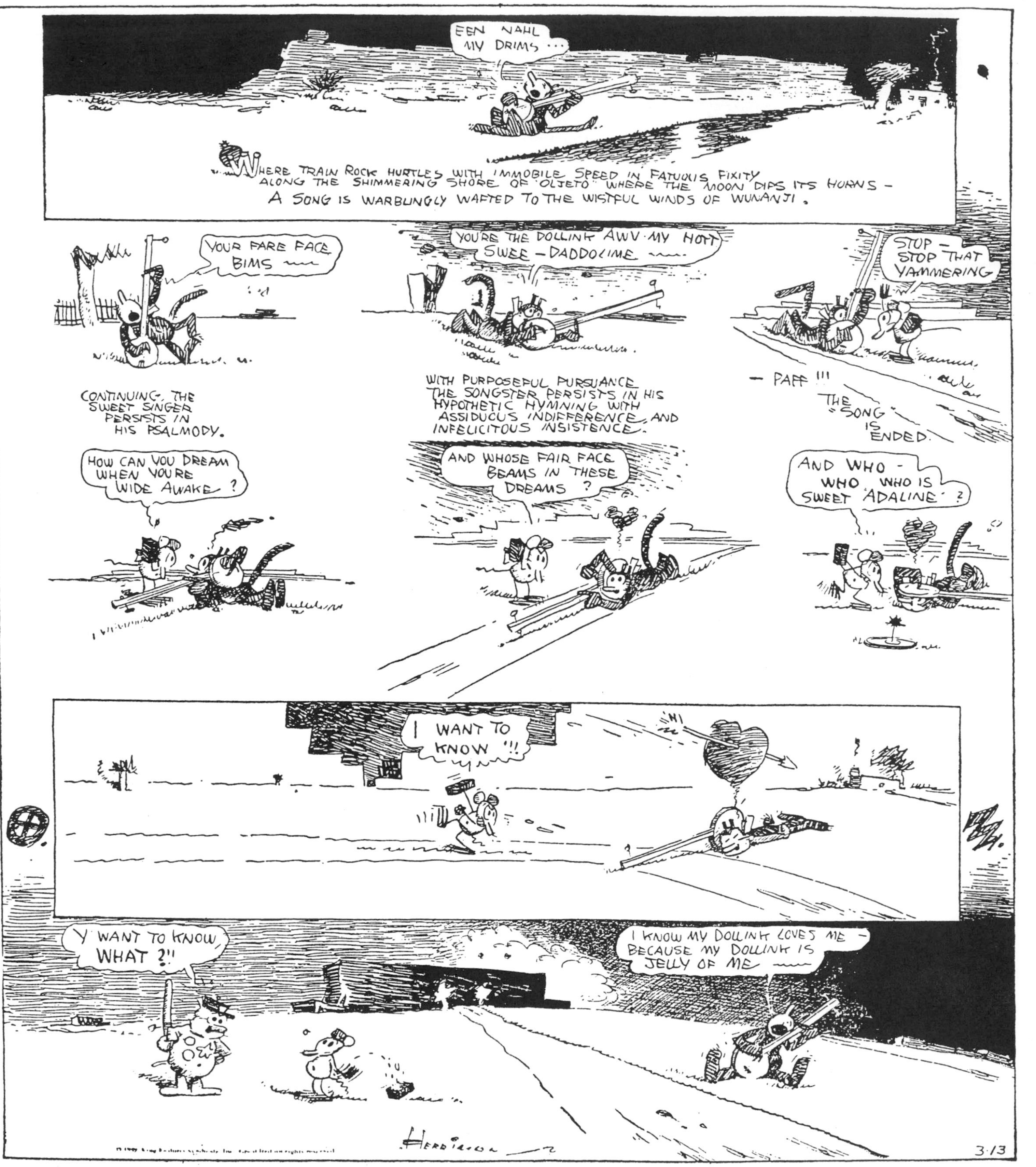
EEN NAHL MY DRIMS ...
WHERE TRAIN ROCK HURTLES WITH IMMOBILE SPEED IN FATUOUS FIXITY ALONG THE SHIMMERING SHORE OF "OLJETO" WHERE THE MOON DIPS ITS HORNS - A SONG IS WARBLINGLY WAFTED TO THE WISTFUL WINDS OF WUNANJI.
YOUR FARE FACE BIMS
CONTINUING, THE SWEET SINGER PERSISTS IN HIS PSALMODY.
YOU'RE THE DOLLINK AWV MY HOTT SWEE - DADDOLIME
WITH PURPOSEFUL PURSUANCE THE SONGSTER PERSISTS IN HIS HYPOTHETIC HYMNING WITH ASSIDUOUS INDIFFERENCE, AND INFELICITOUS INSISTENCE.
STOP - STOP THAT YAMMERING
- PAFF !!!
THE SONG IS ENDED.
HOW CAN YOU DREAM WHEN YOU'RE WIDE AWAKE ?
AND WHOSE FAIR FACE BEAMS IN THESE DREAMS ?
AND WHO - WHO, WHO IS SWEET 'ADALINE' ?
I WANT TO KNOW !!!
Y' WANT TO KNOW, WHAT ?!!
I KNOW MY DOLLINK LOVES ME - BECAUSE MY DOLLINK IS JELLY OF ME
HERRIMAN
3-13

March 13th, 1932.

KRAZY KAT ❖ ❖ By Herriman

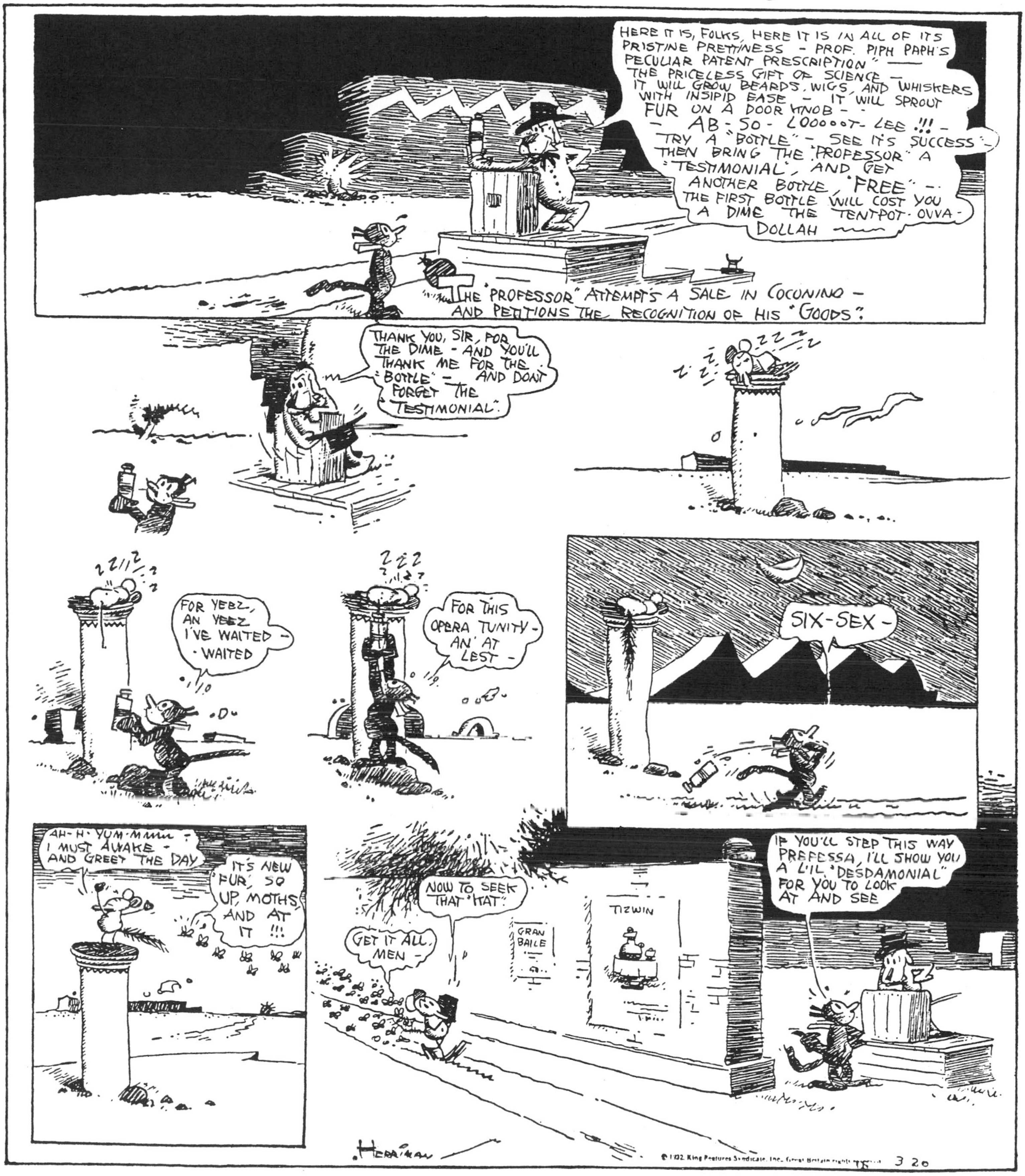

HERE IT IS, FOLKS, HERE IT IS IN ALL OF ITS PRISTINE PRETTINESS - PROF. PIPH PAPH'S PECULIAR PATENT PRESCRIPTION" —— THE PRICELESS GIFT OF SCIENCE — IT WILL GROW BEARDS, WIGS, AND WHISKERS WITH INSIPID EASE - IT WILL SPROUT FUR ON A DOOR KNOB - - AB - SO - LOOOOOT - LEE !!! - TRY A "BOTTLE" - SEE IT'S SUCCESS - THEN BRING THE "PROFESSOR" A "TESTMONIAL", AND GET ANOTHER BOTTLE "FREE" - - THE FIRST BOTTLE WILL COST YOU A DIME THE TENTPOT - OVVA - DOLLAH
THE "PROFESSOR" ATTEMPT'S A SALE IN COCONINO - AND PETITIONS THE RECOGNITION OF HIS "GOODS".
THANK YOU, SIR, FOR THE DIME - AND YOU'LL THANK ME FOR THE "BOTTLE" - AND DON'T FORGET THE "TESTMONIAL".
Z Z Z Z Z Z Z
Z Z Z Z
FOR YEEZ, AN YEEZ I'VE WAITED - - WAITED
Z Z Z
FOR THIS OPERA TUNITY - AN' AT LEST -
SIX - SEX -
AH - H - YUM - MMM - I MUST AWAKE - AND GREET THE DAY
IT'S NEW FUR, SO UP, MOTHS AND AT IT !!!
NOW TO SEEK THAT "KAT"
GET IT ALL, MEN -
GRAN BAILE
TIZWIN
IF YOU'LL STEP THIS WAY PREFESSA, I'LL SHOW YOU A L'IL "DESDAMONIAL" FOR YOU TO LOOK AT AND SEE
HERRIMAN
© 1932, King Features Syndicate, Inc.
3 20

March 20th, 1932.

KRAZY KAT ⁘ ⁘ By Herriman

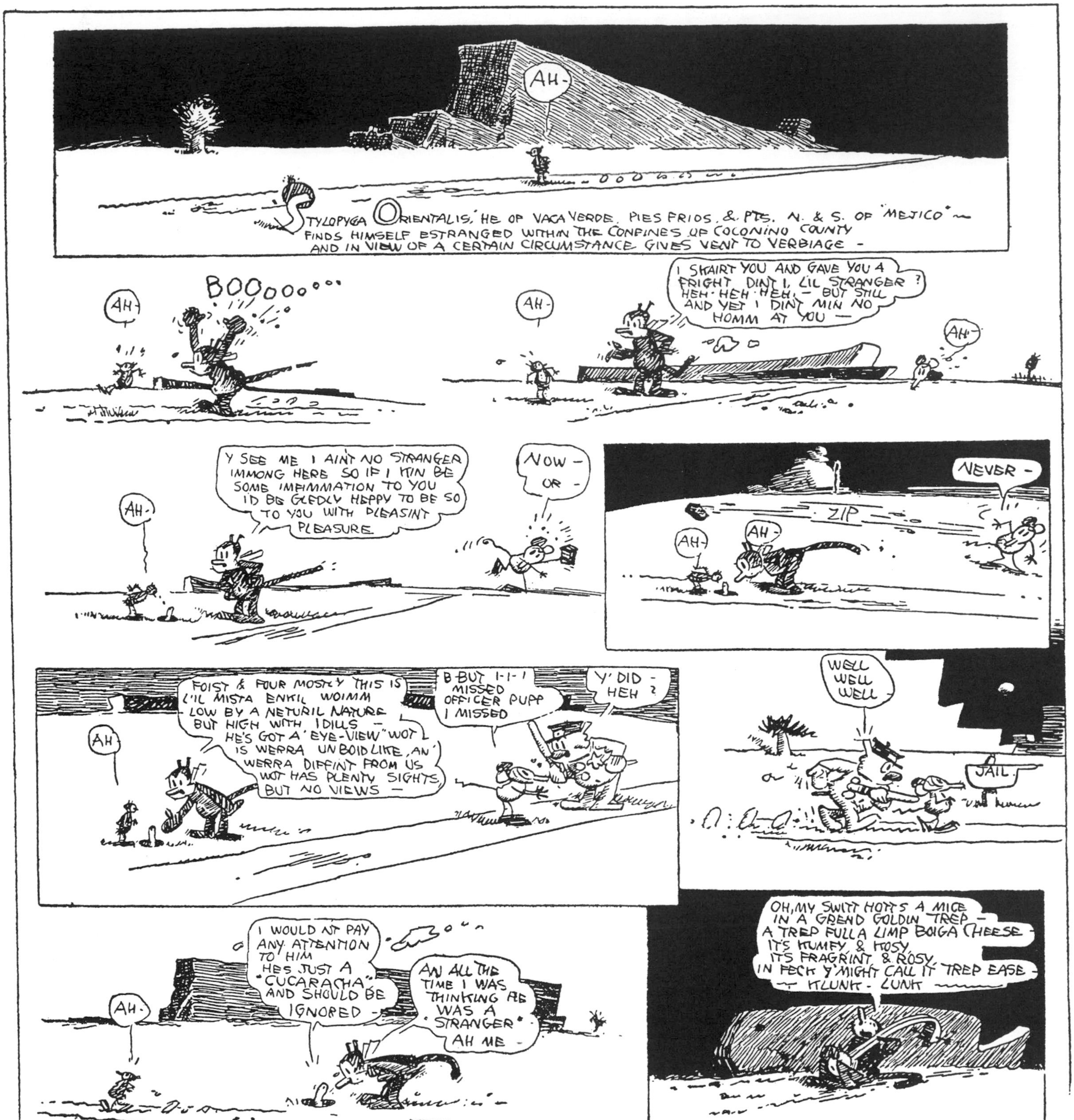

AH-
STYLOPYGA ORIENTALIS, HE OF VACA VERDE, PIES FRIOS, & PTS. N. & S. OF "MEJICO" — FINDS HIMSELF ESTRANGED WITHIN THE CONFINES OF COCONINO COUNTY AND IN VIEW OF A CERTAIN CIRCUMSTANCE GIVES VENT TO VERBIAGE -
AH-
BOOOOOOO
AH-
I SKAIRT YOU AND GAVE YOU A FRIGHT DINT I, LIL STRANGER? HEH·HEH·HEH, — BUT STILL AND YET I DINT MIN NO HOMM AT YOU —
AH-
AH-
Y SEE ME I AINT NO STRANGER IMMONG HERE SO IF I KIN BE SOME INFIMMATION TO YOU ID BE GLEDLY HEPPY TO BE SO TO YOU WITH PLEASINT PLEASURE
NOW — OR -
NEVER -
ZIP
AH-
AH-
AH
FOIST & FOUR MOSTLY THIS IS L'IL MISTA ENKIL WOIMM LOW BY A NETURIL NATURE BUT HIGH WITH IDILLS — HE'S GOT A 'EYE-VIEW" WOT IS WERRA UNBOIDLIKE, AN' WERRA DIFFINT FROM US WOT HAS PLENTY SIGHTS, BUT NO VIEWS —
B-BUT I-I-I MISSED OFFICER PUPP I MISSED
Y' DID - HEH?
WELL WELL WELL
JAIL
AH-
I WOULD NT PAY ANY ATTENTION TO HIM HES JUST A "CUCARACHA" AND SHOULD BE IGNORED -
AN ALL THE TIME I WAS THINKING HE WAS A "STRANGER" AH ME -
OH, MY SWITT HOT'S A MICE IN A GREND GOLDIN TREP — A TREP FULLA LIMP BOIGA CHEESE - ITS KUMFY, & KOSY, ITS FRAGRINT & ROSY, IN FECK Y'MIGHT CALL IT TREP EASE - KLUNK - LUNK
3·27 · HERRIMAN

March 27th, 1932.

KRAZY KAT ⁘ ⁘ By Herriman

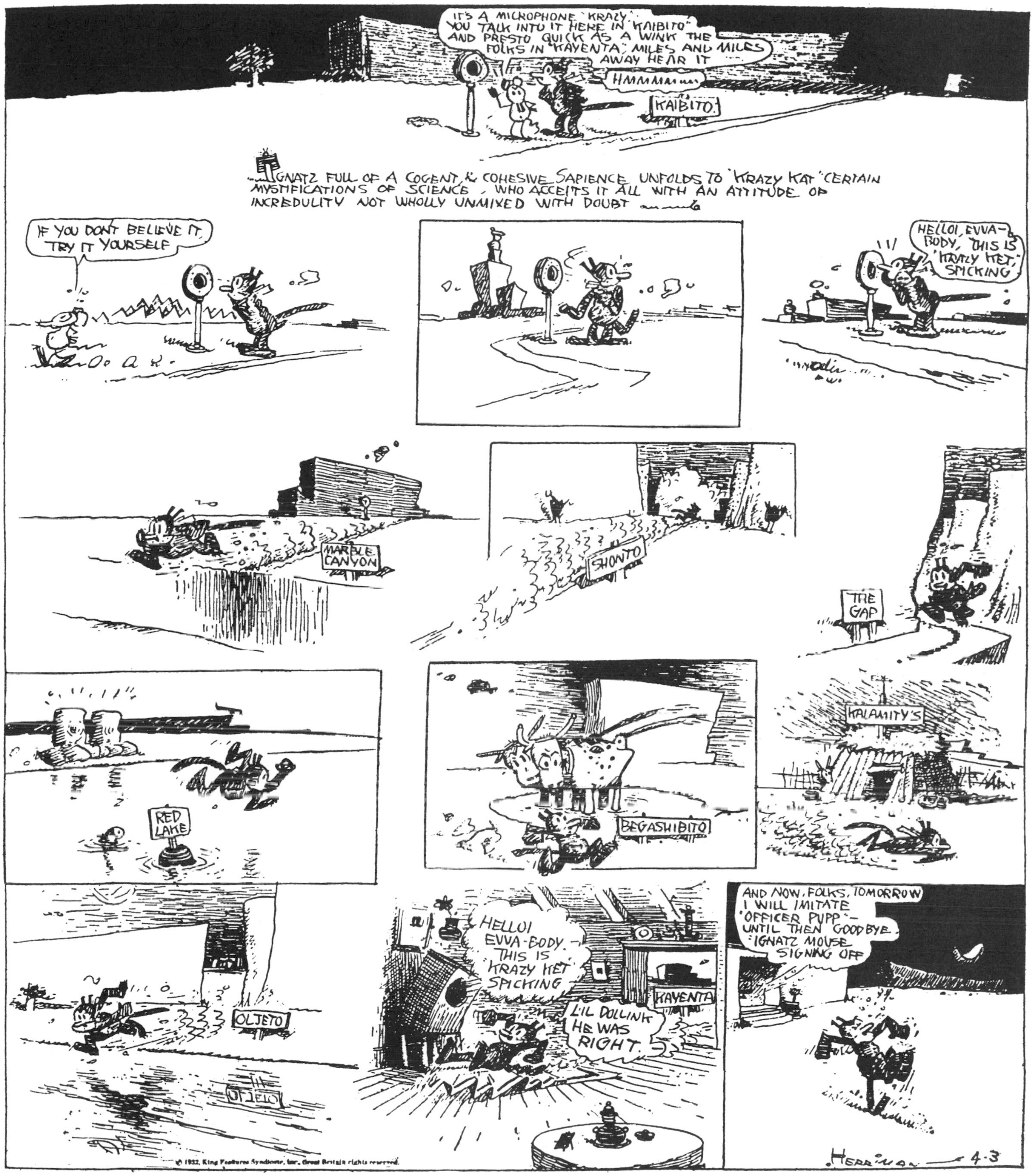
IT'S A MICROPHONE 'KRAZY' YOU TALK INTO IT HERE IN 'KAIBITO' AND PRESTO QUICK AS A WINK THE FOLKS IN 'KAYENTA', MILES AND MILES AWAY HEAR IT
HMMMM
KAIBITO
IGNATZ FULL OF A COGENT & COHESIVE SAPIENCE UNFOLDS TO 'KRAZY KAT' CERTAIN MYSTIFICATIONS OF SCIENCE - WHO ACCEPTS IT ALL WITH AN ATTITUDE OF INCREDULITY NOT WHOLLY UNMIXED WITH DOUBT
IF YOU DON'T BELIEVE IT, TRY IT YOURSELF
HELLO! EVVA-BODY, THIS IS 'KRAZY KET,' SPICKING
MARBLE CANYON
SHONTO
THE GAP
RED LAKE
BEGASHIBITO
KALAMITY'S
OLJETO
HELLO! EVVA-BODY - THIS IS KRAZY KET SPICKING
KAYENTA
L'IL DOLLINK HE WAS RIGHT.
AND NOW, FOLKS, TOMORROW I WILL IMITATE 'OFFICER PUPP' - UNTIL THEN GOODBYE. IGNATZ MOUSE SIGNING OFF
© 1932, King Features Syndicate, Inc., Great Britain rights reserved.
HERRIMAN 4-3

April 3rd, 1932.

KRAZY KAT ⁘ ⁘ By Herriman

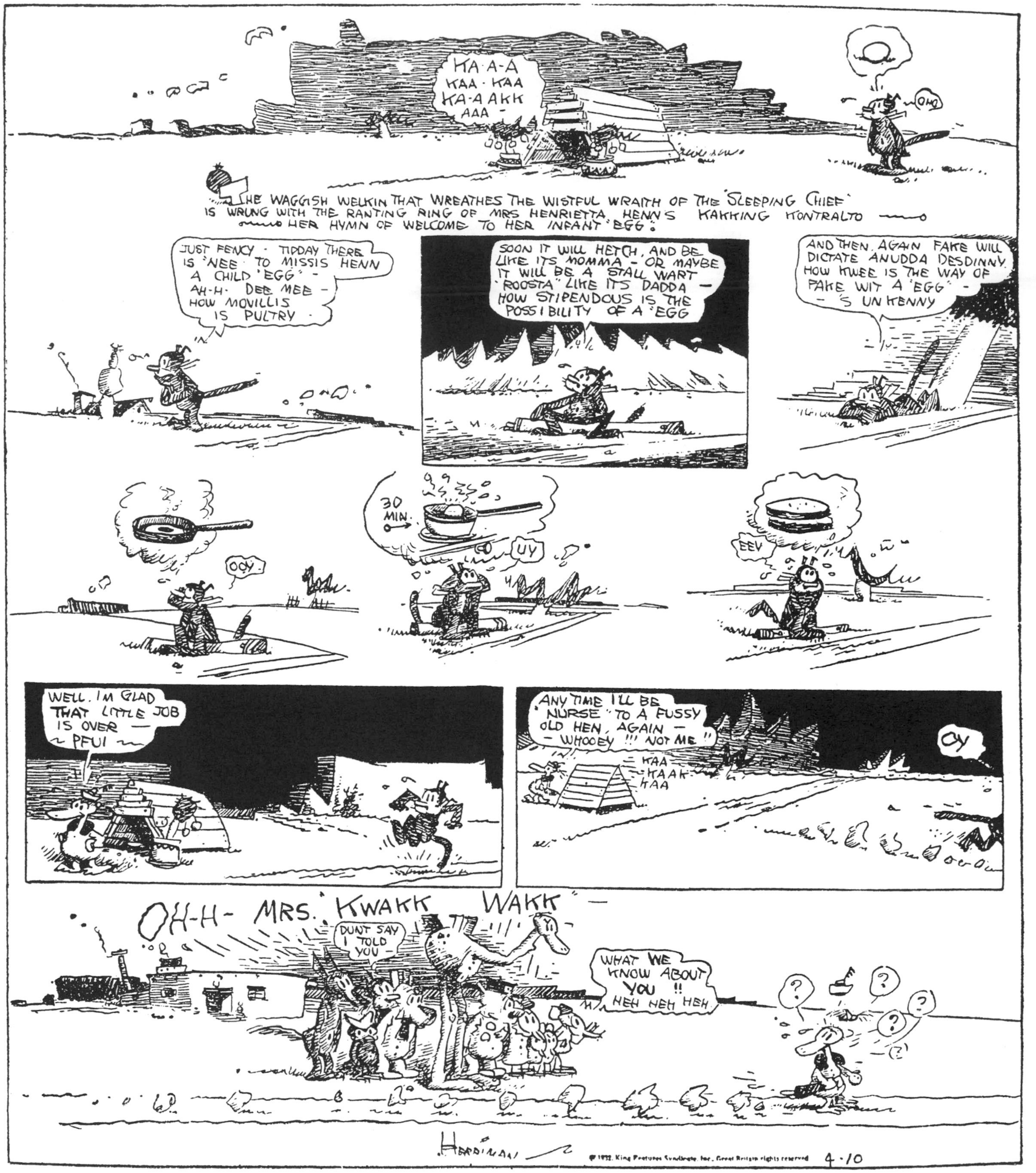

KA-A-A KAA-KAA KA-A-AKK AAA -
OHO
THE WAGGISH WELKIN THAT WREATHES THE WISTFUL WRAITH OF THE "SLEEPING CHIEF" IS WRUNG WITH THE RANTING RING OF MRS HENRIETTA HENN'S KAKKING KONTRALTO — HER HYMN OF WELCOME TO HER INFANT "EGG".
JUST FENCY - TIDDAY THERE IS "NEE" TO MISSIS HENN A CHILD "EGG" - AH-H- DEE MEE - HOW MOVILLIS IS PULTRY -
SOON IT WILL HETCH, AND BE LIKE ITS MOMMA - OR MAYBE IT WILL BE A STALL WART "ROOSTA" LIKE ITS DADDA - HOW STIPENDOUS IS THE POSSIBILITY OF A "EGG"
AND THEN, AGAIN FAKE WILL DICTATE ANUDDA DESDINNY. HOW KWEE IS THE WAY OF FAKE WIT A "EGG" - - 'S UN KENNY
OOY
30 MIN.
UY
EEV
WELL. I'M GLAD THAT LITTLE JOB IS OVER - PFUI
ANY TIME I'LL BE "NURSE" TO A FUSSY OLD HEN, AGAIN - - WHOOEY !!! NOT ME"!
KAA KAAK KAA
OY
OH-H- MRS. "KWAKK WAKK" -
DUNT SAY I TOLD YOU -
WHAT WE KNOW ABOUT YOU !! HEH HEH HEH
HERRIMAN
© 1932, King Features Syndicate, Inc., Great Britain rights reserved
4-10

April 10th, 1932.

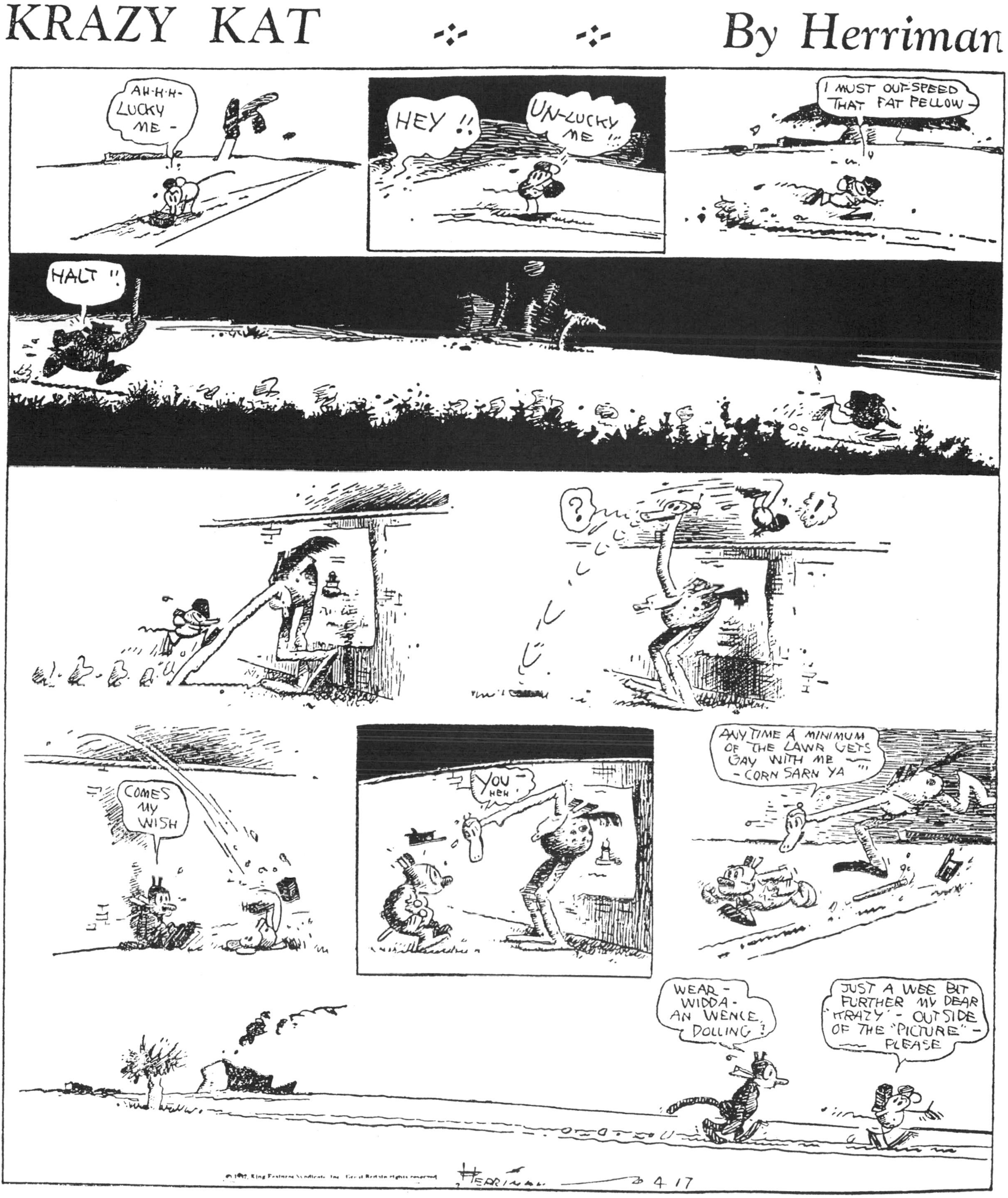
KRAZY KAT
By Herriman
AH-H-H- LUCKY ME -
HEY !!
UN-LUCKY ME !!
I MUST OUT-SPEED THAT FAT FELLOW -
HALT !!
?
!
COMES MY WISH
YOU HEH
ANY TIME A MINIMUM OF THE LAWR GETS GAY WITH ME — - CORN SARN YA
WEAR - WIDDA - AN WENCE, DOLLING ?
JUST A WEE BIT FURTHER MY DEAR "KRAZY" - OUTSIDE OF THE "PICTURE" - PLEASE
HERRIMAN
4 17

April 17th, 1932.

KRAZY KAT ∴ ∴ By Herriman

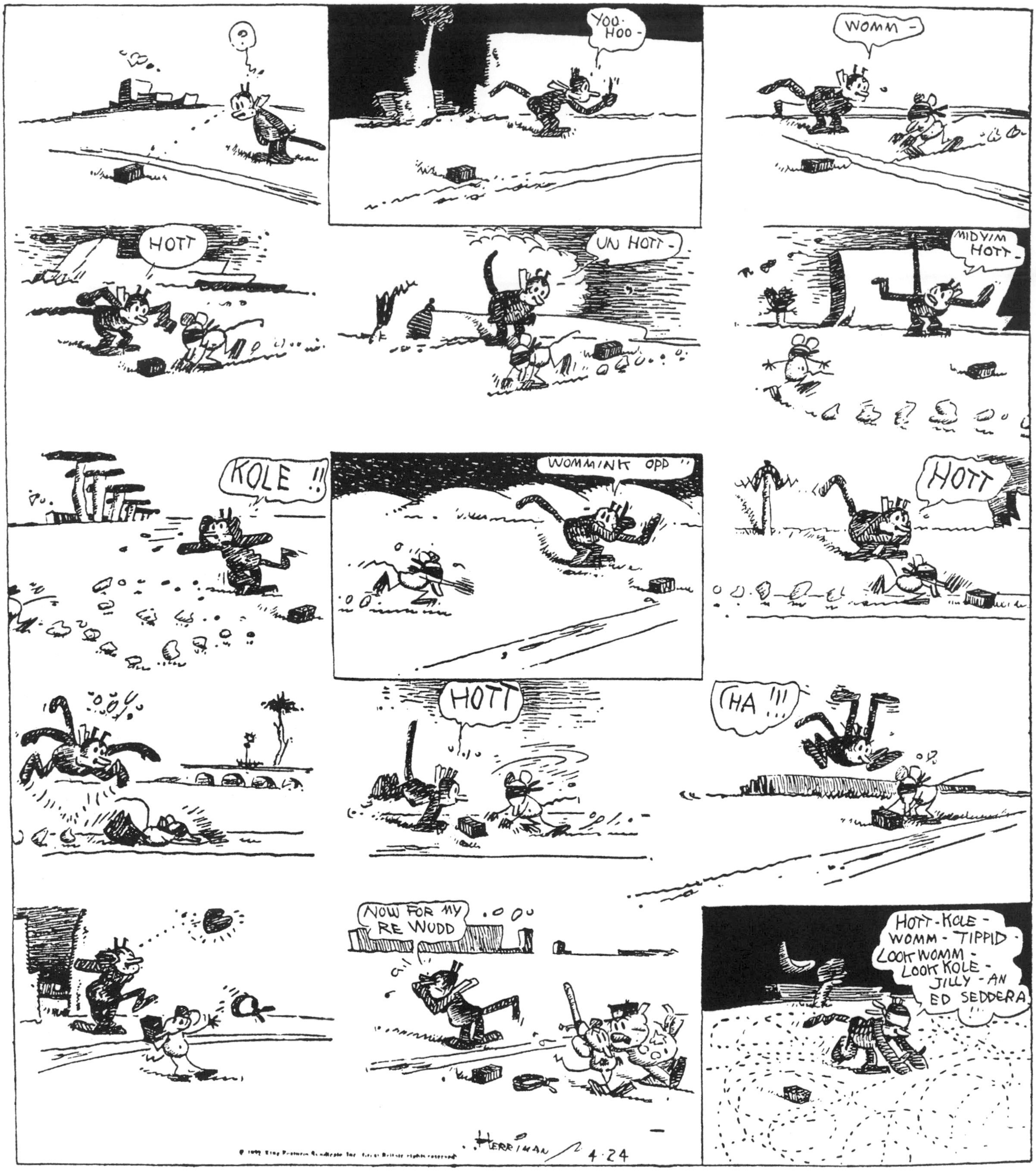

YOU-HOO -
WOMM -
HOTT
UN HOTT -
MIDYIM HOTT -
KOLE !!
WOMMINK OPP
HOTT
HOTT
HA !!!
NOW FOR MY RE WUDD
HOTT-KOLE - WOMM - TIPPID - LOOK WOMM - LOOK KOLE - JILLY - AN ED SEDDERA
HERRIMAN 4-24

April 24th, 1932.

KRAZY KAT By Herriman

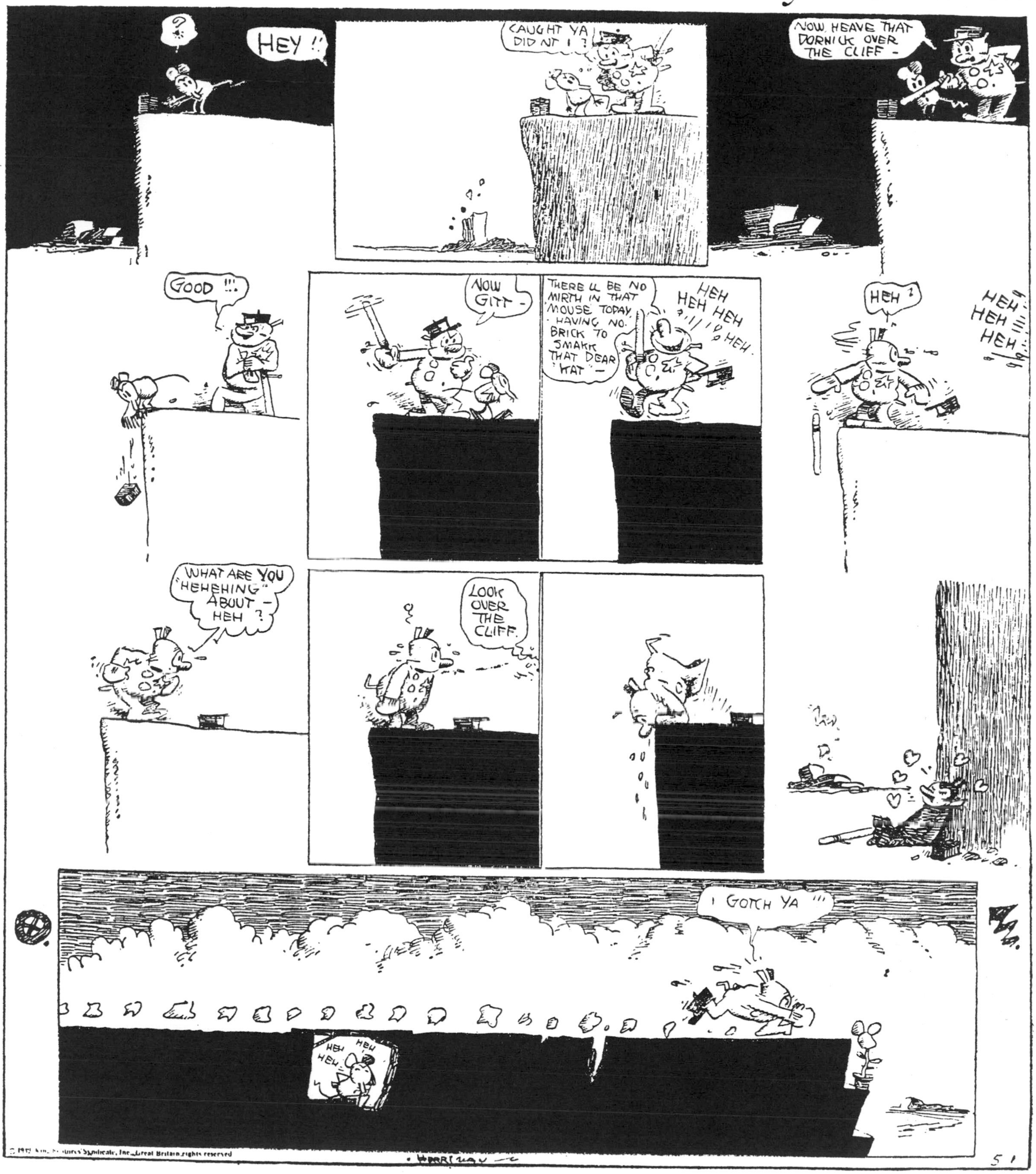

?
HEY !!
CAUGHT YA DID NT I ?
NOW, HEAVE THAT DORNICK OVER THE CLIFF -
GOOD !!!
NOW GITT -
THERE LL BE NO MIRTH IN THAT MOUSE TODAY, HAVING NO BRICK TO SMAKK THAT DEAR KAT -
HEH HEH HEH HEH
HEH ?
HEH HEH HEH
WHAT ARE YOU "HEHEHING" ABOUT - HEH ?
LOOK OVER THE CLIFF.
I GOTCH YA
HEH HEH HEH
HERRIMAN
5 1

May 1st, 1932.

KRAZY KAT By Herriman

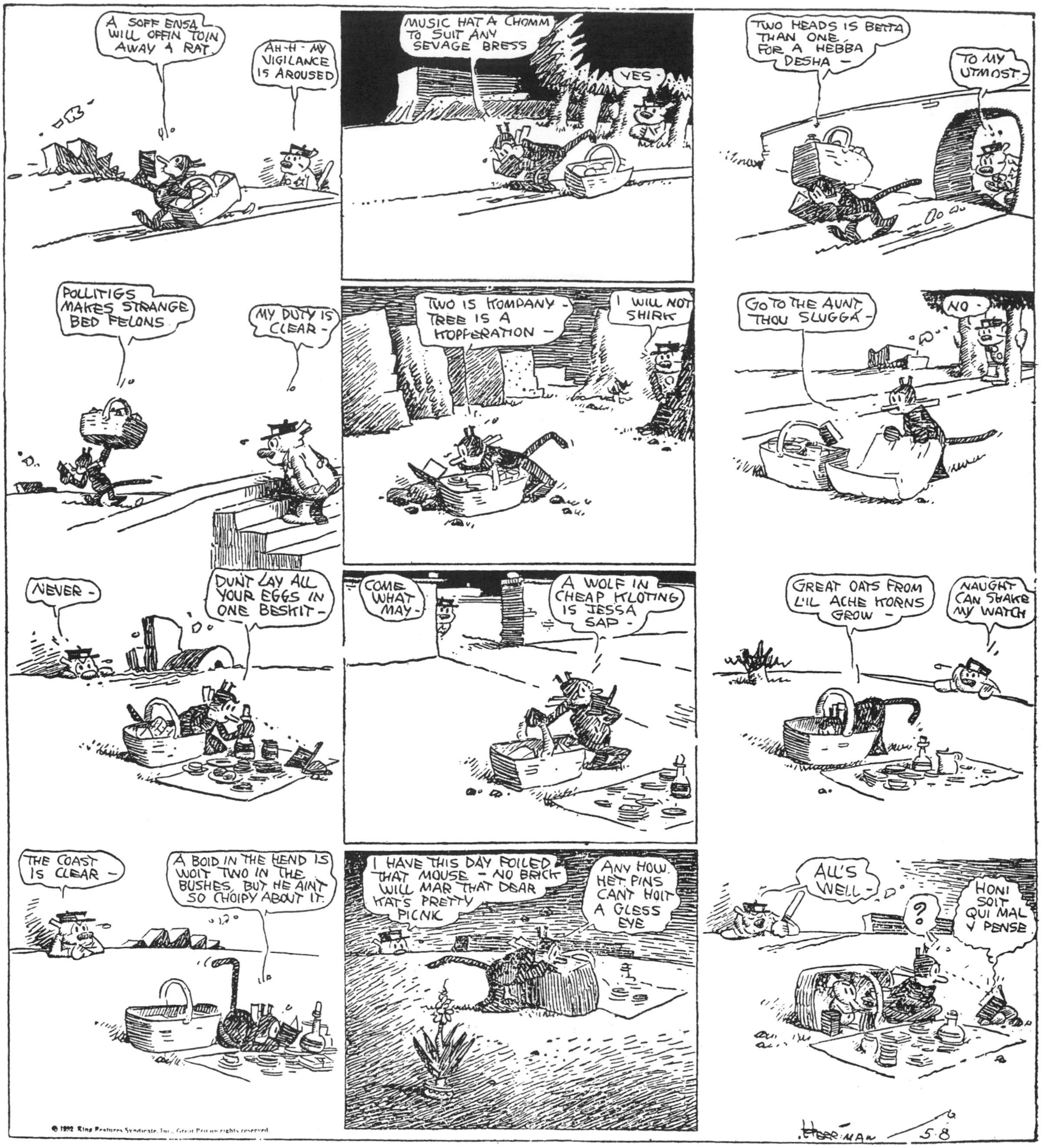
A SOFF ENSA WILL OFFIN TOIN AWAY A RAT.
AH-H - MY VIGILANCE IS AROUSED
MUSIC HAT A CHOMM TO SUIT ANY SEVAGE BRESS
YES -
TWO HEADS IS BETTA THAN ONE FOR A HEBBA DESHA -
TO MY UTMOST -
POLLITICS MAKES STRANGE BED FELONS
MY DUTY IS CLEAR -
TWO IS KOMPANY - TREE IS A KOPPERATION -
I WILL NOT SHIRK
GO TO THE AUNT THOU SLUGGA -
NO -
NEVER -
DUNT LAY ALL YOUR EGGS IN ONE BESKIT -
COME WHAT MAY -
A WOLF IN CHEAP KLOTING IS JESSA SAP -
GREAT OATS FROM L'IL ACHE KORNS GROW -
NAUGHT CAN SHAKE MY WATCH
THE COAST IS CLEAR -
A BOID IN THE HEND IS WOIT TWO IN THE BUSHES, BUT HE AINT SO CHOIPY ABOUT IT.
I HAVE THIS DAY FOILED THAT MOUSE - NO BRICK WILL MAR THAT DEAR KAT'S PRETTY PICNK
ANY HOW, HET PINS CANT HOIT A GLESS EYE
ALL'S WELL -
?
HONI SOIT QUI MAL Y PENSE
HERRIMAN 5-8

May 8th, 1932.

KRAZY KAT ∴ ∴ By Herriman

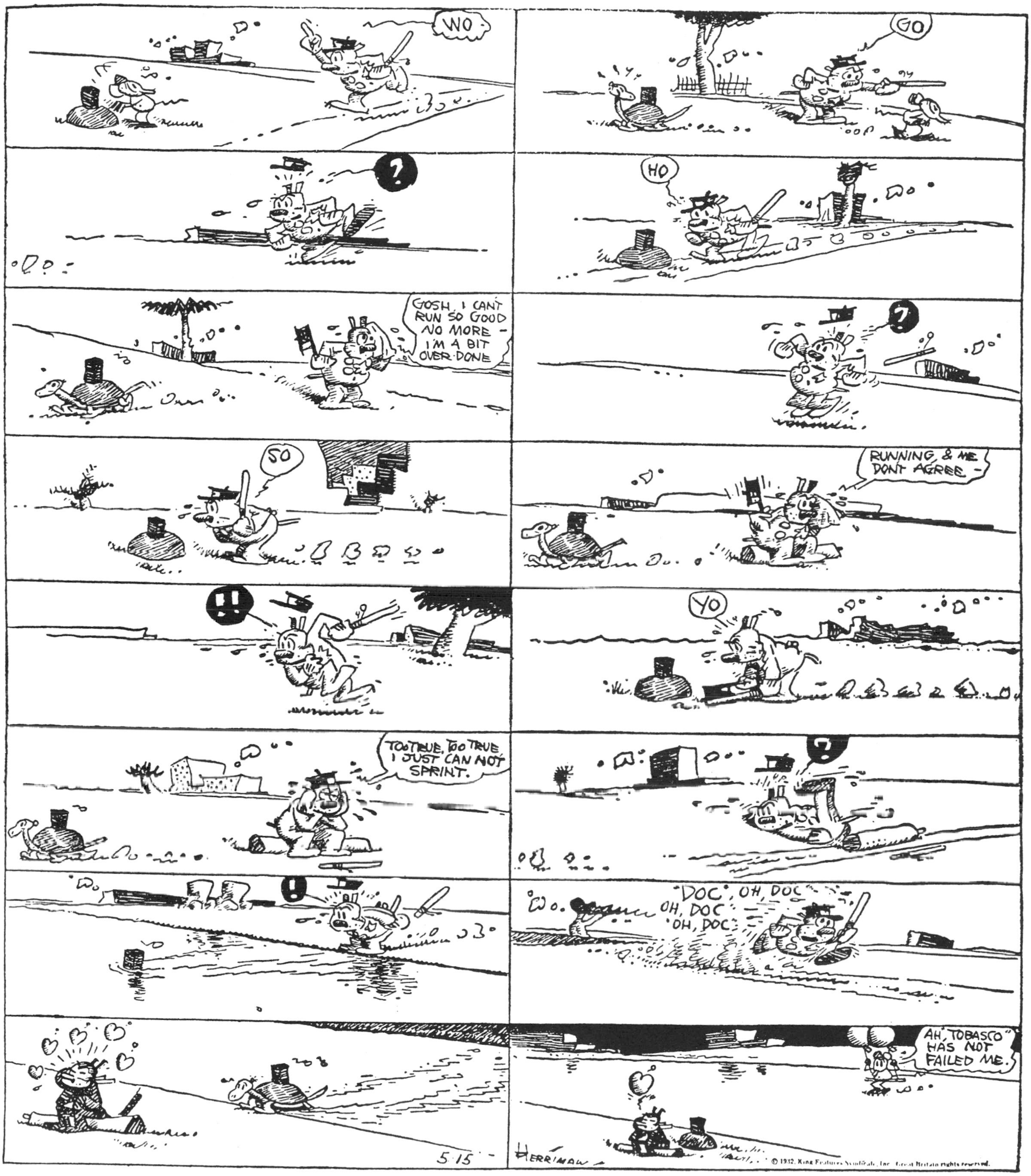
WO
GO
?
HO
GOSH, I CAN'T RUN SO GOOD NO MORE – I'M A BIT OVER-DONE
?
SO
RUNNING & ME DON'T AGREE –
!
YO
TOO TRUE, TOO TRUE I JUST CAN NOT SPRINT.
?
!
"DOC", OH, DOC
OH, DOC
OH, DOC
AH, "TOBASCO" HAS NOT FAILED ME.
5.15
HERRIMAN

May 15th, 1932.

KRAZY KAT ⁘ ⁘ By Herriman

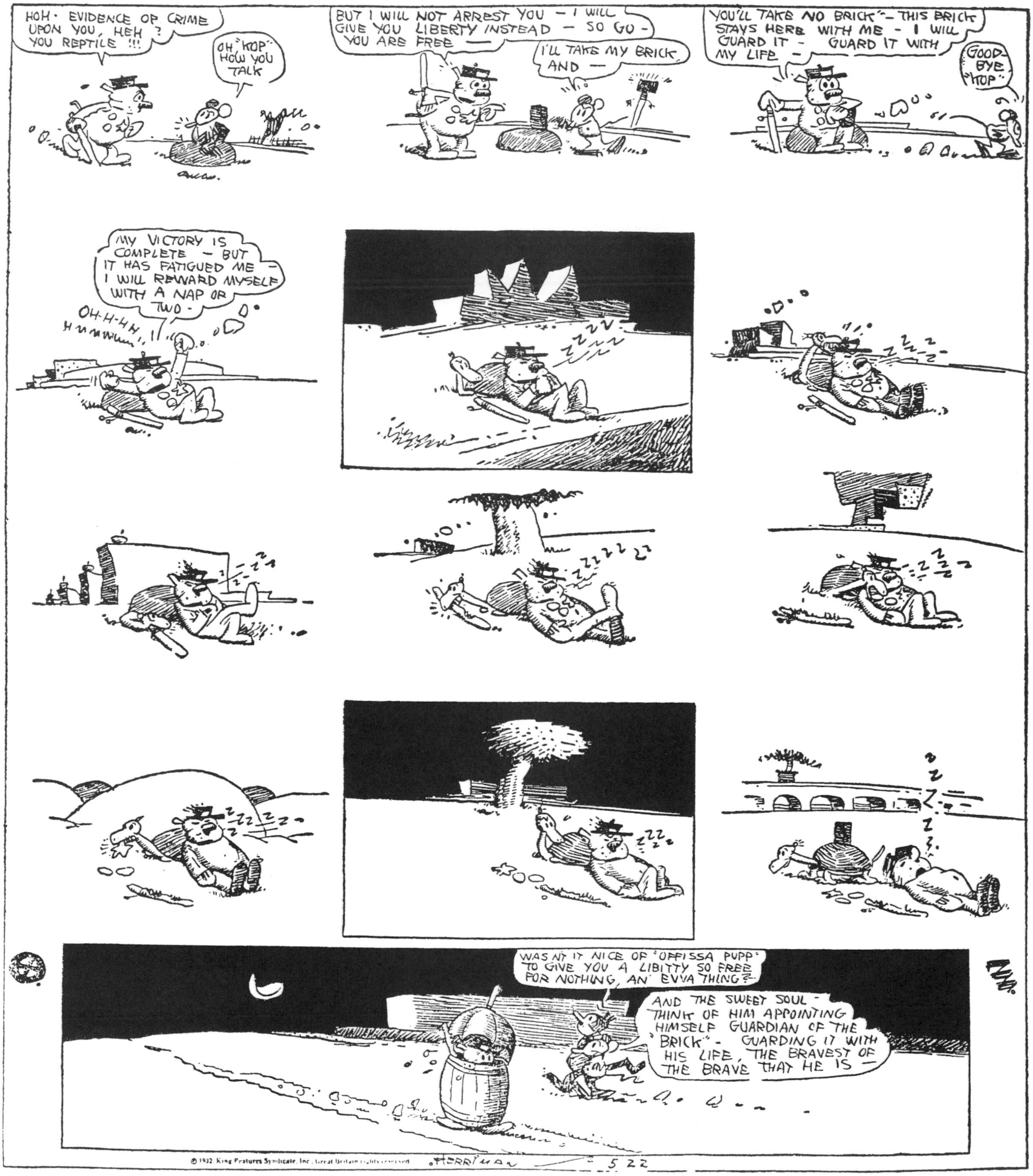

HOH - EVIDENCE OF CRIME UPON YOU, HEH ? YOU REPTILE !!!
OH "KOP" HOW YOU TALK
BUT I WILL NOT ARREST YOU - I WILL GIVE YOU LIBERTY INSTEAD - SO GO - YOU ARE FREE -
I'LL TAKE MY BRICK AND -
YOU'LL TAKE NO BRICK - THIS BRICK STAYS HERE WITH ME - I WILL GUARD IT - GUARD IT WITH MY LIFE -
GOOD-BYE "KOP"
MY VICTORY IS COMPLETE - BUT IT HAS FATIGUED ME - I WILL REWARD MYSELF WITH A NAP OR TWO -
OH-H-HH, HMMMM
WAS N'T IT NICE OF "OFFISSA PUPP" TO GIVE YOU A LIBITTY SO FREE FOR NOTHING, AN' EVVA THING?
AND THE SWEET SOUL - THINK OF HIM APPOINTING HIMSELF GUARDIAN OF THE "BRICK" - GUARDING IT WITH HIS LIFE, THE BRAVEST OF THE BRAVE THAT HE IS -
HERRIMAN 5 22

May 22nd, 1932.

KRAZY KAT ·:· ·:· By Herriman

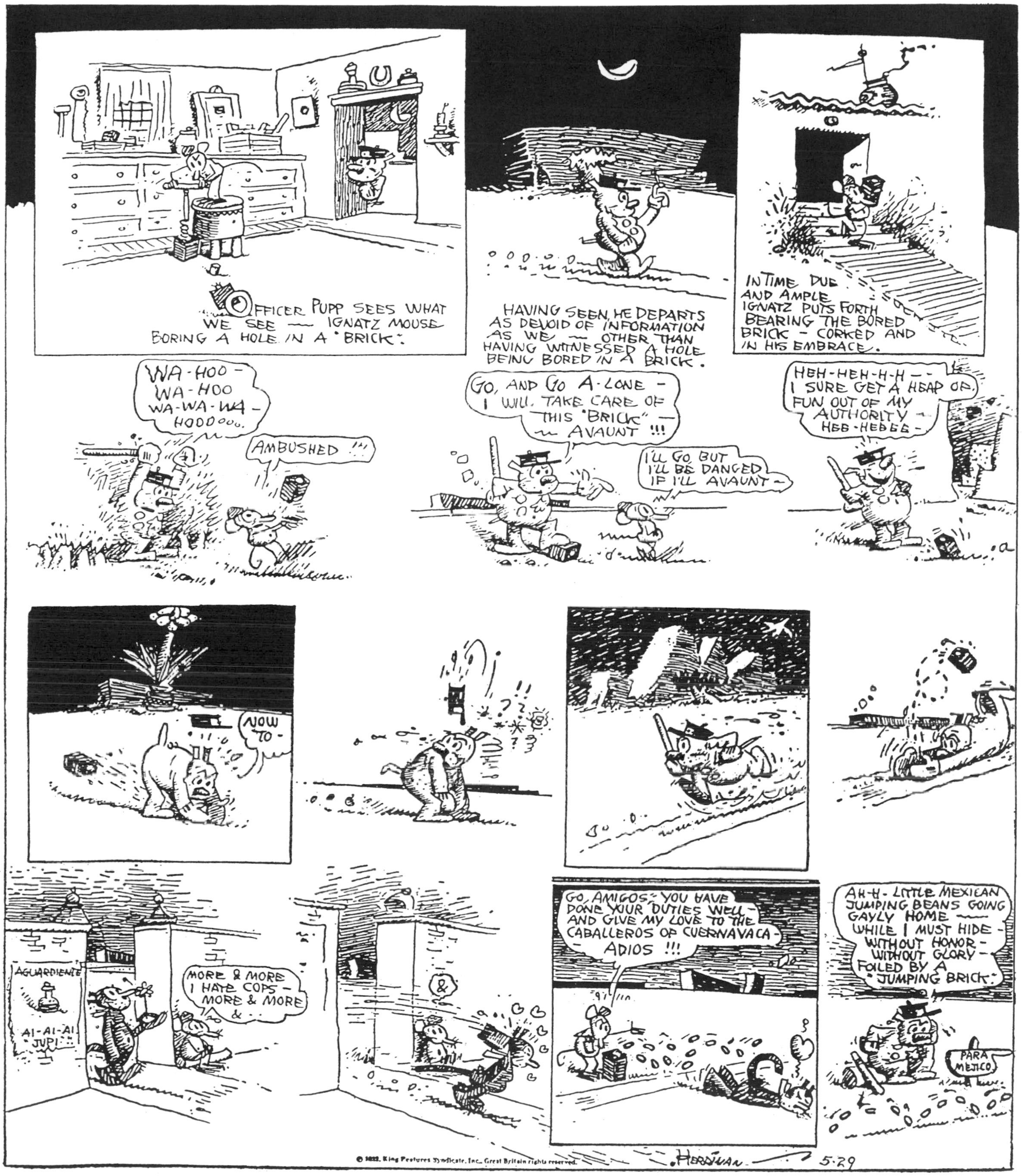

OFFICER PUPP SEES WHAT WE SEE — IGNATZ MOUSE BORING A HOLE IN A "BRICK".
HAVING SEEN, HE DEPARTS AS DEVOID OF INFORMATION AS WE — OTHER THAN HAVING WITNESSED A HOLE BEING BORED IN A BRICK.
IN TIME DUE AND AMPLE IGNATZ PUTS FORTH BEARING THE BORED BRICK - CORKED AND IN HIS EMBRACE.
WA-HOO - WA-HOO WA-WA-WA - HOOD ooo.
AMBUSHED !!!
GO, AND GO A-LONE - I WILL TAKE CARE OF THIS "BRICK" — — AVAUNT !!!
I'LL GO, BUT I'LL BE DANCED IF I'LL AVAUNT —
HEH-HEH-H-H — - I SURE GET A HEAP OF. FUN OUT OF MY AUTHORITY — HEB-HEBEE -
NOW TO -
MORE & MORE I HATE COPS - MORE & MORE &
AGUARDIENTE
AI-AI-AI JUPI
&
GO, AMIGOS, YOU HAVE DONE YOUR DUTIES WELL - AND GIVE MY LOVE TO THE CABALLEROS OF CUERNAVACA - ADIOS !!!
AH-H - LITTLE MEXICAN JUMPING BEANS GOING GAYLY HOME —— WHILE I MUST HIDE - WITHOUT HONOR - WITHOUT GLORY - FOILED BY A "JUMPING BRICK".
PARA MEJICO.
© King Features Syndicate, Inc. Great Britain rights reserved.
HERRIMAN
5·29

May 29th, 1932.

KRAZY KAT ⁘ ⁘ By Herriman

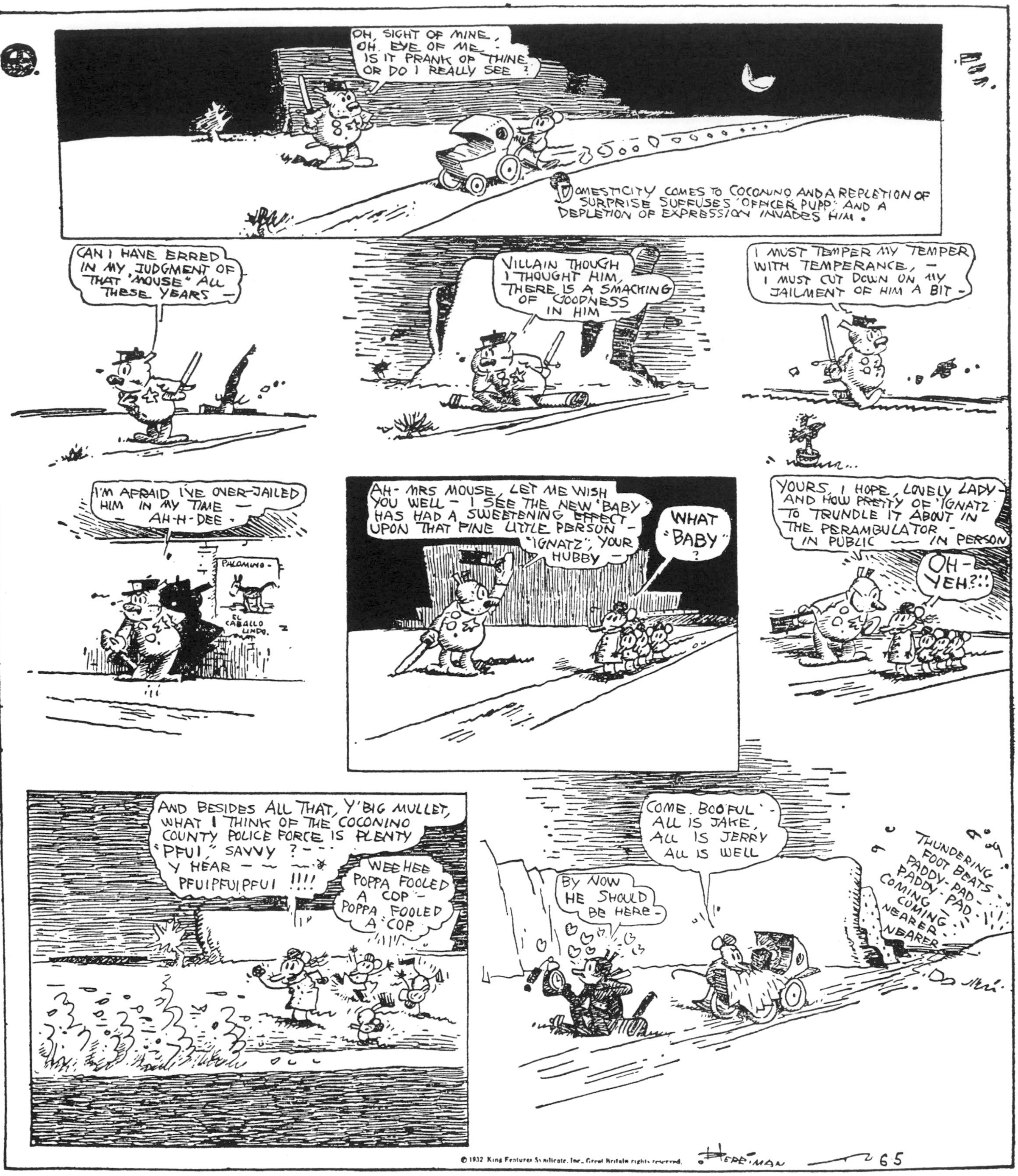

OH, SIGHT OF MINE, OH, EYE OF ME - IS IT PRANK OF THINE, OR DO I REALLY SEE ?
DOMESTICITY COMES TO COCONINO AND A REPLETION OF SURPRISE SUFFUSES 'OFFICER PUPP' AND A DEPLETION OF EXPRESSION INVADES HIM.
CAN I HAVE ERRED IN MY JUDGMENT OF THAT 'MOUSE' ALL THESE YEARS —
VILLAIN THOUGH I THOUGHT HIM, THERE IS A SMACKING OF GOODNESS IN HIM —
I MUST TEMPER MY TEMPER WITH TEMPERANCE, — I MUST CUT DOWN ON MY JAILMENT OF HIM A BIT —
I'M AFRAID I'VE OVER-JAILED HIM IN MY TIME — AH-H-DEE —
PALOMINO
EL CABALLO LINDO.
AH - MRS MOUSE, LET ME WISH YOU WELL — I SEE THE NEW 'BABY' HAS HAD A SWEETENING EFFECT UPON THAT FINE LITTLE PERSON 'IGNATZ', YOUR HUBBY —
WHAT 'BABY' ?
YOURS, I HOPE, LOVELY LADY - AND HOW PRETTY OF 'IGNATZ' TO TRUNDLE IT ABOUT IN THE PERAMBULATOR - IN PUBLIC — IN PERSON
OH - YEH ?!!
AND BESIDES ALL THAT, Y'BIG MULLET, WHAT I THINK OF THE COCONINO COUNTY POLICE FORCE IS PLENTY 'PFUI', SAVVY ? — Y HEAR — PFUIPFUIPFUI !!!!
WEE HEE POPPA FOOLED A COP - POPPA FOOLED A COP.
COME. BOO'FUL - ALL IS JAKE, ALL IS JERRY ALL IS WELL
BY NOW HE SHOULD BE HERE -
THUNDERING FOOT BEATS PADDY-PAD PADDY-PAD COMING COMING NEARER NEARER
© 1932 King Features Syndicate, Inc., Great Britain rights reserved.
HERRIMAN 6-5

June 5th, 1932.

KRAZY KAT ⁘ ⁘ By Herriman

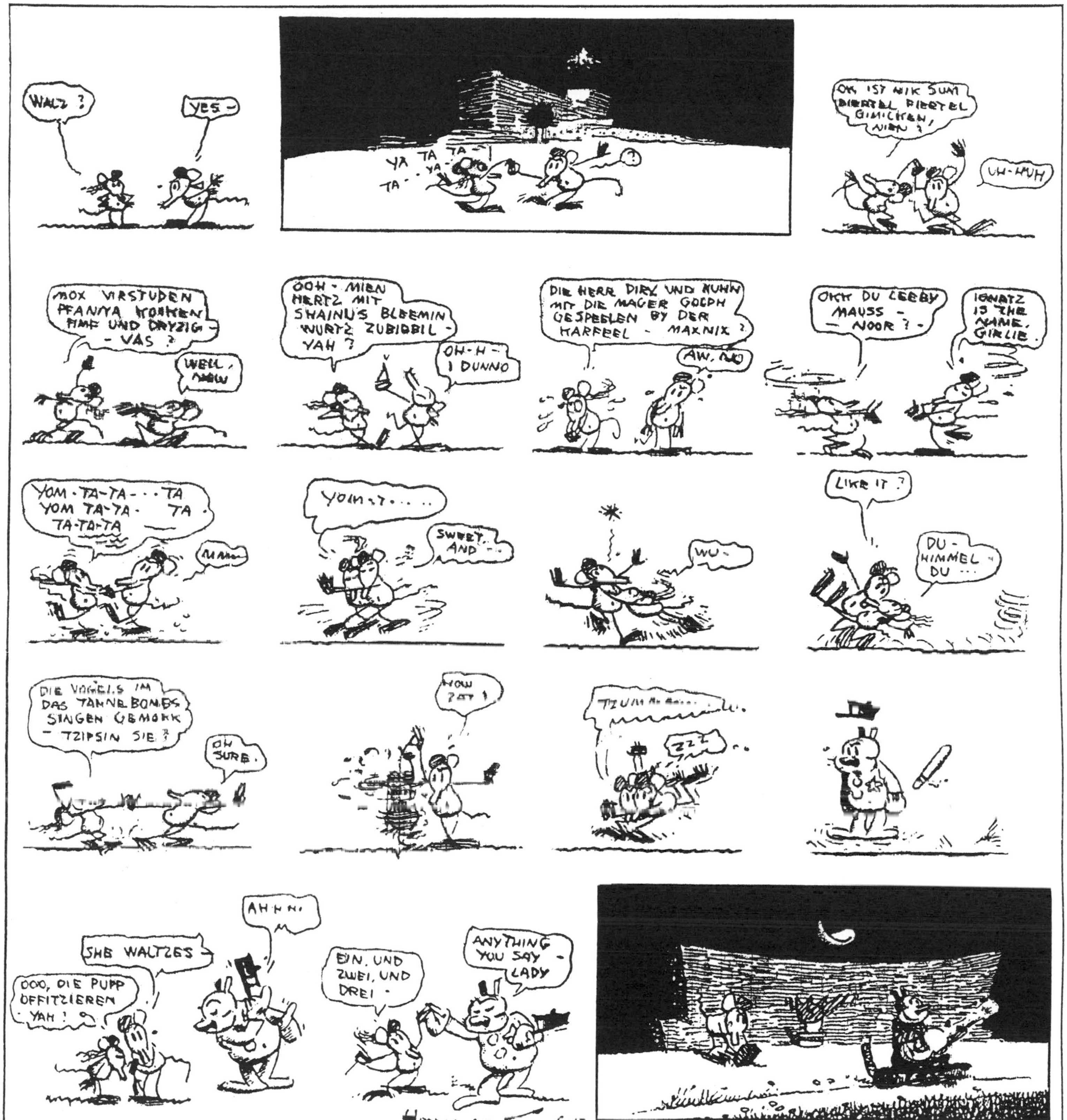

WALZ ?
YES -
YA TA TA - TA - YA - TA
OH, IST NIK SUM DIERTEL PIERTEL GIMICKEN, NIEN ?
UH-HUH
MOX VIRSTUDEN PFANIYA KOHHEN FIMF UND DRYZIG - VAS ?
WELL,
OOH - MIEN HERTZ MIT SHAINU'S BLEEMIN WURTZ ZUBIBBIL - YAH ?
OH-H - I DUNNO
DIE HERR DIRX UND KUHN MIT DIE MAGER GOLDH GESPEELEN BY DER HARFEEL - MAXNIX ?
AW, NO
OKH DU LEEBY MAUSS - - NOOR ? -
IGNATZ IS THE NAME, GIRLIE.
YOM - TA-TA - - - TA YOM TA-TA - TA TA-TA-TA
YOM - - - - - -
SWEET AND - -
WU -
LIKE IT ?
DU - HIMMEL DU - - -
DIE VOGELS IM DAS TANNEBOMBS SINGEN GEMOKK - TZIPSIN SIE ?
OH SURE.
NOW PAT !
ZZZ
SHE WALTZES -
OOO, DIE PUPP OFFITZIEREN - YAH !
AH-H-N!
EIN, UND ZWEI, UND DREI -
ANYTHING YOU SAY LADY -
HERRIMAN
6-12

June 12th, 1932.

KRAZY KAT ∴ ∴ By Herriman

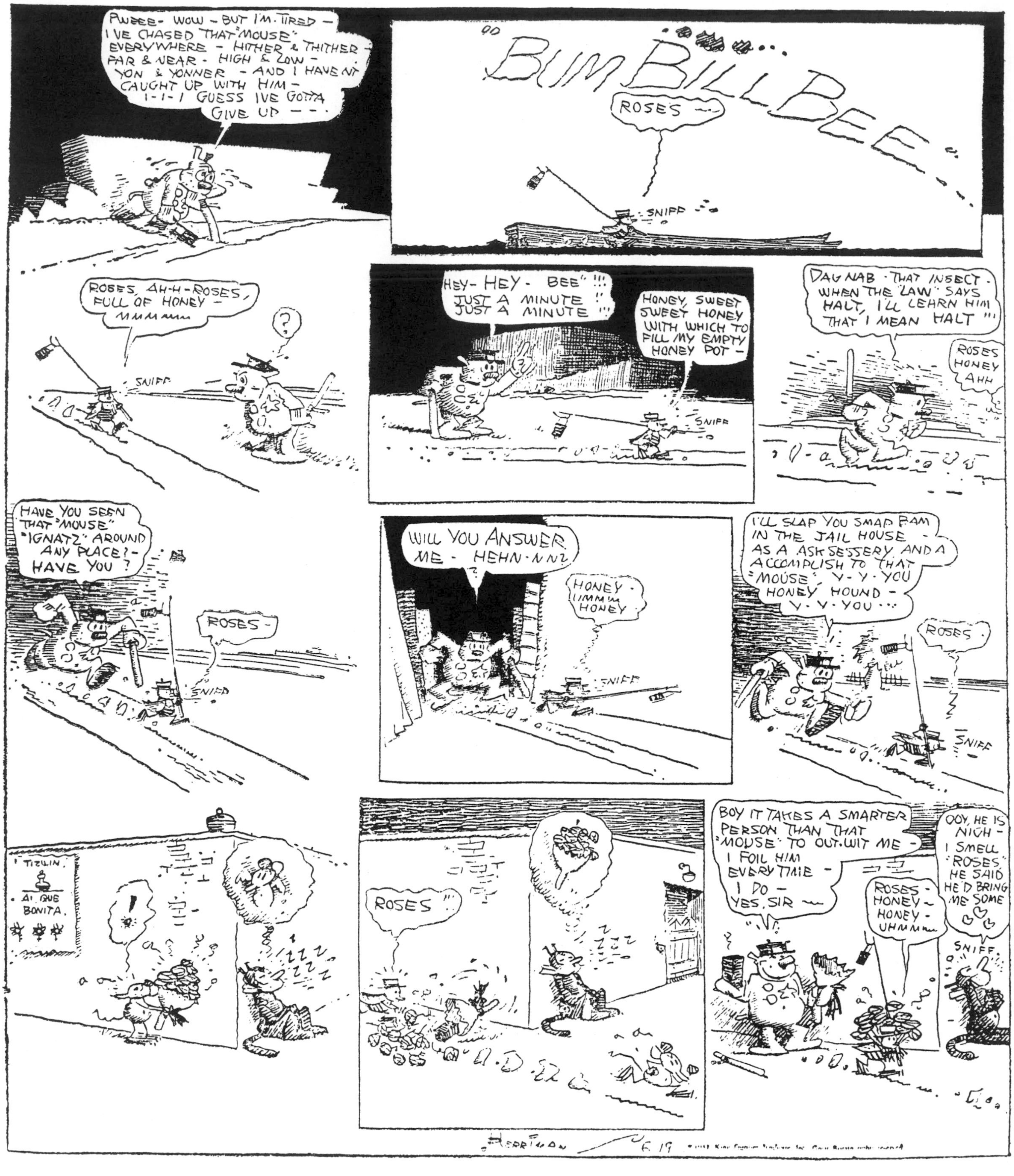
PWEEE- WOW - BUT I'M TIRED - I'VE CHASED THAT "MOUSE" EVERYWHERE - HITHER & THITHER - FAR & NEAR - HIGH & LOW - YON & YONNER - AND I HAVEN'T CAUGHT UP WITH HIM - I-I-I GUESS I'VE GOTTA GIVE UP ---
"BUM BILL BEE"
ROSES --
SNIFF
ROSES, AH-H-ROSES, FULL OF HONEY - MMMMM
?
SNIFF
HEY- HEY- BEE" !!! JUST A MINUTE !! JUST A MINUTE !!!
HONEY, SWEET SWEET HONEY WITH WHICH TO FILL MY EMPTY HONEY POT -
SNIFF
DAG NAB THAT INSECT - WHEN THE "LAW" SAYS HALT, I'LL LEHRN HIM THAT I MEAN HALT !!!
ROSES HONEY AHH
HAVE YOU SEEN THAT "MOUSE" "IGNATZ" AROUND ANY PLACE? - HAVE YOU ?
ROSES -
SNIFF
WILL YOU ANSWER ME - HEHN-NNZ
HONEY - UMMM HONEY
SNIFF
I'LL SLAP YOU SMAP BAM IN THE JAIL HOUSE - AS A ASK SESSERY AND A ACCOMPLISH TO THAT "MOUSE", Y-Y-YOU HONEY HOUND - Y-Y-YOU ...
ROSES
SNIFF
TIZWIN
AI QUE BONITA
!
ZZZZ
ROSES !!!
ZZZ
BOY IT TAKES A SMARTER PERSON THAN THAT "MOUSE" TO OUT-WIT ME - I FOIL HIM EVERY TIME - I DO - YES, SIR ~
ROSES - HONEY - HONEY - UHMMM
OOY, HE IS NIGH - I SMELL "ROSES" HE SAID HE'D BRING ME SOME
SNIFF
HERRIMAN 6.19

June 19th, 1932.

KRAZY KAT ⁘ ⁘ By Herriman

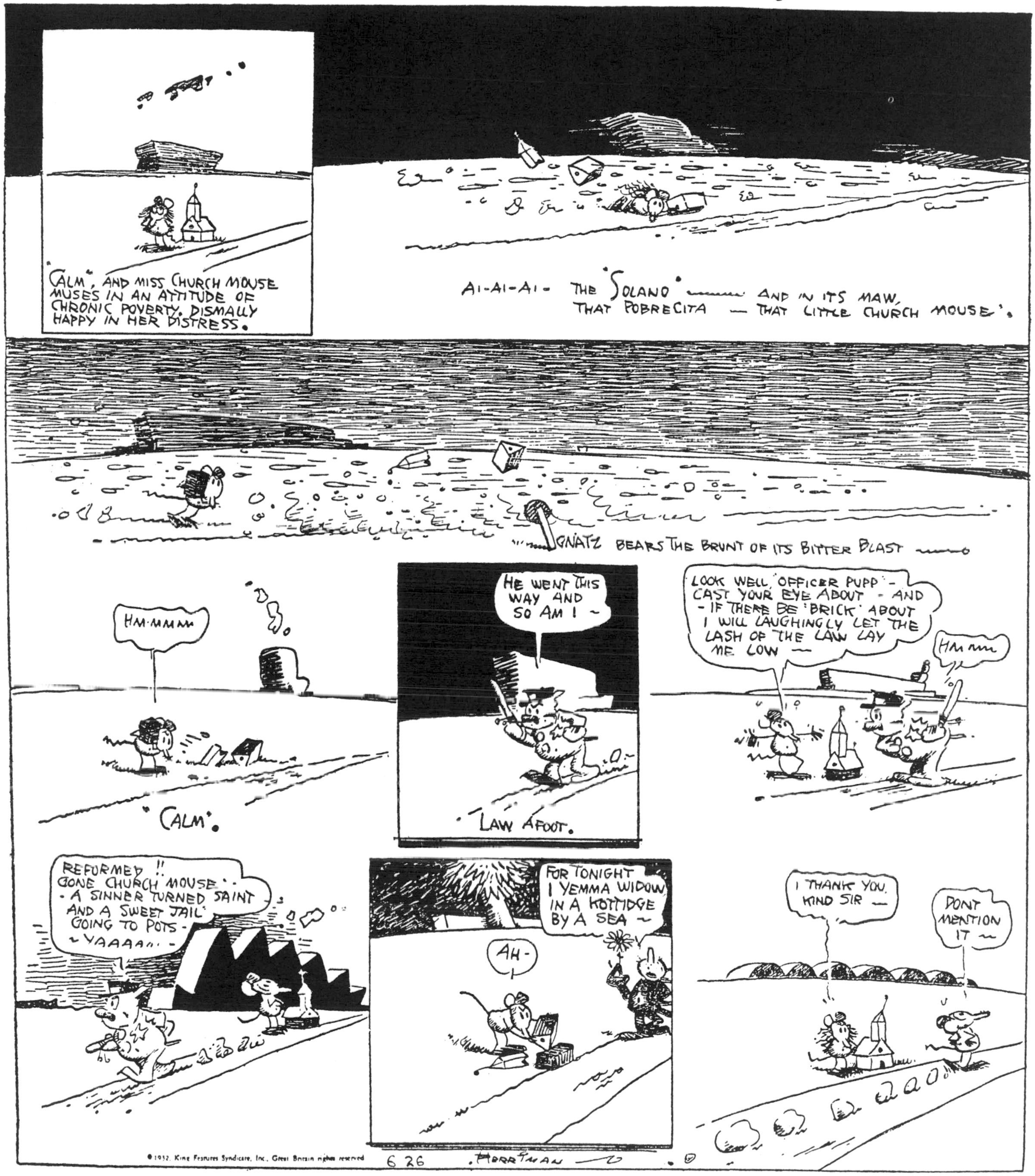

"CALM", AND MISS CHURCH MOUSE MUSES IN AN ATTITUDE OF CHRONIC POVERTY. DISMALLY HAPPY IN HER DISTRESS.
AI-AI-AI- THE "SOLANO" AND IN ITS MAW, THAT POBRECITA — THAT LITTLE CHURCH MOUSE".
IGNATZ BEARS THE BRUNT OF ITS BITTER BLAST
HM-MMM
"CALM".
HE WENT THIS WAY AND SO AM I ~
LAW AFOOT.
LOOK WELL, OFFICER PUPP - CAST YOUR EYE ABOUT - AND - IF THERE BE 'BRICK' ABOUT I WILL LAUGHINGLY LET THE LASH OF THE LAW LAY ME LOW —
HM MM
REFORMED !! GONE CHURCH MOUSE - - A SINNER TURNED SAINT AND A SWEET JAIL GOING TO POTS - ~YAAAA.. -
FOR TONIGHT I YEMMA WIDOW IN A KOTTIDGE BY A SEA ~
AH-
I THANK YOU, KIND SIR —
DONT MENTION IT ~
© 1932, King Features Syndicate, Inc., Great Britain rights reserved
6 26
HERRIMAN

June 26th, 1932.

KRAZY KAT By Herriman

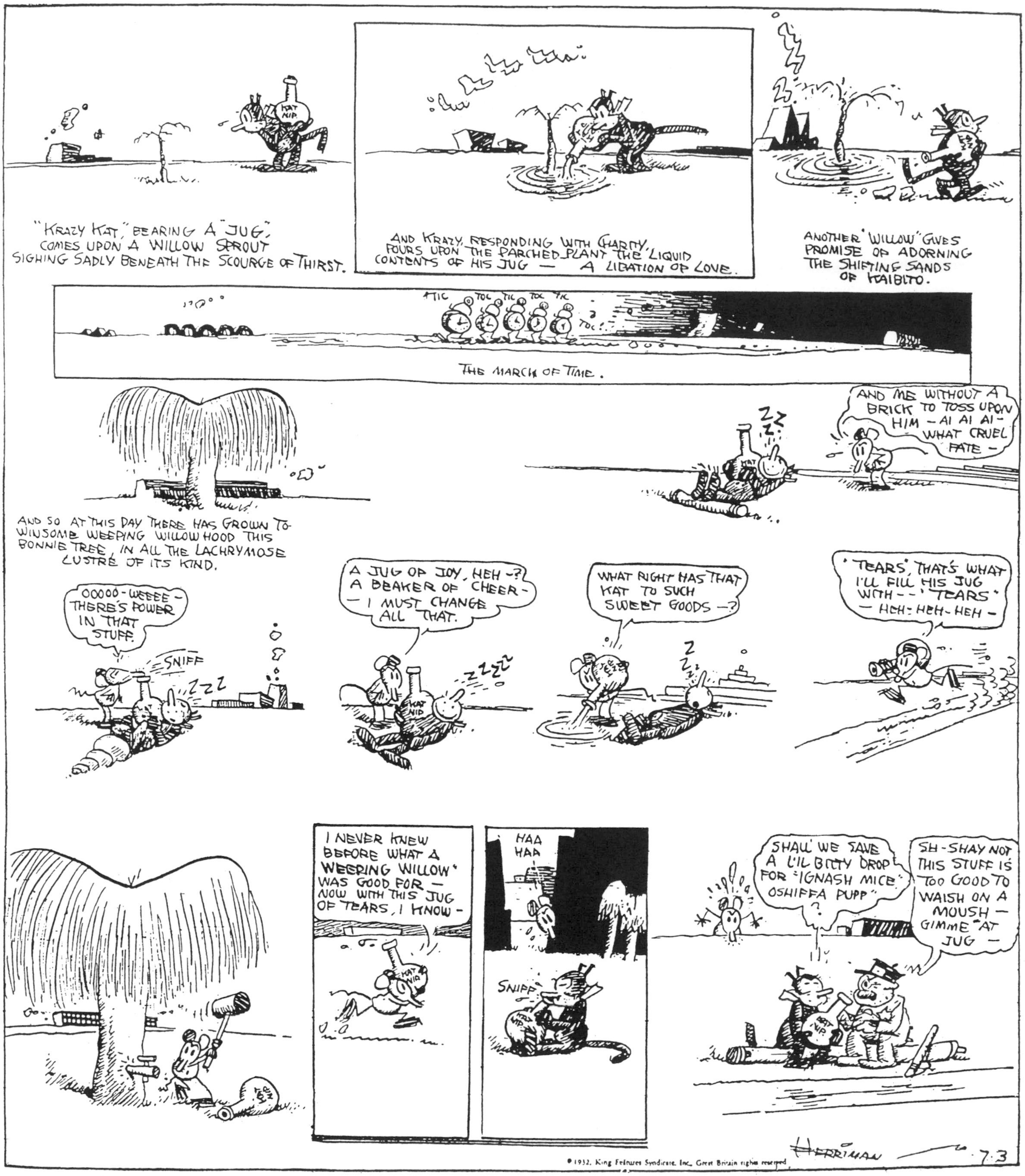

KAT NIP
"Krazy Kat," bearing a "jug," comes upon a willow sprout sighing sadly beneath the scourge of thirst.
And Krazy, responding with charity, pours upon the parched plant the liquid contents of his jug — a libation of love.
Another "willow" gives promise of adorning the shifting sands of Kaibito.
TIC TOC TIC TOC TIC TOC
The march of time.
And so at this day there has grown to winsome weeping willow hood this bonnie tree, in all the lachrymose lustre of its kind.
KAT
And me without a brick to toss upon him — ai ai ai — what cruel fate —
Z Z Z
Ooooo-weeee — there's power in that stuff.
SNIFF
A jug of joy, heh —? A beaker of cheer — I must change all that.
KAT NIP
What right has that kat to such sweet goods —?
"Tears," that's what I'll fill his jug with — "tears" — heh-heh-heh —
I never knew before what a "weeping willow" was good for — now with this jug of tears, I know —
KAT NIP
HAA HAA
SNIFF
Shall we save a li'l bitty drop for "Ignash Mice" oshiffa pupp"?
Sh-shay not this stuff is too good to waish on a moush — gimme "at jug —
Herriman 7·3
© 1932, King Features Syndicate, Inc. Great Britain rights reserved.

July 3rd, 1932.

KRAZY KAT ∴ ∴ By Herriman

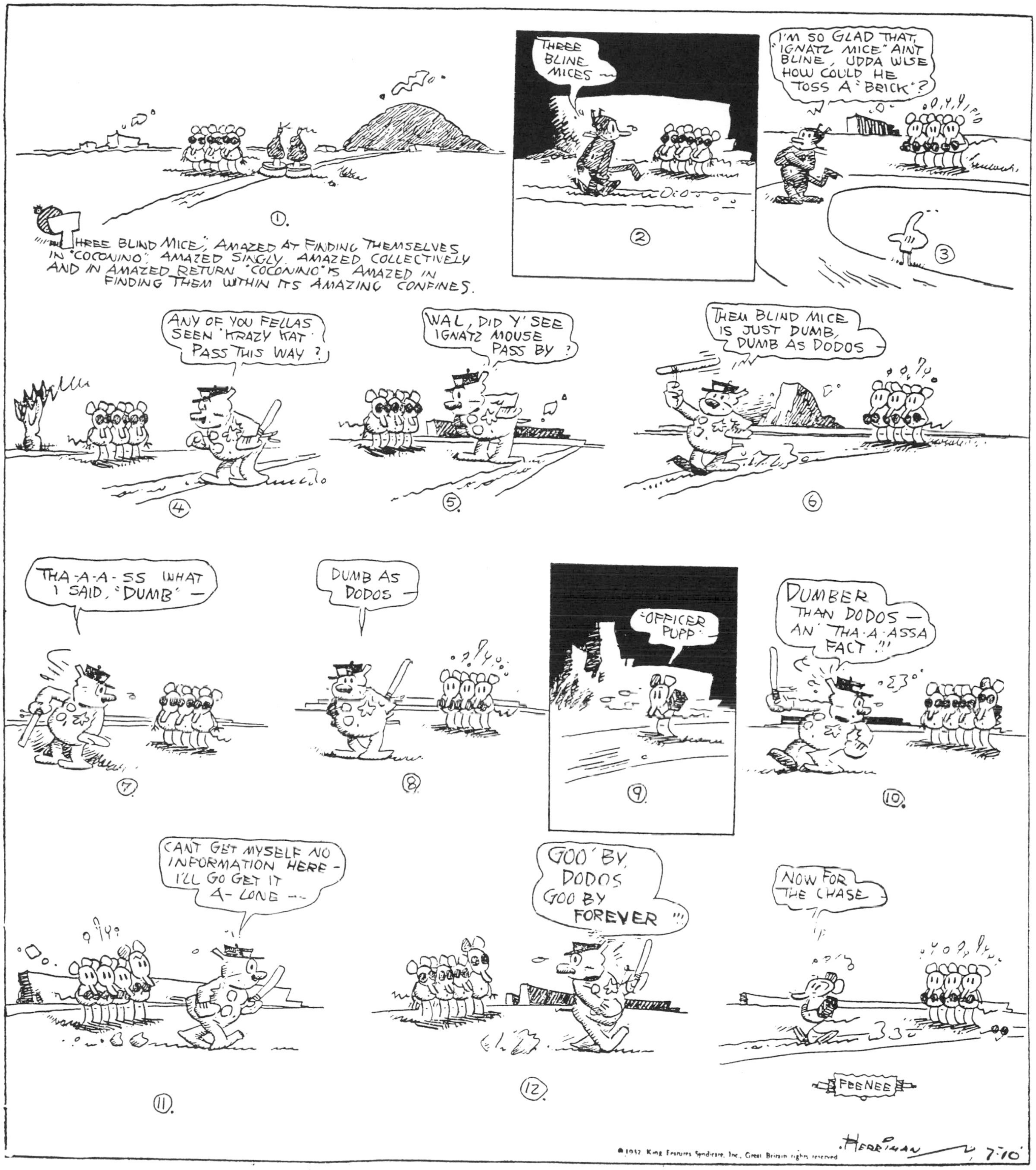

"THREE BLIND MICE", AMAZED AT FINDING THEMSELVES IN "COCONINO", AMAZED SINGLY, AMAZED COLLECTIVELY AND IN AMAZED RETURN "COCONINO" IS AMAZED IN FINDING THEM WITHIN ITS AMAZING CONFINES.
THREE BLINE MICES —
I'M SO GLAD THAT, "IGNATZ MICE" AINT BLINE, UDDA WISE HOW COULD HE TOSS A "BRICK"?
ANY OF YOU FELLAS SEEN "KRAZY KAT" PASS THIS WAY?
WAL, DID Y' SEE IGNATZ MOUSE PASS BY?
THEM BLIND MICE IS JUST DUMB, DUMB AS DODOS —
THA-A-A-SS WHAT I SAID, "DUMB" —
DUMB AS DODOS —
"OFFICER PUPP"
DUMBER THAN DODOS — AN' THA-A-ASSA FACT!!!
CAN'T GET MYSELF NO INFORMATION HERE - I'LL GO GET IT A-LONE —
GOO' BY, DODOS GOO BY FOREVER!!!
NOW FOR THE CHASE
FEENEE
©1932 King Features Syndicate, Inc., Great Britain rights reserved
HERRIMAN 7·10

July 10th, 1932.

KRAZY KAT ⁘ ⁘ By Herriman

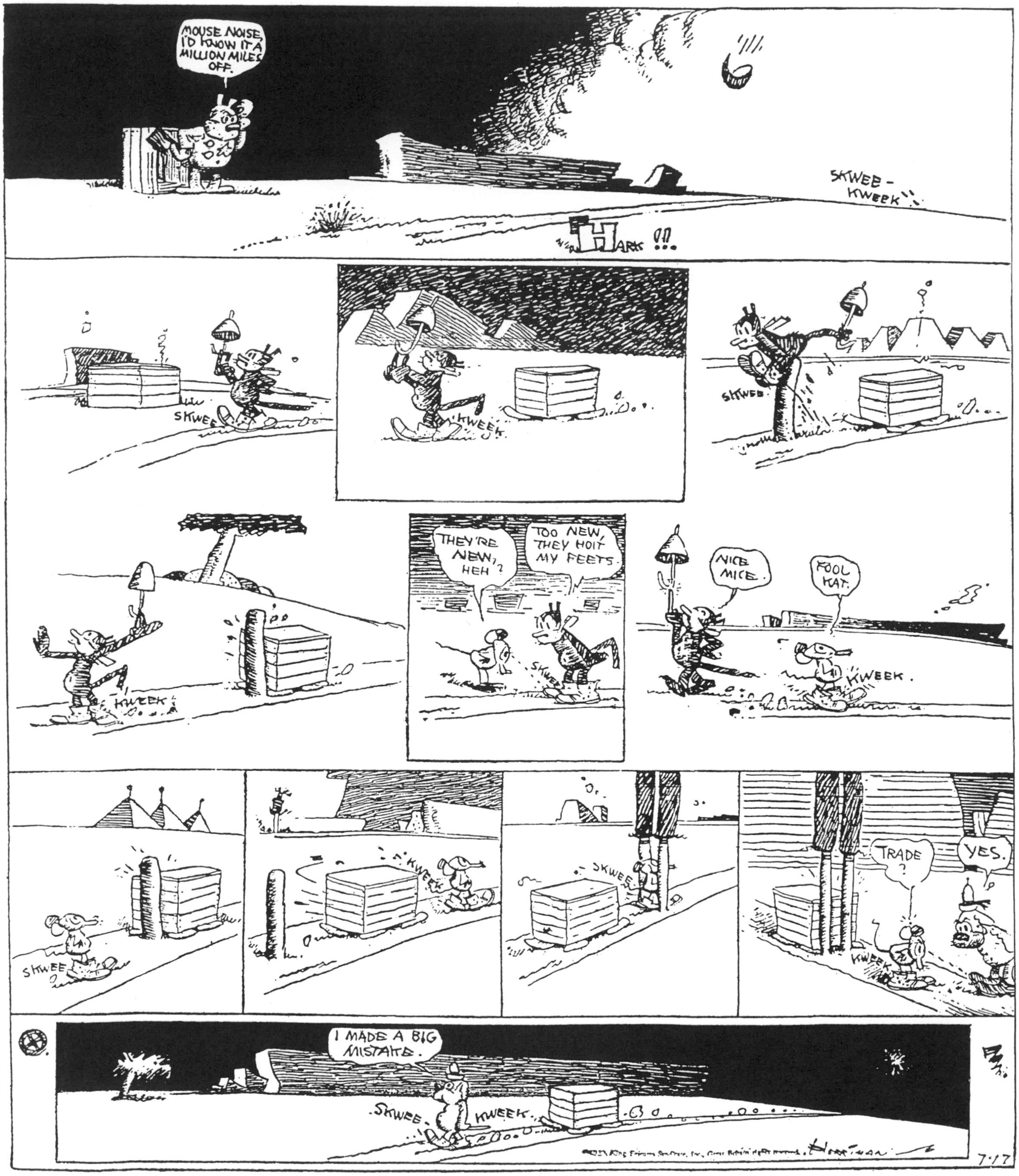
MOUSE NOISE, I'D KNOW IT A MILLION MILES OFF.
SKWEE - KWEEK
HARK !!!
SKWEE
KWEEK
SKWEE
KWEEK
THEY'RE NEW, HEH ?
TOO NEW, THEY HOIT MY FEETS.
SKWEE
NICE MICE.
FOOL KAT.
KWEEK.
SKWEE
KWEEK
SKWEE
TRADE ?
YES.
KWEEK
I MADE A BIG MISTAKE.
SKWEE.
KWEEK.
HERRIMAN
7·17

July 17th, 1932.

KRAZY KAT ⁘ ⁘ By Herriman

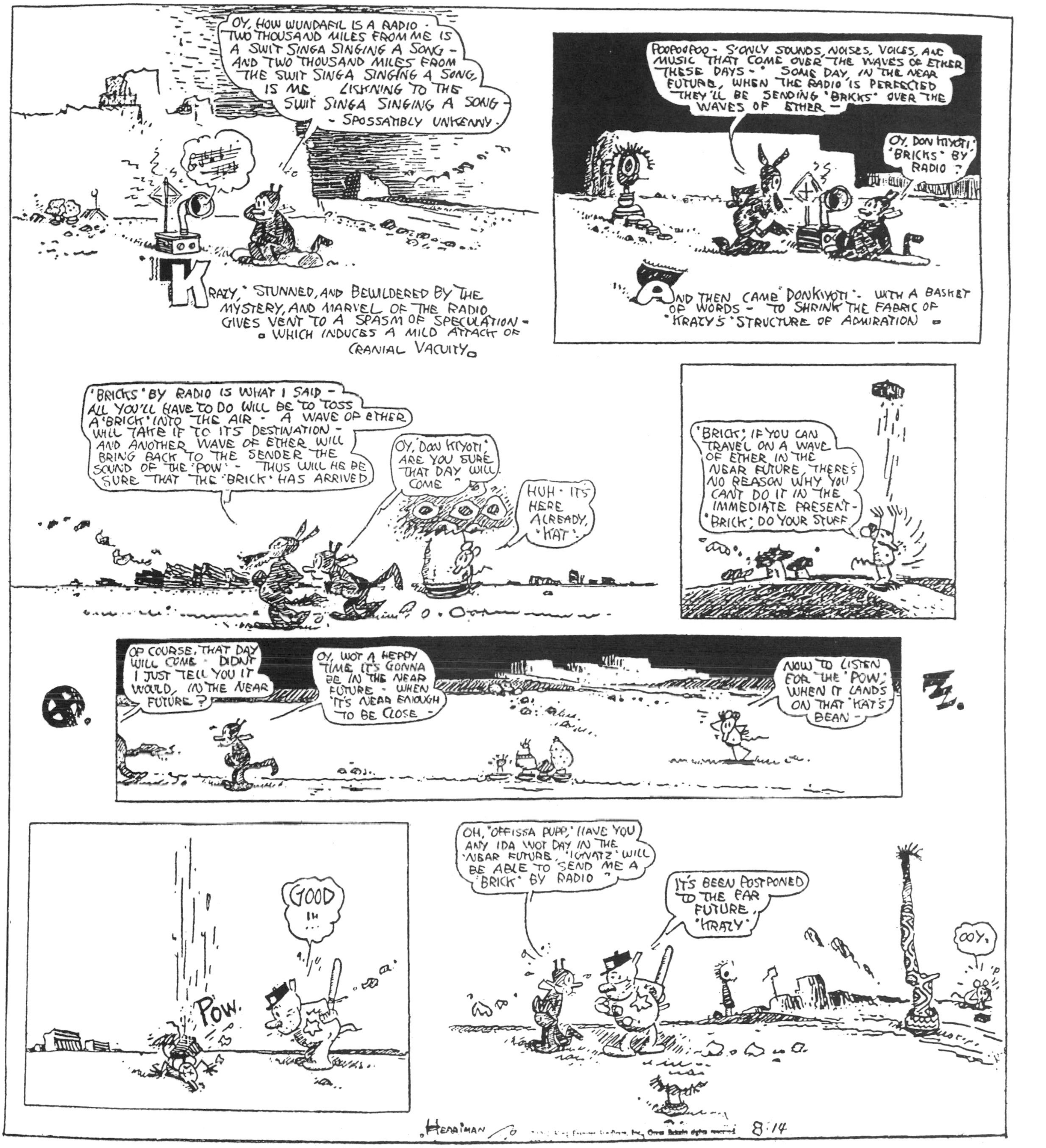

OY, HOW WUNDAFIL IS A RADIO - TWO THOUSAND MILES FROM ME IS A SWIT SINGA SINGING A SONG - AND TWO THOUSAND MILES FROM THE SWIT SINGA SINGING A SONG, IS ME LISKNING TO THE SWIT SINGA SINGING A SONG - SPOSSAMBLY UNKENNY -
KRAZY, STUNNED, AND BEWILDERED BY THE MYSTERY, AND MARVEL OF THE RADIO GIVES VENT TO A SPASM OF SPECULATION - WHICH INDUCES A MILD ATTACK OF CRANIAL VACUITY
POOPOOPOO - S'ONLY SOUNDS, NOISES, VOICES, AND MUSIC THAT COME OVER THE WAVES OF ETHER THESE DAYS - SOME DAY, IN THE NEAR FUTURE, WHEN THE RADIO IS PERFECTED THEY'LL BE SENDING 'BRICKS' OVER THE WAVES OF ETHER -
OY, DON KIYOTI, 'BRICKS' BY RADIO ?
AND THEN CAME 'DONKIYOTI' - WITH A BASKET OF WORDS - TO SHRINK THE FABRIC OF 'KRAZY'S' STRUCTURE OF ADMIRATION
'BRICKS' BY RADIO IS WHAT I SAID - ALL YOU'LL HAVE TO DO WILL BE TO TOSS A 'BRICK' INTO THE AIR - A WAVE OF ETHER WILL TAKE IT TO ITS DESTINATION - AND ANOTHER WAVE OF ETHER WILL BRING BACK TO THE SENDER THE SOUND OF THE 'POW' - THUS WILL HE BE SURE THAT THE 'BRICK' HAS ARRIVED
OY, DON KIYOTI, ARE YOU SURE THAT DAY WILL COME
HUH - ITS HERE ALREADY, 'KAT'
'BRICK,' IF YOU CAN TRAVEL ON A WAVE OF ETHER IN THE NEAR FUTURE, THERE'S NO REASON WHY YOU CAN'T DO IT IN THE IMMEDIATE PRESENT - 'BRICK,' DO YOUR STUFF
OF COURSE, THAT DAY WILL COME - DIDN'T I JUST TELL YOU IT WOULD, IN THE NEAR FUTURE ?
OY, WOT A HEPPY TIME IT'S GONNA BE IN THE NEAR FUTURE - WHEN IT'S NEAR ENOUGH TO BE CLOSE -
NOW TO LISTEN FOR THE 'POW,' WHEN IT LANDS ON THAT 'KAT'S' BEAN -
GOOD
POW.
OH, 'OFFISSA PUPP,' HAVE YOU ANY IDA WOT DAY IN THE 'NEAR FUTURE,' 'IGNATZ' WILL BE ABLE TO SEND ME A 'BRICK' BY RADIO
IT'S BEEN POSTPONED TO THE FAR FUTURE, 'KRAZY'
OOY.
HERRIMAN
8-14

August 14th, 1932.

KRAZY KAT ⁘ ⁘ By Herriman

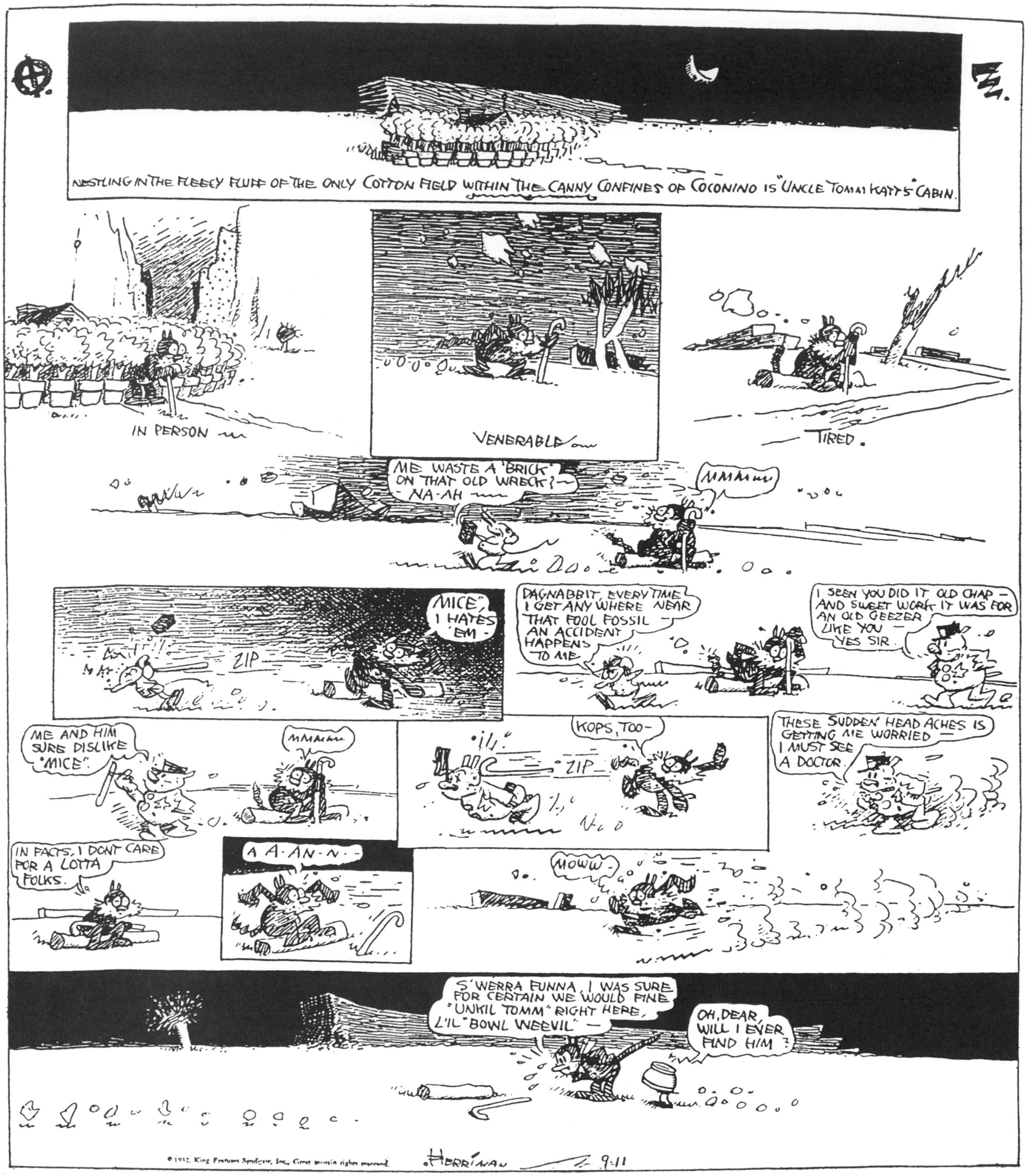
NESTLING IN THE FLEECY FLUFF OF THE ONLY COTTON FIELD WITHIN THE CANNY CONFINES OF COCONINO IS "UNCLE TOMM KATT'S" CABIN.
IN PERSON
VENERABLE
TIRED.
ME WASTE A 'BRICK' ON THAT OLD WRECK? — NA-AH
MMMM
"MICE", I HATES 'EM
ZIP
DAGNABBIT, EVERY TIME I GET ANY WHERE NEAR THAT FOOL FOSSIL AN ACCIDENT HAPPENS TO ME
I SEEN YOU DID IT, OLD CHAP — AND SWEET WORK IT WAS FOR AN OLD GEEZER LIKE YOU — YES SIR
ME AND HIM SURE DISLIKE "MICE".
MMMM
KOPS, TOO —
ZIP
THESE SUDDEN HEAD ACHES IS GETTING ME WORRIED — I MUST SEE A DOCTOR.
IN FACTS, I DON'T CARE FOR A LOTTA FOLKS.
A A-AN-N —
MOWW
S'WERRA FUNNA, I WAS SURE FOR CERTAIN WE WOULD FINE "UNKIL TOMM" RIGHT HERE, L'IL' "BOWL WEEVIL" —
OH, DEAR, WILL I EVER FIND HIM?
© 1932, King Features Syndicate, Inc., Great Britain rights reserved.
HERRIMAN 9-11

September 11th, 1932.

KRAZY KAT ∴ ∴ By Herriman

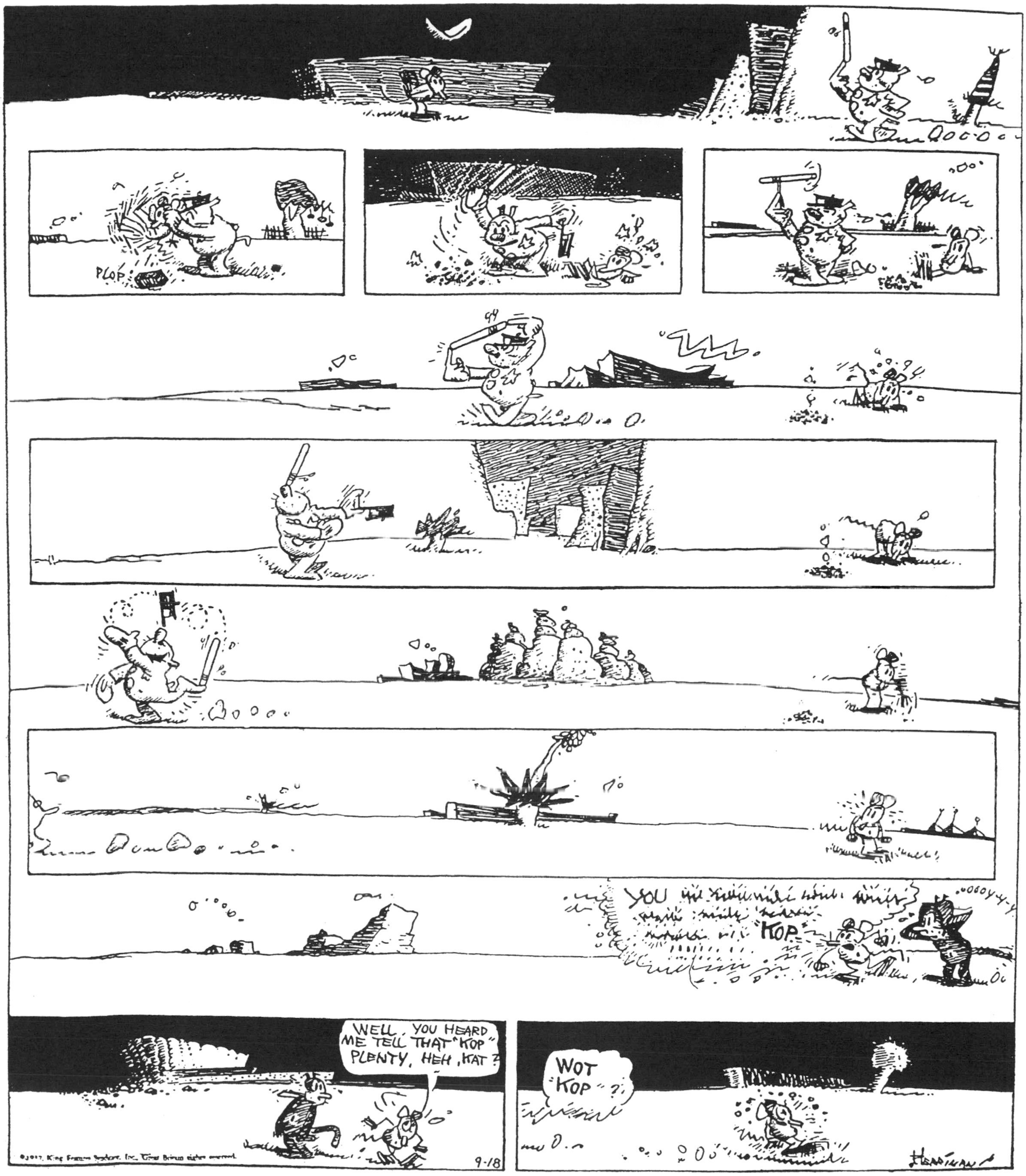
PLOP
YOU
KOP
WELL, YOU HEARD ME TELL THAT "KOP" PLENTY, HEH, KAT?
9-18
WOT KOP ?
HERRIMAN

September 18th, 1932.

KRAZY KAT ·:· ·:· By Herriman

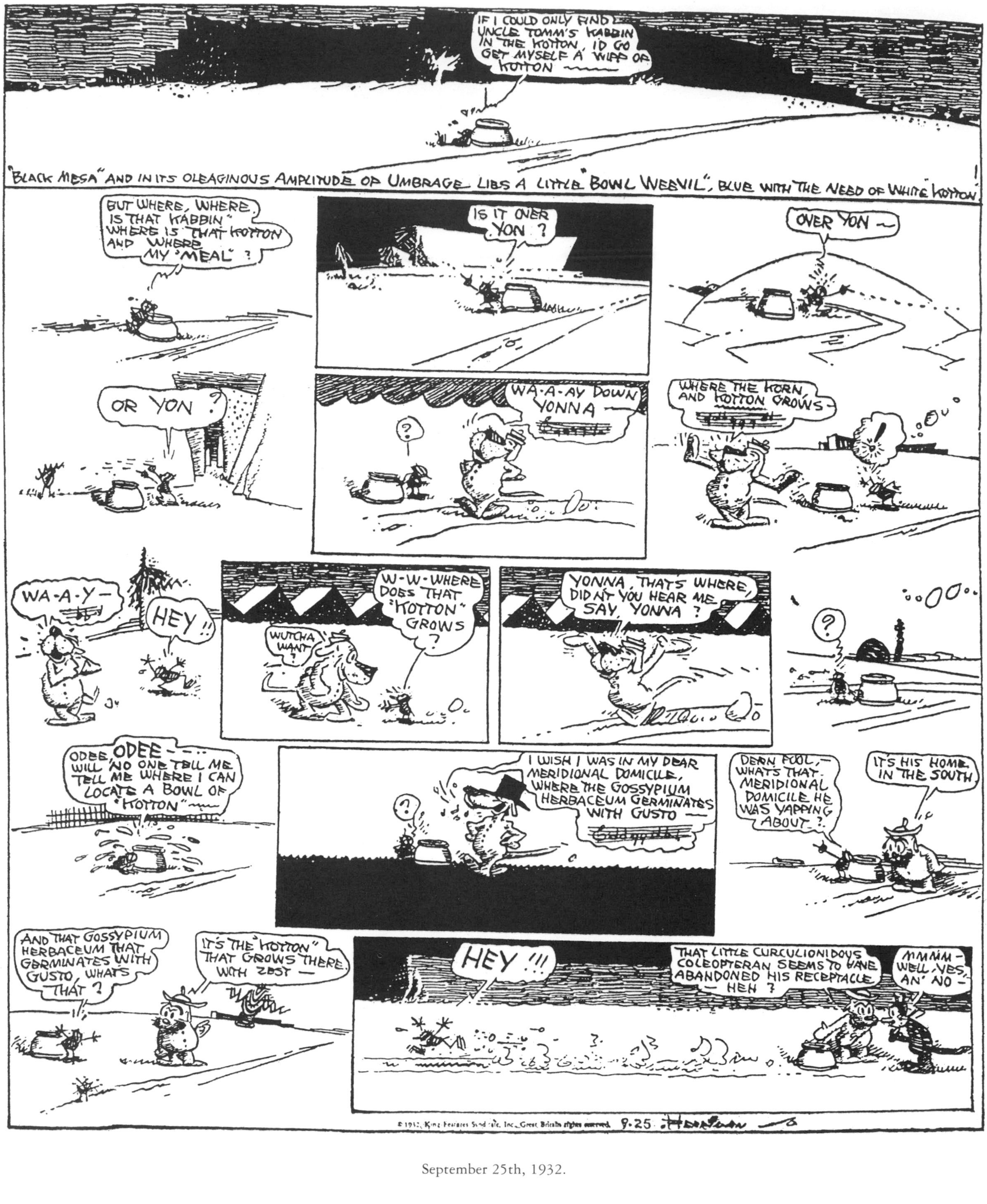

IF I COULD ONLY FIND UNCLE TOMM'S KABBIN IN THE KOTTON, I'D GO GET MYSELF A' WIFF OF KOTTON ~~~
"BLACK MESA" AND IN ITS OLEAGINOUS AMPLITUDE OF UMBRAGE LIBS A LITTLE "BOWL WEEVIL", BLUE WITH THE NEED OF WHITE KOTTON!
BUT WHERE, WHERE, IS THAT "KABBIN" WHERE IS THAT KOTTON AND WHERE MY "MEAL"?
IS IT OVER YON?
OVER YON ~
OR YON?
WA-A-AY DOWN YONNA ~
?
WHERE THE KORN, AND KOTTON GROWS ~
!
WA-A-Y ~
HEY!!
WUTCHA WANT?
W-W-WHERE DOES THAT "KOTTON" GROWS?
YONNA, THAT'S WHERE, DID'NT YOU HEAR ME SAY, YONNA?
?
ODEE, ODEE ~~ WILL NO ONE TELL ME TELL ME WHERE I CAN LOCATE A BOWL OF "KOTTON" ~~~
I WISH I WAS IN MY DEAR MERIDIONAL DOMICILE, WHERE THE GOSSYPIUM HERBACEUM GERMINATES WITH GUSTO ~
?
DERN FOOL, ~ WHATS THAT MERIDIONAL DOMICILE HE WAS YAPPING ABOUT?
IT'S HIS HOME IN THE SOUTH
AND THAT GOSSYPIUM HERBACEUM THAT GERMINATES WITH GUSTO, WHAT'S THAT?
IT'S THE "KOTTON" THAT GROWS THERE WITH ZEST ~
HEY!!!
THAT LITTLE CURCULIONIDOUS COLEOPTERAN SEEMS TO HAVE ABANDONED HIS RECEPTACLE ~ HEH?
MMMM ~ WELL, YES, AN' NO ~
9-25 HERRIMAN

September 25th, 1932.

KRAZY KAT ∴ ∴ By Herriman

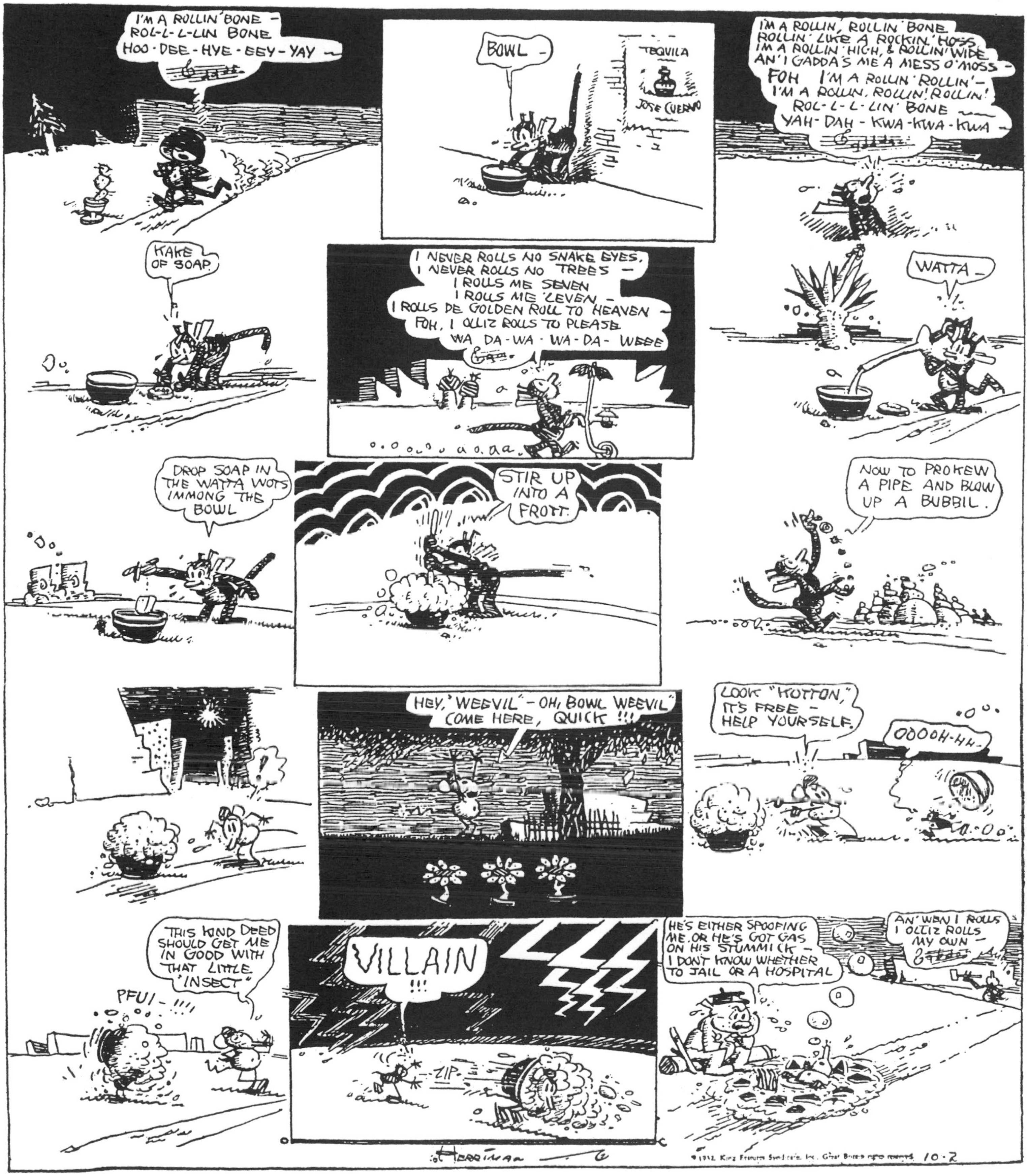

I'M A ROLLIN' BONE - ROL-L-L-LIN BONE HOO-DEE-HYE-EEY-YAY -
BOWL -
TEQUILA
JOSE CUERVO
I'M A ROLLIN', ROLLIN' BONE ROLLIN' LIKE A ROCKIN' HOSS, I'M A ROLLIN' HIGH, & ROLLIN' WIDE AN' I GADDA'S ME A MESS O' MOSS - FOH I'M A ROLLIN' ROLLIN' - I'M A ROLLIN, ROLLIN', ROLLIN' ROL-L-L-LIN' BONE YAH-DAH-KWA-KWA-KWA -
KAKE OF SOAP.
I NEVER ROLLS NO SNAKE EYES, I NEVER ROLLS NO TREES - I ROLLS ME SEVEN I ROLLS ME 'LEVEN - I ROLLS DE GOLDEN ROLL TO HEAVEN - FOH, I OLLIZ ROLLS TO PLEASE WA DA-WA-WA-DA-WEEE
WATTA -
DROP SOAP IN THE WATTA WOTS IMMONG THE BOWL
STIR UP INTO A FROTT.
NOW TO PROKEW A PIPE AND BLOW UP A BUBBIL.
HEY, 'WEEVIL' - OH, BOWL WEEVIL' COME HERE, QUICK !!!
LOOK "KOTTON," IT'S FREE - HELP YOURSELF.
OOOOH-HH-
THIS KIND DEED SHOULD GET ME IN GOOD WITH THAT LITTLE 'INSECT'
PFU! - !!!
VILLAIN !!!
ZIP
HE'S EITHER SPOOFING ME, OR HE'S GOT GAS ON HIS STUMMICK - I DON'T KNOW WHETHER TO JAIL OR A HOSPITAL
AN' WEN I ROLLS I OLLIZ ROLLS MY OWN -
HERRIMAN
10-2

October 2nd, 1932.

KRAZY KAT ∴ ∴ By Herriman

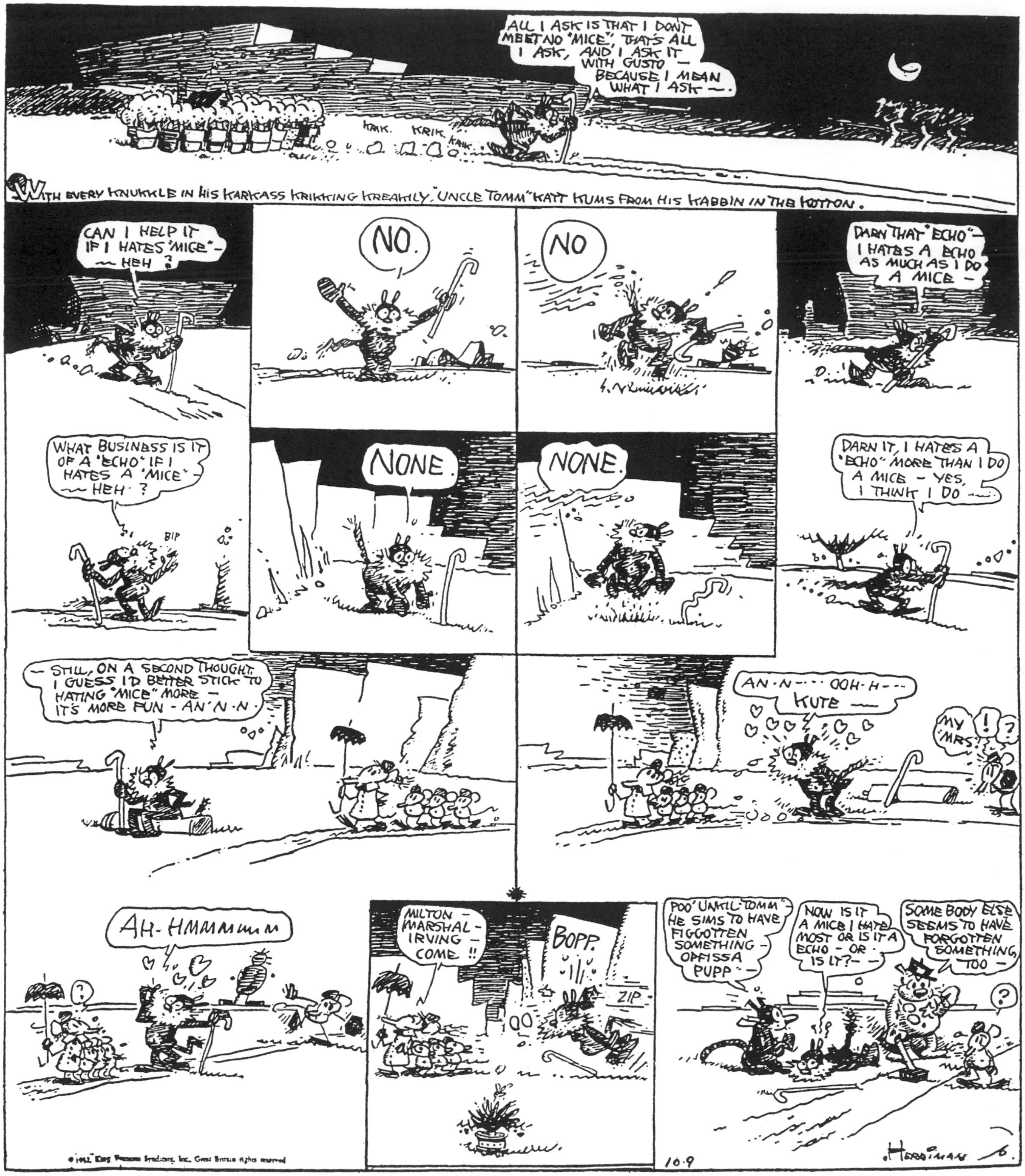
ALL I ASK IS THAT I DON'T MEET NO "MICE", THAT'S ALL I ASK, AND I ASK IT WITH GUSTO — BECAUSE I MEAN WHAT I ASK —.
KRIK. KRIK. KRIK.
WITH EVERY KNUKKLE IN HIS KARKASS KRIKKING KREAKILY, "UNCLE TOMM" KATT KUMS FROM HIS KABBIN IN THE KOTTON.
CAN I HELP IT IF I HATES "MICE" — HEH ?
NO.
NO
DARN THAT "ECHO" — I HATES A ECHO AS MUCH AS I DO A MICE —
WHAT BUSINESS IS IT OF A "ECHO" IF I HATES A "MICE" — HEH ?
BIP
NONE.
NONE.
DARN IT, I HATES A "ECHO" MORE THAN I DO A MICE — YES, I THINK I DO —
— STILL, ON A SECOND THOUGHT, I GUESS I'D BETTER STICK TO HATING "MICE" MORE — IT'S MORE FUN — AN-N-N.
AN-N--- OOH-H--- KUTE —
MY MRS
AH-HMMMMM
MILTON — MARSHAL — IRVING COME !!
BOPP.
ZIP
POO' UNKILL "TOMM" HE SIMS TO HAVE FIGGOTTEN SOMETHING — OFFISSA PUPP —
NOW IS IT A MICE I HATE MOST OR IS IT A ECHO — OR IS IT? —
SOME BODY ELSE SEEMS TO HAVE FORGOTTEN SOMETHING, TOO —
10-9

October 9th, 1932.

KRAZY KAT ⁘ ⁘ By Herriman

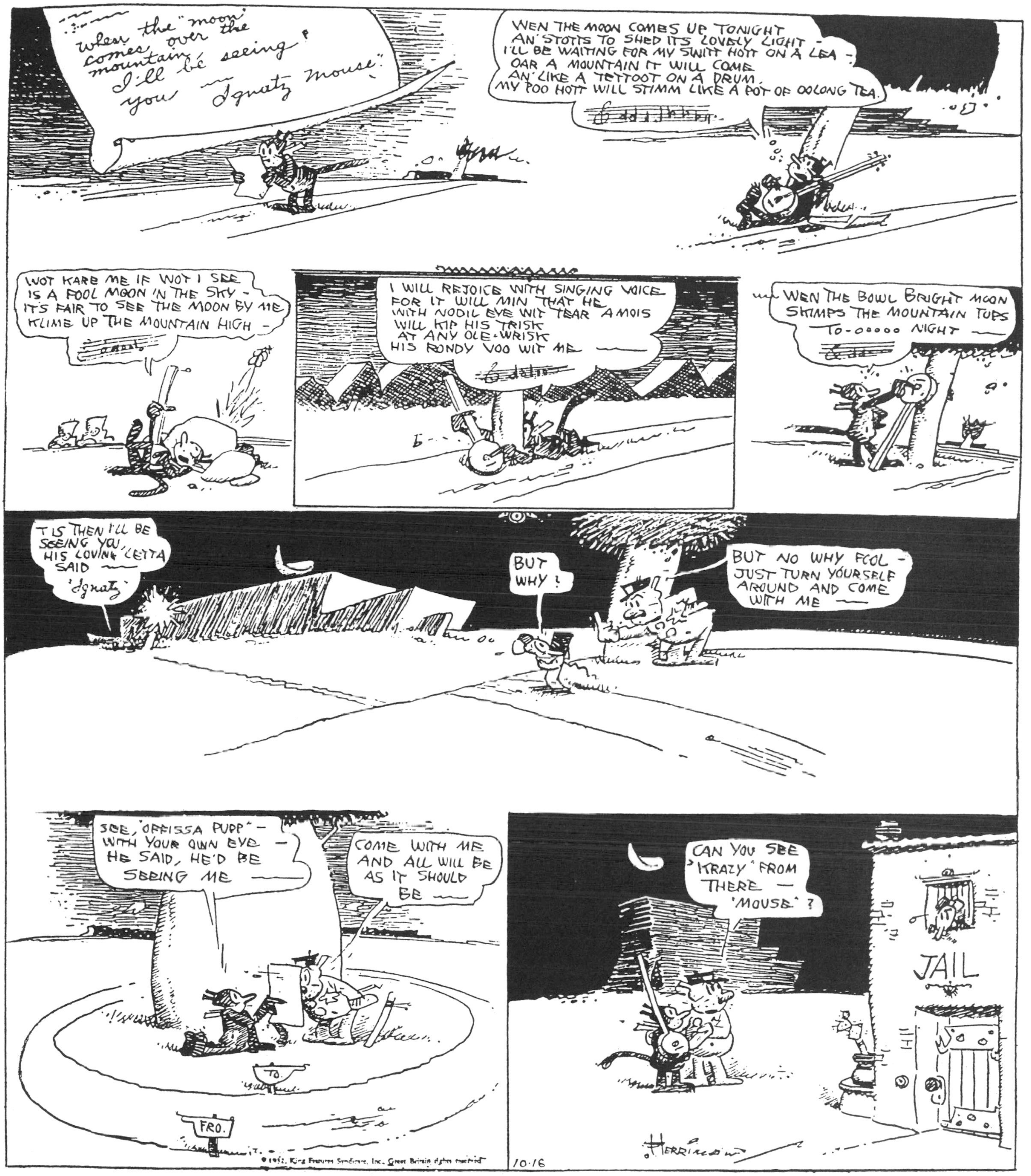

When the "moon" comes over the mountain, I'll be seeing you — "Ignatz Mouse."
WEN THE MOON COMES UP TONIGHT AN' STOTTS TO SHED ITS LOVELY LIGHT - I'LL BE WAITING FOR MY SWITT HOTT ON A LEA - OAR A MOUNTAIN IT WILL COME AN' LIKE A TETTOOT ON A DRUM, MY POO HOTT WILL STIMM LIKE A POT OF OOLONG TEA.
WOT KARE ME IF WOT I SEE IS A FOOL MOON IN THE SKY - IT'S FAIR TO SEE THE MOON BY ME KLIME UP THE MOUNTAIN HIGH -
I WILL REJOICE WITH SINGING VOICE FOR IT WILL MIN THAT HE WITH NODIL EYE WIT TEAR AMOIS WILL KIP HIS TRISK AT ANY OLE-WRISK HIS RONDY VOO WIT ME
WEN THE BOWL BRIGHT MOON SKIMPS THE MOUNTAIN TUPS TO-OOOOO NIGHT
T'IS THEN I'LL BE SEEING YOU, HIS LOVING LETTA SAID — 'Ignatz'
BUT WHY!
BUT NO WHY FOOL - JUST TURN YOURSELF AROUND AND COME WITH ME
SEE, 'OFFISSA PUPP' - WITH YOUR OWN EYE - HE SAID, HE'D BE SEEING ME
COME WITH ME AND ALL WILL BE AS IT SHOULD BE
CAN YOU SEE 'KRAZY' FROM THERE — 'MOUSE'?
JAIL
TO.
FRO.
HERRIMAN
10-16

October 16th, 1932.

KRAZY KAT ⁘ ⁘ By Herriman

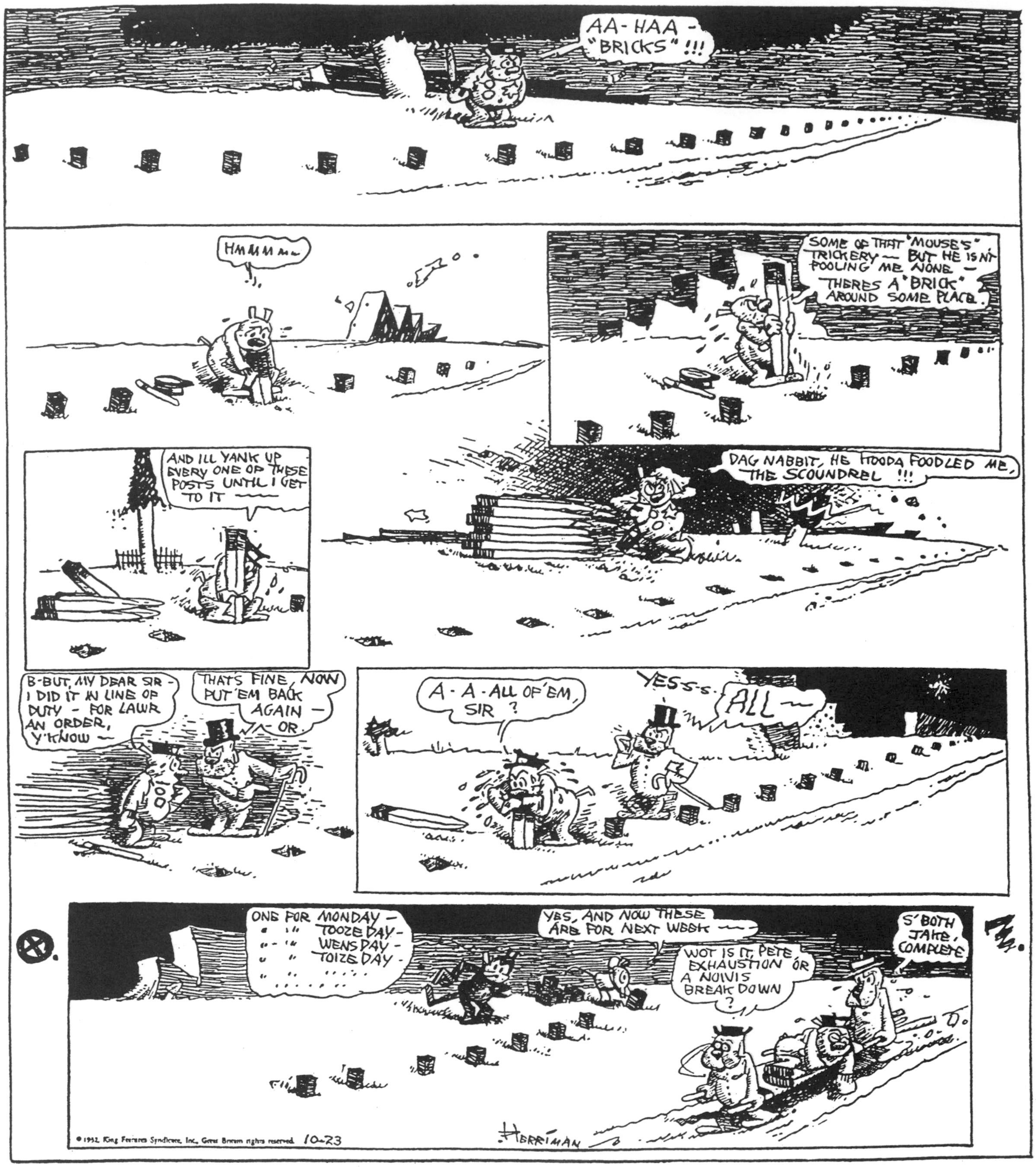

AA-HAA - "BRICKS" !!!
HMMMM
SOME OF THAT "MOUSE'S" TRICKERY — BUT HE IS'NT FOOLING ME NONE — THERES A "BRICK" AROUND SOME PLACE.
AND ILL YANK UP EVERY ONE OF THESE POSTS UNTIL I GET TO IT —
DAG NABBIT, HE HOODA FOODLED ME, THE SCOUNDREL !!!
B-BUT, MY DEAR SIR - I DID IT IN LINE OF DUTY - FOR LAWR AN ORDER, Y'KNOW —
THAT'S FINE, NOW PUT 'EM BACK AGAIN — - OR.
A-A-ALL OF 'EM, SIR ?
YES-S-S
ALL —
ONE FOR MONDAY - " " TOOZE DAY - " " WENS DAY - " " TOIZE DAY -
YES, AND NOW THESE ARE FOR NEXT WEEK —
WOT IS IT, PETE, EXHAUSTION OR A NUIVIS BREAK DOWN ?
S' BOTH JAKE, COMPLETE
© 1932, King Features Syndicate, Inc., Great Britain rights reserved. 10-23
HERRIMAN

October 23rd, 1932.

KRAZY KAT ⁘ ⁘ By Herriman

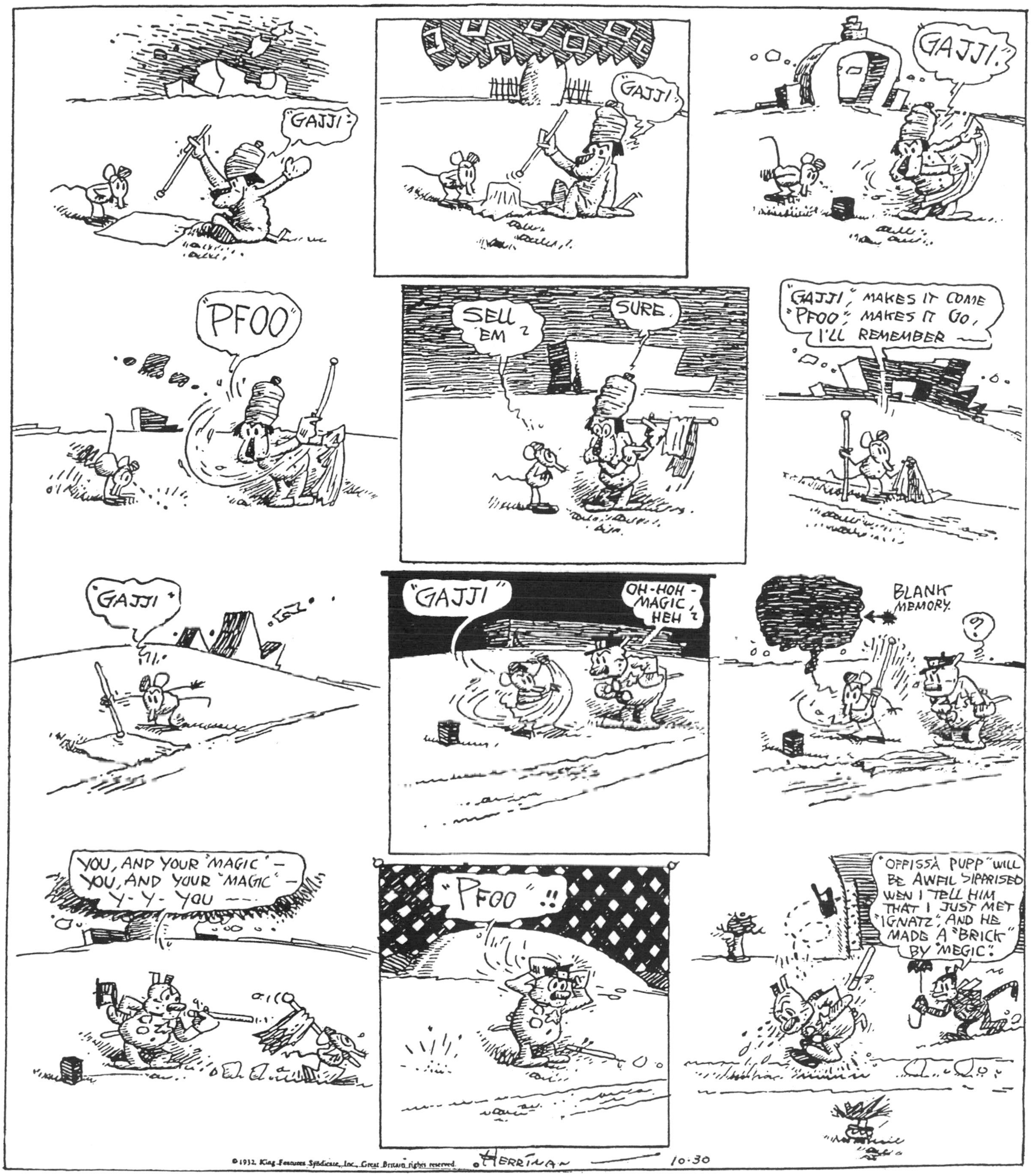

"GAJJI"
"GAJJI"
"GAJJI"
"PFOO"
SELL 'EM?
SURE
"GAJJI," MAKES IT COME
"PFOO," MAKES IT GO,
I'LL REMEMBER
"GAJJI"
"GAJJI"
OH-HOH - MAGIC, HEH?
BLANK MEMORY.
?
YOU, AND YOUR "MAGIC" - YOU, AND YOUR "MAGIC" - Y-Y- YOU
"PFOO" !!
"OFFISSA PUPP" WILL BE AWFIL SIPPRISED WEN I TELL HIM THAT I JUST MET "IGNATZ", AND HE MADE A "BRICK" BY "MEGIC".
©1932, King Features Syndicate, Inc., Great Britain rights reserved.
HERRIMAN
10-30

October 30th, 1932.

KRAZY KAT ⁘ ⁘ By Herriman

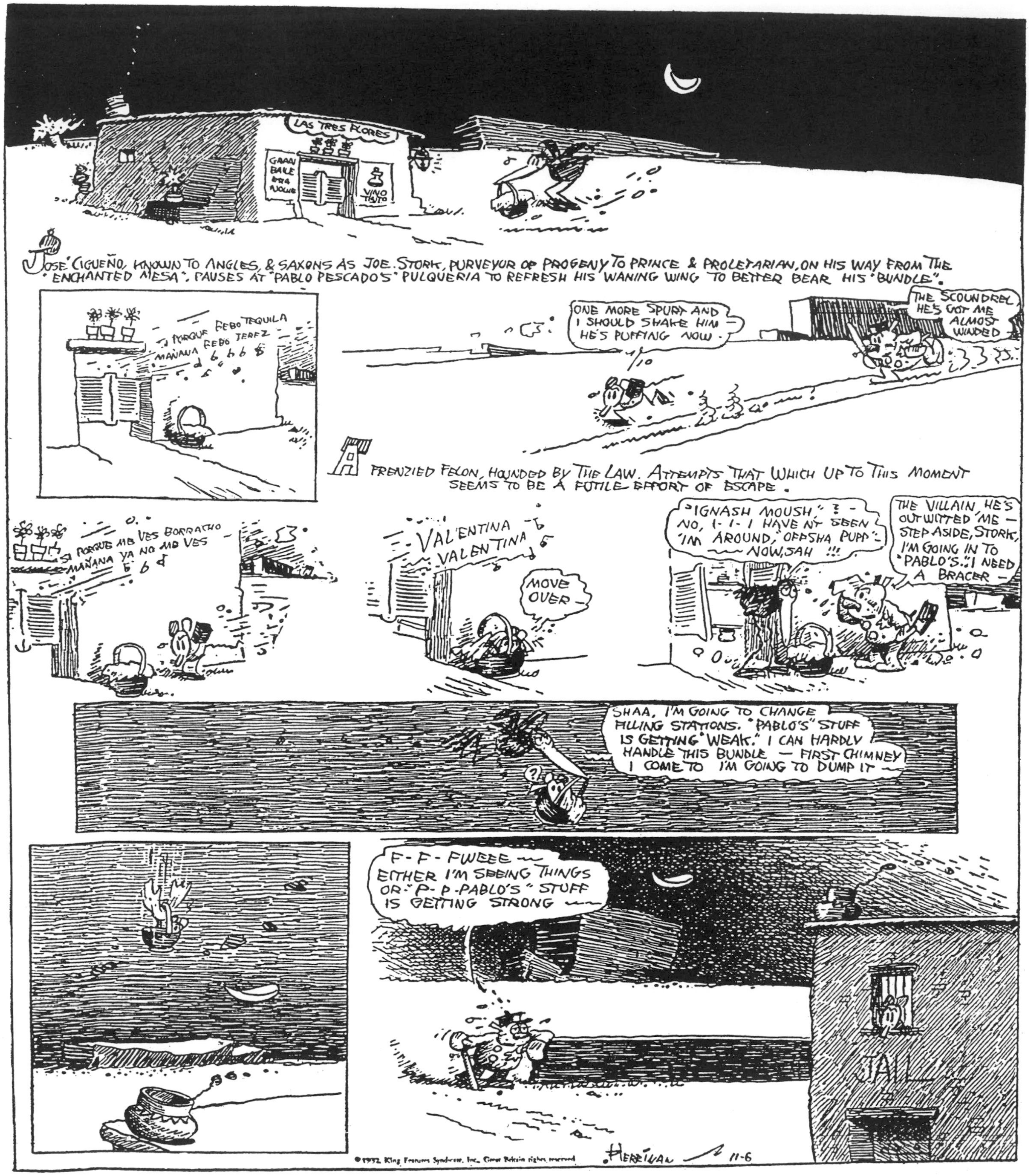

LAS TRES FLORES
GRAN BAILE ESTA NOCHE
VINO TINTO
JOSE' CIGUEÑO, KNOWN TO ANGLES, & SAXONS AS JOE. STORK, PURVEYOR OF PROGENY TO PRINCE & PROLETARIAN, ON HIS WAY FROM THE "ENCHANTED MESA", PAUSES AT "PABLO PESCADO'S" PULQUERIA TO REFRESH HIS WANING WING TO BETTER BEAR HIS "BUNDLE".
SI PORQUE FEBO TEQUILA MAÑANA FEBO JEREZ
ONE MORE SPURT AND I SHOULD SHAKE HIM — HE'S PUFFING NOW.
THE SCOUNDREL, HE'S GOT ME ALMOST WINDED —
A FRENZIED FELON, HOUNDED BY THE LAW. ATTEMPTS THAT WHICH UP TO THIS MOMENT SEEMS TO BE A FUTILE EFFORT OF ESCAPE.
SI PORQUE ME VES BORRACHO MAÑANA YA NO ME VES
VAL'ENTINA VALENTINA
MOVE OVER —
"IGNASH MOUSH," ? — NO, I-I-I HAVE N'T SEEN 'IM AROUND, OFFSHA PUPP — NOW, SAH !!!
THE VILLAIN, HE'S OUTWITTED ME — STEP ASIDE, STORK, I'M GOING IN TO "PABLO'S." I NEED A BRACER —
SHAA, I'M GOING TO CHANGE FILLING STATIONS. "PABLO'S" STUFF IS GETTING "WEAK." I CAN HARDLY HANDLE THIS BUNDLE — FIRST CHIMNEY I COME TO I'M GOING TO DUMP IT —
F-F-FWEEE — EITHER I'M SEEING THINGS OR "P-P-PABLO'S" STUFF IS GETTING STRONG —
JAIL
HERRIMAN 11-6

November 6th, 1932.

KRAZY KAT ⁘ ⁘ By Herriman

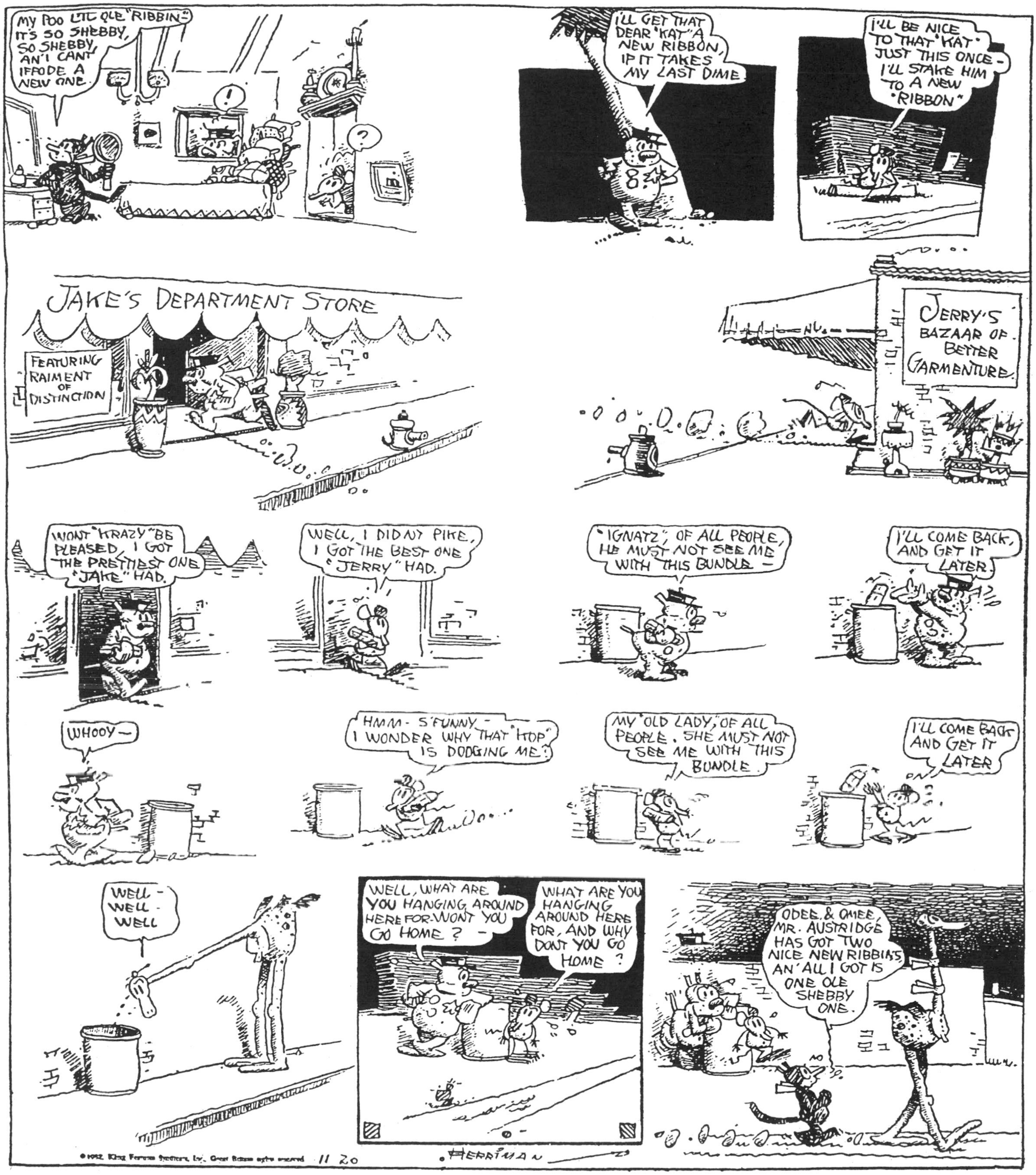

MY POO LIT-OLE "RIBBIN"- IT'S SO SHEBBY, SO SHEBBY, AN' I CAN'T IFFODE A NEW ONE.
I'LL GET THAT DEAR "KAT" A NEW RIBBON, IF IT TAKES MY LAST DIME.
I'LL BE NICE TO THAT "KAT" JUST THIS ONCE - I'LL STAKE HIM TO A NEW "RIBBON"
JAKE'S DEPARTMENT STORE
FEATURING RAIMENT OF DISTINCTION
JERRY'S BAZAAR OF BETTER GARMENTURE
WONT "KRAZY" BE PLEASED, I GOT THE PRETTIEST ONE "JAKE" HAD.
WELL, I DIDN'T PIKE, I GOT THE BEST ONE "JERRY" HAD.
"IGNATZ", OF ALL PEOPLE, HE MUST NOT SEE ME WITH THIS BUNDLE -
I'LL COME BACK, AND GET IT LATER.
WHOOY -
HMM - S'FUNNY - I WONDER WHY THAT "KOP" IS DODGING ME?
MY "OLD LADY," OF ALL PEOPLE. SHE MUST NOT SEE ME WITH THIS BUNDLE.
I'LL COME BACK AND GET IT LATER
WELL - WELL - WELL
WELL, WHAT ARE YOU HANGING AROUND HERE FOR - WONT YOU GO HOME? -
WHAT ARE YOU HANGING AROUND HERE FOR, AND WHY DONT YOU GO HOME?
ODEE & OMEE, MR. AUSTRIDGE HAS GOT TWO NICE NEW RIBBINS AN' ALL I GOT IS ONE OLE SHEBBY ONE.
11 20
HERRIMAN

November 20th, 1932.

KRAZY KAT ⁘ ⁘ By Herriman

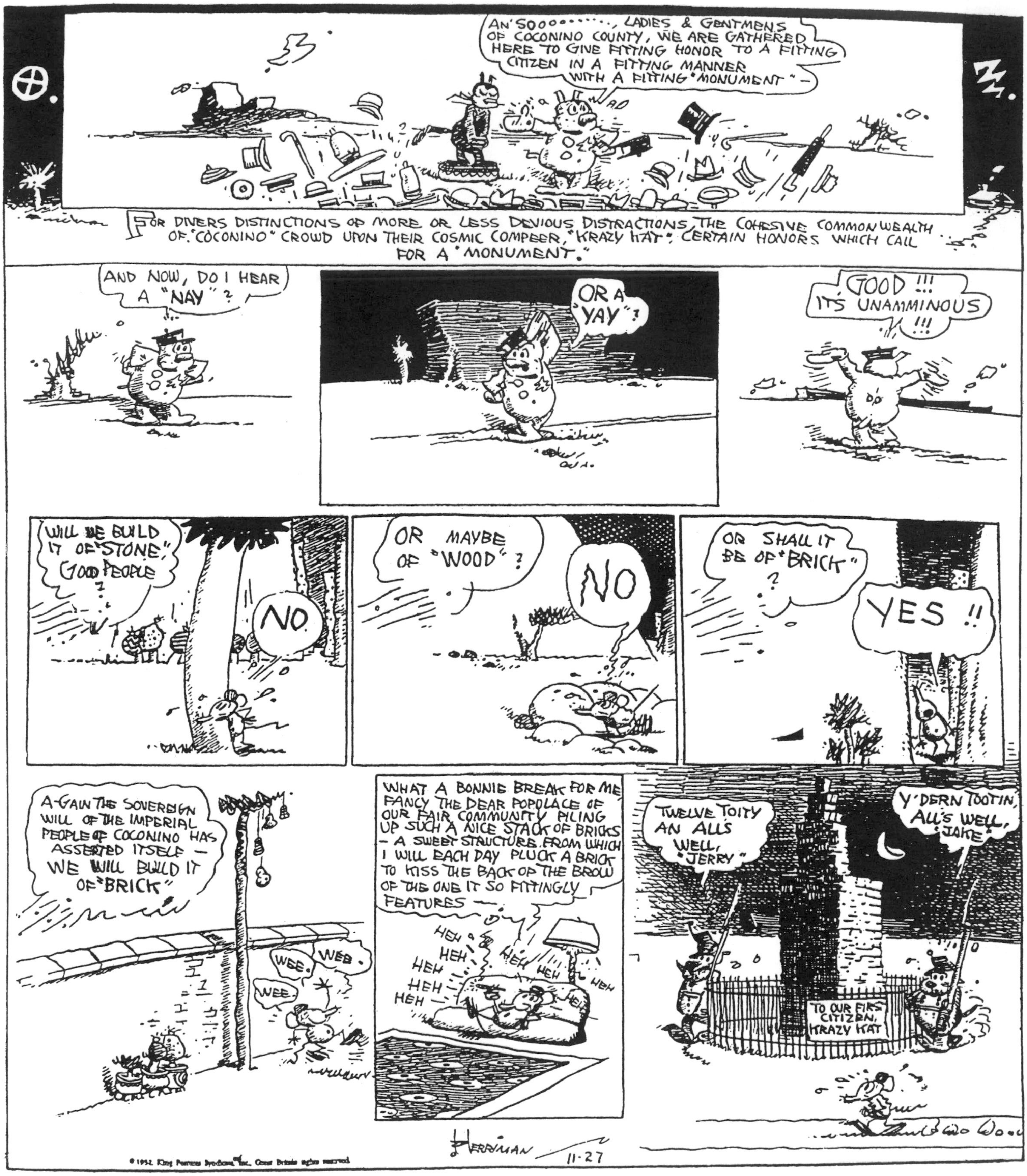

AN' SOOO......., LADIES & GENTMENS OF COCONINO COUNTY, WE ARE GATHERED HERE TO GIVE FITTING HONOR TO A FITTING CITIZEN IN A FITTING MANNER WITH A FITTING "MONUMENT" —
FOR DIVERS DISTINCTIONS OF MORE OR LESS DEVIOUS DISTRACTIONS, THE COHESIVE COMMONWEALTH OF "COCONINO" CROWD UPON THEIR COSMIC COMPEER, "KRAZY KAT", CERTAIN HONORS WHICH CALL FOR A "MONUMENT."
AND NOW, DO I HEAR A "NAY"?
OR A "YAY"?
GOOD !!! ITS UNAMMINOUS !!!
WILL WE BUILD IT OF "STONE", GOOD PEOPLE ?
NO.
OR MAYBE OF "WOOD"?
NO
OR SHALL IT BE OF "BRICK"?
YES !!
A-GAIN THE SOVEREIGN WILL OF THE IMPERIAL PEOPLE OF COCONINO HAS ASSERTED ITSELF — WE WILL BUILD IT OF "BRICK"
WEE. WEE. WEE.
WHAT A BONNIE BREAK FOR ME FANCY THE DEAR POPULACE OF OUR FAIR COMMUNITY PILING UP SUCH A NICE STACK OF BRICKS — A SWEET STRUCTURE FROM WHICH I WILL EACH DAY PLUCK A BRICK TO KISS THE BACK OF THE BROW OF THE ONE IT SO FITTINGLY FEATURES —
HEH HEH HEH HEH HEH HEH HEH HEH HEH
TWELVE TOITY AN ALLS WELL, "JERRY"
Y'DERN TOOTIN, ALL'S WELL, "JAKE"
TO OUR FIRST CITIZEN, KRAZY KAT
HERRIMAN 11-27

November 27th, 1932.

KRAZY KAT ⁘ ⁘ By Herriman

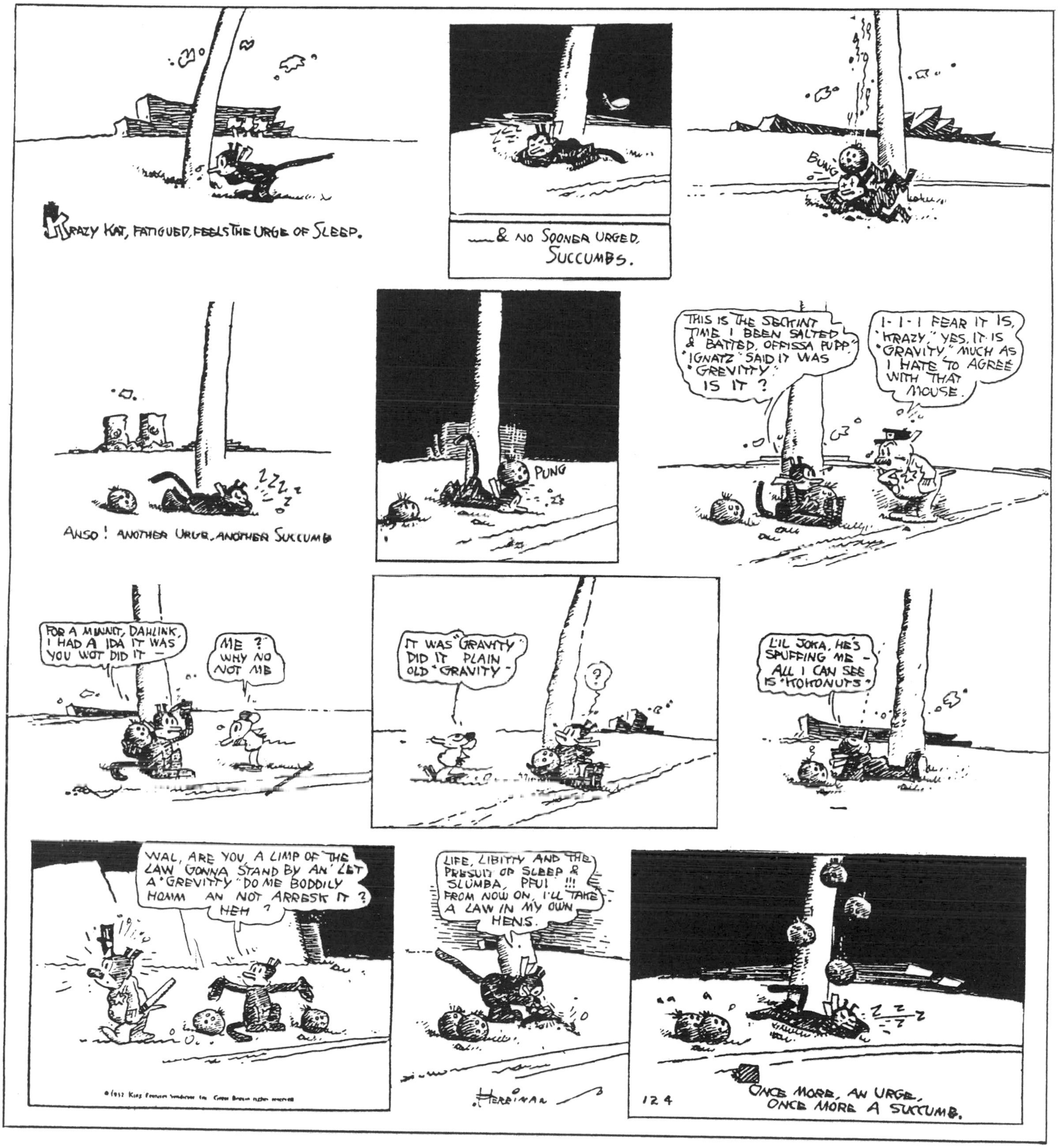
KRAZY KAT, FATIGUED, FEELS THE URGE OF SLEEP.
— & NO SOONER URGED, SUCCUMBS.
BUNG
ANSO! ANOTHER URGE, ANOTHER SUCCUMB
PUNG
THIS IS THE SECKINT TIME I BEEN SALTED & BATTED, OFFISSA PUPP. "IGNATZ" SAID IT WAS "GREVITTY." IS IT ?
I-I-I FEAR IT IS, "KRAZY," YES, IT IS "GRAVITY," MUCH AS I HATE TO AGREE WITH THAT MOUSE.
FOR A MINNIT, DAHLINK, I HAD A IDA IT WAS YOU WOT DID IT —
ME ? WHY NO NOT ME
IT WAS "GRAVITY" DID IT PLAIN OLD "GRAVITY" —
?
L'IL JOKA, HE'S SPUFFING ME — ALL I CAN SEE IS "KOKONUTS"
WAL, ARE YOU, A LIMP OF THE LAW GONNA STAND BY AN' LET A "GREVITTY" DO ME BODDILY HOMM AN NOT ARRESK IT ?
HEH ?
LIFE, LIBITTY AND THE PRESUIT OF SLEEP & SLUMBA, PFUI !!! FROM NOW ON, I'LL TAKE A LAW IN MY OWN HENS.
HERRIMAN
12 4
ONCE MORE, AN URGE, ONCE MORE A SUCCUMB.

December 4th, 1932.

KRAZY KAT ⁘ ⁘ By Herriman

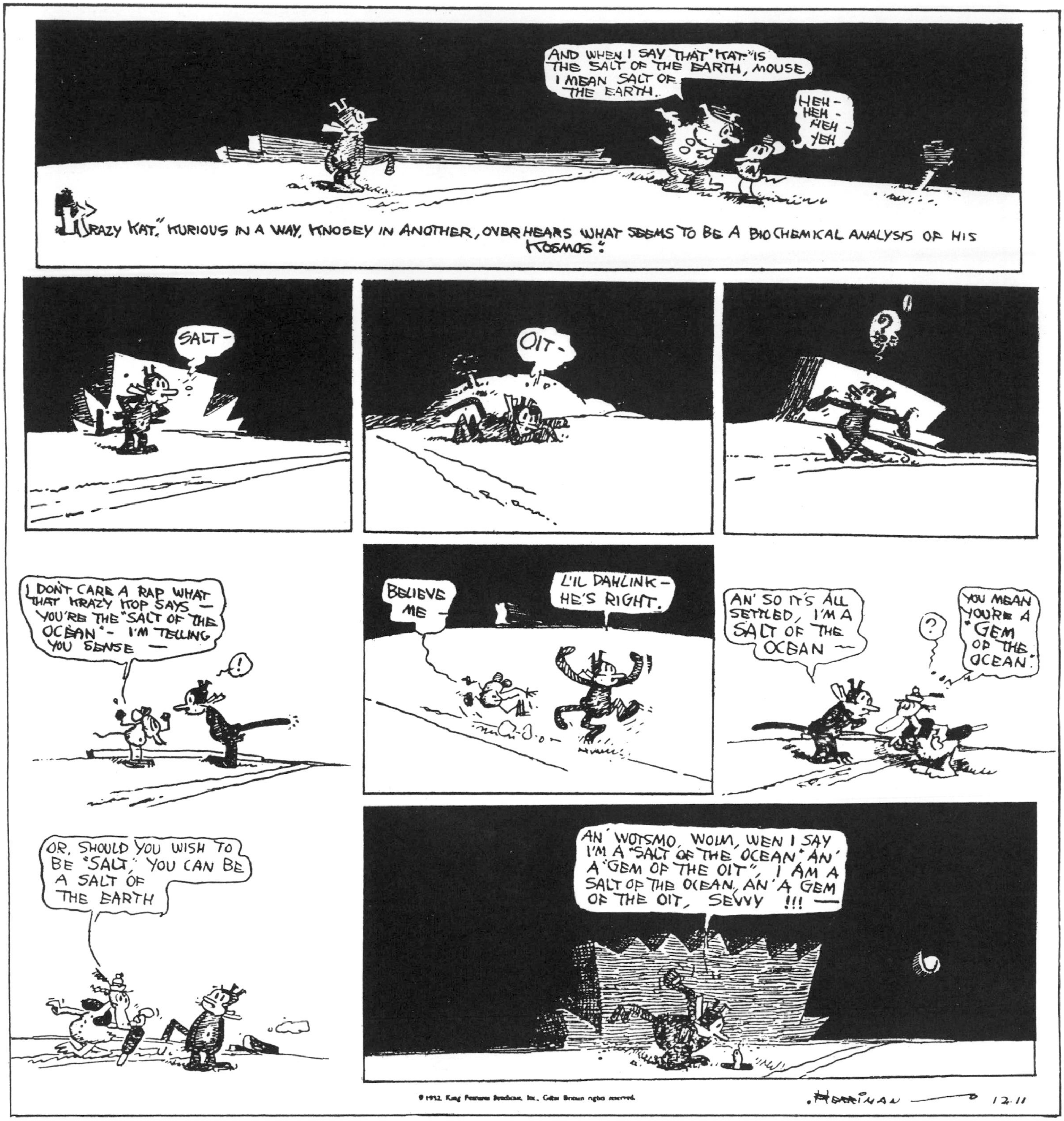

AND WHEN I SAY THAT "KAT" IS THE SALT OF THE EARTH, MOUSE I MEAN SALT OF THE EARTH.
HEH-HEH-HEH-YEH
"KRAZY KAT," KURIOUS IN A WAY, KNOBEY IN ANOTHER, OVERHEARS WHAT SEEMS TO BE A BIOCHEMICAL ANALYSIS OF HIS KOSMOS:
SALT-
OIT-
?
I DON'T CARE A RAP WHAT THAT KRAZY KOP SAYS — YOU'RE THE "SALT OF THE OCEAN" - I'M TELLING YOU SENSE —
!
BELIEVE ME —
L'IL DAHLINK — HE'S RIGHT.
AN' SO IT'S ALL SETTLED, I'M A SALT OF THE OCEAN —
?
YOU MEAN YOU'RE A "GEM OF THE OCEAN."
OR, SHOULD YOU WISH TO BE "SALT," YOU CAN BE A SALT OF THE EARTH
AN' WOTSMO, WOIM, WEN I SAY I'M A "SALT OF THE OCEAN" AN' A "GEM OF THE OIT", I AM A SALT OF THE OCEAN, AN' A GEM OF THE OIT, SEVVY !!! —
HERRIMAN 12.11

December 11th, 1932.

KRAZY KAT ∴ ∴ By Herriman

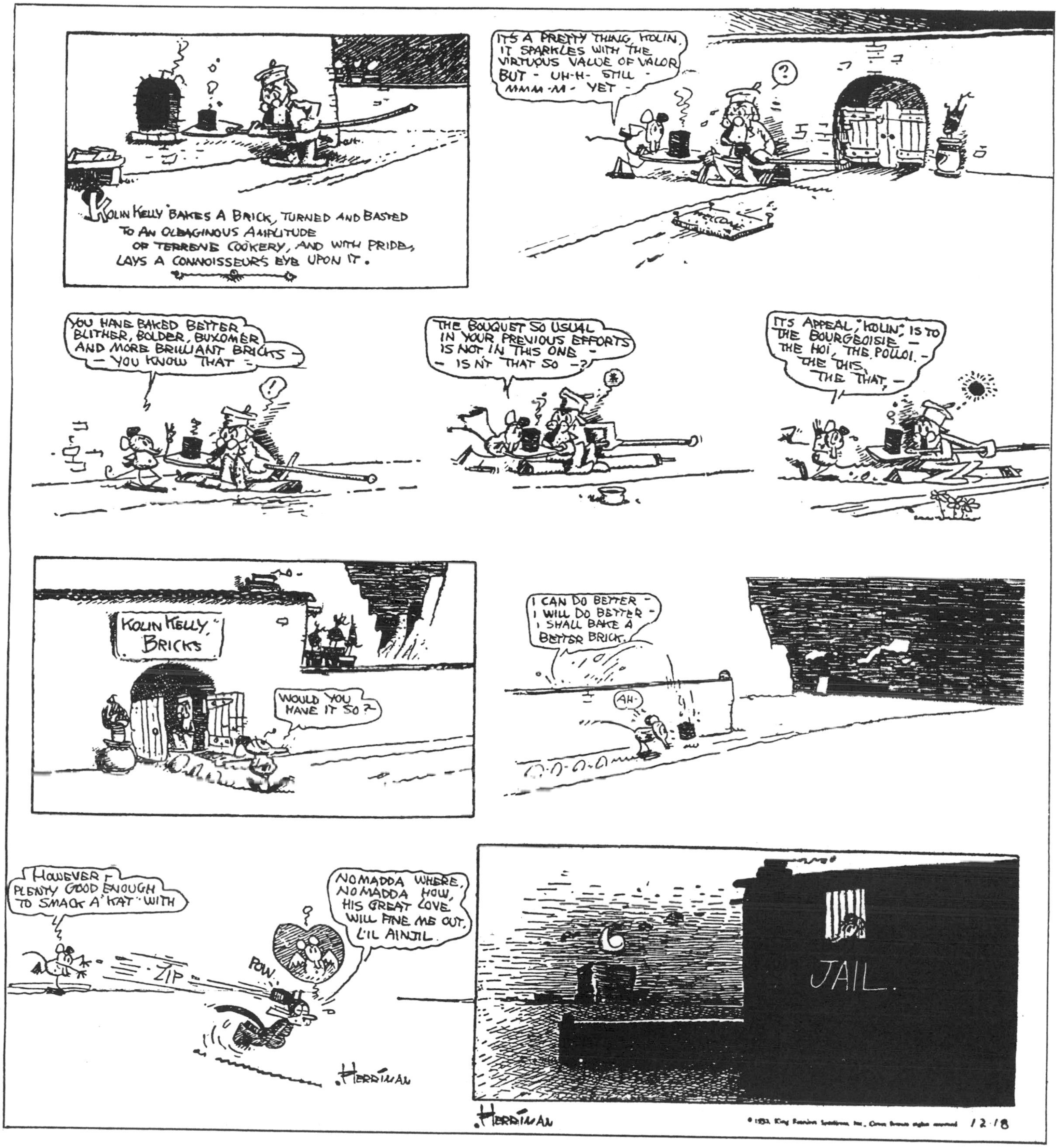
KOLIN KELLY BAKES A BRICK, TURNED AND BASTED TO AN OLEAGINOUS AMPLITUDE OF TERRENE COOKERY, AND WITH PRIDE, LAYS A CONNOISSEUR'S EYE UPON IT.
ITS A PRETTY THING, KOLIN, IT SPARKLES WITH THE VIRTUOUS VALUE OF VALOR BUT - UH-H- STILL - MMM-M- YET -
YOU HAVE BAKED BETTER BLITHER, BOLDER, BUXOMER AND MORE BRILLIANT BRICKS — — YOU KNOW THAT —
THE BOUQUET SO USUAL IN YOUR PREVIOUS EFFORTS IS NOT IN THIS ONE — — IS N'T THAT SO —?
ITS APPEAL, "KOLIN" IS TO THE BOURGEOISIE — THE HOI, THE POLLOI. — THE "THIS," THE "THAT," —
KOLIN KELLY BRICKS
WOULD YOU HAVE IT SO ?
I CAN DO BETTER — I WILL DO BETTER — I SHALL BAKE A BETTER BRICK.
AH-
HOWEVER — PLENTY GOOD ENOUGH TO SMACK A "KAT" WITH
ZIP
POW
NOMADDA WHERE, NOMADDA HOW, HIS GREAT LOVE WILL FINE ME OUT. L'IL AINJIL.
HERRIMAN
JAIL.
HERRIMAN
12-18

December 18th, 1932.

KRAZY KAT ∴ ∴ By Herriman

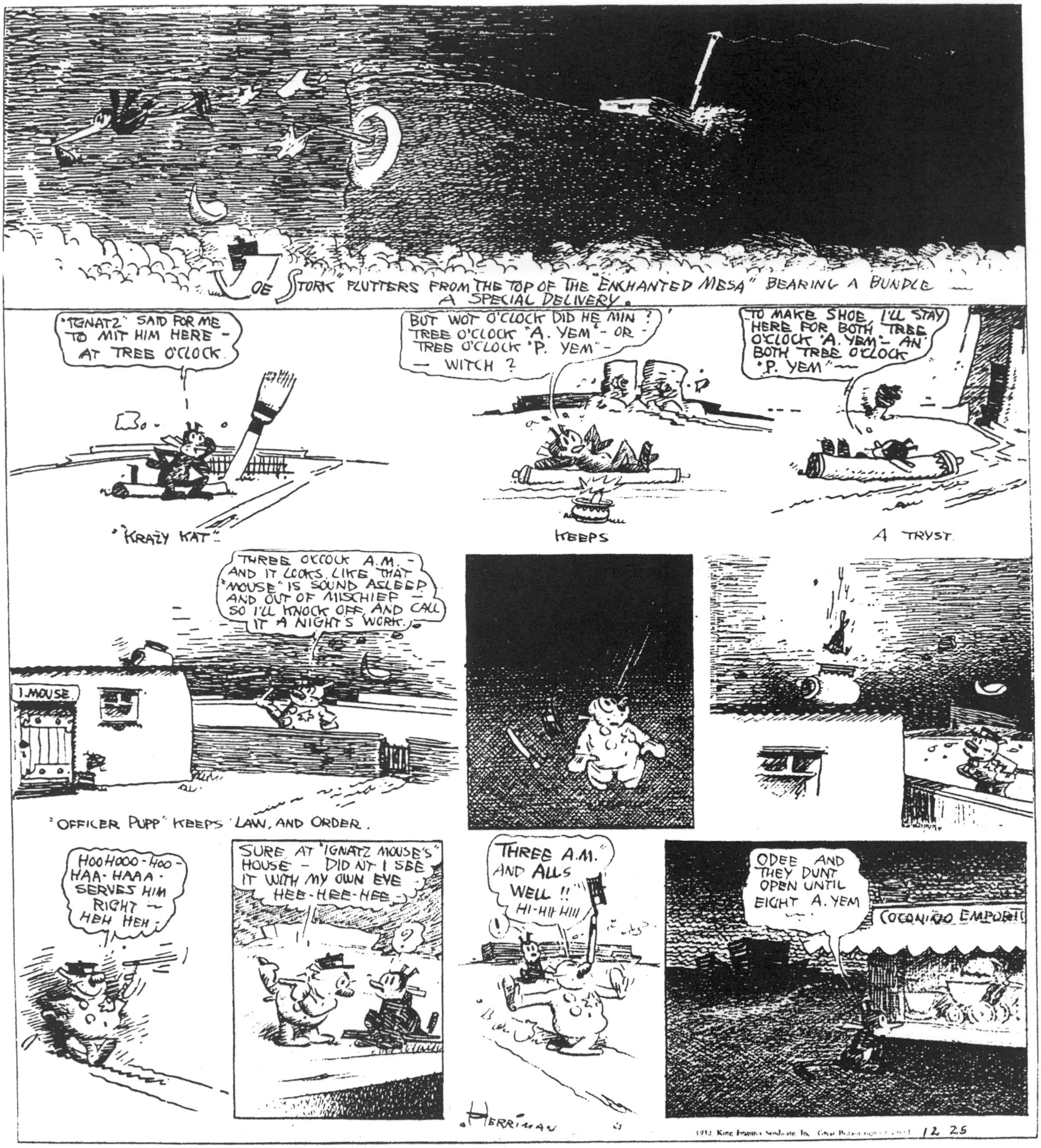
"JOE STORK" FLUTTERS FROM THE TOP OF THE "ENKHANTED MESA" BEARING A BUNDLE — A SPECIAL DELIVERY.
"IGNATZ" SAID FOR ME TO MIT HIM HERE - AT TREE O'CLOCK.
"KRAZY KAT"
BUT WOT O'CLOCK DID HE MIN? TREE O'CLOCK "A. YEM" - OR TREE O'CLOCK "P. YEM" - WITCH?
KEEPS
TO MAKE SHOE, I'LL STAY HERE FOR BOTH TREE O'CLOCK "A. YEM" - AN BOTH TREE O'CLOCK "P. YEM" —
A TRYST.
THREE O'CLOCK A.M. - AND IT LOOKS LIKE THAT "MOUSE" IS SOUND ASLEEP AND OUT OF MISCHIEF - SO I'LL KNOCK OFF, AND CALL IT A NIGHT'S WORK.
I. MOUSE
"OFFICER PUPP" KEEPS LAW, AND ORDER.
HOO HOOO - HOO - HAA - HAAA - SERVES HIM RIGHT - HEH HEH -
SURE AT "IGNATZ MOUSE'S" HOUSE - DID N'T I SEE IT WITH MY OWN EYE HEE-HEE-HEE
THREE A.M. AND ALLS WELL !! HI-HI HIII
ODEE AND THEY DUNT OPEN UNTIL EIGHT A. YEM
COCONINO EMPORI
HERRIMAN
12 25

December 25th, 1932.

The Daily Krazy Kat Strip, 1931.

What was going on in the daily *Krazy Kat* kontinuity in 1931? Published in tandem with the Sunday *Kat* pages from 1916 through 1944, the daily strip appeared in some twenty newspapers of obvious good taste and judgement, from the *St Louis Post Dispatch* to the *Baltimore American*. Here is a rich sample of what millions of Americans were reading once upon a kat.

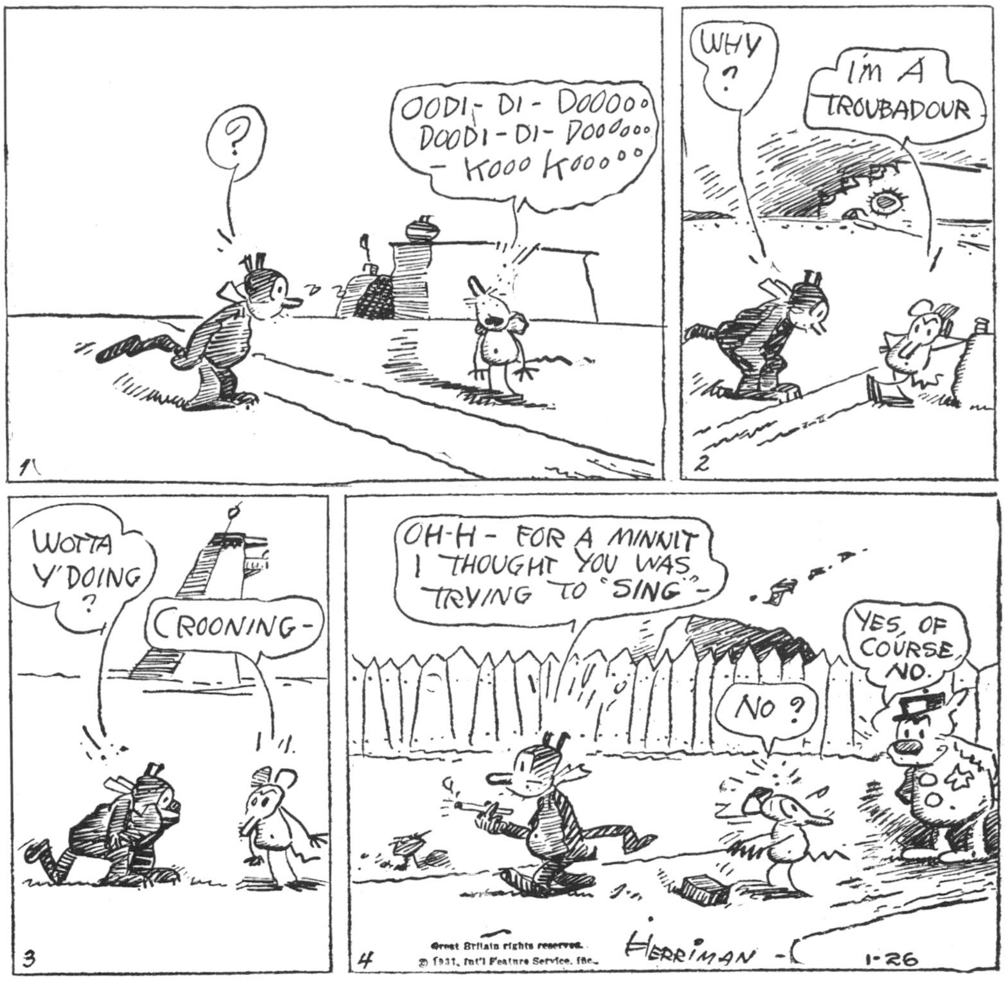
?
OODI- DI- DOOOOO
DOODI-DI-DOOOOOO
- KOOO KOOOOO
WHY ?
I'M A TROUBADOUR
WOTTA Y'DOING ?
CROONING-
OH-H- FOR A MINNIT I THOUGHT YOU WAS TRYING TO "SING"-
NO ?
YES, OF COURSE NO.
Great Britain rights reserved.
© 1931, Int'l Feature Service, Inc.
HERRIMAN
1-26

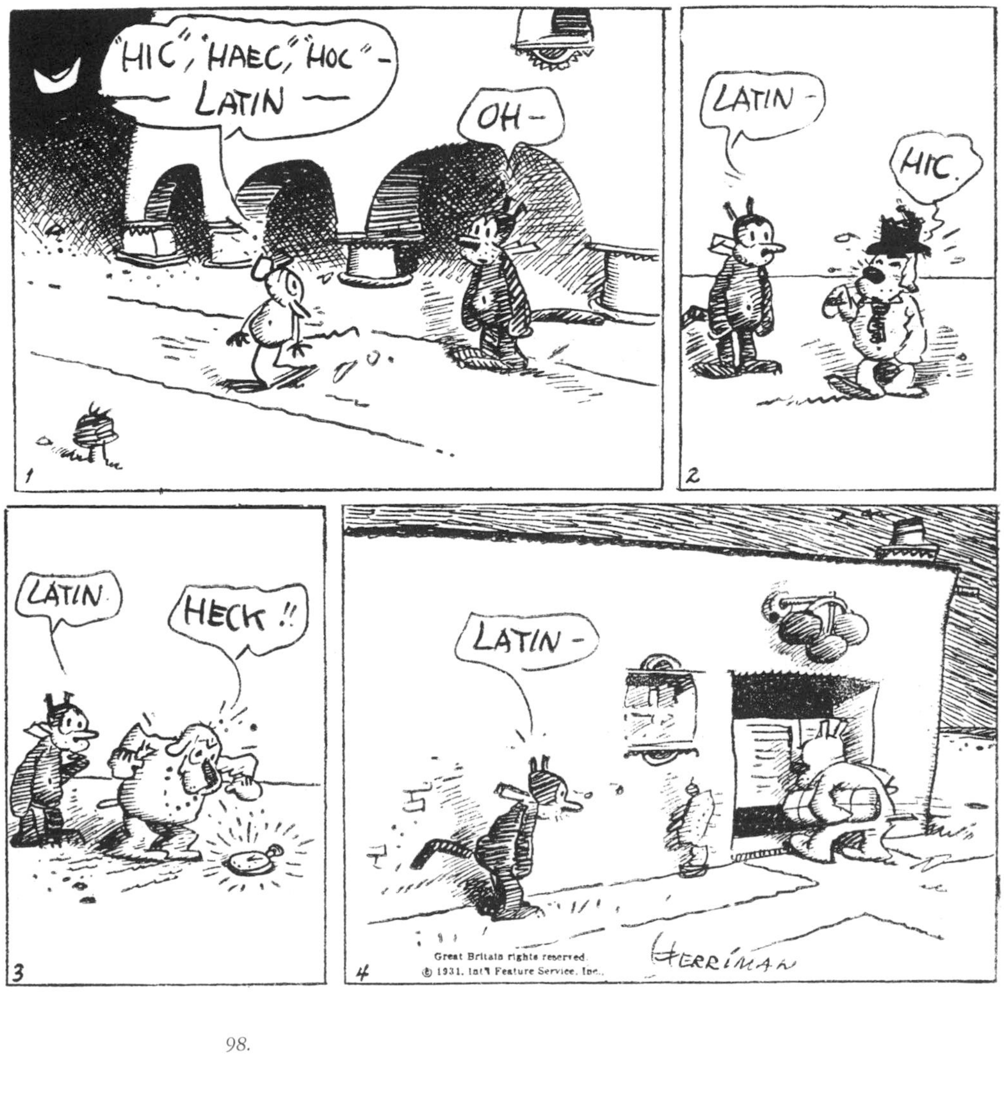
"HIC", "HAEC", "HOC" -
— LATIN —
OH-
LATIN -
HIC.
LATIN
HECK !!
LATIN -
Great Britain rights reserved.
© 1931, Int'l Feature Service, Inc.
HERRIMAN

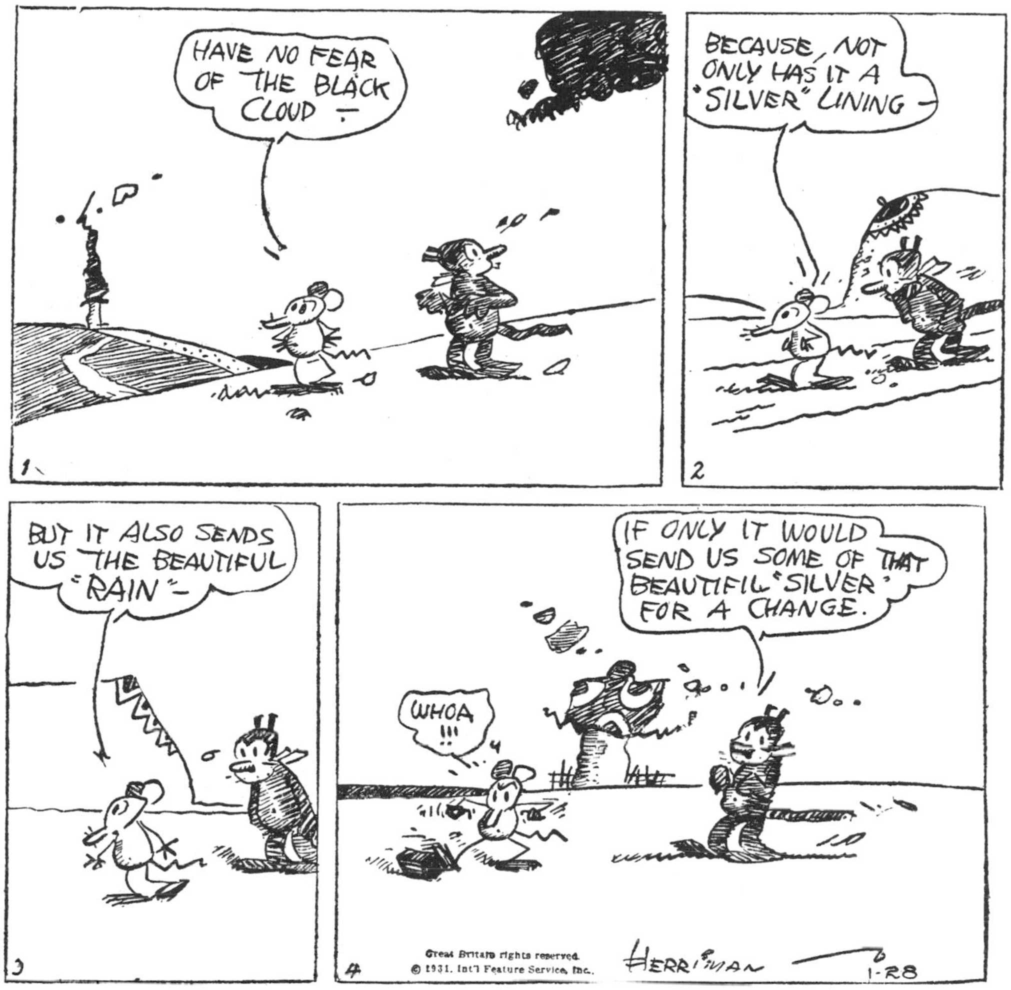
HAVE NO FEAR OF THE BLACK CLOUD -
BECAUSE, NOT ONLY HAS IT A "SILVER" LINING -
BUT IT ALSO SENDS US THE BEAUTIFUL "RAIN" -
WHOA !!!
IF ONLY IT WOULD SEND US SOME OF THAT BEAUTIFUL "SILVER" FOR A CHANGE.
Great Britain rights reserved.
© 1931, Int'l Feature Service, Inc.
HERRIMAN
1-28

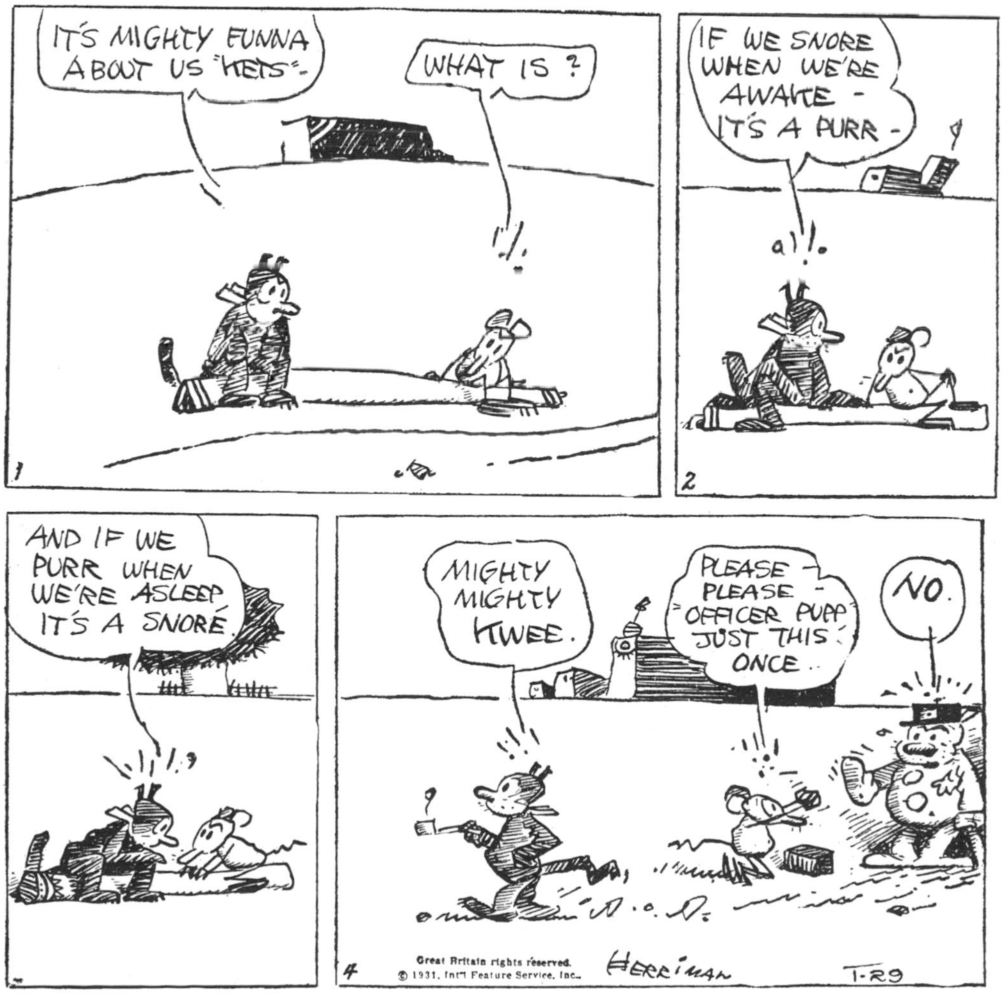
IT'S MIGHTY FUNNA ABOUT US "KETS" -
WHAT IS ?
IF WE SNORE WHEN WE'RE AWAKE - IT'S A PURR -
AND IF WE PURR WHEN WE'RE ASLEEP IT'S A SNORE
MIGHTY MIGHTY KWEE.
PLEASE - PLEASE - OFFICER PUPP JUST THIS ONCE
NO.
Great Britain rights reserved.
© 1931, Int'l Feature Service, Inc.
HERRIMAN
1-29

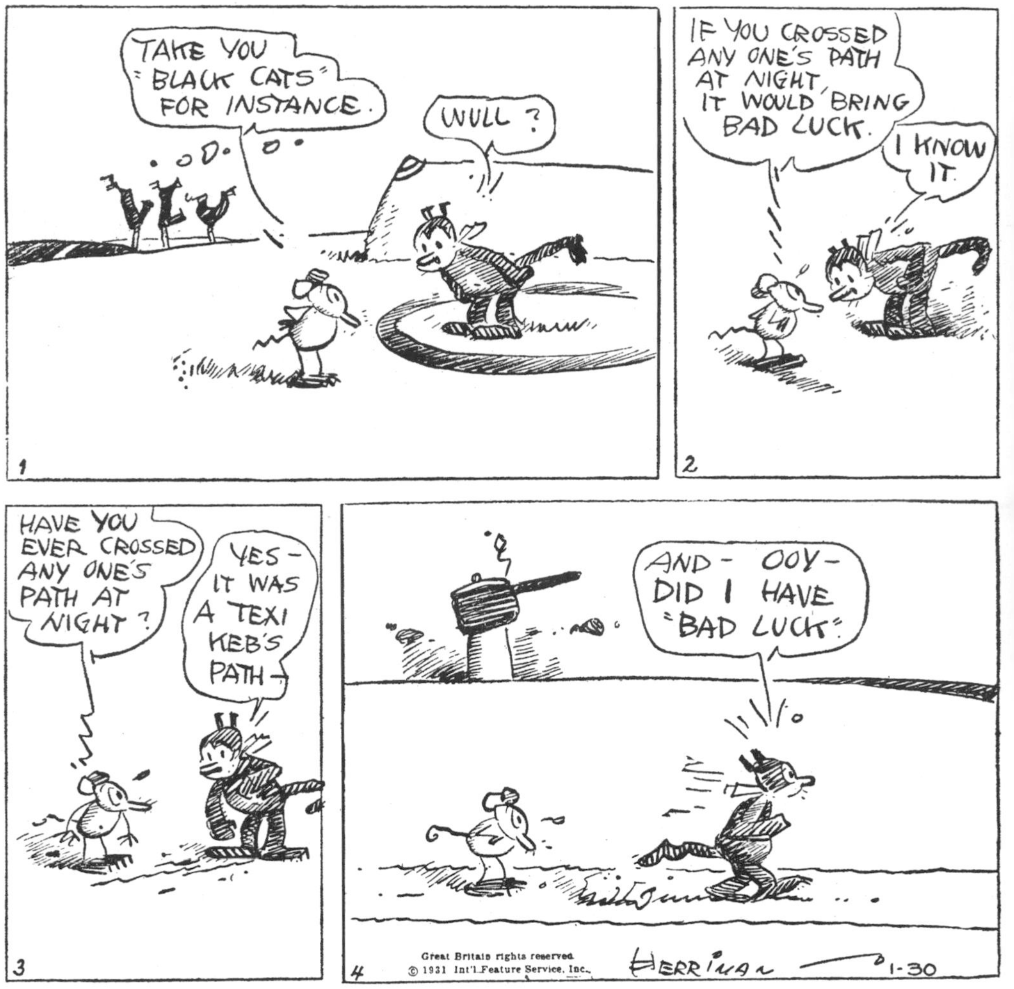
TAKE YOU BLACK CATS FOR INSTANCE.
WULL ?
IF YOU CROSSED ANY ONE'S PATH AT NIGHT, IT WOULD BRING BAD LUCK.
I KNOW IT.
HAVE YOU EVER CROSSED ANY ONE'S PATH AT NIGHT ?
YES - IT WAS A TEXI KEB'S PATH -
AND - OOY - DID I HAVE BAD LUCK
Great Britain rights reserved.
© 1931 Int'l Feature Service, Inc.
HERRIMAN
1-30

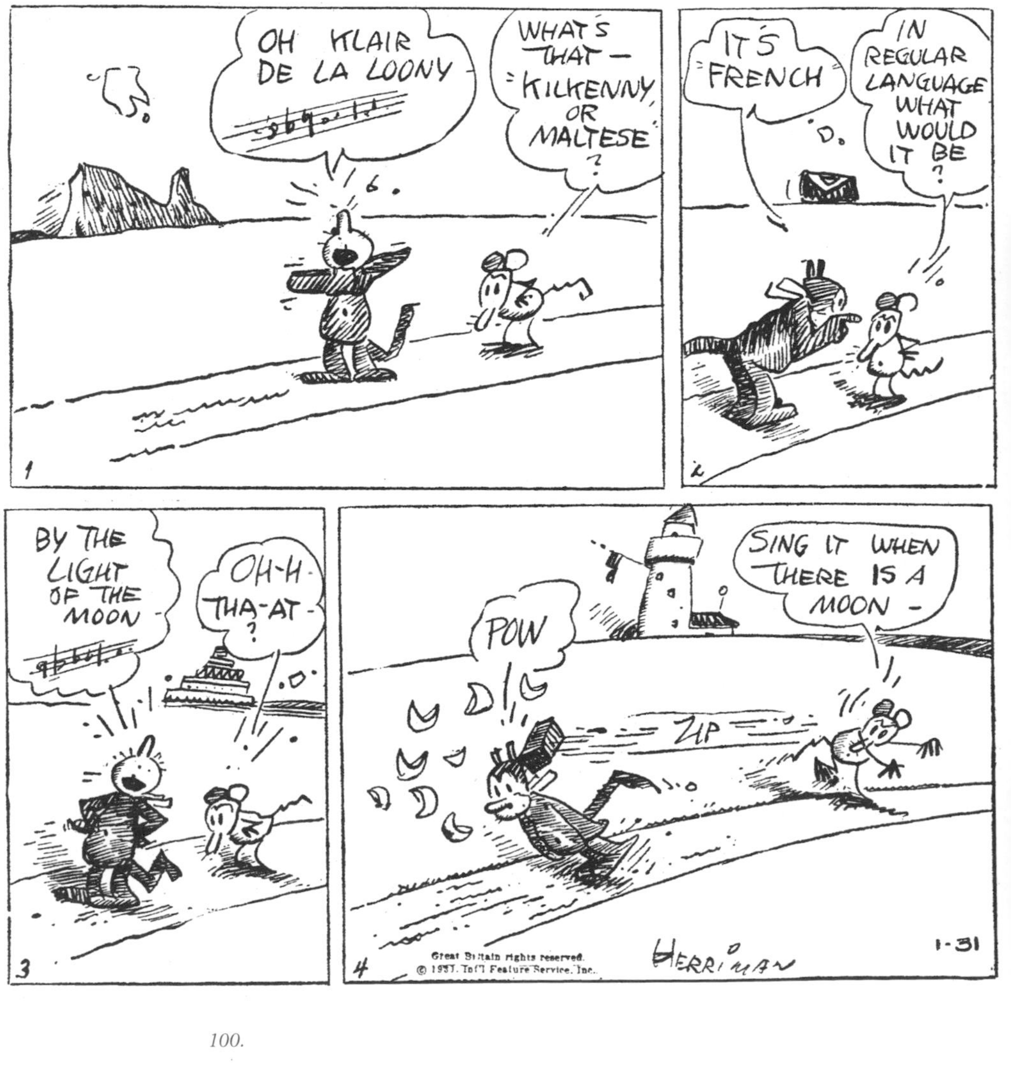
OH KLAIR DE LA LOONY
WHAT'S THAT - KILKENNY, OR MALTESE ?
IT'S FRENCH
IN REGULAR LANGUAGE WHAT WOULD IT BE ?
BY THE LIGHT OF THE MOON -
OH-H THA-AT ?
POW
ZIP
SING IT WHEN THERE IS A MOON -
Great Britain rights reserved.
© 1931 Int'l Feature Service, Inc.
HERRIMAN
1-31

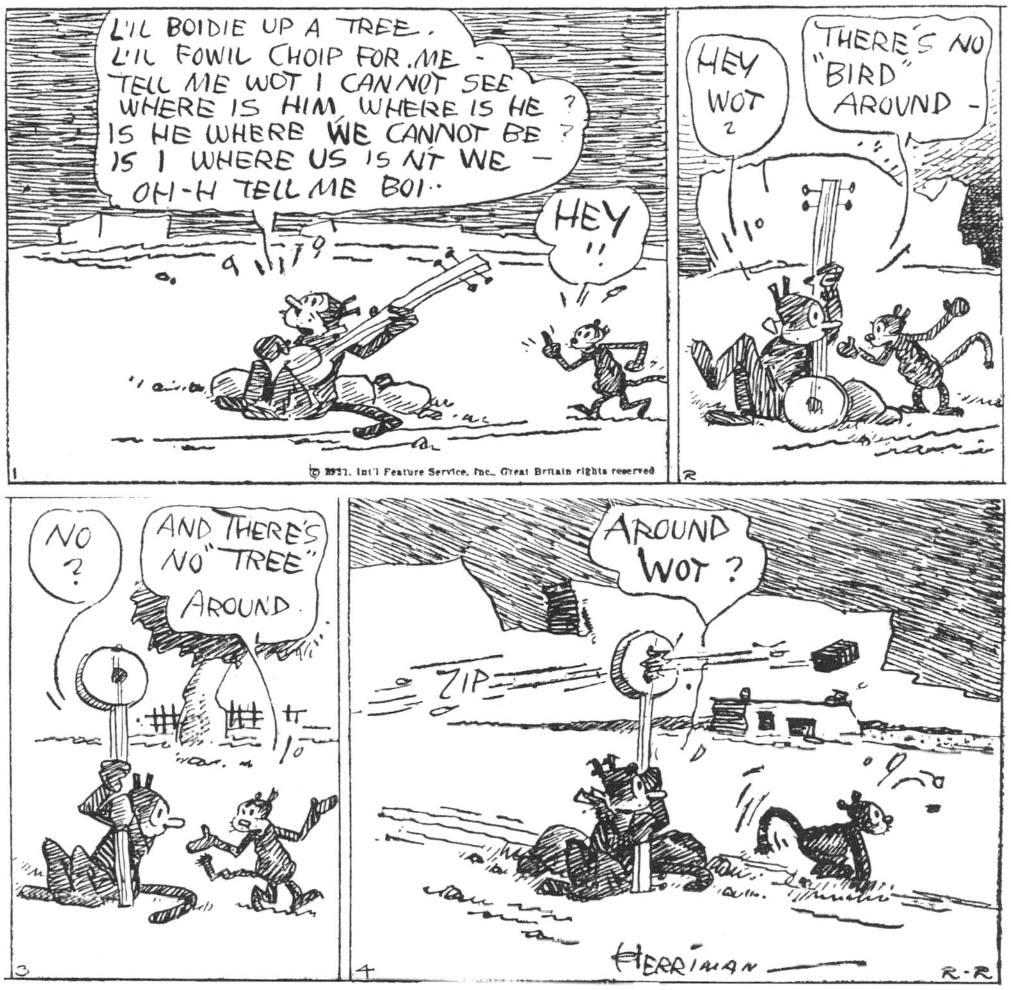
L'IL BOIDIE UP A TREE.
L'IL FOWIL CHOIP FOR ME -
TELL ME WOT I CANNOT SEE
WHERE IS HIM, WHERE IS HE ?
IS HE WHERE WE CANNOT BE ?
IS I WHERE US IS N'T WE -
OH-H TELL ME BOI..
HEY !!
© 1931, Int'l Feature Service, Inc., Great Britain rights reserved
HEY WOT ?
THERE'S NO "BIRD" AROUND -
NO ?
AND THERE'S NO "TREE" AROUND.
AROUND WOT ?
ZIP
HERRIMAN

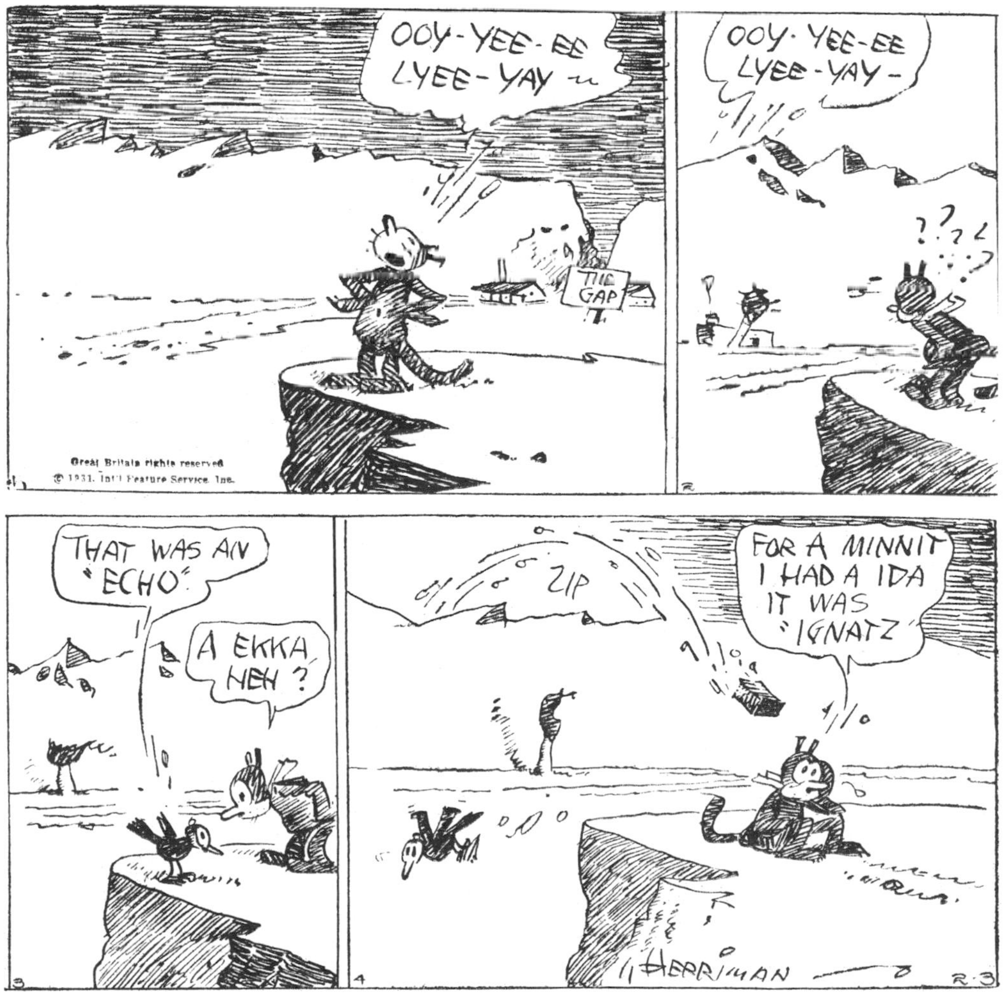
OOY-YEE-EE LYEE-YAY
THE GAP
Great Britain rights reserved
© 1931, Int'l Feature Service, Inc.
OOY-YEE-EE LYEE-YAY -
THAT WAS AN "ECHO"
A EKKA, HEH ?
ZIP
FOR A MINNIT I HAD A IDA IT WAS "IGNATZ"
HERRIMAN

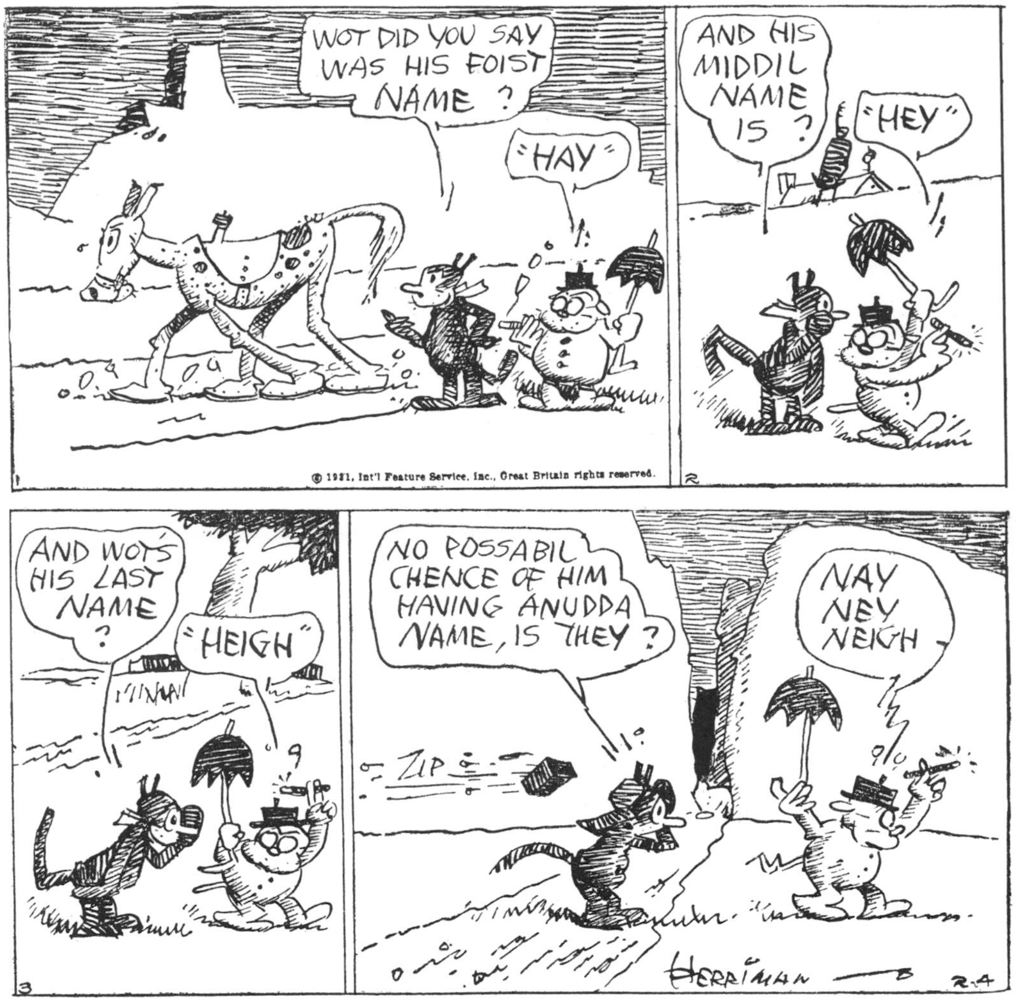
WOT DID YOU SAY WAS HIS FOIST NAME ?
"HAY"
© 1931, Int'l Feature Service, Inc., Great Britain rights reserved.
AND HIS MIDDIL NAME IS ?
"HEY"
AND WOT'S HIS LAST NAME ?
"HEIGH"
NO POSSABIL CHENCE OF HIM HAVING ANUDDA NAME, IS THEY ?
ZIP
NAY NEY NEIGH
HERRIMAN

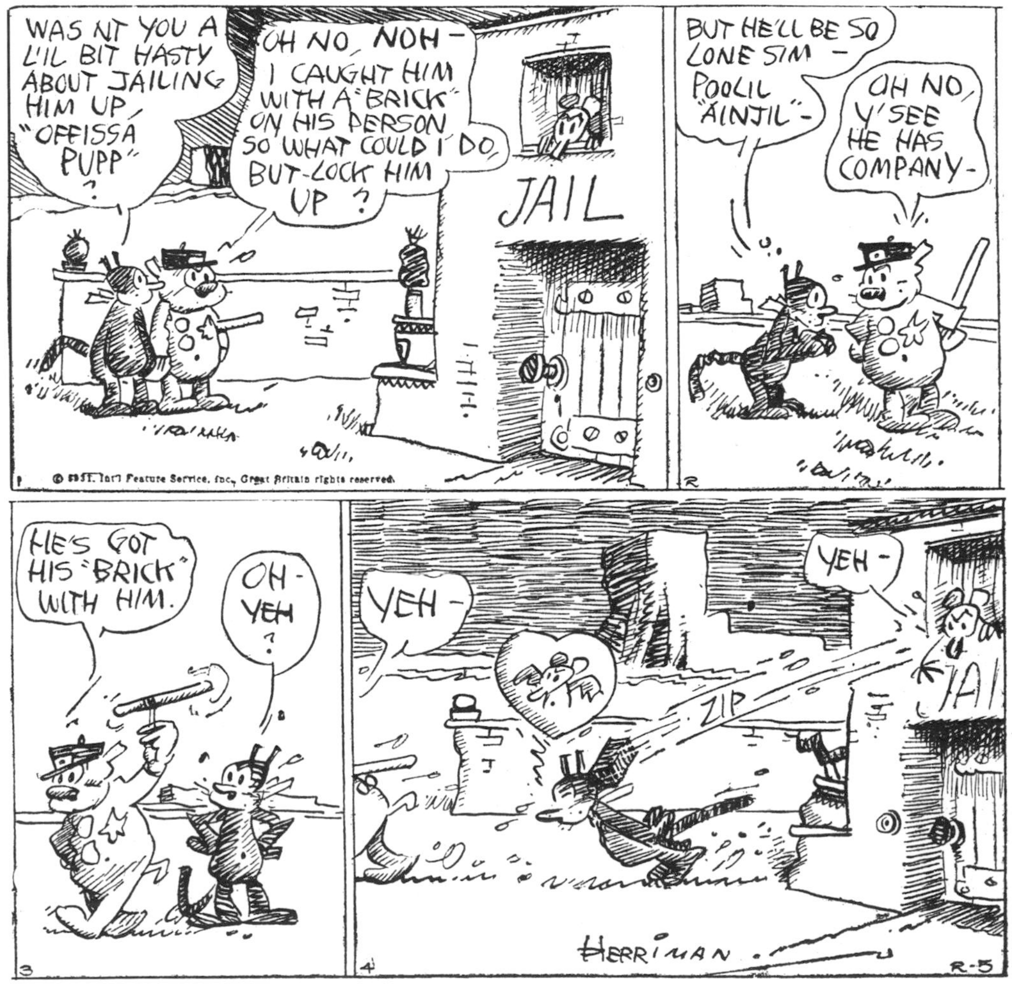
WAS NT YOU A L'IL BIT HASTY ABOUT JAILING HIM UP, "OFFISSA PUPP" ?
OH NO, NOH - I CAUGHT HIM WITH A "BRICK" ON HIS PERSON SO WHAT COULD I DO, BUT-LOCK HIM UP ?
JAIL
© 1931, Int'l Feature Service, Inc., Great Britain rights reserved.
BUT HE'LL BE SO LONE SIM - POOLIL "AINJIL" -
OH NO, Y'SEE HE HAS COMPANY -
HE'S GOT HIS "BRICK" WITH HIM.
OH - YEH ?
YEH -
ZIP
YEH -
HERRIMAN

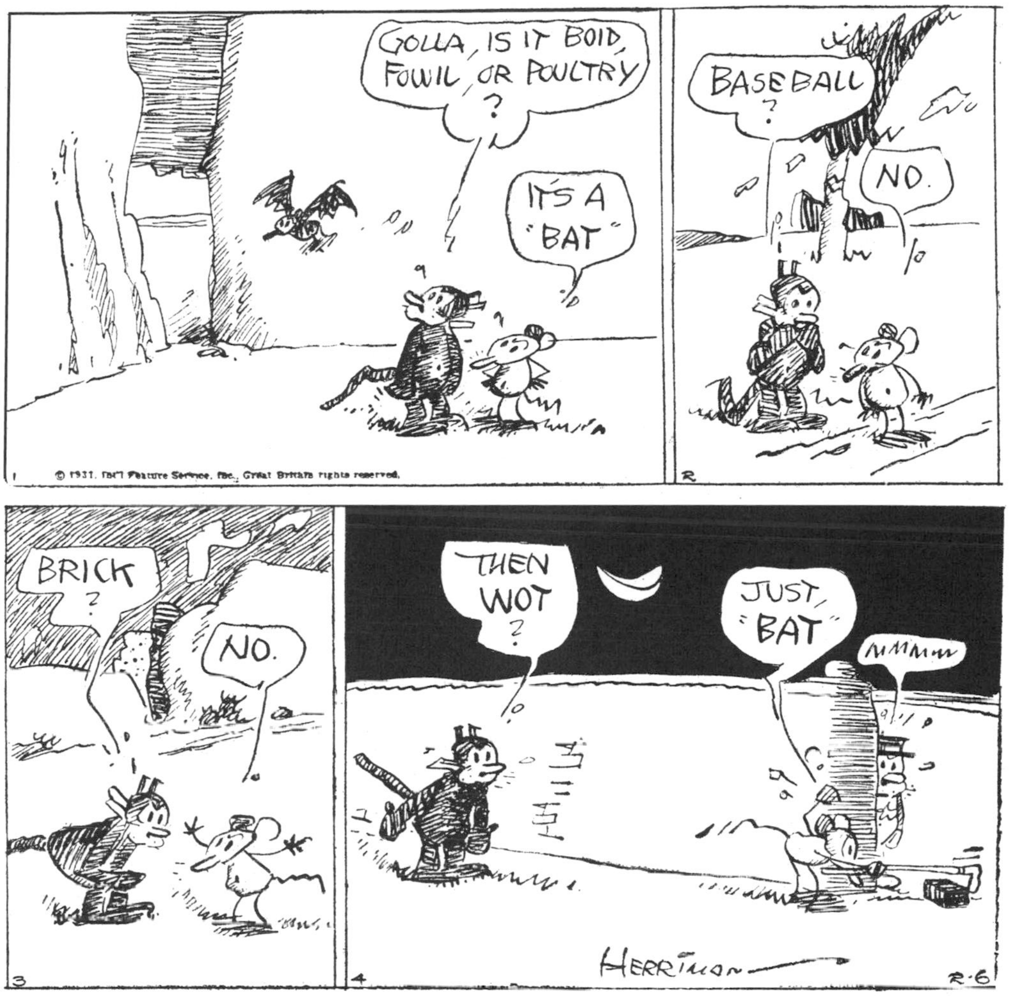

GOLLA, IS IT BOID, FOWL, OR POULTRY ?
IT'S A "BAT"
© 1931, Int'l Feature Service, Inc., Great Britain rights reserved.
BASEBALL ?
NO.
BRICK ?
NO.
THEN WOT ?
JUST "BAT"
HERRIMAN

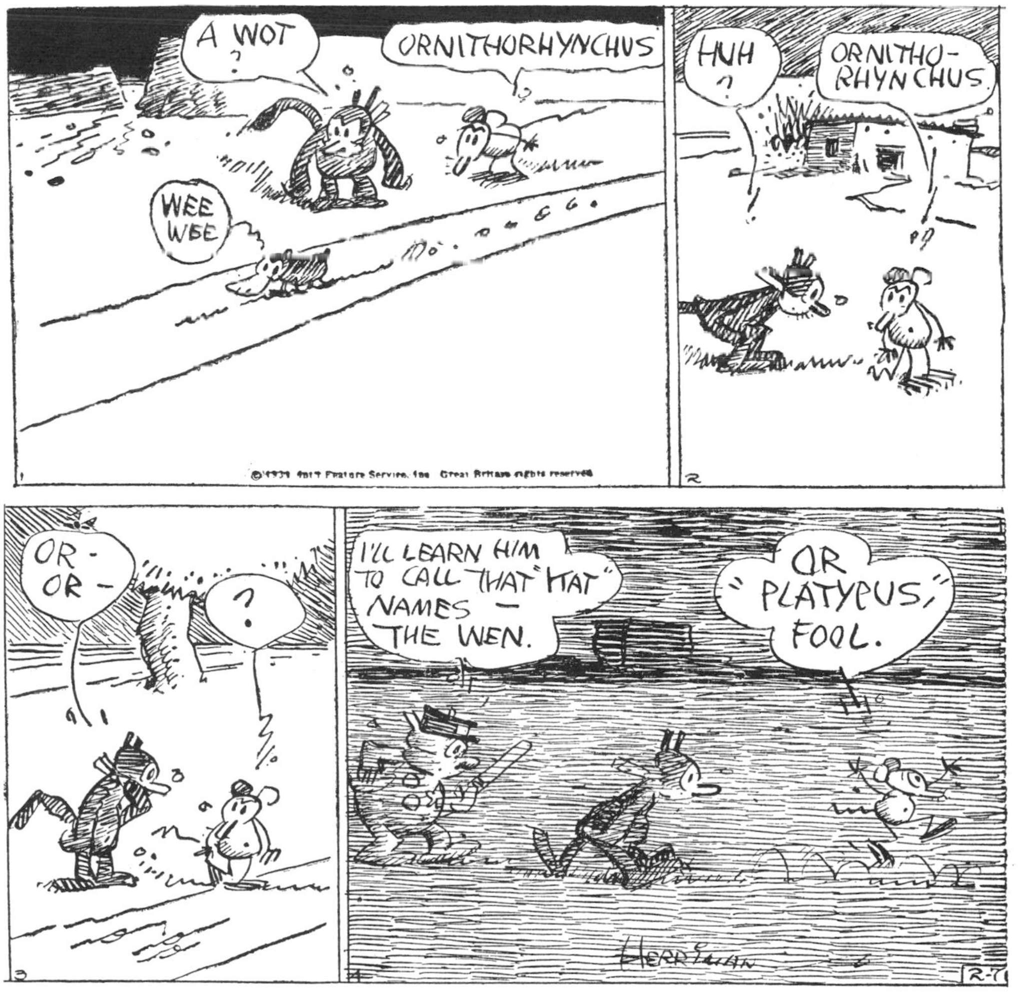

A WOT ?
ORNITHORHYNCHUS
WEE WEE
HUH ?
ORNITHO-RHYNCHUS.
OR - OR -
?
I'LL LEARN HIM TO CALL THAT "KAT" NAMES — THE WEN.
OR "PLATYPUS," FOOL.
HERRIMAN

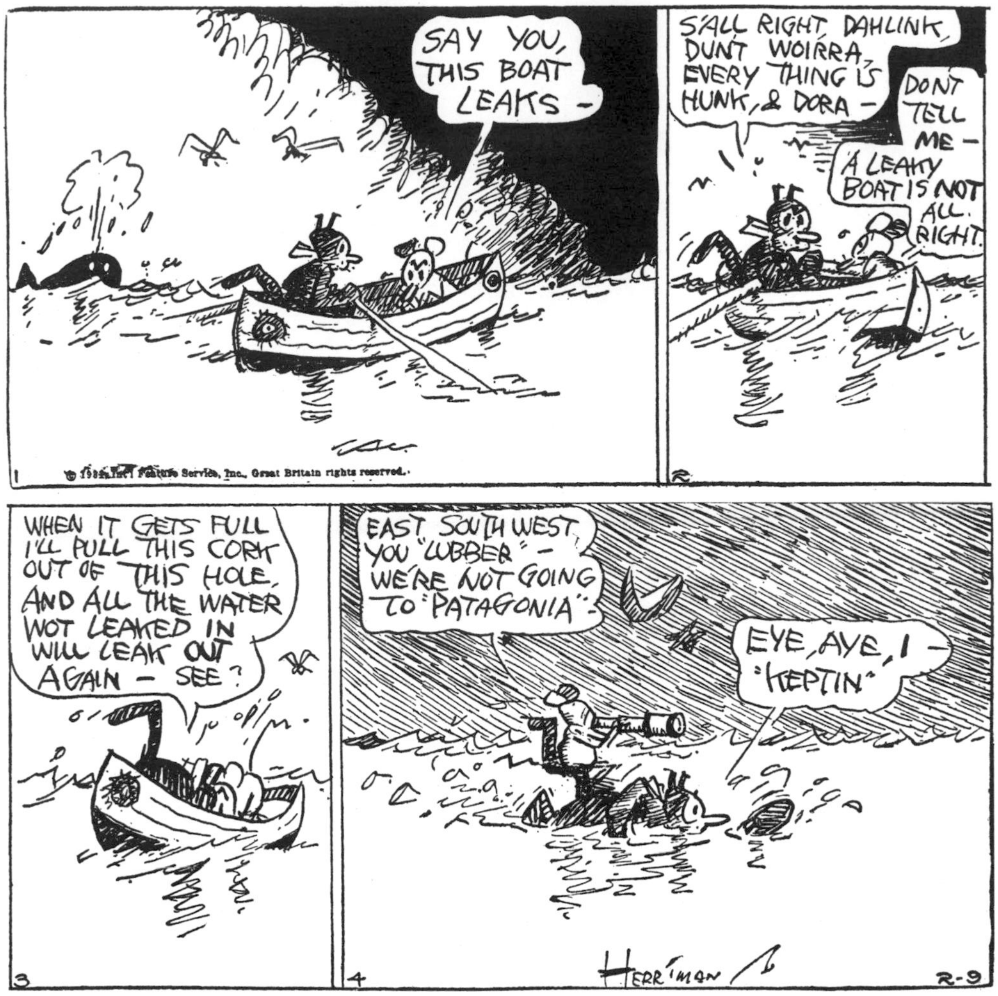
SAY YOU, THIS BOAT LEAKS -
© 1934, Int'l Feature Service, Inc., Great Britain rights reserved.
S'ALL RIGHT, DAHLINK, DUNT WOIRRA, EVERY THING IS HUNK, & DORA -
DON'T TELL ME - A LEAKY BOAT IS NOT ALL RIGHT.
WHEN IT GETS FULL I'LL PULL THIS CORK OUT OF THIS HOLE, AND ALL THE WATER WOT LEAKED IN WILL LEAK OUT AGAIN - SEE?
EAST SOUTH WEST, YOU "LUBBER" - WE'RE NOT GOING TO "PATAGONIA" -
EYE, AYE, I - "KEPTIN"
HERRIMAN
2-9

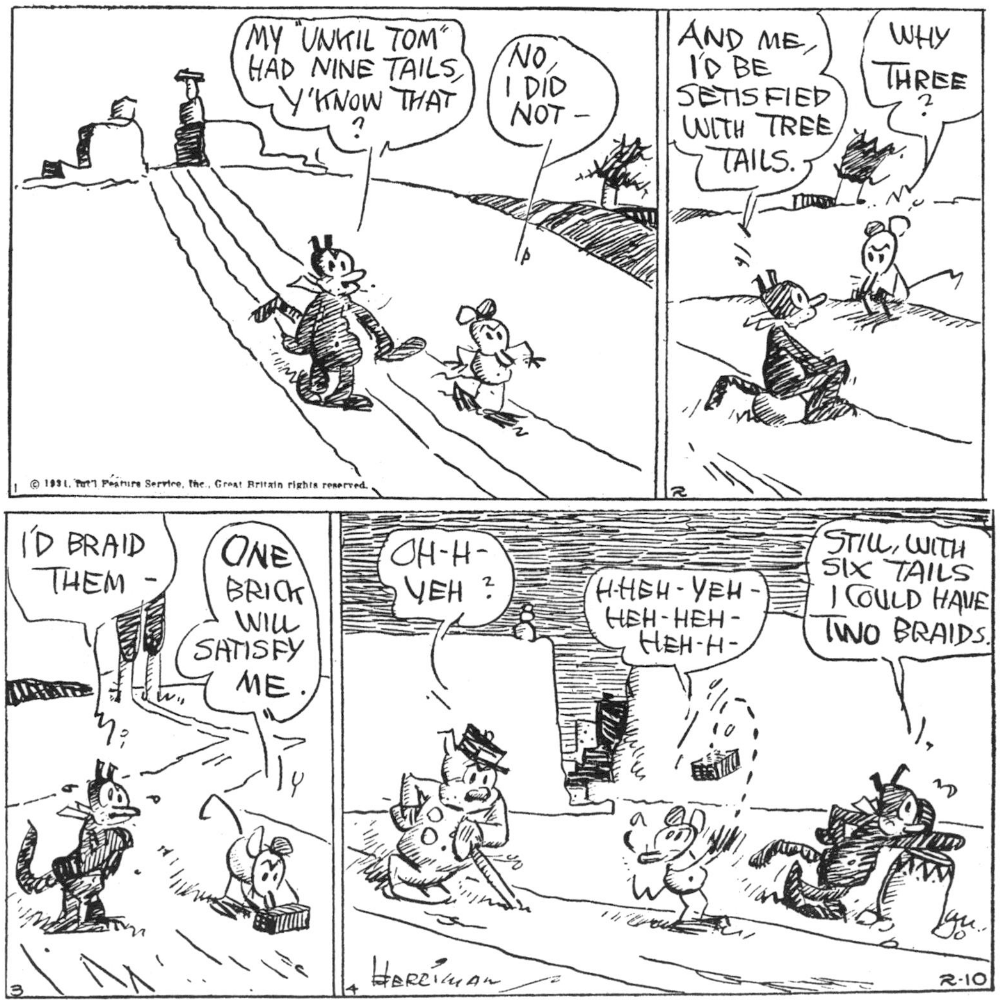
MY "UNKIL TOM" HAD NINE TAILS, Y'KNOW THAT?
NO, I DID NOT -
© 1934, Int'l Feature Service, Inc., Great Britain rights reserved.
AND ME, I'D BE SETISFIED WITH TREE TAILS.
WHY THREE?
I'D BRAID THEM -
ONE BRICK WILL SATISFY ME.
OH-H- YEH?
H-HEH - YEH - HEH-HEH - HEH-H-
STILL, WITH SIX TAILS I COULD HAVE TWO BRAIDS.
HERRIMAN
2-10

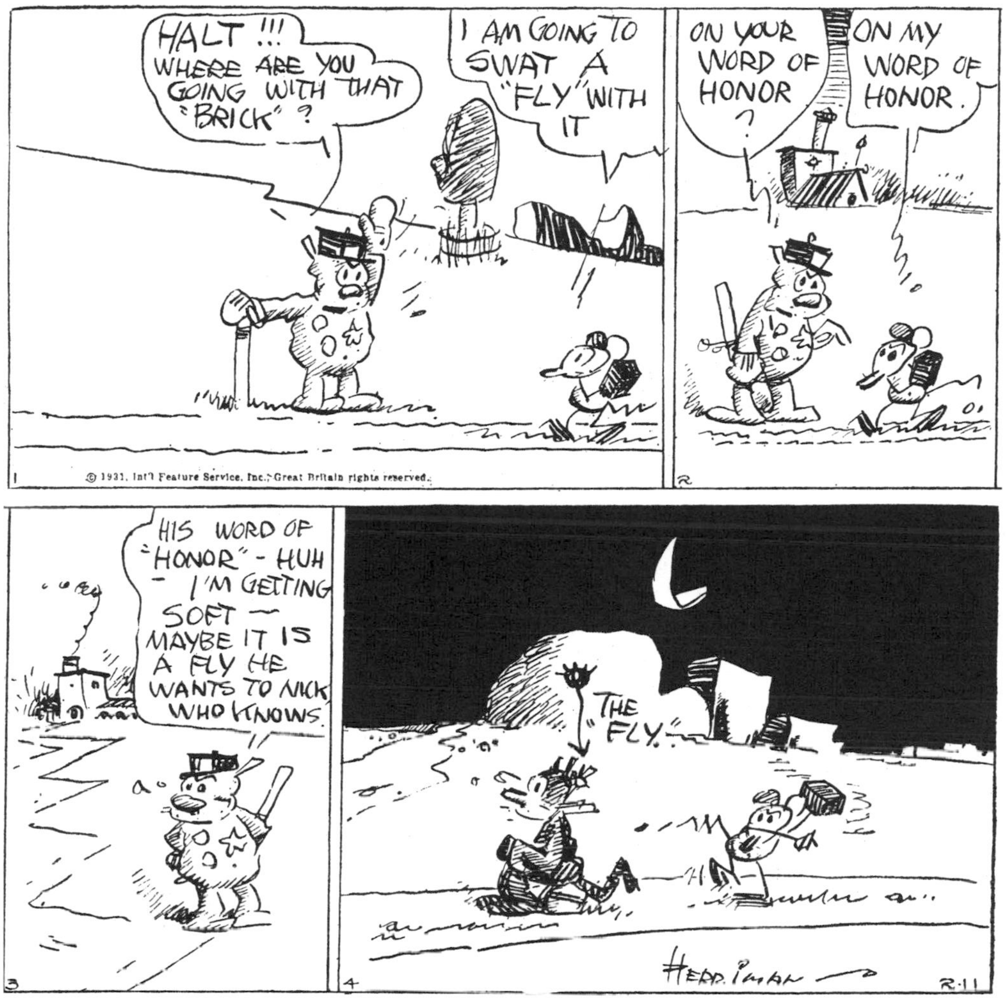
HALT!!! WHERE ARE YOU GOING WITH THAT "BRICK"?
I AM GOING TO SWAT A "FLY" WITH IT
ON YOUR WORD OF HONOR?
ON MY WORD OF HONOR.
HIS WORD OF "HONOR" - HUH - I'M GETTING SOFT - MAYBE IT IS A FLY HE WANTS TO NICK WHO KNOWS.
"THE FLY"
HERRIMAN
R.11
© 1931, Int'l Feature Service, Inc., Great Britain rights reserved.

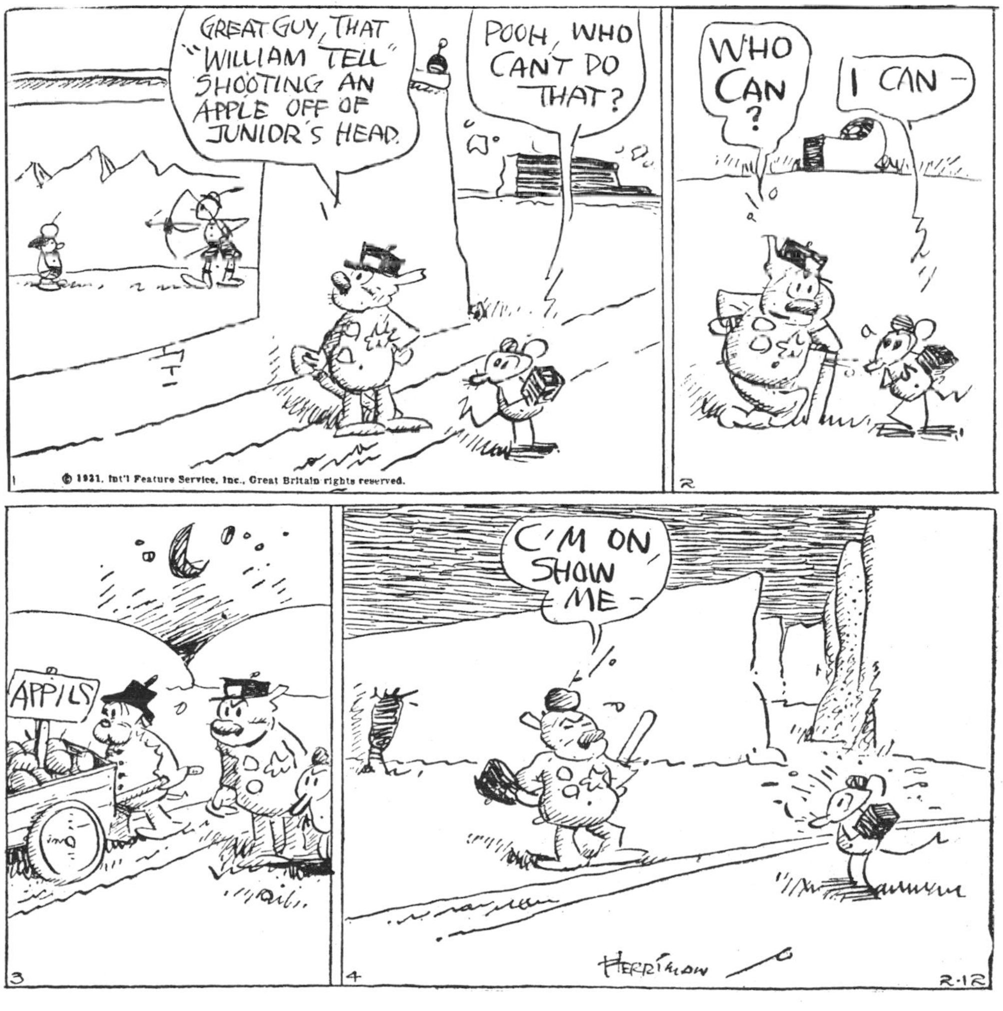
GREAT GUY, THAT "WILLIAM TELL" SHOOTING AN APPLE OFF OF JUNIOR'S HEAD.
POOH, WHO CAN'T DO THAT?
WHO CAN?
I CAN -
APPILS
C'M ON SHOW ME -
HERRIMAN
R.12
© 1931, Int'l Feature Service, Inc., Great Britain rights reserved.

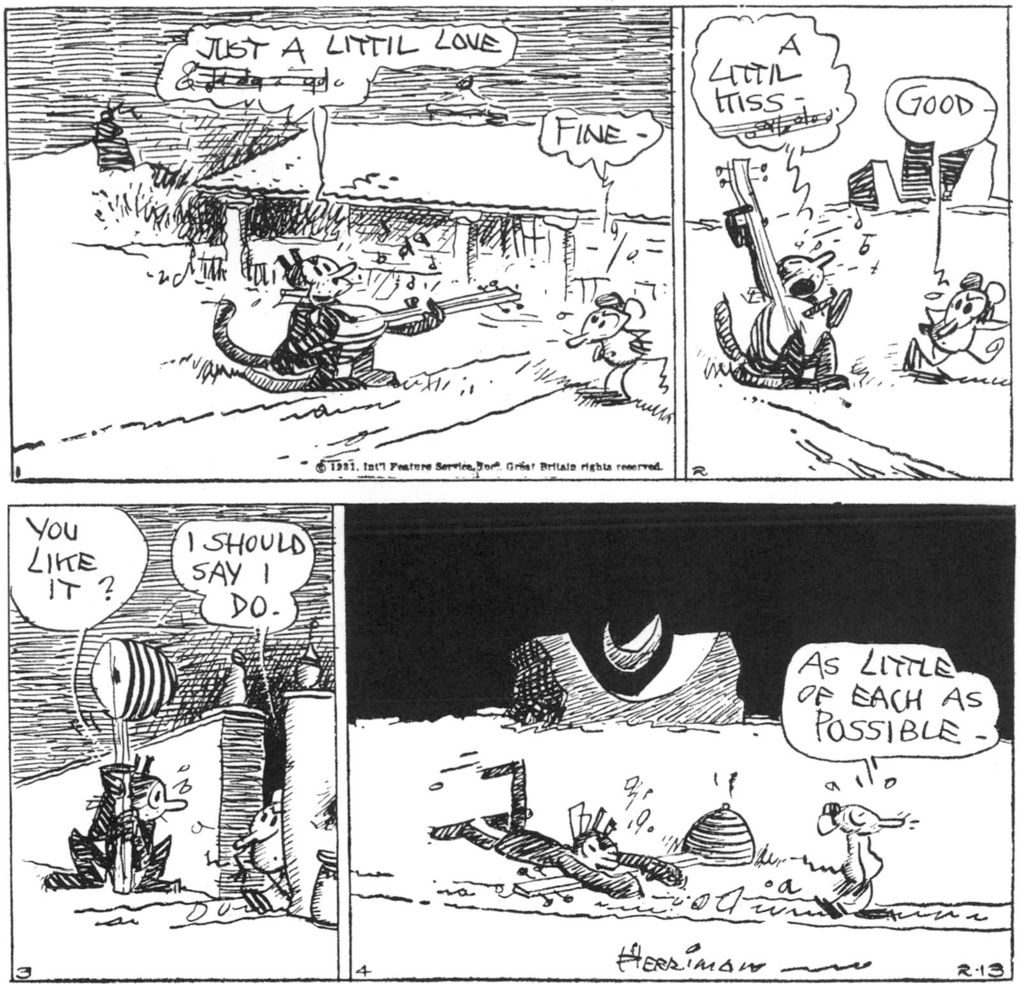

JUST A LITTIL LOVE
FINE -
A LITTIL KISS -
GOOD -
© 1931, Int'l Feature Service, Inc. Great Britain rights reserved.
YOU LIKE IT ?
I SHOULD SAY I DO.
AS LITTLE OF EACH AS POSSIBLE -
HERRIMAN
2-13

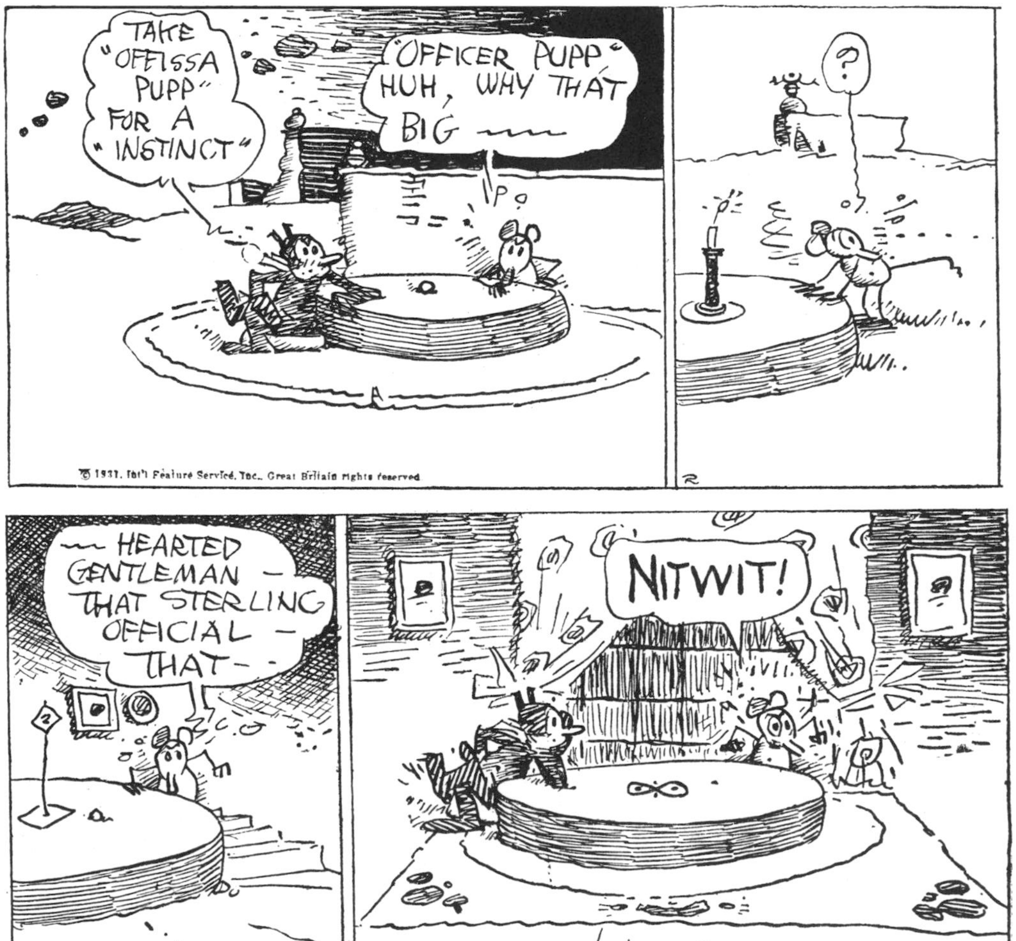

TAKE "OFFISSA PUPP" FOR A "INSTINCT"
"OFFICER PUPP" HUH, WHY THAT BIG
?
© 1931, Int'l Feature Service, Inc., Great Britain rights reserved
— HEARTED GENTLEMAN — THAT STERLING OFFICIAL — THAT -
NITWIT!
HERRIMAN
2-14

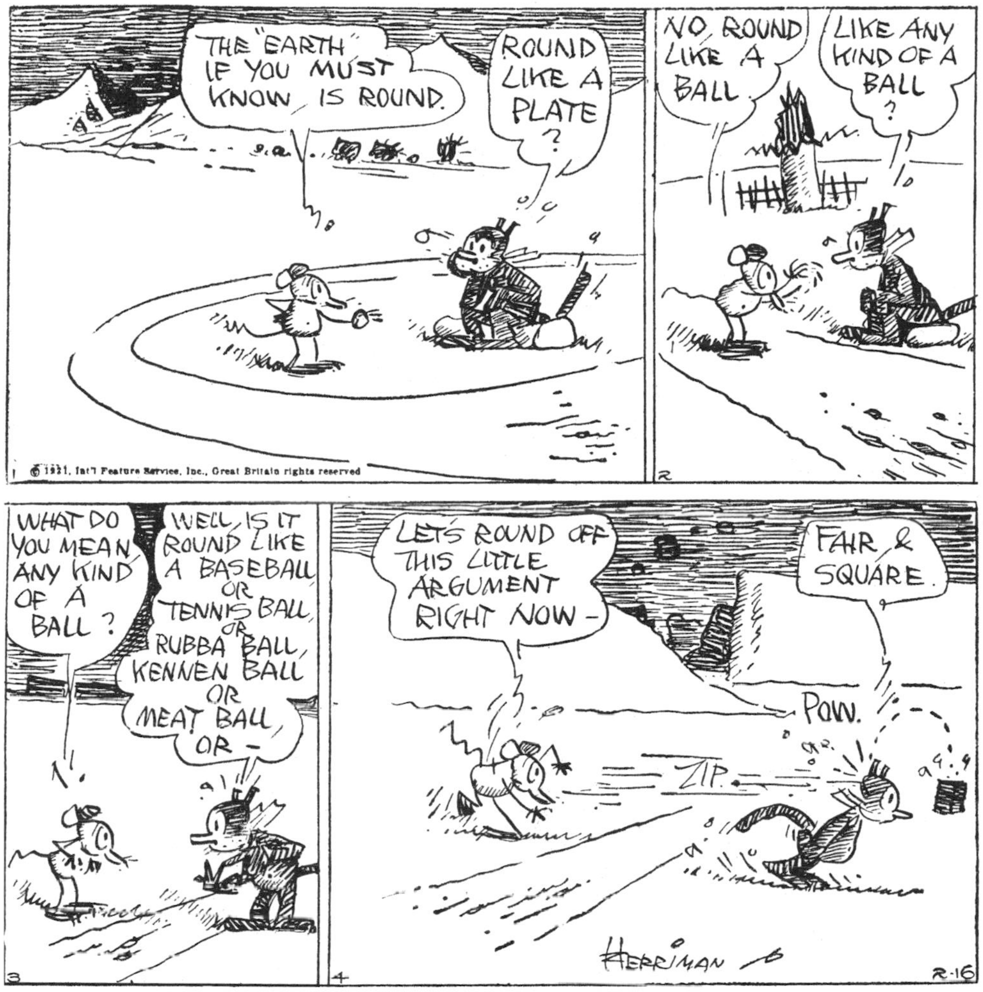
THE "EARTH" IF YOU MUST KNOW, IS ROUND.
ROUND LIKE A PLATE ?
© 1921, Int'l Feature Service, Inc., Great Britain rights reserved
NO, ROUND LIKE A BALL.
LIKE ANY KIND OF A BALL ?
WHAT DO YOU MEAN ANY KIND OF A BALL ?
WELL, IS IT ROUND LIKE A BASEBALL OR TENNIS BALL, OR RUBBA BALL, KENNEN BALL OR MEAT BALL, OR -
LETS ROUND OFF THIS LITTLE ARGUMENT RIGHT NOW -
FAIR & SQUARE.
POW.
ZIP.
HERRIMAN
R-16

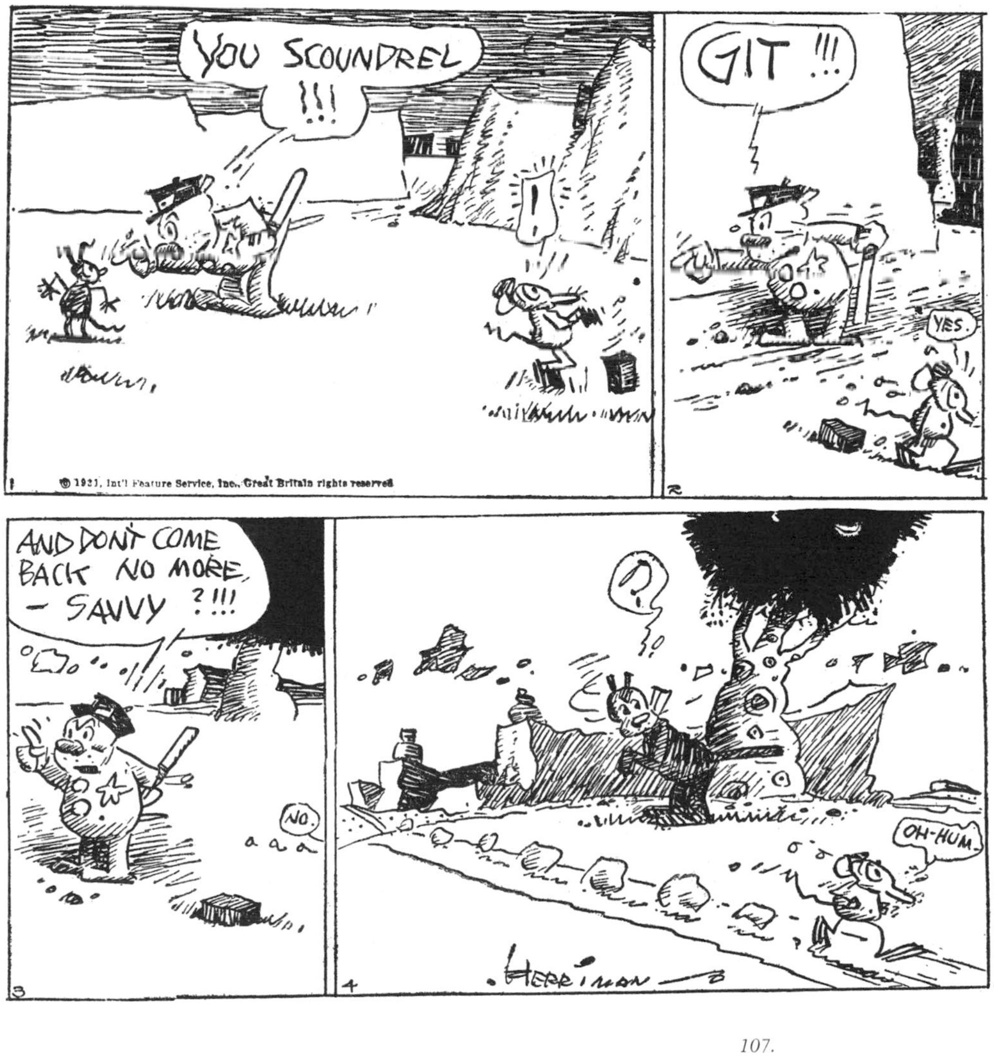
YOU SCOUNDREL !!!
!
© 1921, Int'l Feature Service, Inc., Great Britain rights reserved
GIT !!!
YES.
AND DON'T COME BACK NO MORE, - SAVVY ?!!!
NO.
?
OH-HUM.
HERRIMAN

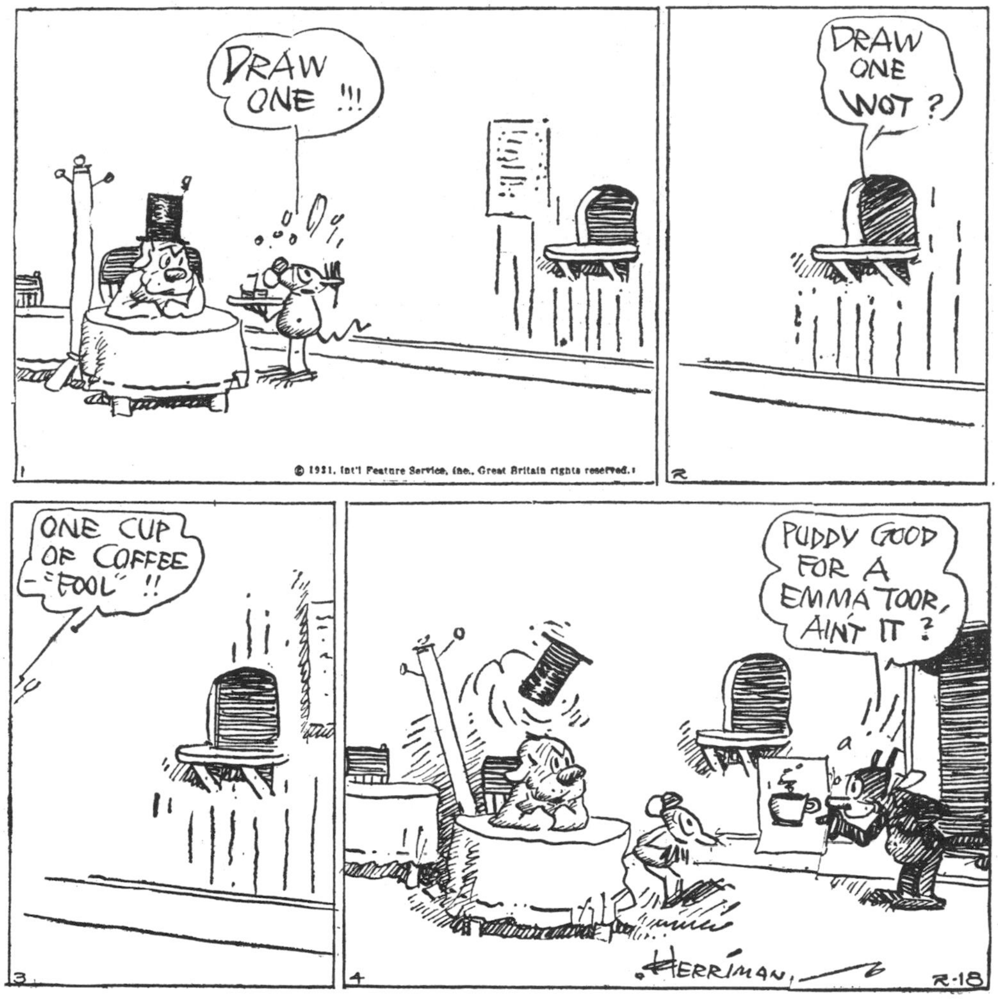
DRAW ONE !!!
© 1921, Int'l Feature Service, Inc., Great Britain rights reserved.
DRAW ONE WOT ?
ONE CUP OF COFFEE -"FOOL" !!
PUDDY GOOD FOR A EMMA TOOR, AINT IT ?
HERRIMAN
2-18

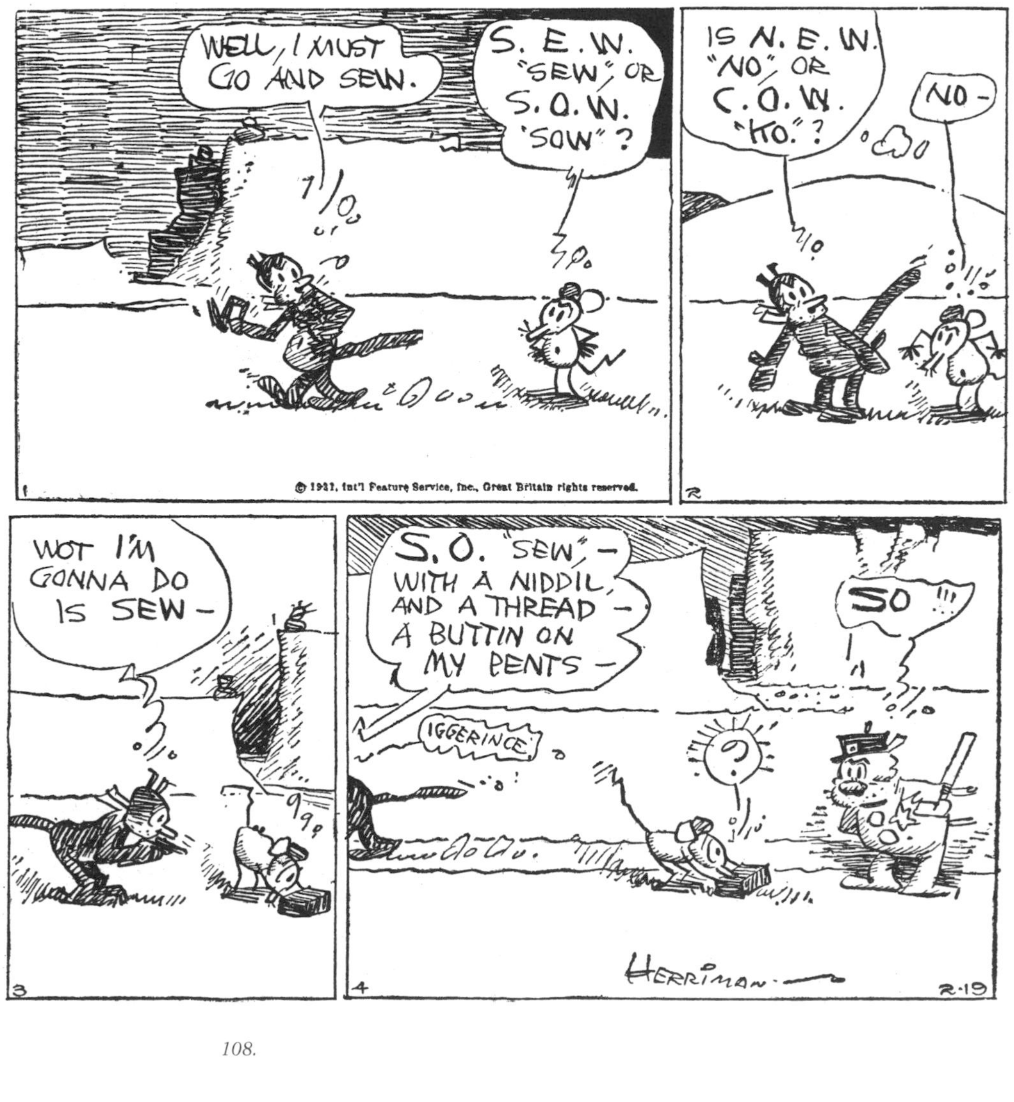
WELL, I MUST GO AND SEW.
S. E. W. "SEW" OR S. O. W. "SOW" ?
© 1921, Int'l Feature Service, Inc., Great Britain rights reserved.
IS N. E. W. "NO" OR C. O. W. "KO." ?
NO -
WOT I'M GONNA DO IS SEW -
S. O. "SEW", - WITH A NIDDIL, AND A THREAD - A BUTTIN ON MY PENTS -
IGGERINCE
SO !!!
HERRIMAN
2-19

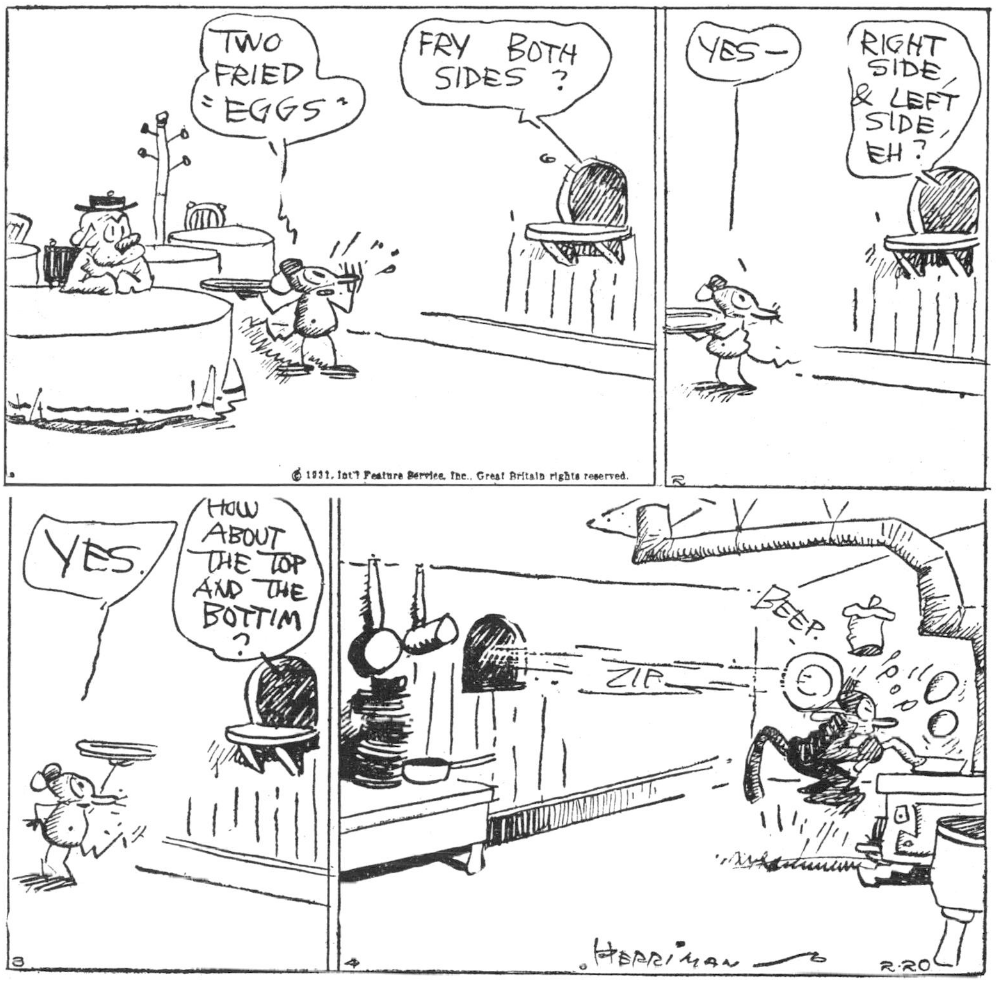
TWO FRIED =EGGS=
FRY BOTH SIDES ?
© 1931, Int'l Feature Service, Inc., Great Britain rights reserved.
YES—
RIGHT SIDE, & LEFT SIDE, EH ?
YES.
HOW ABOUT THE TOP AND THE BOTTIM ?
BEEP
ZIP
HERRIMAN
R.20

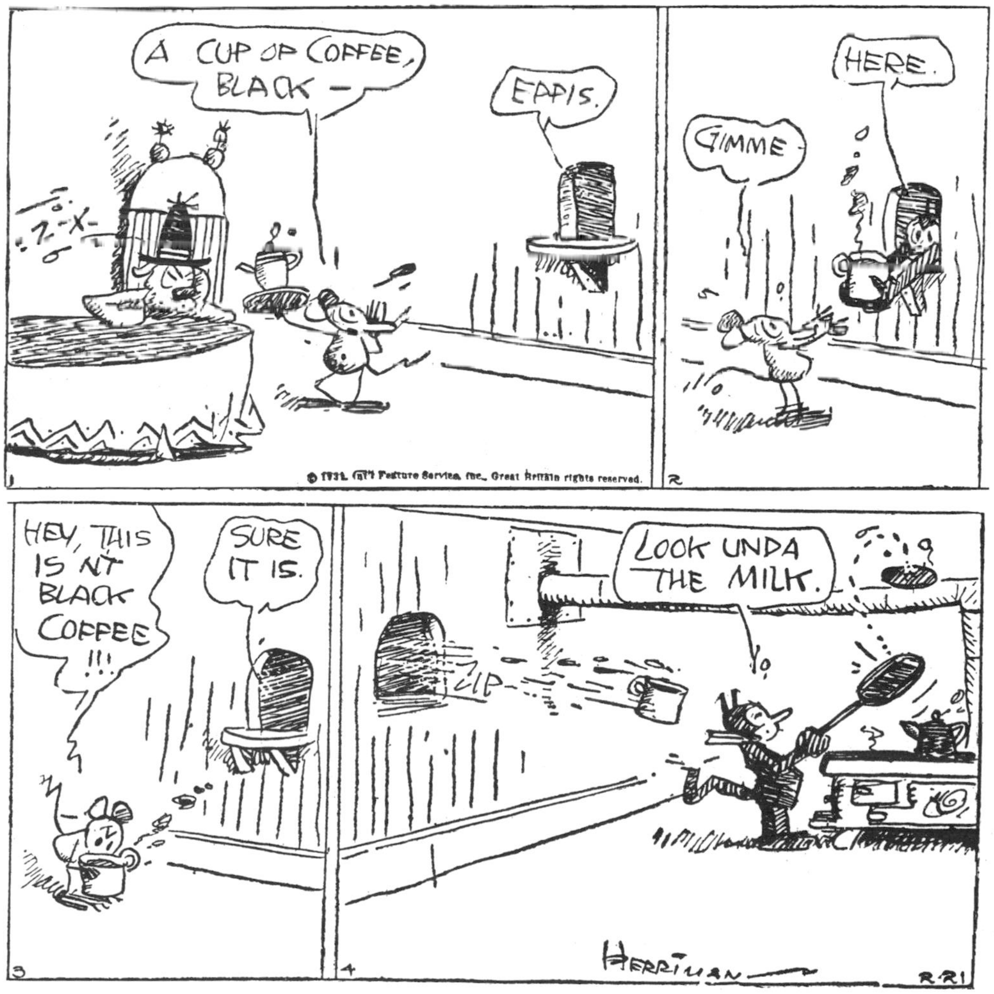
A CUP OF COFFEE, BLACK —
EPPIS.
Z-X-
© 1931, Int'l Feature Service, Inc., Great Britain rights reserved.
HERE.
GIMME
HEY, THIS IS N'T BLACK COFFEE !!!
SURE IT IS.
LOOK UNDA THE MILK.
ZIP
HERRIMAN
R.21

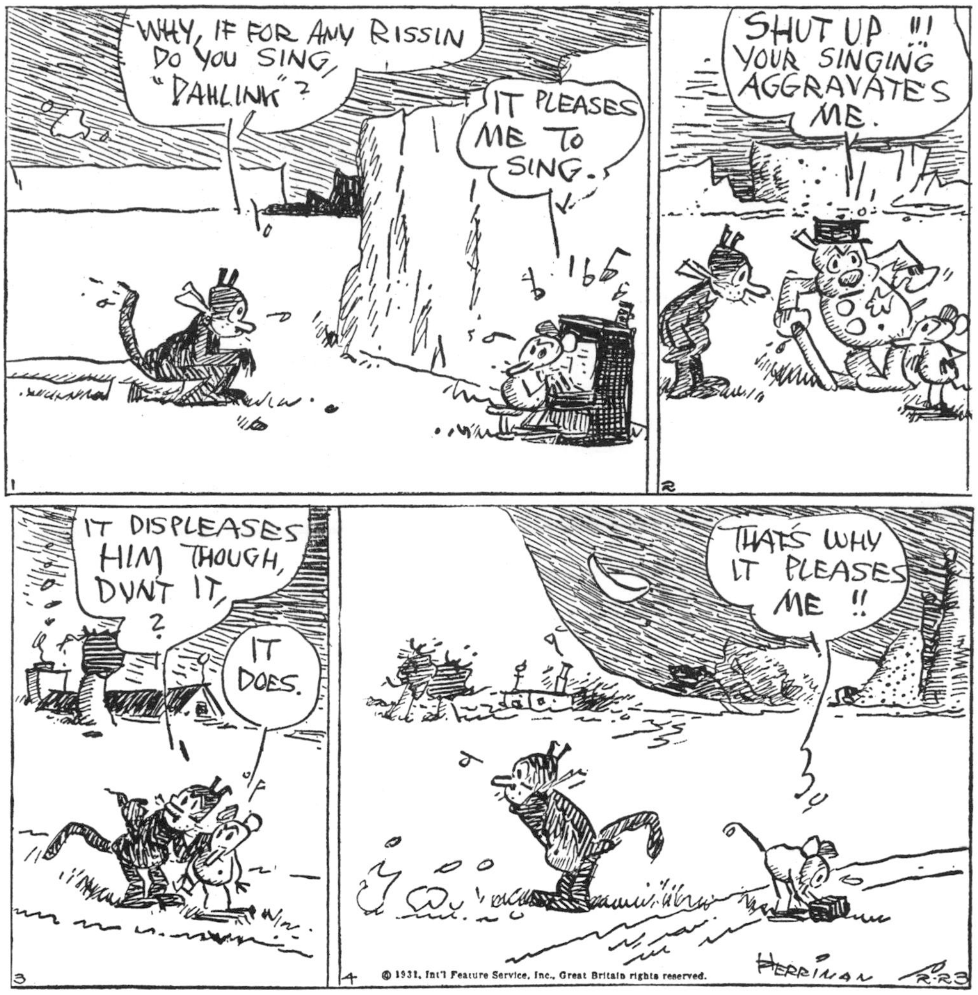
WHY, IF FOR ANY RISSIN DO YOU SING "DAHLINK"?
IT PLEASES ME TO SING.
SHUT UP !!! YOUR SINGING AGGRAVATES ME.
IT DISPLEASES HIM THOUGH, DUNT IT?
IT DOES.
THATS WHY IT PLEASES ME !!
© 1931, Int'l Feature Service, Inc., Great Britain rights reserved.
HERRIMAN

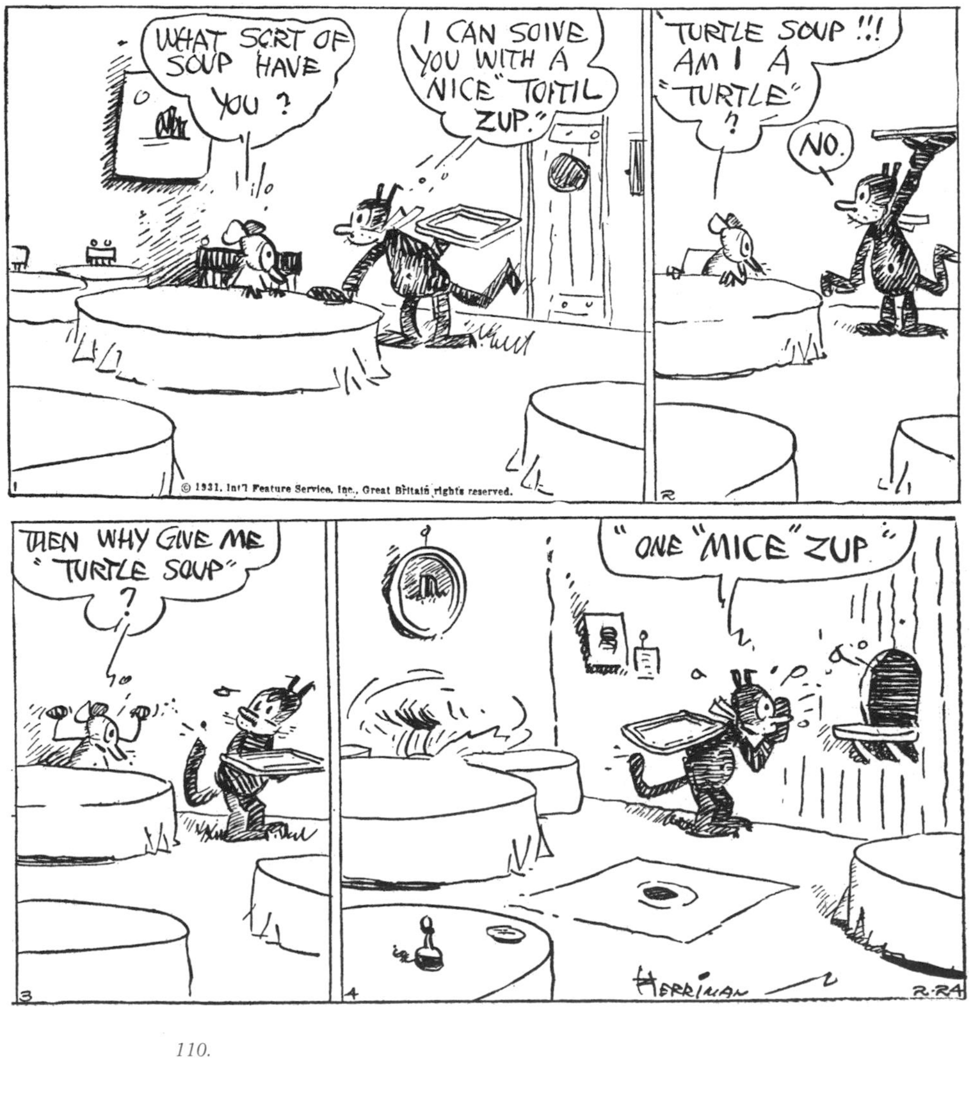
WHAT SORT OF SOUP HAVE YOU?
I CAN SOIVE YOU WITH A NICE "TOITIL ZUP."
TURTLE SOUP !!! AM I A "TURTLE"?
NO.
© 1931, Int'l Feature Service, Inc., Great Britain rights reserved.
THEN WHY GIVE ME "TURTLE SOUP"?
"ONE "MICE" ZUP"
HERRIMAN

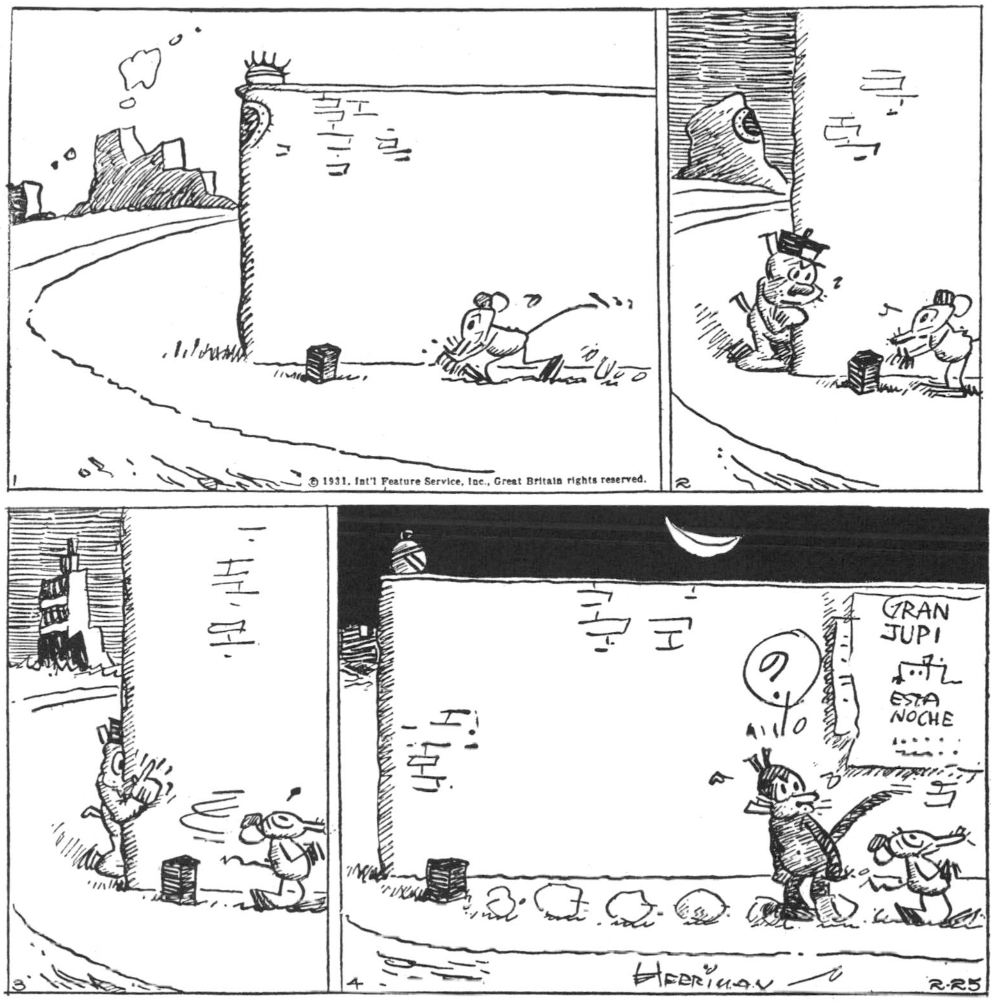
© 1931, Int'l Feature Service, Inc., Great Britain rights reserved.
GRAN JUPI
ESTA NOCHE
HERRIMAN

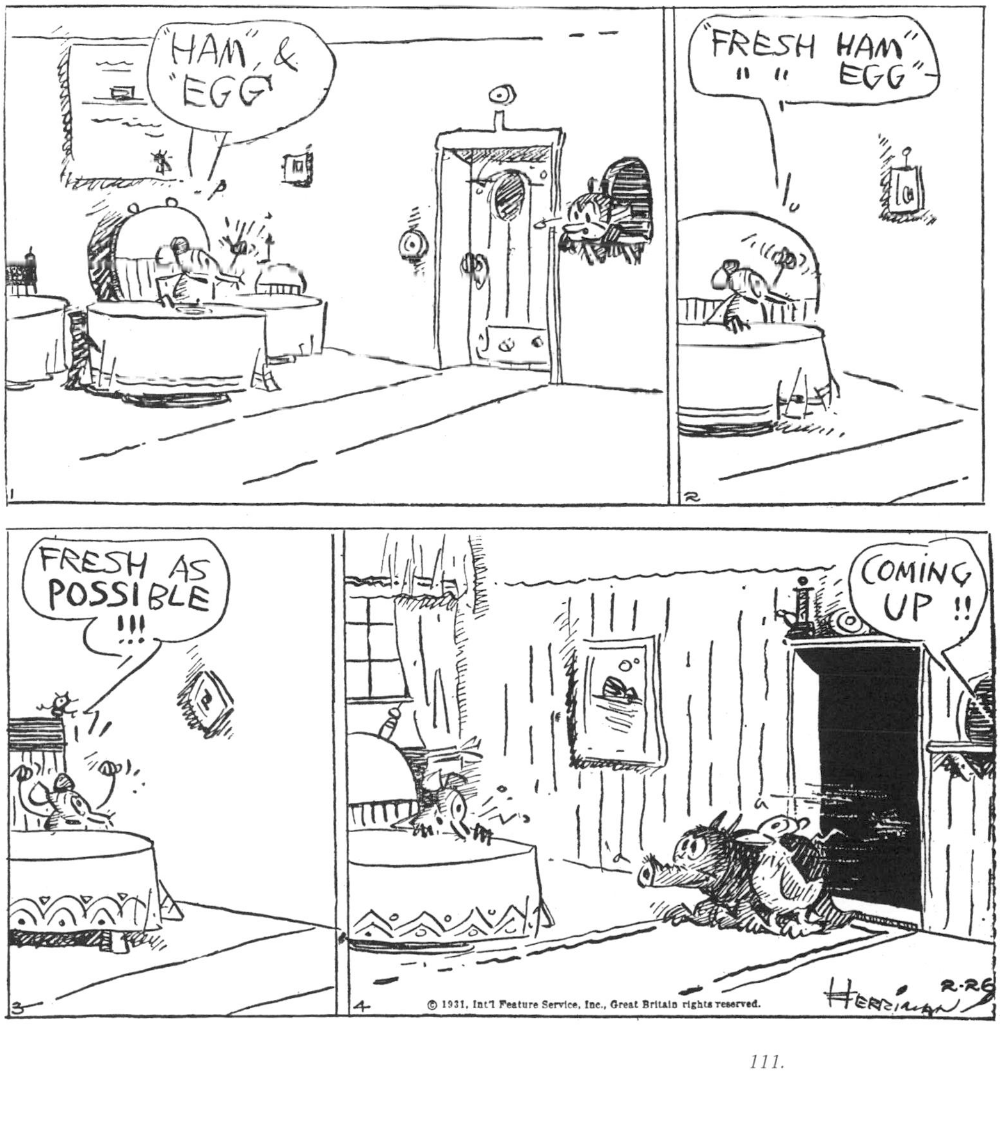
"HAM" & "EGG"
"FRESH HAM"
" " EGG"
FRESH AS POSSIBLE !!!
COMING UP !!
© 1931, Int'l Feature Service, Inc., Great Britain rights reserved.
HERRIMAN

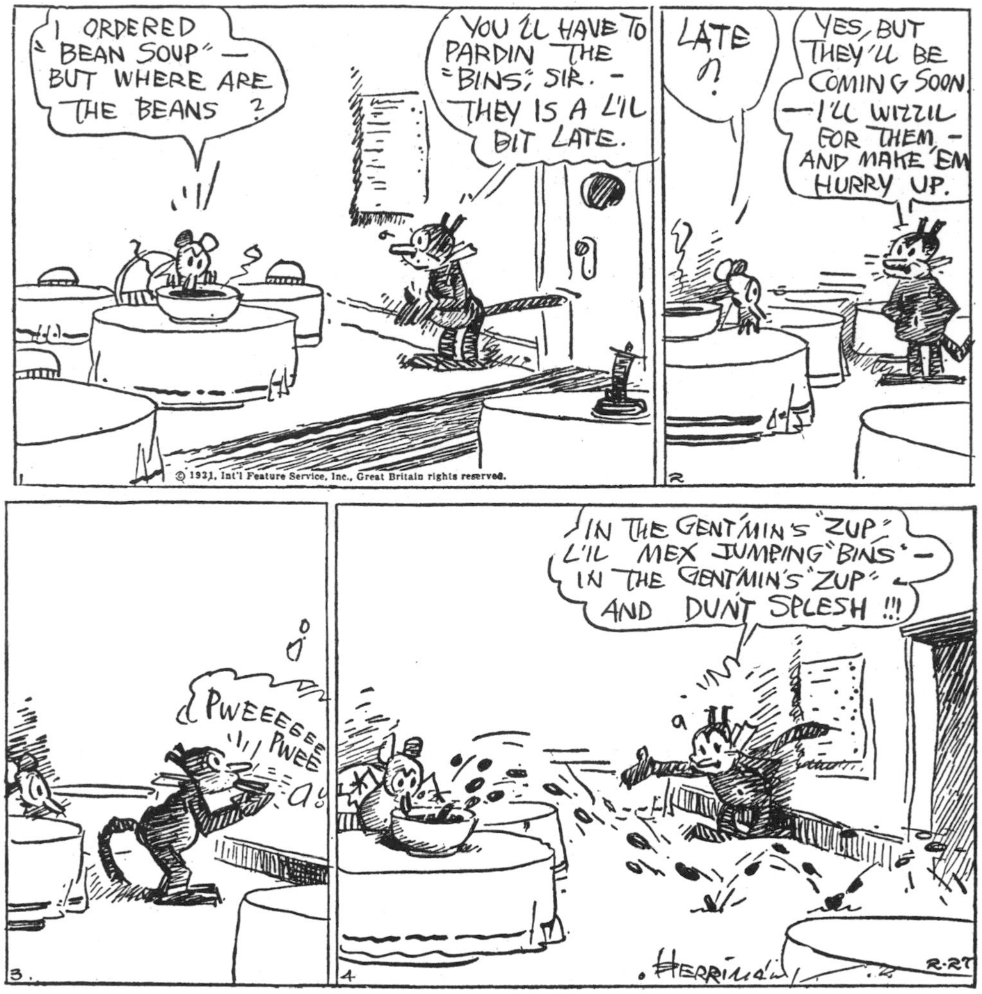
I ORDERED BEAN SOUP" — BUT WHERE ARE THE BEANS ?
YOU'LL HAVE TO PARDIN THE "BINS", SIR. — THEY IS A L'IL BIT LATE.
© 1931, Int'l Feature Service, Inc., Great Britain rights reserved.
LATE ?
YES, BUT THEY'LL BE COMING SOON. — I'LL WIZZIL FOR THEM, — AND MAKE 'EM HURRY UP.
PWEEEEEEE PWEE
IN THE GENT'MIN'S "ZUP" L'IL "MEX JUMPING "BINS" — IN THE GENT'MIN'S "ZUP" AND DUNT SPLESH !!!
HERRIMAN
2-27

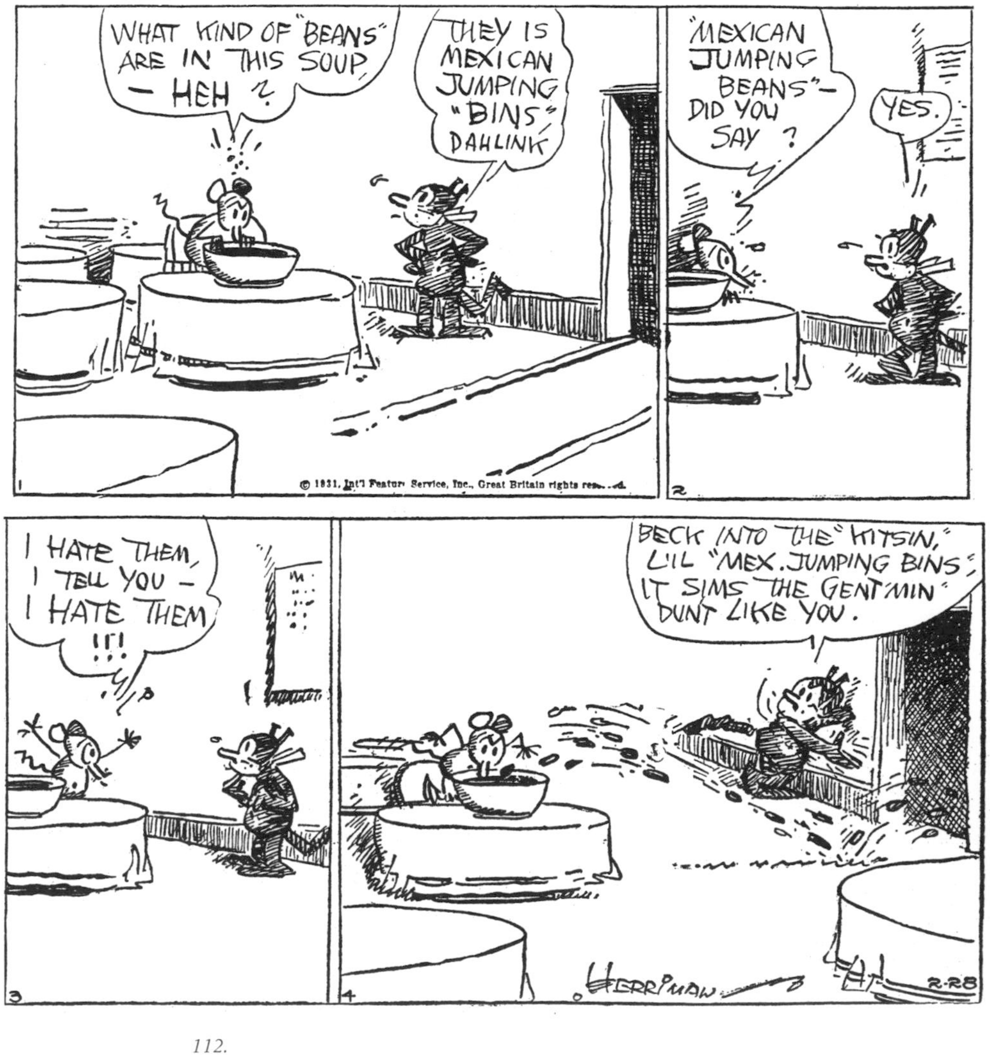
WHAT KIND OF "BEANS" ARE IN THIS SOUP — HEH ?
THEY IS MEXICAN JUMPING "BINS" DAHLINK
© 1931, Int'l Feature Service, Inc., Great Britain rights reserved.
"MEXICAN JUMPING BEANS" — DID YOU SAY ?
YES.
I HATE THEM, I TELL YOU — I HATE THEM !!!
BECK INTO THE "KITSIN," L'IL "MEX. JUMPING BINS", IT SIMS THE GENT'MIN" DUNT LIKE YOU.
HERRIMAN
2-28

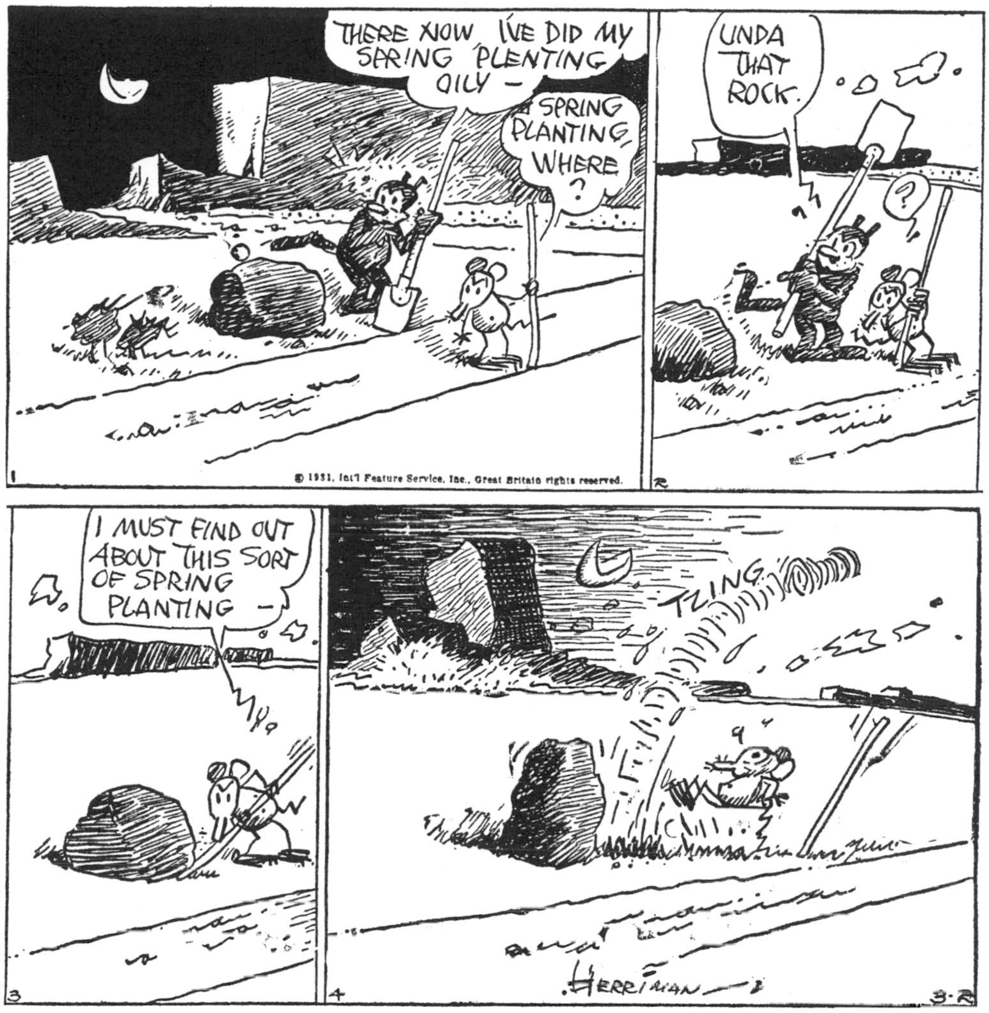
THERE NOW, I'VE DID MY SPRING PLENTING OILY –
SPRING PLANTING, WHERE ?
UNDA THAT ROCK.
I MUST FIND OUT ABOUT THIS SORT OF SPRING PLANTING –
TZING
HERRIMAN
3-2
© 1931, Int'l Feature Service, Inc., Great Britain rights reserved.

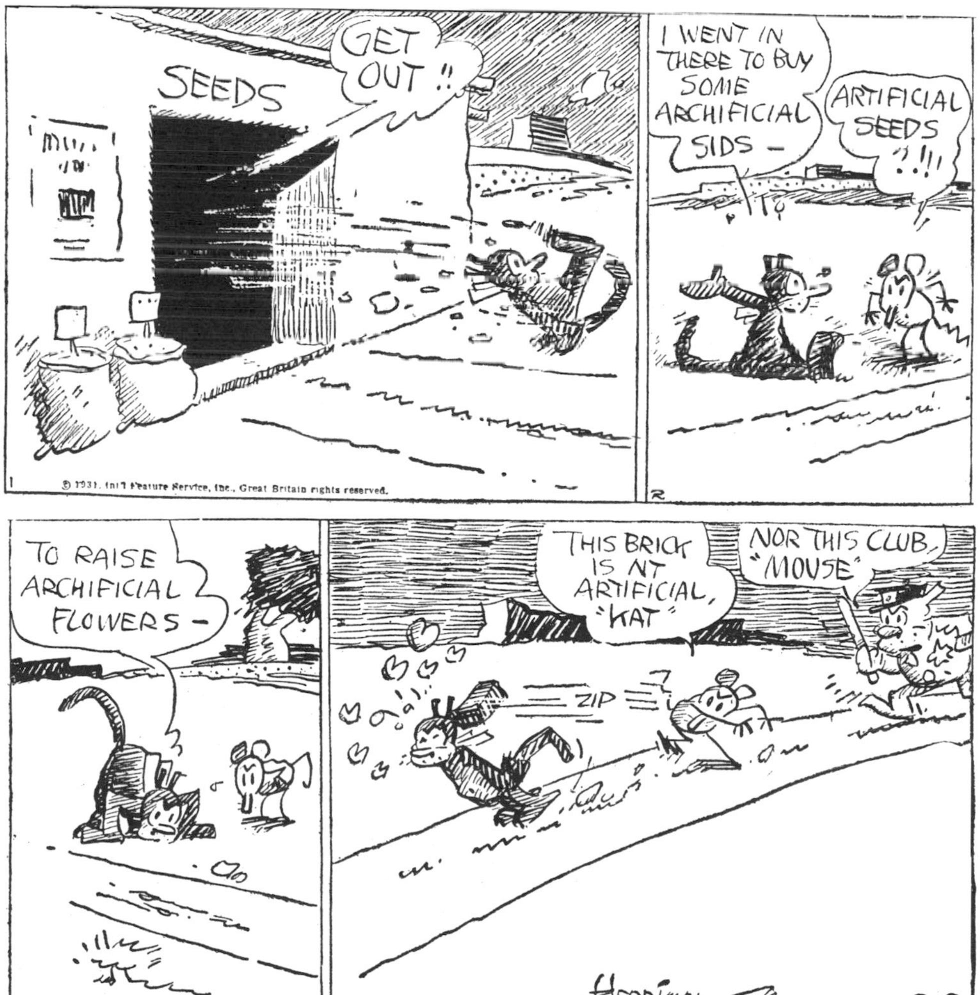
SEEDS
GET OUT !!
I WENT IN THERE TO BUY SOME ARCHIFICIAL SIDS –
ARTIFICIAL SEEDS ?!!!
TO RAISE ARCHIFICIAL FLOWERS –
THIS BRICK IS N'T ARTIFICIAL, "KAT"
NOR THIS CLUB, "MOUSE"
ZIP
HERRIMAN
3-3
© 1931, Int'l Feature Service, Inc., Great Britain rights reserved.

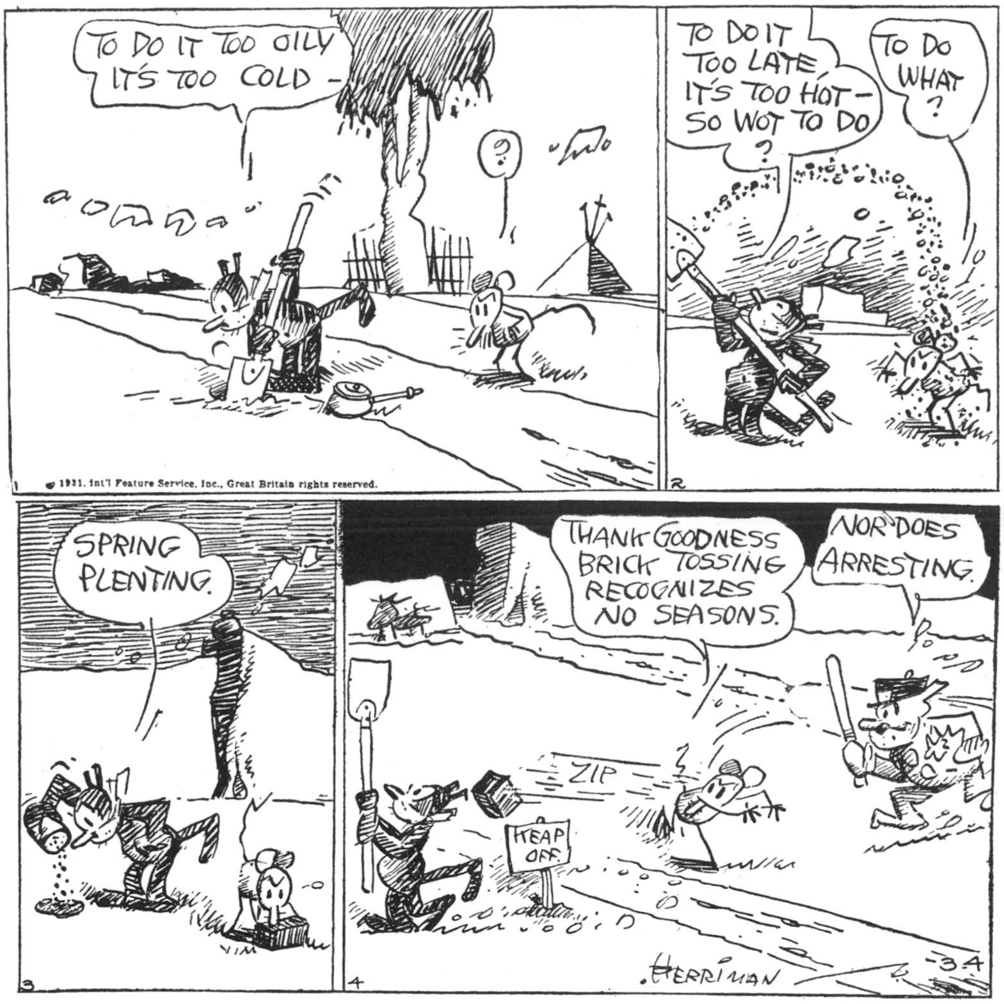
TO DO IT TOO OILY IT'S TOO COLD –
?
TO DO IT TOO LATE, IT'S TOO HOT – SO WOT TO DO ?
TO DO WHAT ?
© 1931, Int'l Feature Service, Inc., Great Britain rights reserved.
SPRING PLENTING.
THANK GOODNESS BRICK TOSSING RECOGNIZES NO SEASONS.
NOR DOES ARRESTING.
ZIP
HEAP OFF.
HERRIMAN
3-4

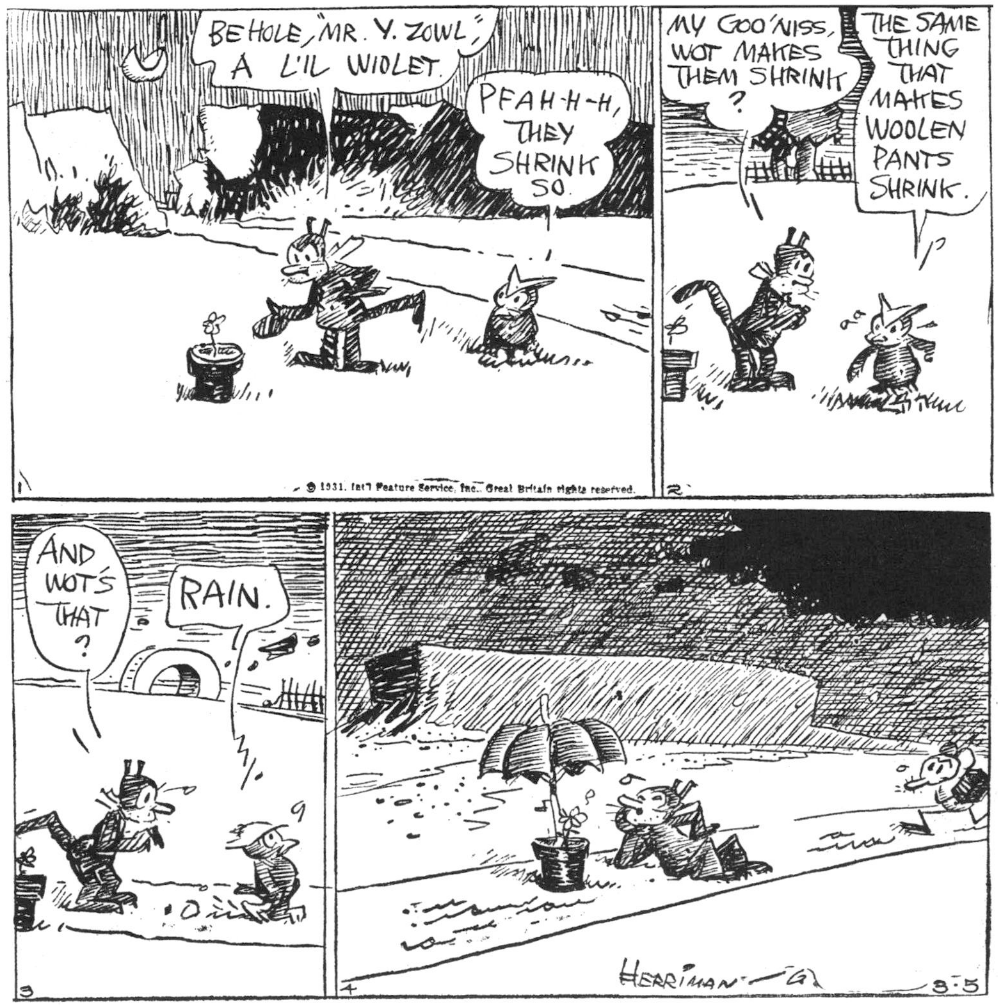
BE HOLE, MR. Y. ZOWL, A L'IL WIOLET.
PFAH-H-H, THEY SHRINK SO.
© 1931, Int'l Feature Service, Inc., Great Britain rights reserved.
MY GOO'NISS, WOT MAKES THEM SHRINK ?
THE SAME THING THAT MAKES WOOLEN PANTS SHRINK.
AND WOT'S THAT ?
RAIN.
HERRIMAN
3-5

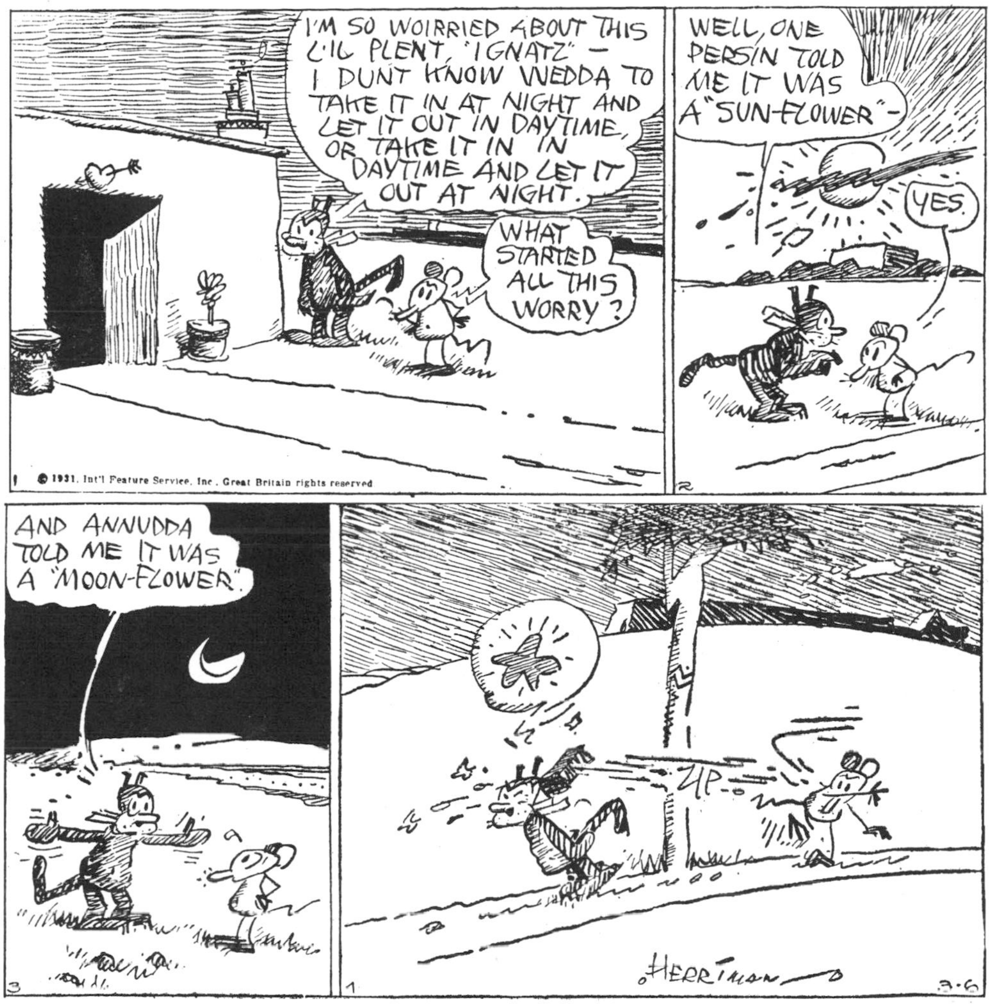
I'M SO WOIRRIED ABOUT THIS L'IL PLENT, "IGNATZ" — I DUNT KNOW WEDDA TO TAKE IT IN AT NIGHT AND LET IT OUT IN DAYTIME, OR TAKE IT IN IN DAYTIME AND LET IT OUT AT NIGHT.
WHAT STARTED ALL THIS WORRY?
© 1931, Int'l Feature Service, Inc. Great Britain rights reserved
WELL, ONE PERSIN TOLD ME IT WAS A "SUN-FLOWER" —
YES.
AND ANNUDDA TOLD ME IT WAS A "MOON-FLOWER".
ZIP
HERRIMAN
3-6

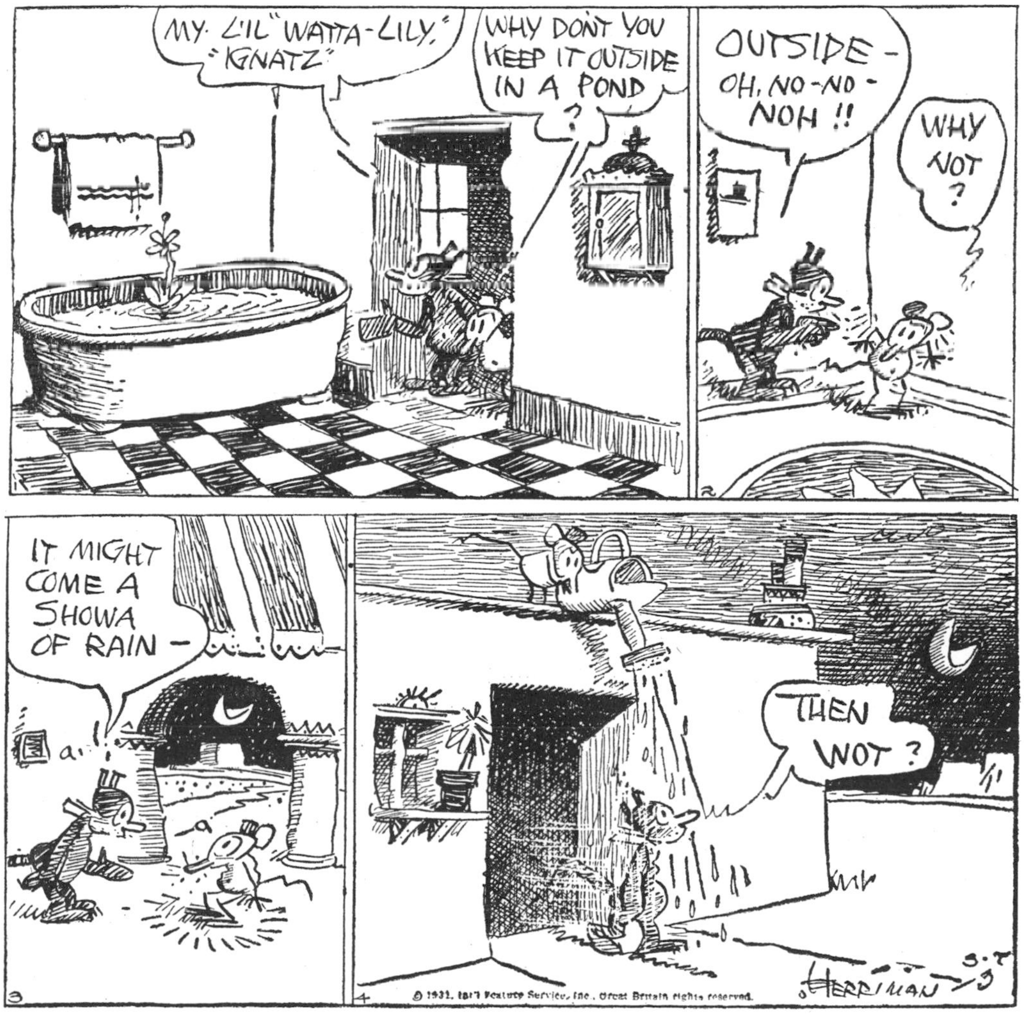
MY L'IL "WATTA-LILY," "IGNATZ"
WHY DON'T YOU KEEP IT OUTSIDE IN A POND ?
OUTSIDE — OH, NO-NO-NOH !!
WHY NOT ?
IT MIGHT COME A SHOWA OF RAIN —
THEN WOT ?
© 1931, Int'l Feature Service, Inc. Great Britain rights reserved.
HERRIMAN
3-7

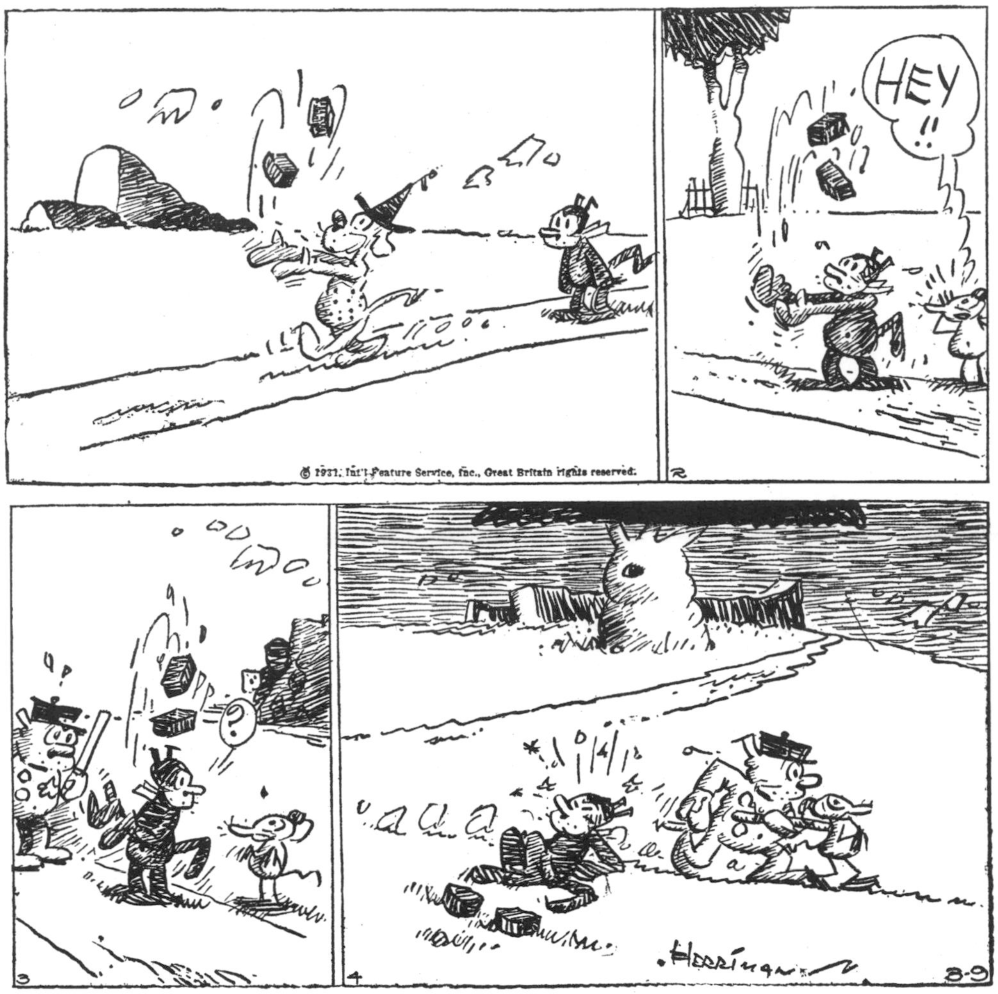
HEY !!
© 1931, Int'l Feature Service, Inc., Great Britain rights reserved.
HERRIMAN
8-9

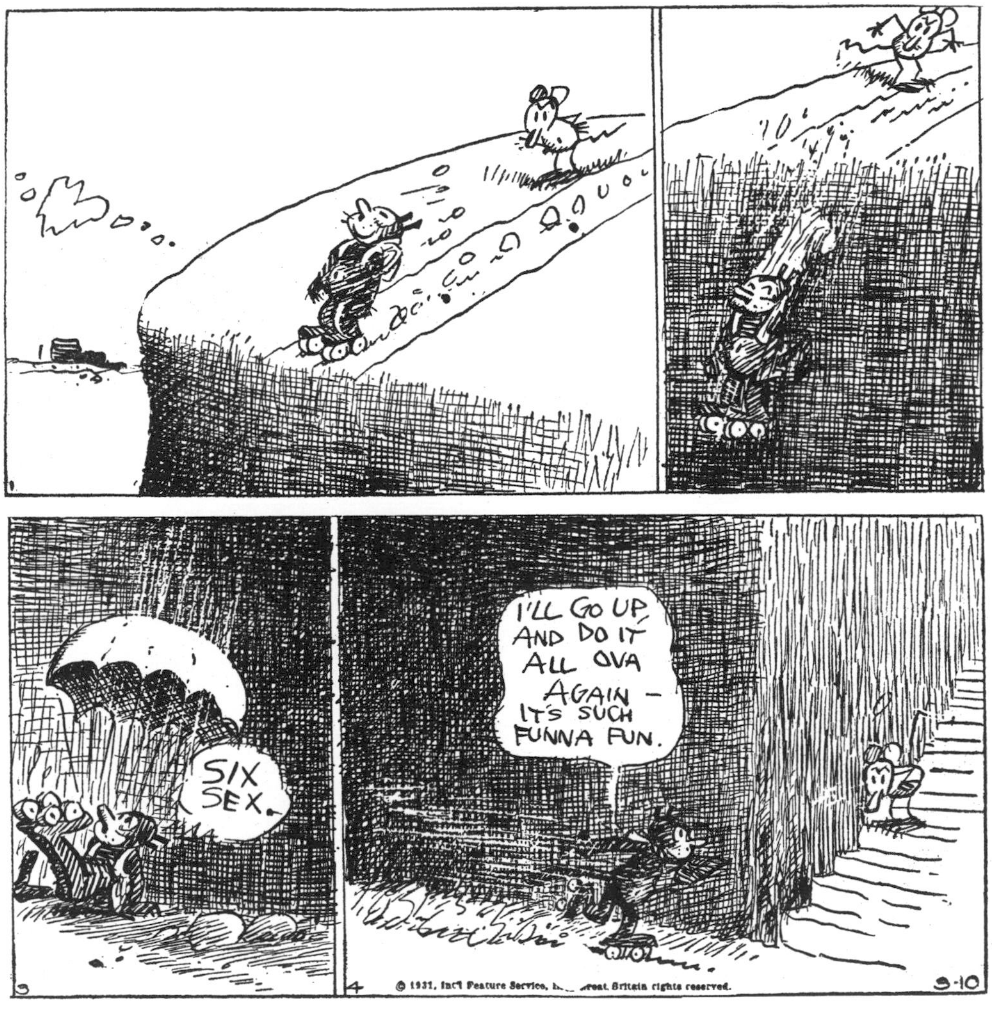
SIX SEX.
I'LL GO UP AND DO IT ALL OVA AGAIN — IT'S SUCH FUNNA FUN.
9-10

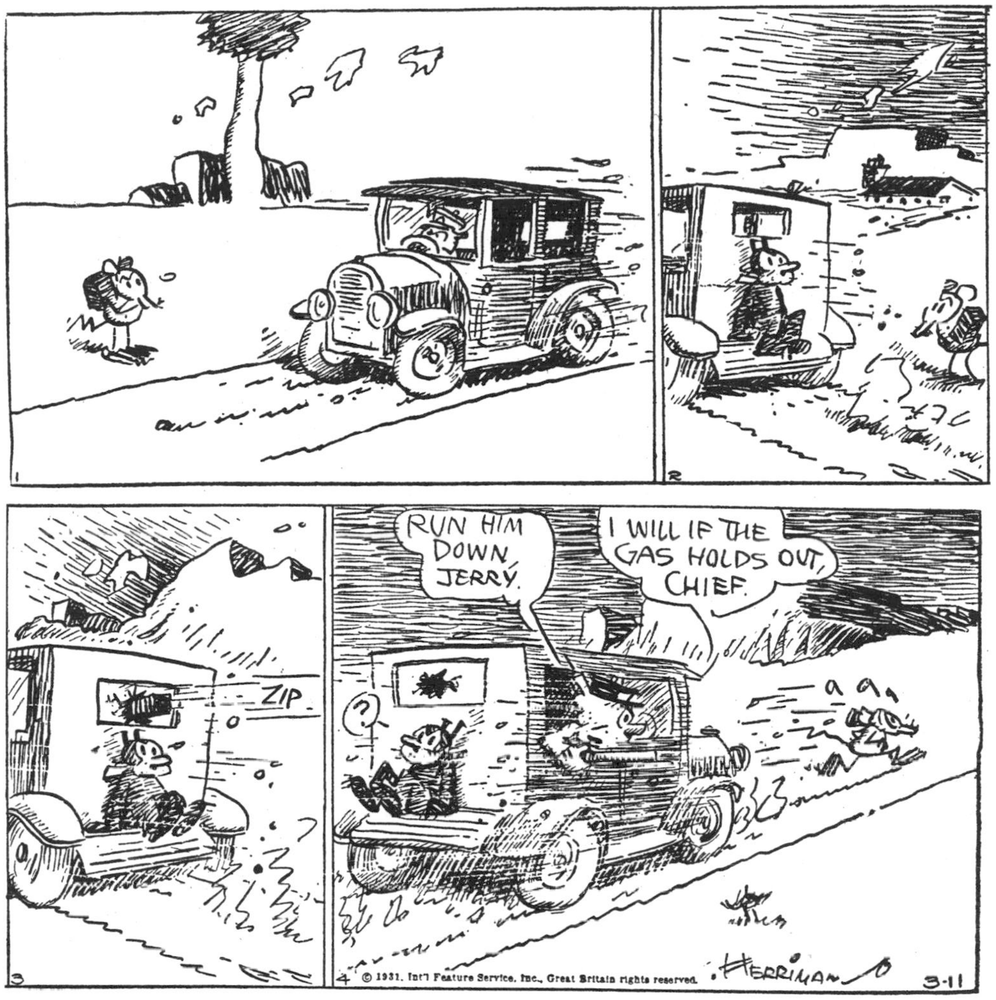
ZIP
RUN HIM DOWN, JERRY.
I WILL IF THE GAS HOLDS OUT, CHIEF.
© 1931, Int'l Feature Service, Inc., Great Britain rights reserved.
HERRIMAN
3-11

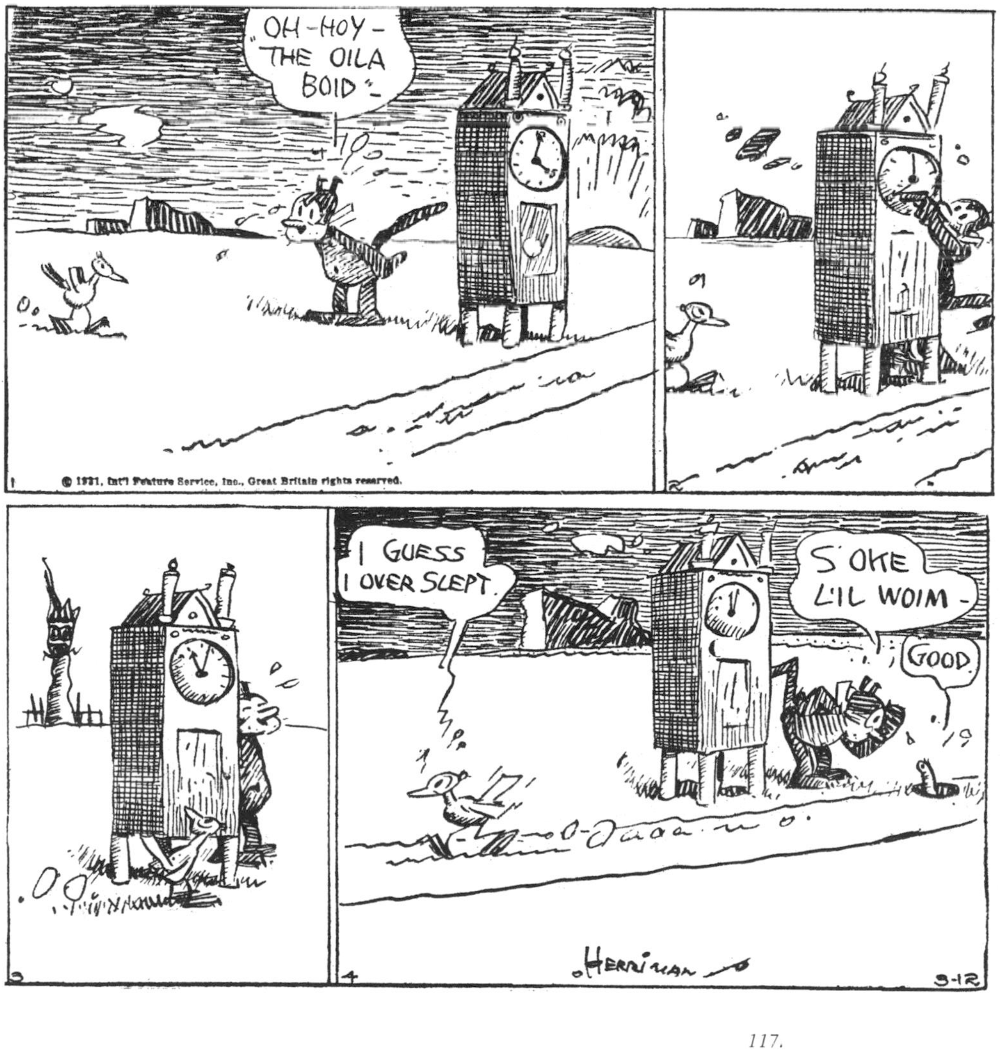
OH-HOY- THE OILA BOID-
© 1931, Int'l Feature Service, Inc., Great Britain rights reserved.
I GUESS I OVER SLEPT.
S'OKE L'IL WOIM-
GOOD.
HERRIMAN
3-12

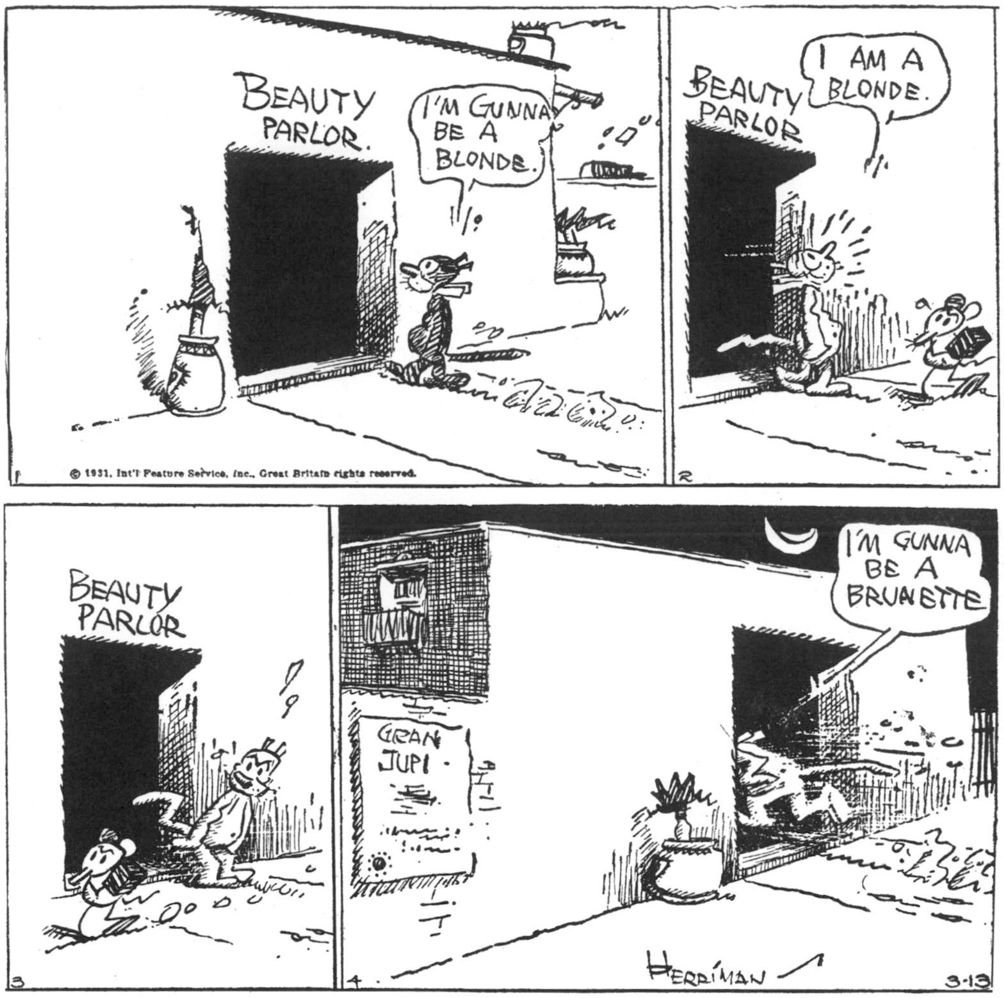
BEAUTY PARLOR.
I'M GUNNA BE A BLONDE.
© 1931, Int'l Feature Service, Inc., Great Britain rights reserved.
BEAUTY PARLOR
I AM A BLONDE.
BEAUTY PARLOR
GRAN JUPI
I'M GUNNA BE A BRUNETTE
HERRIMAN
3-13

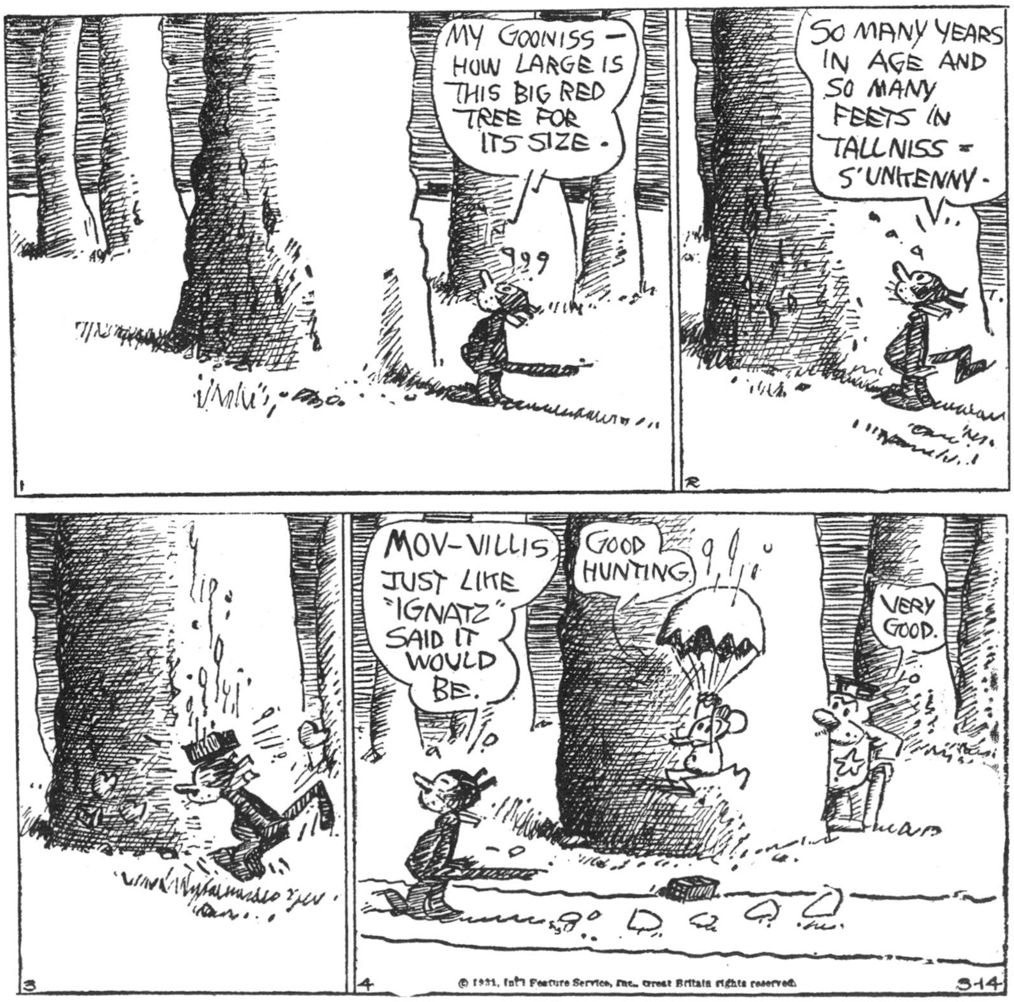
MY GOONISS— HOW LARGE IS THIS BIG RED TREE FOR ITS SIZE.
SO MANY YEARS IN AGE AND SO MANY FEETS IN TALLNISS = S'UNKENNY.
MOV-VILLIS JUST LIKE "IGNATZ" SAID IT WOULD BE.
GOOD HUNTING.
VERY GOOD.
© 1931, Int'l Feature Service, Inc., Great Britain rights reserved.
3-14

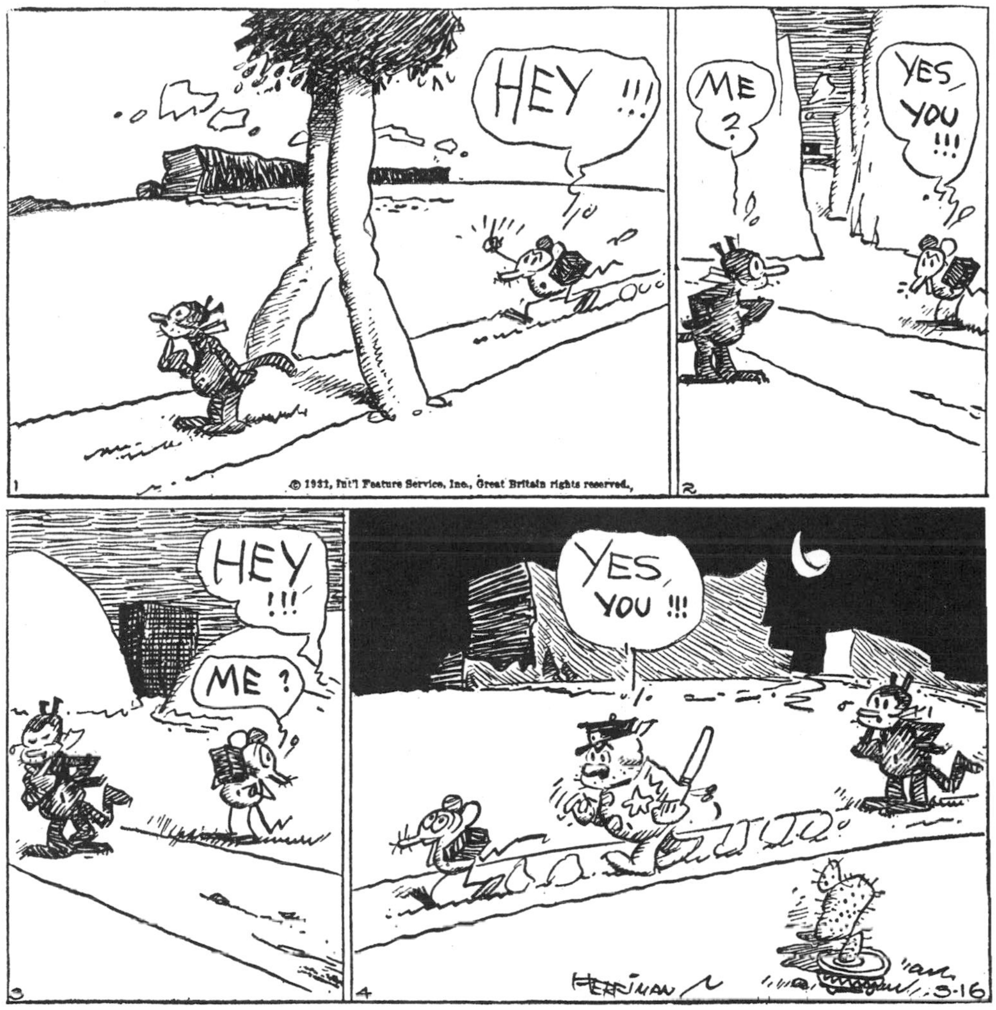
HEY !!!
ME ?
YES, YOU !!!
© 1931, Int'l Feature Service, Inc., Great Britain rights reserved.
HEY !!!
ME ?
YES, YOU !!!
HERRIMAN
3-16

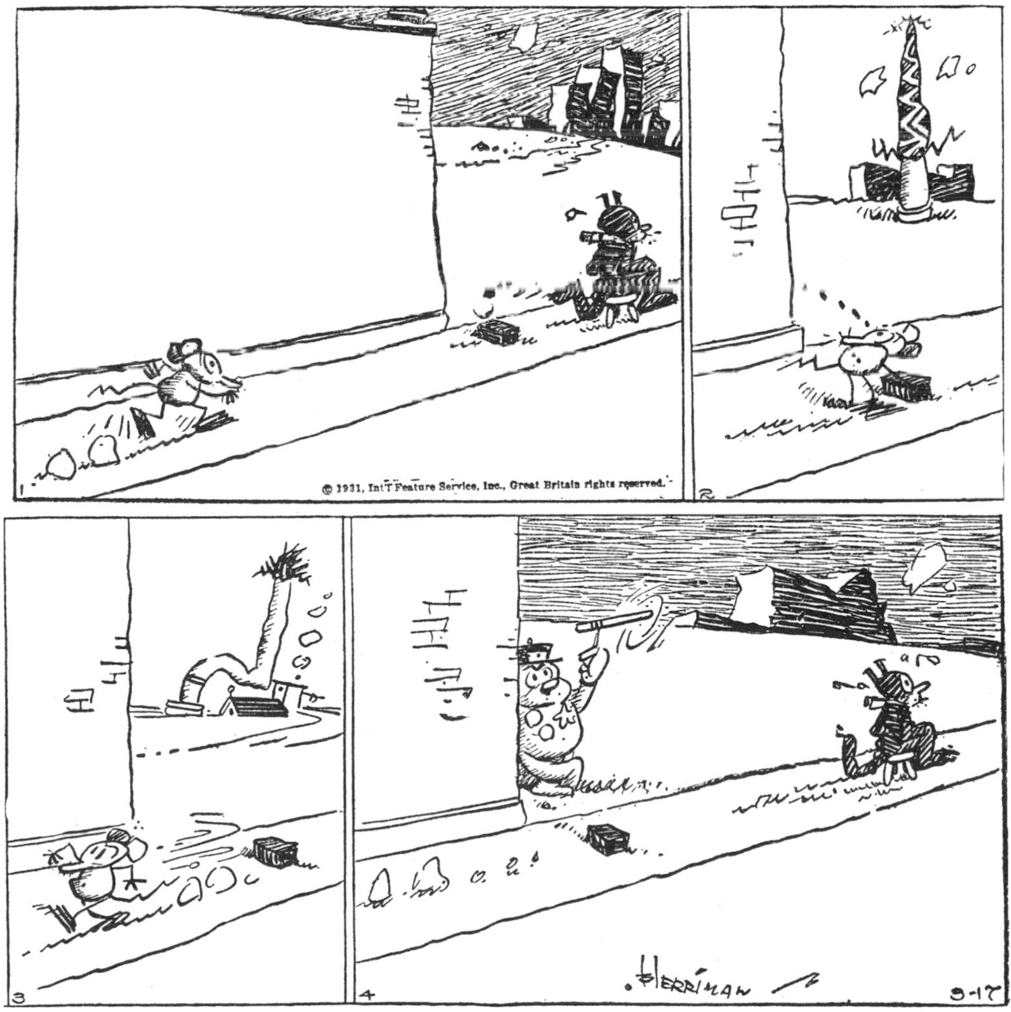
© 1931, Int'l Feature Service, Inc., Great Britain rights reserved.
HERRIMAN
3-17

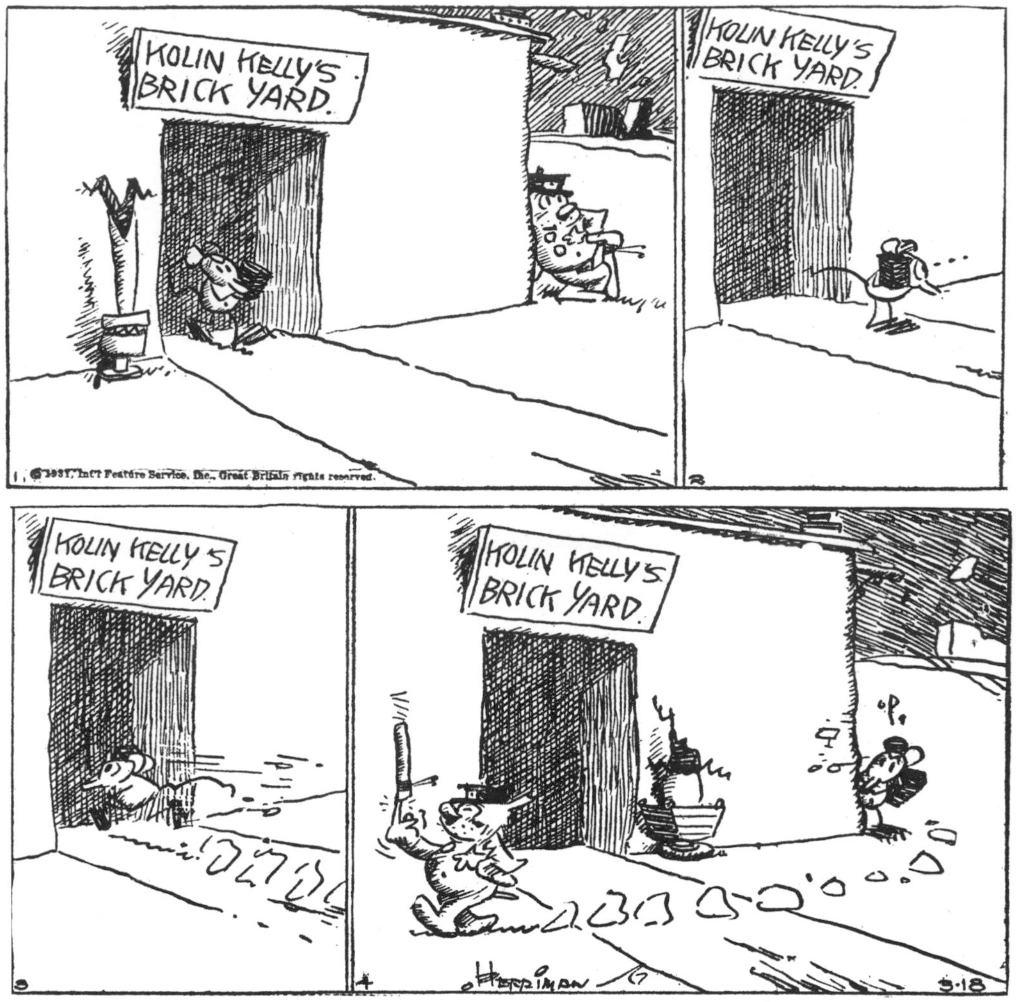
KOLIN KELLY'S BRICK YARD.
© 1931, Int'l Feature Service, Inc., Great Britain rights reserved.
KOLIN KELLY'S BRICK YARD.
KOLIN KELLY'S BRICK YARD.
KOLIN KELLY'S BRICK YARD.
HERRIMAN
3-18

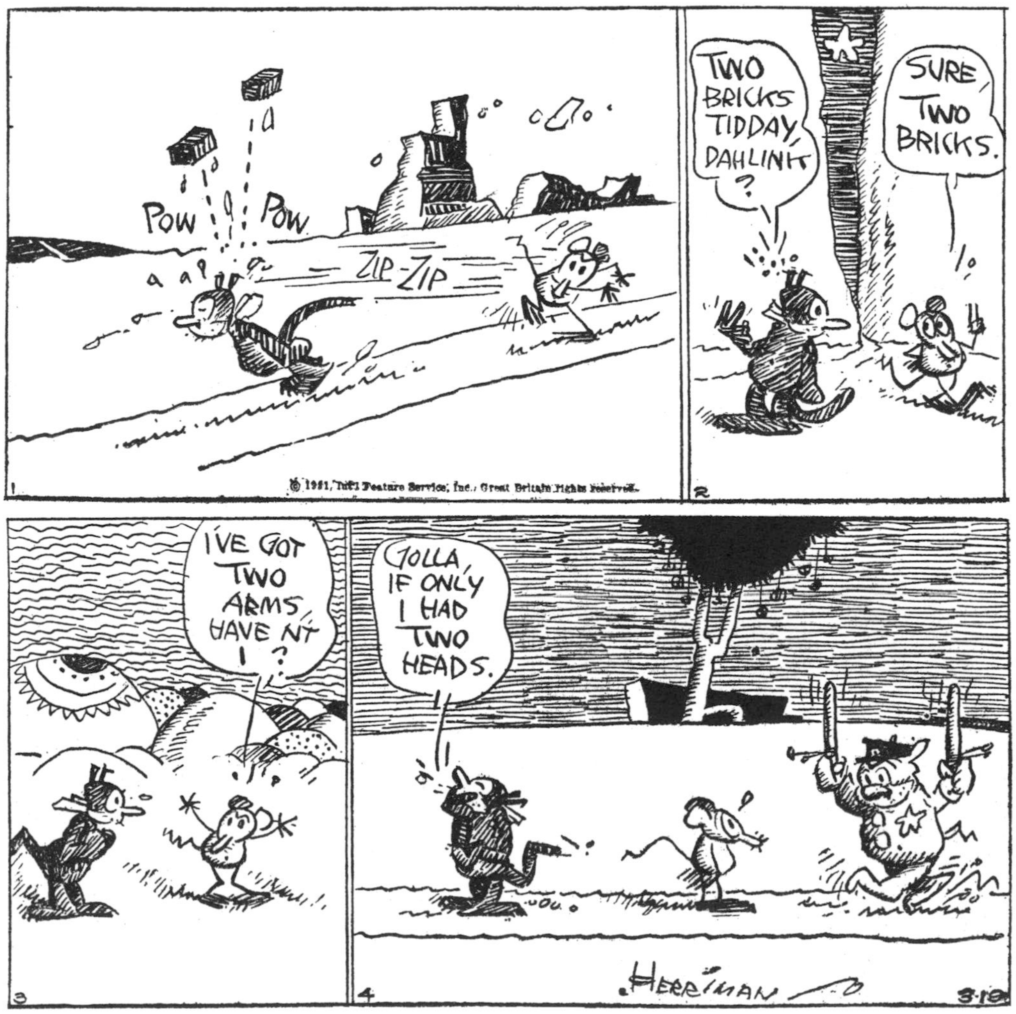
POW
POW
ZIP-ZIP
© 1931, Int'l Feature Service, Inc., Great Britain rights reserved.
TWO BRICKS TIDDAY, DAHLINK ?
SURE, TWO BRICKS.
I'VE GOT TWO ARMS HAVE N'T I ?
GOLLA, IF ONLY I HAD TWO HEADS.
HERRIMAN
3-19

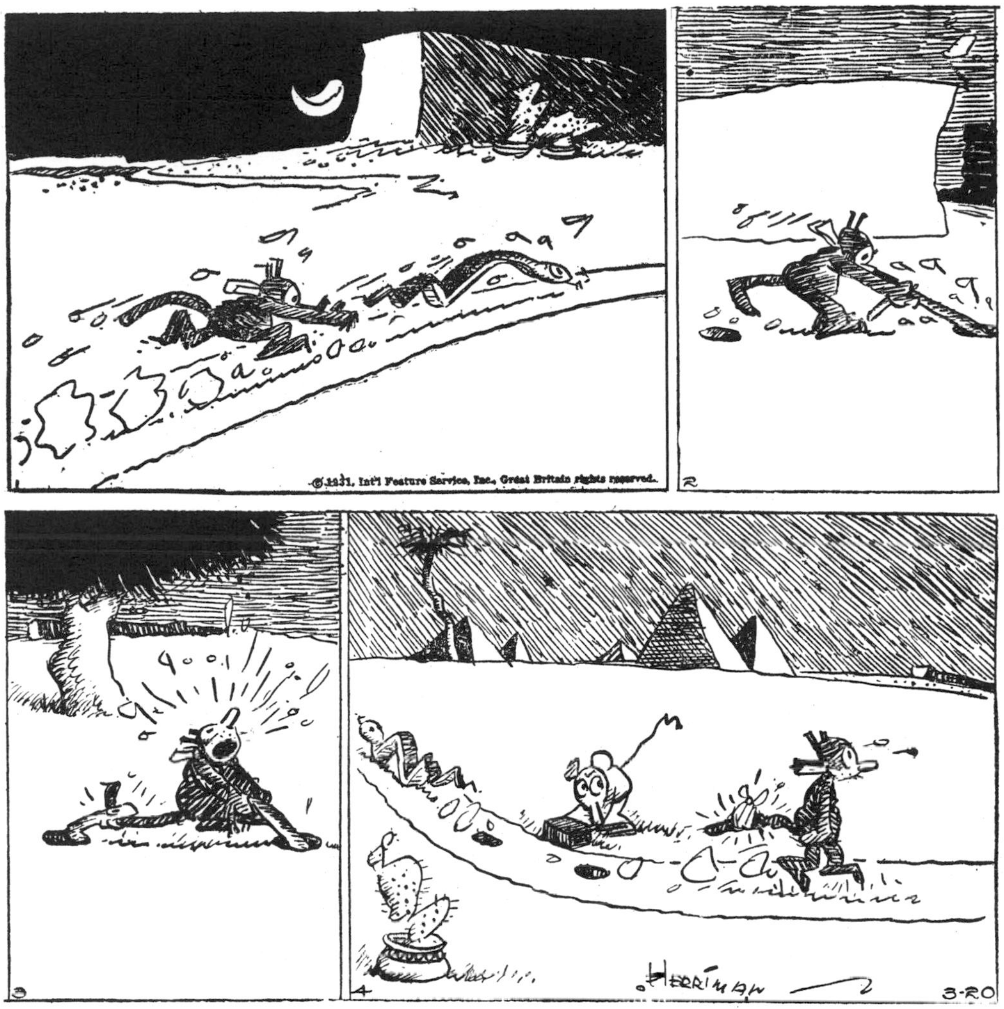
© 1931, Int'l Feature Service, Inc., Great Britain rights reserved.
HERRIMAN
3-20

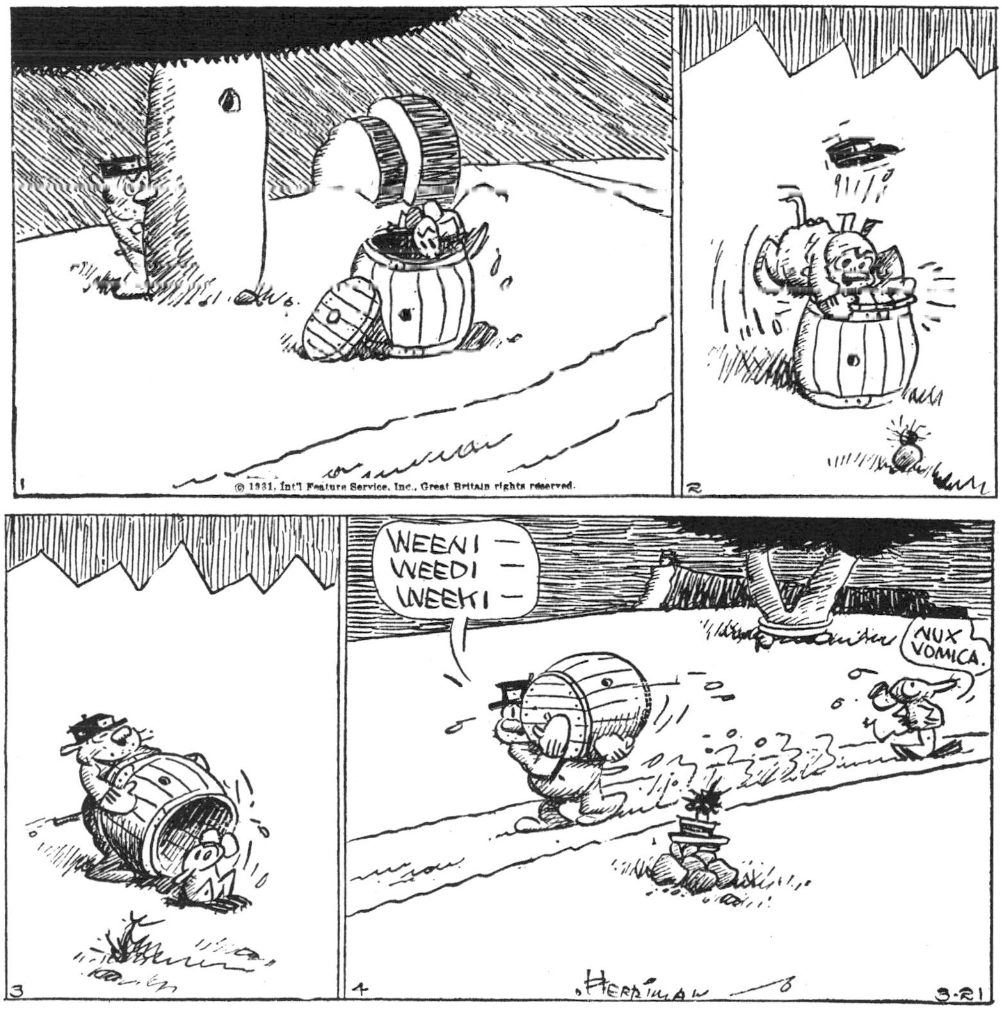
© 1931, Int'l Feature Service, Inc., Great Britain rights reserved.
WEENI — WEEDI — WEEKI —
NUX VOMICA.
HERRIMAN
3-21

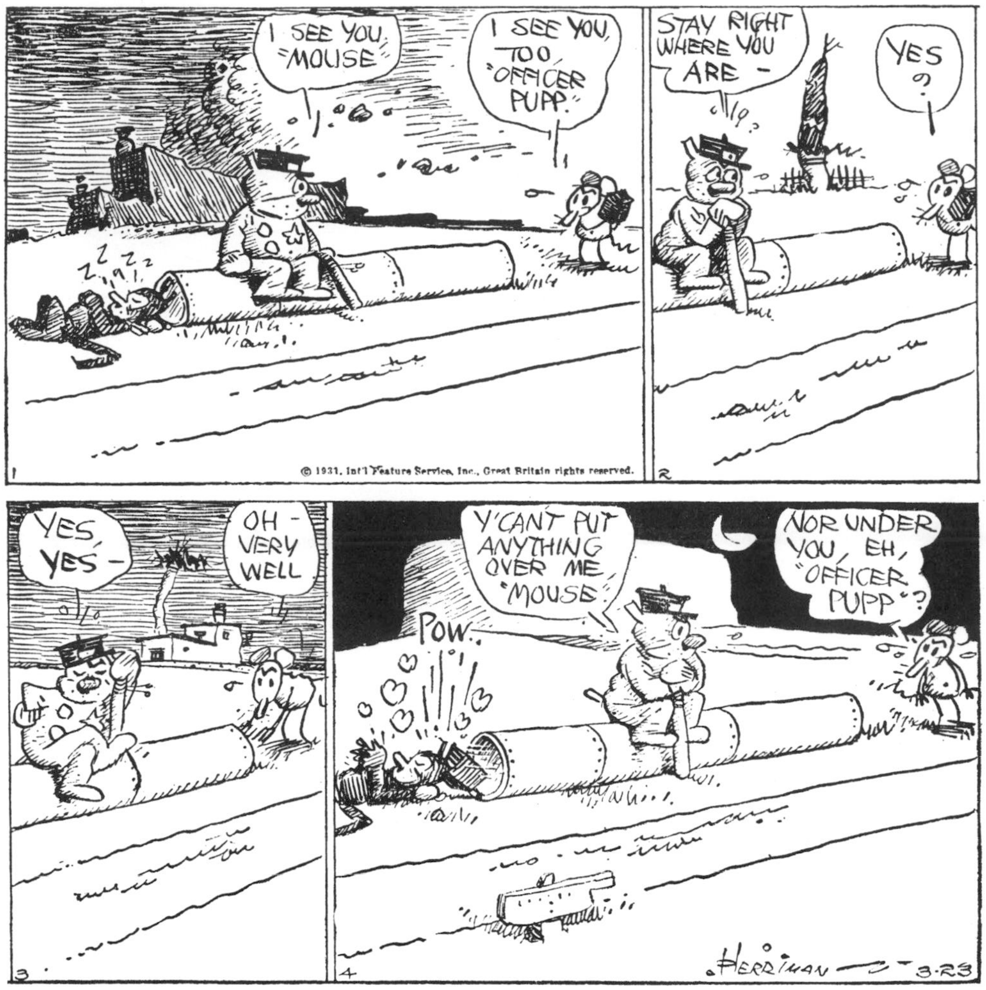
I SEE YOU, "MOUSE"
I SEE YOU, TOO, "OFFICER PUPP."
© 1931, Int'l Feature Service, Inc., Great Britain rights reserved.
STAY RIGHT WHERE YOU ARE –
YES ?
YES, YES –
OH – VERY WELL
Y'CAN'T PUT ANYTHING OVER ME, "MOUSE"
POW
NOR UNDER YOU, EH, "OFFICER PUPP"?
HERRIMAN
3-23

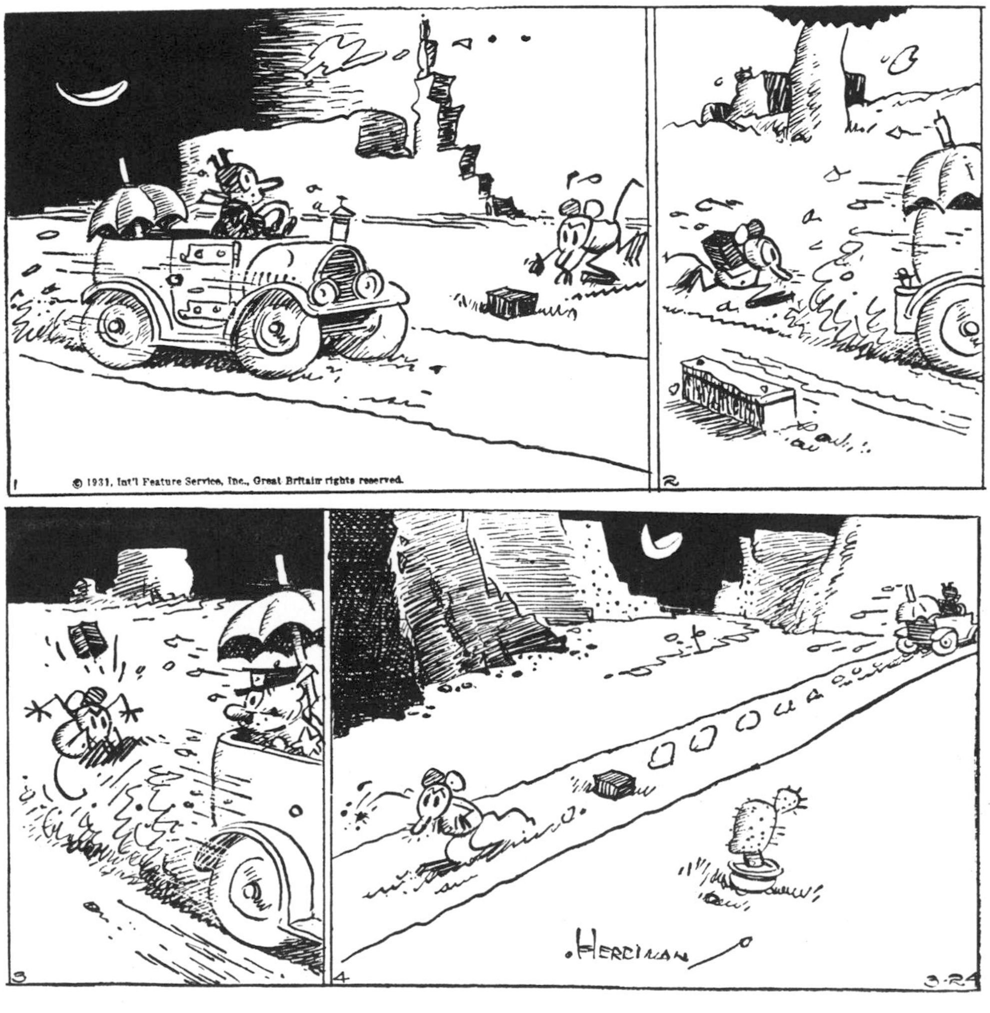
© 1931, Int'l Feature Service, Inc., Great Britain rights reserved.
HERRIMAN
3-24

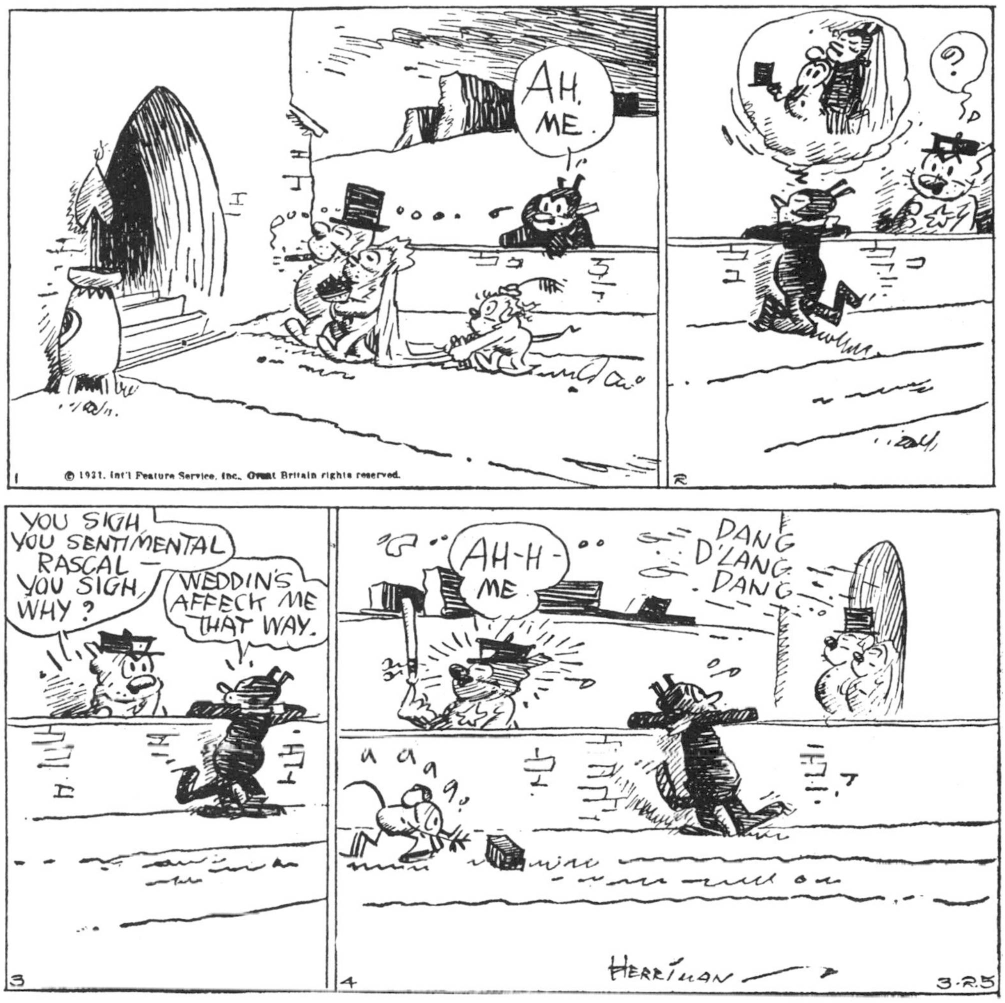
AH, ME.
© 1921, Int'l Feature Service, Inc., Great Britain rights reserved.
YOU SIGH, YOU SENTIMENTAL RASCAL — YOU SIGH, WHY?
WEDDIN'S AFFECK ME THAT WAY.
AH-H ME
DANG D'LANG DANG
HERRIMAN
3-25

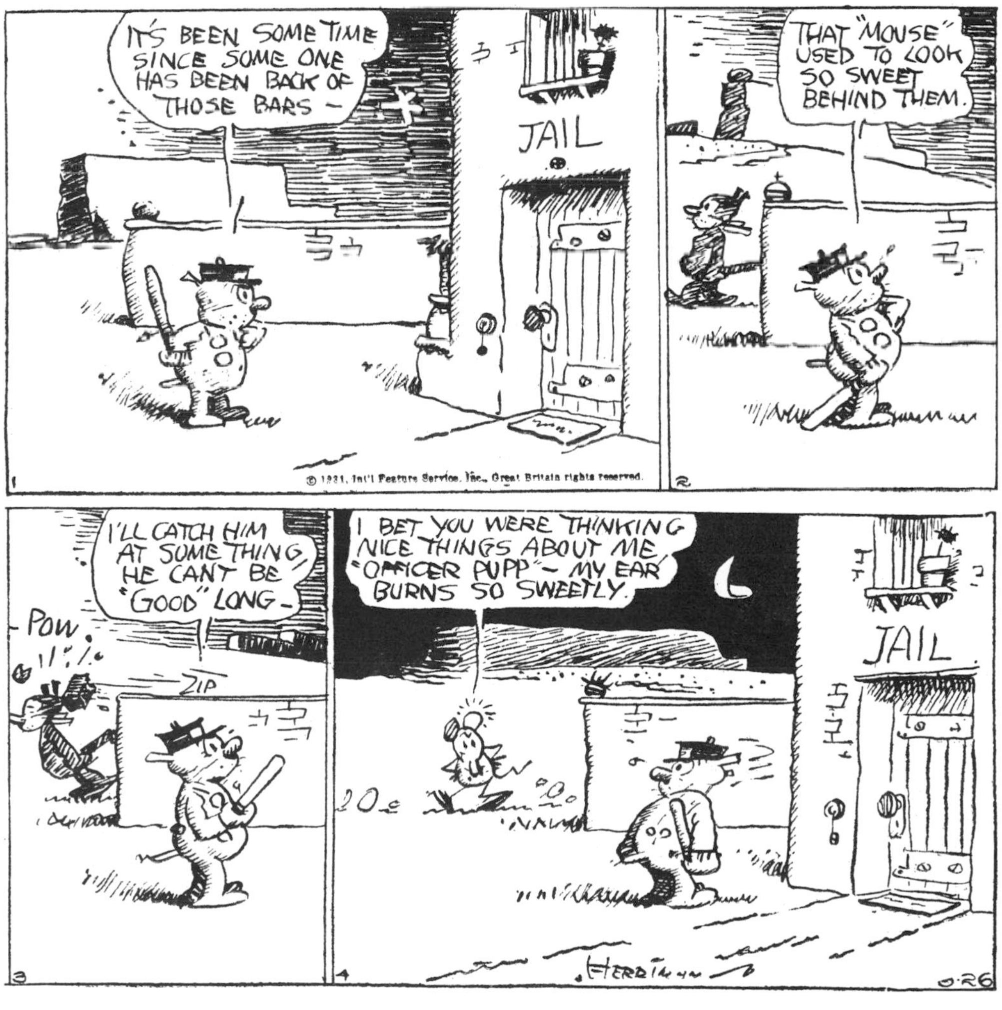
IT'S BEEN SOME TIME SINCE SOME ONE HAS BEEN BACK OF THOSE BARS —
JAIL
© 1921, Int'l Feature Service, Inc., Great Britain rights reserved.
THAT "MOUSE" USED TO LOOK SO SWEET BEHIND THEM.
I'LL CATCH HIM AT SOME THING, HE CAN'T BE "GOOD" LONG —
POW
ZIP
I BET YOU WERE THINKING NICE THINGS ABOUT ME "OFFICER PUPP" — MY EAR BURNS SO SWEETLY.
JAIL
HERRIMAN

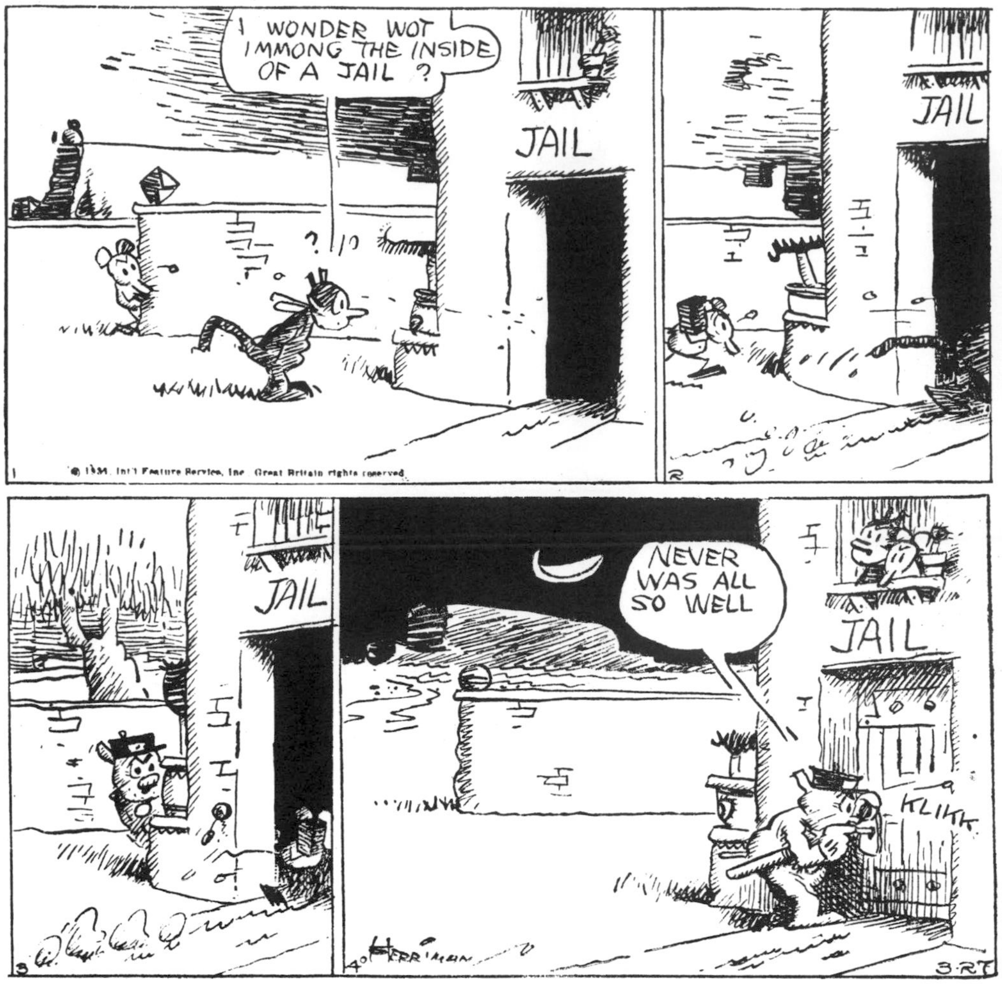
I WONDER WOT IMMONG THE INSIDE OF A JAIL ?
JAIL
Int'l Feature Service, Inc. Great Britain rights reserved.
JAIL
JAIL
NEVER WAS ALL SO WELL
JAIL
KLIKK
HERRIMAN
3-27

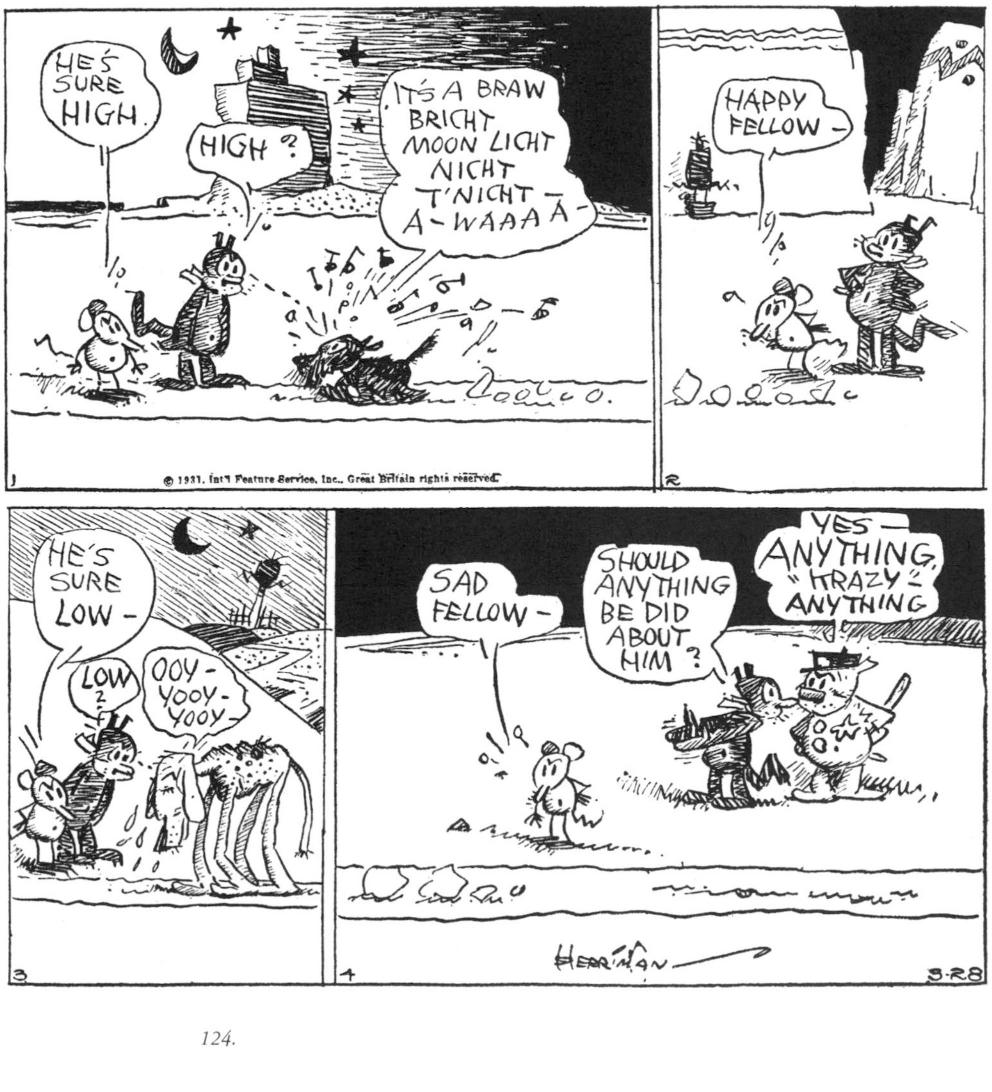
HE'S SURE HIGH.
HIGH ?
IT'S A BRAW BRICHT MOON LICHT NICHT T'NICHT – A-WAAA Ā
© 1931, Int'l Feature Service, Inc., Great Britain rights reserved.
HAPPY FELLOW –
HE'S SURE LOW –
LOW ?
OOY- YOOY- YOOY
SAD FELLOW –
SHOULD ANYTHING BE DID ABOUT HIM ?
YES – ANYTHING, "KRAZY" – ANYTHING
HERRIMAN
3-28

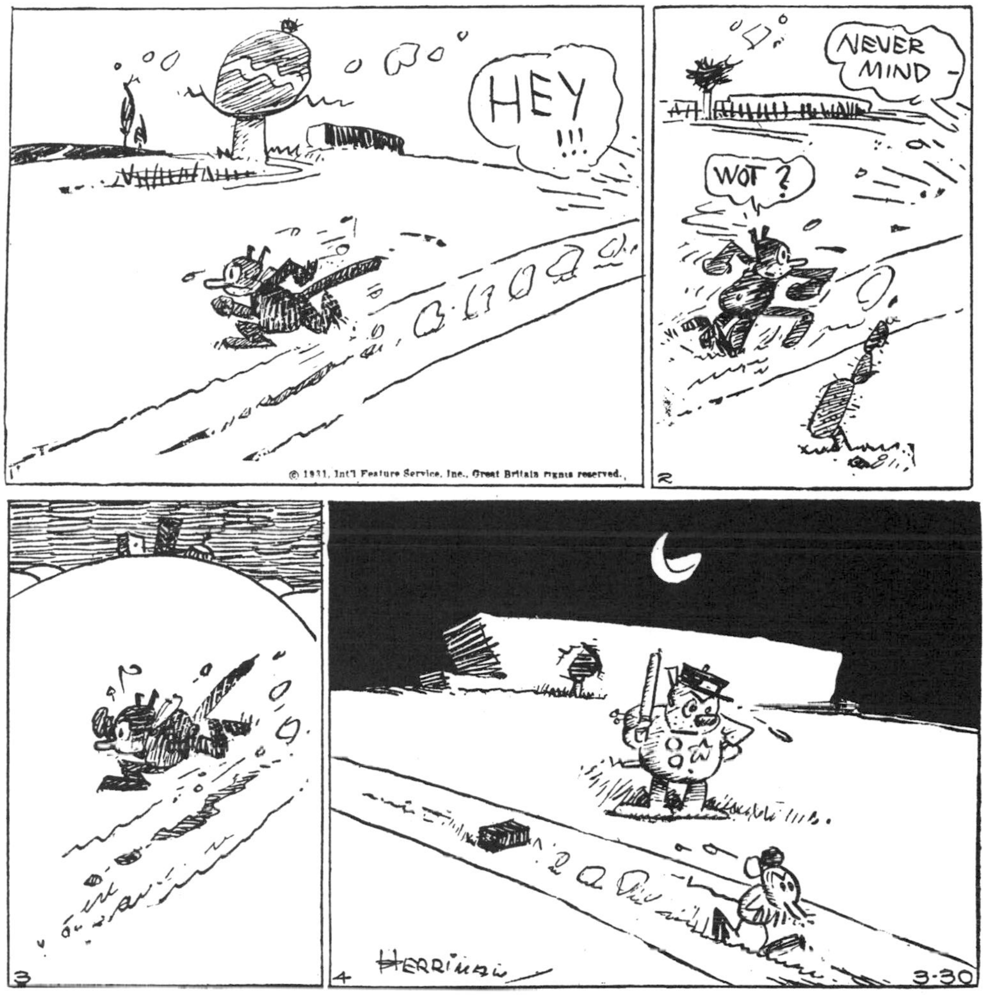
HEY !!!
NEVER MIND -
WOT ?
HERRIMAN
3-30

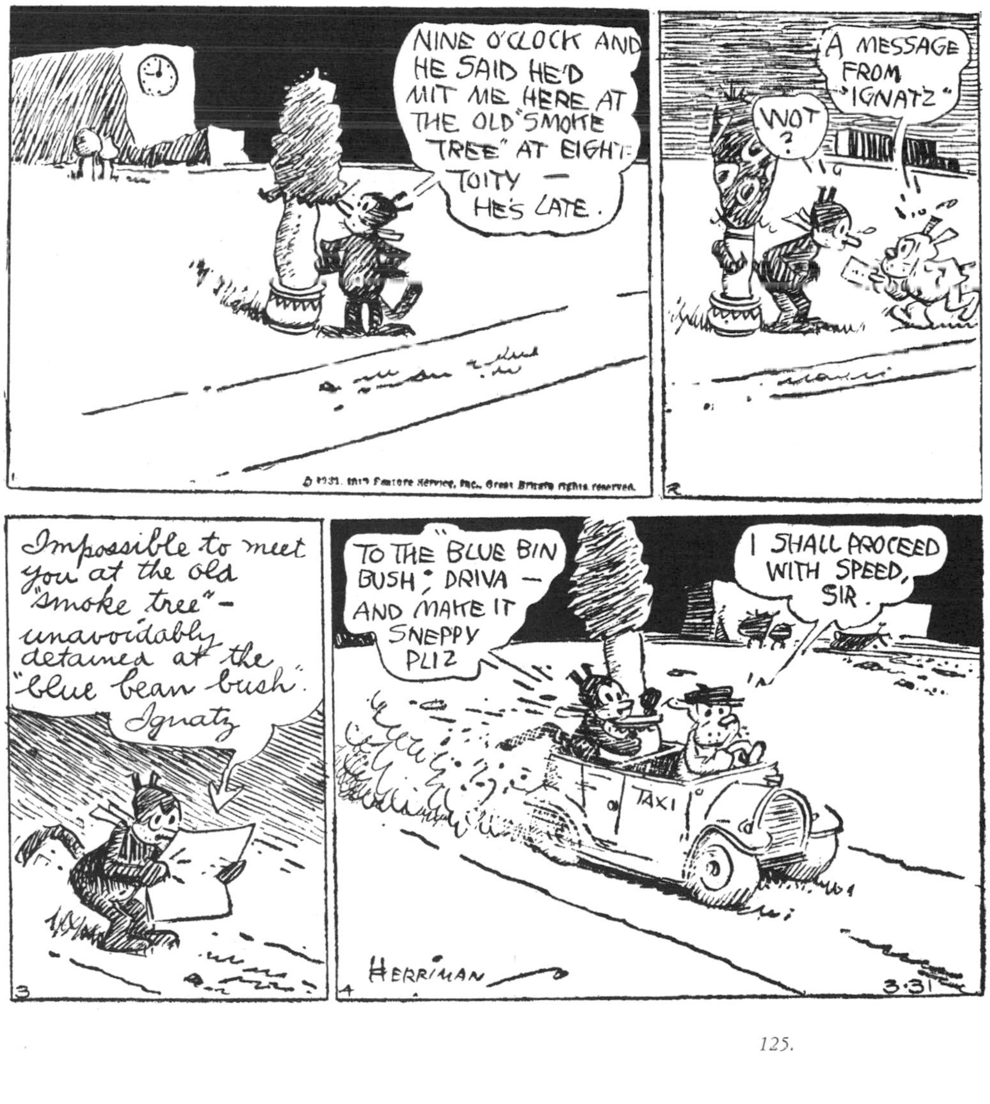
NINE O'CLOCK AND HE SAID HE'D MIT ME HERE AT THE OLD "SMOKE TREE" AT EIGHT-TOITY — HE'S LATE.
A MESSAGE FROM "IGNATZ"
WOT ?
Impossible to meet you at the old "smoke tree" - unavoidably detained at the "blue bean bush". Ignatz
TO THE "BLUE BIN BUSH" DRIVA — AND MAKE IT SNEPPY PLIZ
I SHALL PROCEED WITH SPEED, SIR.
TAXI
HERRIMAN
3-31

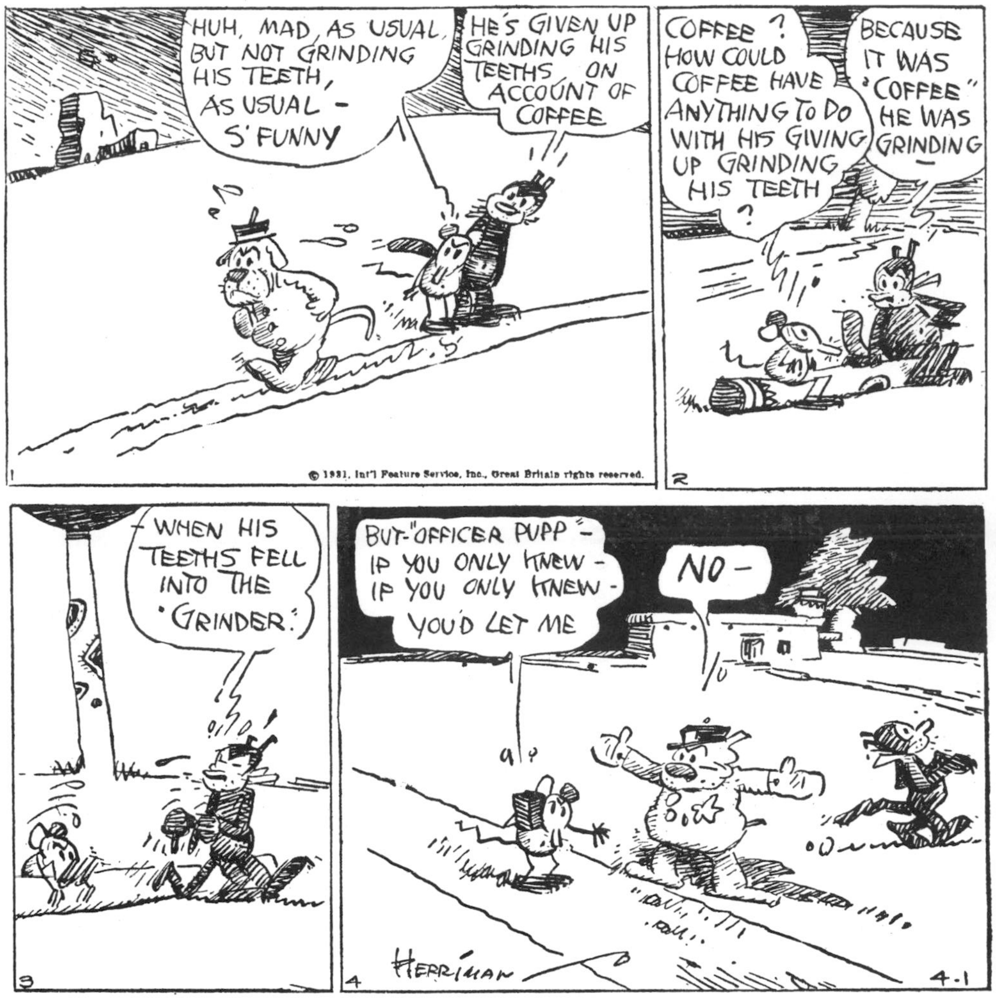
HUH, MAD, AS USUAL, BUT NOT GRINDING HIS TEETH, AS USUAL - S'FUNNY
HE'S GIVEN UP GRINDING HIS TEETHS ON ACCOUNT OF COFFEE
COFFEE? HOW COULD COFFEE HAVE ANYTHING TO DO WITH HIS GIVING UP GRINDING HIS TEETH?
BECAUSE IT WAS "COFFEE" HE WAS GRINDING -
WHEN HIS TEETHS FELL INTO THE "GRINDER."
BUT-"OFFICER PUPP" - IF YOU ONLY KNEW - IF YOU ONLY KNEW - YOU'D LET ME
NO-
© 1931, Int'l Feature Service, Inc., Great Britain rights reserved.
HERRIMAN
4-1

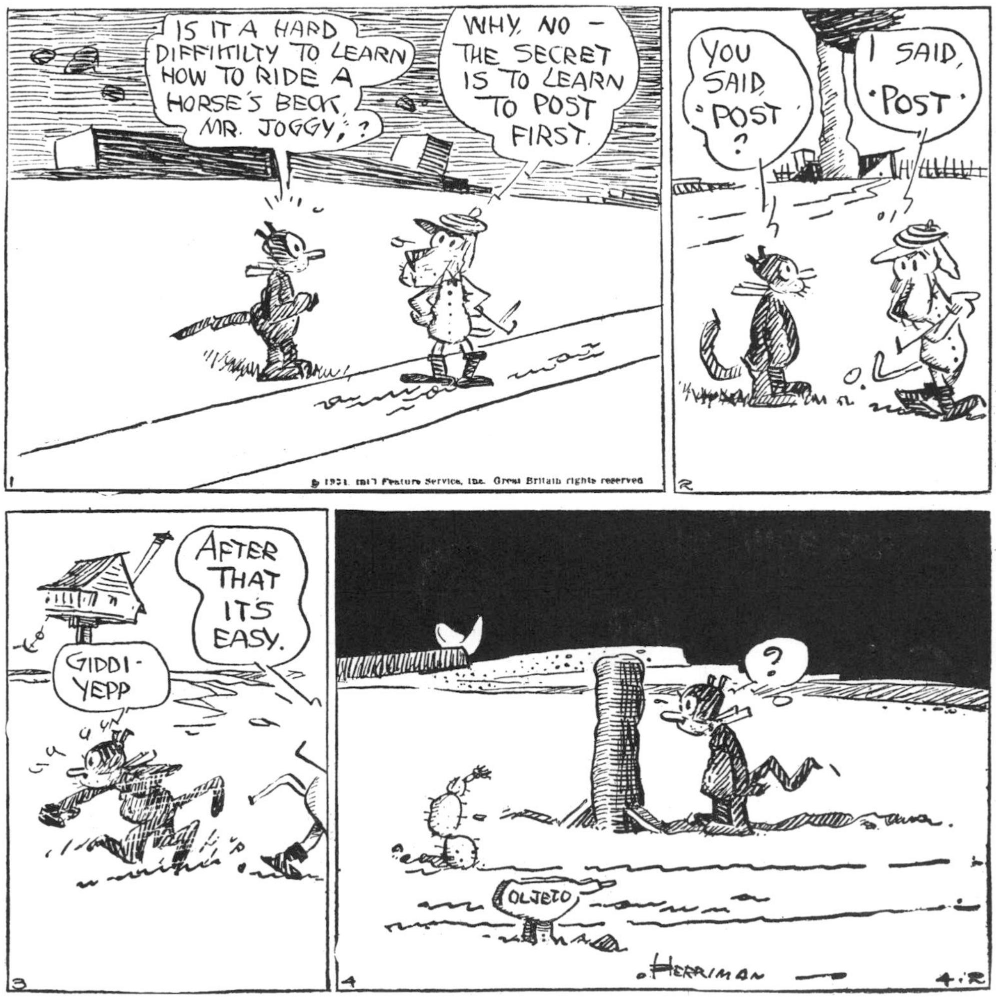
IS IT A HARD DIFFIKILTY TO LEARN HOW TO RIDE A HORSE'S BECK, MR. JOGGY, ?
WHY, NO - THE SECRET IS TO LEARN TO POST FIRST.
YOU SAID "POST"?
I SAID, "POST"
AFTER THAT IT'S EASY.
GIDDI-YEPP
?
OLJETO
HERRIMAN
© 1931, Int'l Feature Service, Inc., Great Britain rights reserved.
4-2

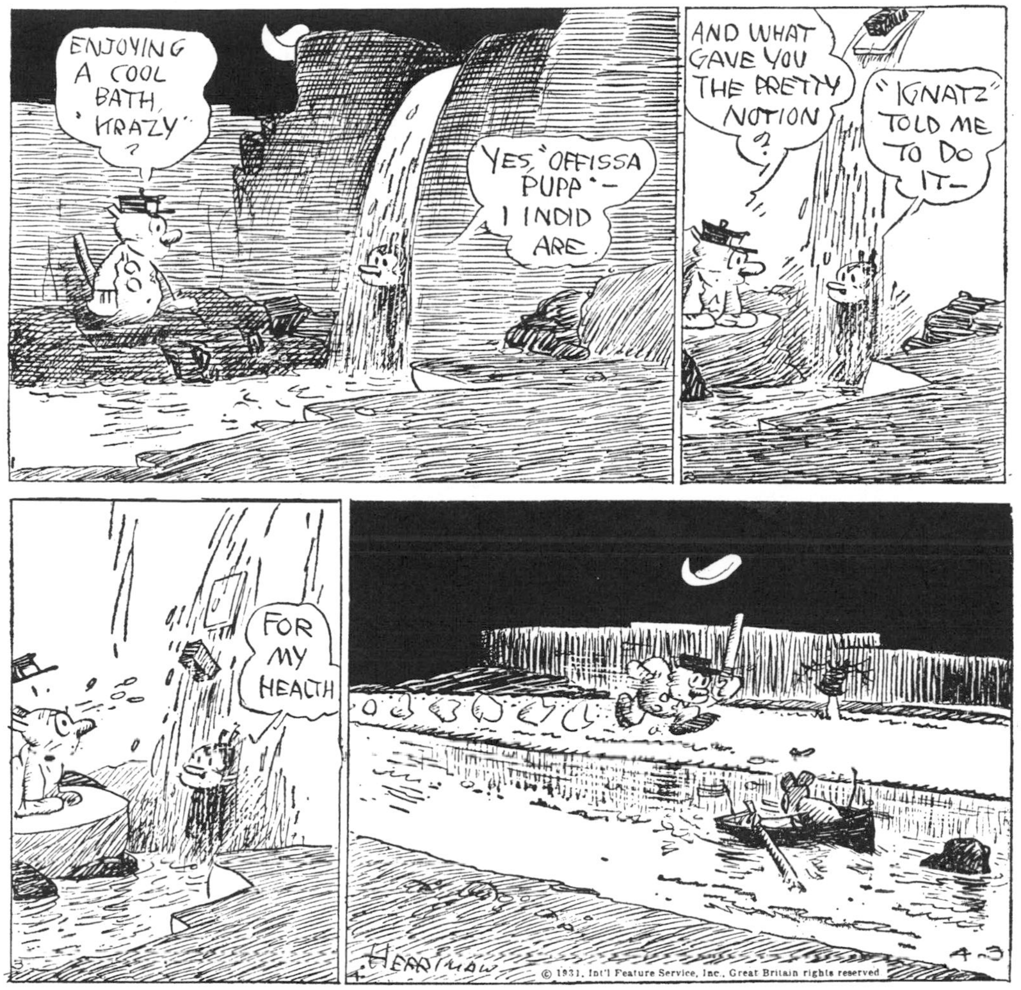

ENJOYING A COOL BATH, "KRAZY" ?
YES, "OFFISSA PUPP" – I INDID ARE.
AND WHAT GAVE YOU THE PRETTY NOTION ?
"IGNATZ" TOLD ME TO DO IT –
FOR MY HEALTH
HERRIMAN
© 1931, Int'l Feature Service, Inc., Great Britain rights reserved
4-3

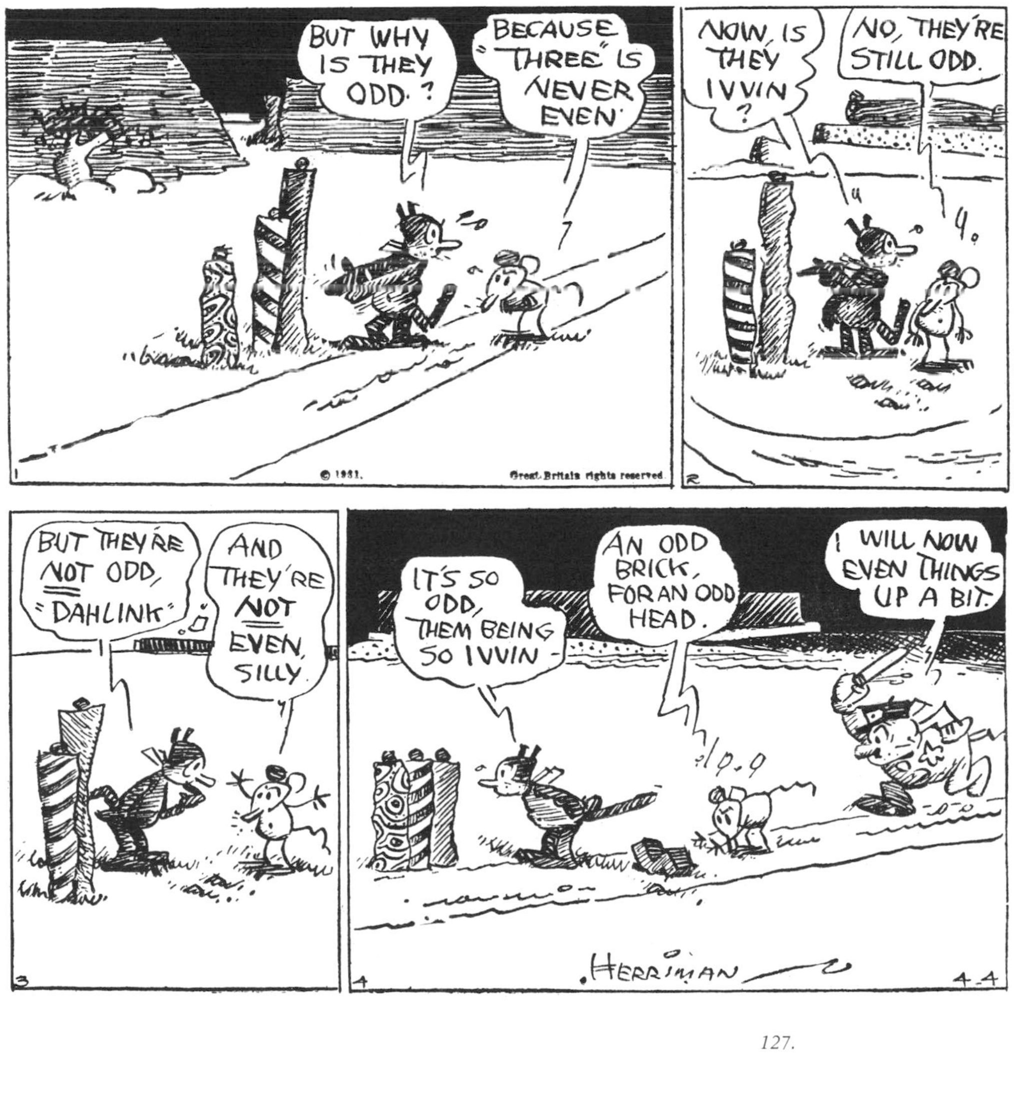

BUT WHY IS THEY ODD ?
BECAUSE "THREE" IS NEVER EVEN
© 1931.
Great Britain rights reserved
NOW, IS THEY IVVIN ?
NO, THEY'RE STILL ODD.
BUT THEY'RE NOT ODD, "DAHLINK"
AND THEY'RE NOT EVEN, SILLY
IT'S SO ODD, THEM BEING SO IVVIN –
AN ODD BRICK, FOR AN ODD HEAD.
I WILL NOW EVEN THINGS UP A BIT.
HERRIMAN
4-4

The IGNATZ MOUSE DEBAFFLER PAGE.

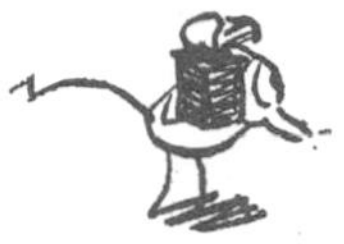

Komments on Mysteries of the Master's Drawing Mesa.

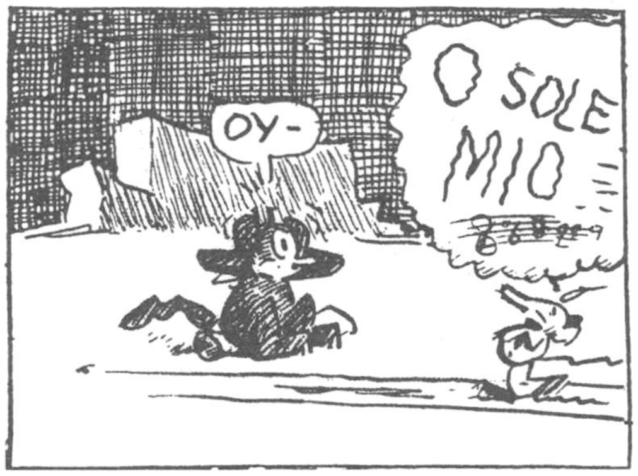
OY-
O SOLE MIO

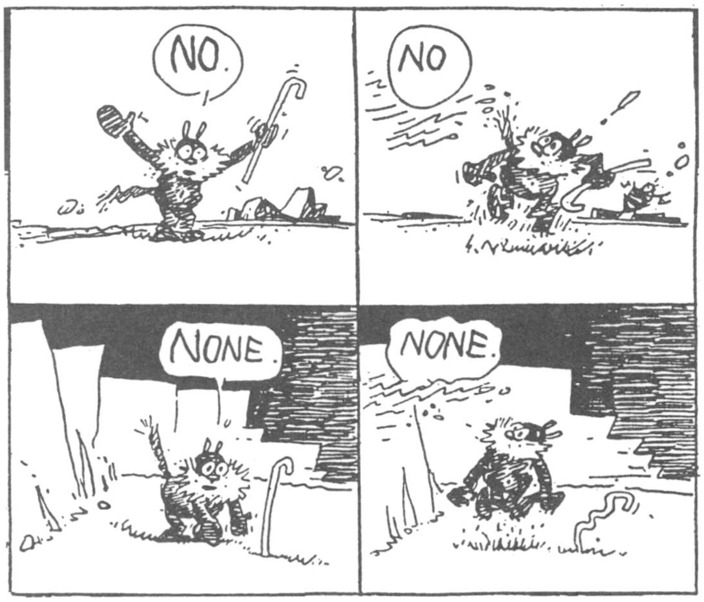
NO.
NO
NONE.
NONE.

5/3/31: This page baffles me. Is the black cloud an Indian smoke signal, which Krazy recognizes and so returns to his snooze? Apparently not, since Krazy says, "Rain IS coming, ain't it?" Is Krazy's pillow a rolled-up sleeping bag which gives him security against a deluge? Unlikely, since there is no final panel showing our kat bagged kontentedly against a downpour. Obviously the response of Ignatz and Offisa Pupp is shown to be highly haywire — but what is the reader tipoff?

6/28/31: The Krazy Katbird makes a rare appearance in this one, second in line in the avian parade. The remarkable piety of Ignatz Mouse displayed here may be no more than a pipedream of the happily inhaling Krazy, quite possibly just potluck on his part.

10/25/31: A series of syndikat mistitling of *Krazy Kat* episodes begins here, ending abruptly when the old man in New York noticed it. Not the sort of goof you wanted to make if you relished your job at King Features.

1/24/32: First of four odd releases of earlier Krazy pages with the decorative central panel as discussed before in these pages. The others are 2/21/32, 2/28/32, and 3/6/32. Herriman labels the last one "Intermission."

1/31/32 & 2/7/32: "I yamma wee hee doh eenna kottidge by the sea" as sung by Krazy in the penultimate panel of 1/31 becomes "I yamma window, etc.," in the second panel lyrics of 2/7; here is certainly a quintessence of mobile backgrounds for the Herriman scholar to ponder and admire.

7/10/32: Herewith a major mystery of the Herriman mesa — where did Ignatz glom the specs in panel 10?

8/14/32: Radio was the big new household consumer item in 1932, and here Krazy reflects on the possibilities of brick delivery by a mouse to kat hookup.

10/9/32: Uncle Tomm Kat, introducd here for just one episode, becomes a major continuing character at this time in the daily *Krazy Kat* strip.